INDIANA UNIVERSITY

Midwestern Pioneer

Volume II / In Mid-Passage

INDIANA UNIVERSITY

Midwestern Pioneer

Vol. II / In Mid-Passage

THOMAS D. CLARK

INDIANA UNIVERSITY PRESS

Bloomington & London

Published in Canada by Fitzhenry & Whiteside Limited, Don Mills, Ontario

Library of Congress catalog card number: 74-126207

ISBN: 0-253-32995-7

Manufactured in the United States of America

To my granddaughter
Elizabeth Marye Stone

CONTENTS

List of Illustrations

following page 142

PREFACE

DURING THE latter quarter of the nineteenth century, Indiana University experienced many of the changes associated with American higher education in this era of expansion. By the turn of the century the institution was in search of its mission as a "separate" public liberal arts university in an intense age of technological advances and materialism. Three presidents, Jordan, Coulter, and Swain, had given the institution sound leadership, and in the case of David Starr Jordan, guidance was imaginative and exciting. The grooves of the course to the future were etched in depth, but the traditions still remained those of liberal arts education with special emphasis in the areas of the biological or life sciences.

When William Julian (Lowe) Bryan came to the office of President in 1902 he was well adapted in the Jordan-Coulter-Swain philosophy of university administration. At heart Bryan was a midwestern rural patrician, conservative in social and religious philosophy, yet liberal in intellectual outlook. He was, in fact and in spirit, harmonious with the contemporaneous views of William James. He was knowledgeable about the work of G. Stanley Hall, Chauncey Wright, Charles Peirce, and the Harris group of Saint Louis. Bryan was himself a pioneer of genuine promise in the field of psychology which was just then splitting off from philosophy.

William Lowe Bryan was in fact a complex and paradoxical person. He possessed an abundance of rare human leadership capacity without the endowment of aggressive administrative talent. The world of earthy Indiana politics in which he had to function during most of his years in the Indiana University presidency was as far removed from the mores of his personal life as was the folk history of outer Mongolia. Without being either an intellectual or social snob, he found it indeed difficult to unbend to associate comfortably with shortsighted and self-centered men of statehouse and legislative chamber. This he had to leave largely to the trustees,

[x i]

friends of the institution, and the "arrangers" on the university's administrative staff, like John W. Cravens and U. H. Smith.

In the decade and a half prior to 1916, Indiana underwent a grueling period of forming itself into a university, not only in the abstract intellectual sense, but in the much broader pragmatic concept of professionalism. An analysis of the institution at the turn of the century revealed it was set on a calamitous course of singleness of purpose. The great majority of its graduates had become teachers, and the handful who did not entered the practice of law from the struggling lone professional school. This condition had to be corrected at once or the school would fail to rise above the level of a teacher's normal. The struggles of four decades centered largely around efforts to broaden the professional base of the university so as to define for it a clear and relevant mission, but at the same time to fit it into the Indiana educational scheme which gave so much emphasis and support to the applied arts as nurtured in the land-grant college.

The first long step into professionalism after establishment of the School of Law was the organization of a school of medicine. The intense political and intra-professional struggle that went on from 1904 to 1909 involved about every element of political and public opinion in Indiana, and none more fatally than the rivalry for survival between the liberal arts university at Bloomington and the land-grant technological arts university at Lafayette. Somewhat by accident, but even more by design, the two schools became locked in heated contest. It would now be impossible for the historian to bring into full focus all of the in-fighting and jealousies of the Indiana doctors, and especially those who had proprietary interests in medical schools in Fort Wayne and Indianapolis. A close search of the record, published and private and confidential, has yielded the visible facts about the enormously important fight in and out of the legislature to save the medical school for the university. To be sure, there is still more to the story than even these records reveal.

Just as reflective in this troubled chapter of Indiana social history was the remarkably thin wall of protection between the public and private colleges and universities. Had Indiana University lost its medical school campaign it is only reasonable to assume that it would have been defeated in the larger plans to become a competitive professional university operating from an ever-widening base. In another way the medical school conflict bore on the course of Indiana higher education. Everybody, from Governor Thomas Marshall down to the most modest college president, sensed how close the medical school argument had brought higher education to political chaos. It also held up a reflective mirror for both public and private colleges to view in intelligent perspective the senseless rivalries among the institutions, and compromises resulted which allowed the schools to operate harmoniously in the future. This may well have been the date when Hoosiers began their real advance to intellectual maturity; certainly it was a period when they saw the necessity for tolerance.

A reviewer of Volume I commented upon what he conceived to be an overemphasis on financial stringency. This volume likewise comments upon the subject. William Lowe Bryan and the trustees would have readily agreed this was a matter of prime central concern. Remarkably the university was able to expand its offerings, to maintain a minimum capacity plant, support a surprisingly good core faculty, and to give a sense of progress on severely limited budgets. Plucking organizational down from its own academic breast, the university organized itself, often in the most elementary way, into professional schools and services. This no doubt was William Lowe Bryan's most notable achievement, although he said making thirty-five budgets was his major accomplishment. Beginning with the Medical School and winding up with the creation of the School of Music, two decades were marked by dramatic effort to perfect a university organization. At the core of the expansion, the institution maintained highly acceptable academic expansion as was reflected by the establishment of chapters of Sigma Xi and Phi Beta Kappa. At the same time, it was admitted to membership in the American Association of Universities and it participated in the Carnegie retirement plan. The standards by which the institution gauged its development were those of the neighboring schools such as Michigan, Wisconsin, and Northwestern.

Every effort has been made in this volume to associate the development of Indiana University with the changing times of the first four decades of the twentieth century. World War I and its aftermath swept the institution almost completely off its traditional course. There were mixed emotions among administrators and faculty about the role of the university in a troubled world. Its intimate association with the Philippine Islands early in the century had broken any isolative bands which had existed in 1902. The later international incident on the Mexican border had increased interest in national and international affairs. Germany's invasion of Belguim brought to a feverish pitch pro-allied sympathies.

Like David Starr Jordan of Stanford, William Lowe Bryan was a pacifist in the opening period of this global struggle, but his conversion to the allied cause was almost instantaneous, and between late 1915 and 1918 he and his faculty made conduct of the war central to the university's purpose. The record of the university in these years was highly creditable. Lacking money and supplies, still, the academic community made a remarkable showing in rendering all sorts of aid. Indiana University's students and alumni distinguished themselves in the various military services.

In the postwar world Indiana faced the biggest challenges in its history. Radically changed world conditions after 1920 brought a revolution in every phase of institutional operations and human relationships. Bryan, a patrician and puritan, found himself caught up by a baffling age of rapidly shifting social attitudes and decorum. The first shock to his sense of moral and professional propriety was the divorce of Professor Samuel Bannister Harding from his wife. The rise of the Ku Klux Klan and the involvement of Indiana politicians with this sub-rosa body, the social complexities created by prohibition, changing attitudes and behavior between the growing popularity of the automobile and with it increased student mobility, increasing enrollments, and the search for new professorial talent all taxed the energies and moral resources of the administration. The "jazz age" in America caught Indiana University largely unprepared for the acceptance of new social mores.

Closely associated with the jazz age was the eternal struggle to achieve excellence in collegiate athletic competition, especially in football and basketball. Not only did students, alumni, and public seek victory for vanity's sake, but the institutional image in good part came to be measured in terms of its muscle within the "Big Nine" or "Big Ten." Season after season an almost adolescent hope arose, that Indiana University would conquer its ancient rivals and Purdue University first of all. William Lowe Bryan was as ardent as any fan in this desire.

During the years of depression and continuing into the late 1930's Indiana University gathered fresh momentum. Availability of federal funds on a generous matching basis enabled the institution to embark on building and academic programs to meet the demands of a greatly increased student enrollment. Support from the New Deal agencies was indeed a godsend. Construction of new buildings with federal aid gave the university a new sense of progress and emboldened the administration and faculty to undertake intensive introspection to chart a new course to the future. Too, the passage of necessary legislation to permit adoption of a national retirement and annuity plan wrought major changes internally in personnel organization. These decisions indeed ended an era, and cast the struggling Bryan years in a purely historical perspective of having laid dependable foundations.

There was indeed a wide gulf between the athletic fields and the university classrooms. The former became a focal point in the period covered by this volume for the non-intellectual view of the university, the latter a crucible in which the institution's enduring labors were performed, well away from the blare of brass bands, maniacal yells, cheer leaders, and irresponsible fans. The faculty of the Bryan era performed its tasks with remarkable results. It has been impossible to single out each of the faculty yeomen who rendered service. Perhaps an unintentional injustice may in cases be done, but limited space has simply interdicted full treatment.

In large measure the history of a university is that of its various departments and their staff members. The histories of these should be written in special monographs and professorial biographies. The historian of Indiana University, like historians of other public universities, confronts the woes of a "sanitized" personal and professional documentation. What records professors have allowed to survive them have often been culled or destroyed by widows and heirs. As the last chapters of this volume were being written the descendants of a truly distinguished professor destroyed his papers.

There has been, however, no lack of documentary material to sustain the writing of this volume, and I have had free and complete access to them. The documentary records of this university are indeed voluminous and full for this era. Because of the jealousy with which I have had to use precious space I have had, of necessity, to be selective. I have endeavored manfully to make clear most sources by a process of internal documentation rather than using footnotes. The bibliography aims at fullness and explicitness; it indicates the richness of Indiana's institutional archival collection.

Again, I am not a graduate of nor have I in any sentimental manner been associated with Indiana University. I have indeed

lived with it more intensively during the past few years than perhaps any other professor except James Albert Woodburn and
Burton D. Myers. I have viewed the university's past so far as humanly possible through objective eyes. The history of a seminal
American public university is the history of a dedicated human
expression of hope, ambition, of faith in the processes of cultural
refinement, and of the importance of the human intellect in a mate-
rialistic society. Because a university is such a human place it
reflects most of the virtues and frailties of its time and place on the
scale of civilization, and it is most of all current in these expressions.
A historian treads on sensitive ground when he writes about people
who still are living, or more especially who have left loyal descendants. I know from fairly long experience of living in a university
community how sensitive its members can be. This is especially
true where a university engages in a great deal of ceremonial display and rewarding people publicly for all sorts of reasons. If I have
erred in fact or interpretation it has been an act of the hand rather
than the heart.

I know, too, there is a wide gap between what appears in the
formal record and what actually happened—or, more important—
how and why it happened. The formal rules and mandates of faculty
and trustees are like civil laws, they may have become distinguished
only in their neglect and non-observance. The eight-man board of
trustees, 1902–1940, lived close to Indiana University on one side
and next to Indiana public and political life on the other. Many of
them were highly oriented in politics and public affairs. The historian can never expect to recover more than a fragment of what was
said or done in the privacy of "executive meeting," or hotel rooms,
lobbies, and legislative chambers. Every public university has to
have its internal managers or its survival would be constantly
threatened. The recovery of this story is fraught with many difficulties. I have penetrated a bit these vaults of silence in taped
interviews in which the public record has been either modified or
validated. For instance, I got an intimate insight into the operation
of the president's office in an interview with Miss Ruth McNutt just
ten days before her death. Judge John Simpson Hastings was exceedingly generous and informative in a long taped interview in
which he placed the administrative affairs of the university in clear
and human perspective.

Throughout the preparation of this book I have kept in mind

the fact that I was dealing with the history of a peoples' university which set its course in harmony with the Jeffersonian ideal for higher education, and a sense of its place in the maturing society which supported it. The test of the Bryan years in Indiana University was largely a matter of determining how well the institution achieved the elementary dream of preparing a public leadership at all levels of human endeavor, and how well it served public needs for specialized personnel in several basic human fields. It would be so easy to make the judgment that because of his strict personal code of morals and ethical relationships, William Lowe Bryan failed to meet the challenge fully. That, however, would be a judgment both false and harsh. Bryan lived within the context of his times and of the Indiana society which supported the university. He never lost sight of the fundamental fact that the university's challenge was to produce the highest quality graduate possible in as many fields as was wise for the institution to support.

In 1937 he delivered over to new administrative management an institution which had made genuine headway, but, of greater consequence, one with a dependable foundation on which to bring about a realization of the greater dream of a full scale, quality university. The credit belongs to trustees, the president, and a dedicated faculty. In almost a century and a quarter Indiana University had experienced about all of the hardships and challenges which had beset American higher education in general. It took institutional dedication of a host of men to see it through these various moments of history, and to keep alight the flame of enthusiasm for making progress. Even so searching and critical a document as the Self-Study Report of 1939 eloquently documents this fact.

I should like to acknowledge that three chapters from this volume were used, in modified form, by me when I gave the Patten Foundation Lectures in 1971.

It is almost impossible to acknowledge all of the people who have made contributions to the preparation of this volume. I am especially grateful to Mrs. Mary B. Craig and Miss Dolores M. Lahrman of the University Archives who very generously aided me in my search for materials. Barbara Buckley Lambert and Eileen Walters did yeoman service indeed in filing, taking notes, and typing. Their services were indispensable. George Challou, Eric Gilbertson, Leo LaSota, John Woerner, Robert Stinson, Donn Gossom, Howard Jones, James H. Jones, David Warriner, Charles

Zimmerman, Don Zimmer, Kathryn Shoupe, and Loren Fraser were research assistants who kept up the hunt for materials and spent endless hours taking notes. I am especially indebted to Thomas Buckley who has read much of the manuscript, checked most of the quotations, and otherwise performed craftsmanlike chores in the preparation of this volume.

Mrs. Dorothy Collins has ever been a source of refuge when I have needed a reader or help in the procurement of information. Donald F. Carmony has been a most helpful and obliging colleague. Leo Solt has borne much of the administrative brunt of seeing this project along the way, and Mrs. Anne Moore, that never-failing source of information and advice, deserves special credit. The book, however, is my responsibility. I have tried to present as full a story as possible with proper realization that no one can in fact fully capture all of the history of an emerging university on paper.

INDIANA
UNIVERSITY
Midwestern Pioneer

Volume II / In Mid-Passage

[I]

The Throb of a New Century

THE *Arbutus* FOR 1899 closed its pages with a pen and ink vignette of Joseph Swain leading a boy and girl by the hands, followed by a procession of Indiana students. They approached a symbolic future with hope and anticipation registered on their faces. The President had led the university literally by the hand from the nineteenth to the twentieth century and into an era when changing values in American life brought radically different demands upon the institution.

Swain had remained in Bloomington long enough into the twentieth century to see the state and nation embark upon a new phase of history in which the latter had become a rising world power and had assumed burdensome moral, political, and economic obligations. New and heavier demands were made upon citizens and resources alike. In 1890 the Superintendent of the United States Census Bureau declared, statistically at least, the great landed frontier was closed. No longer was this sprawling landed sponge receiving an endless stream of home seekers and adventurers. The forces which had helped spawn the university in 1820 were no longer the active ones in 1900. The changes of three-quarters of a century had revised radically the purposes of the public university. Ingenious railroad builders and financiers had webbed the continent with a gossamer of steel, and corporate bodies had consolidated the last of the independent roads into one of the huge systems. Management had grown arrogant to the point that sharper public controls became mandatory for fiscal and operative regulations. Industrial labor made even more direct demands on employers and had become a social and political force in the making of public decisions. In 1900 approximately 38 percent of the Indiana labor force had entered industrial employment, and within the next decade 53 percent was industrially employed.

Nationally the age of McKinley ended abruptly in 1901 and the age of Roosevelt began within the instant of a pistol shot. This indeed became the age of the new common man; the farmer, industrial laborer, white-collar worker, and a host of other middle-class Americans demanded to be included in legislative considerations. More and more state and federal governments were called upon to render regulatory services in the fields of drug and food inspections, public health, education, resource management, social awareness, and agriculture. The big trusts were brought under further scrutiny in successive reviews by the courts, and court decisions became more meaningful for society as a whole. America was making its transition from a frontier agrarian nation to an industrial one. Demands on public universities now meant they largely had to ignore the academic traditions of higher learning of an earlier agrarian-theocratic society.

There is ample evidence that Joseph Swain sensed the thrust of this change in Bloomington, in Indiana, and in the nation. His speeches, reports, and pleas to the public revealed his anxieties. He left for his successor in 1902 the responsibility of setting the new course for Indiana University in the age of Rooseveltian ferment. Swain departed Bloomington in June, and to all intents and purposes he left the presidency at that time. This his successor recognized and that summer William Lowe Bryan was writing Swain a humorous story of a conversation between Will and Henry James, to which Will replied, "I have not understood a word you have said except your profanity."

Bryan in all of his early enthusiasm had written Swain that he was entranced with William James' new book, *Varieties of Religious Experience*, and he expected to conduct his administration on some of the principles stated in it. On August 28, 1902, Swain viewed the problems of Indiana University through more practical

[4]

eyes which were focused nearer the ground. He told his friend, "I do not think you will find any one thing that will be in any way overwhelming. It is the accumulation of things and the succession of them that bring to one the greatest test. You state that it would all be easy were the work of the college president a question of standing by any abstract principle. The difficulty lies in the complex nature of the situation in seeing the application of principles. If one can have an opportunity to withdraw himself occasionally and not think too many hours at a time on any one problem the perspective is generally clearer. After all you are certainly right in your planting yourself on the idea of James' book on *Varieties of Religious Experience*. The difficulty lies not in doing things but in being perfectly sure what to do. I have faith that things will go onward and upward in Indiana."

Swain knew Bryan would have his worries in the future. He wrote at an undisclosed date, "In my dreams last night, I saw you with two cigars in your mouth at the same time. In answer to my enquiring looks, you said, 'My new life has driven me to it.' " The prophetic fabric of Bryan's new life was disclosed in the most recent decennial census report. Had the trustees and legislators taken time to read the tables of 1890 and 1900 they would have discovered the tide of the age as it swept against the university in the form of comparative statistics. Within the decade Indiana added almost 325,000 people to its 1890 population of 2,192,404. The location of Hoosiers had shifted downward appreciatively from 73.1 rural dwellers to 65.7, a trend which came close to an even balance in 1920.

In Bloomington the university enrollment was overwhelmingly of Hoosier origin. Out of a total yearly class enrollment of 1,203 undergraduates in 1902 there were 65 from outside the state, and ten out of 82 graduate students. This ratio prevailed for 1905. In the latter year there were four Filipinos and two Japanese. Though it is impossible to determine rural or urban origins of students, listed addresses in the catalogue seem to indicate that most had small town or rural farm origins.

The man who in Joseph Swain's fantastic dream held two cigars in his mouth at once was no stranger to Indiana University. Nor was he unfamiliar with its needs and lacks. As vice president since 1893 he knew intimately the aims and frustrations of his predecessor. As noted in the earlier volume of this history, Joseph

Swain had suggested William Lowe Bryan as his successor, and the trustees, voting independently, had selected him unanimously within an hour and a half of receiving Joseph Swain's resignation. Bryan had a proper Hoosier background. Born only two miles east of the campus on November 11, 1860, the son of a Presbyterian minister of Irish descent, he was of the bone and sinew of the institution and the community.

On his ninety-second birthday he said, "I was born of parents such that I am still alive at the age of 92, able to walk a mile without sensible fatigue, able to enjoy day by day a healthy life." His parents, Bryan said, had guarded him against "injuries from hornets and rattlesnakes and many other greater dangers." He was schooled at home in English speech, the Bible, McGuffey's readers, and other subjects considered worthy at the time. For seventeen years Bryan learned about the challenges of life on the slopes of a hillside farm. Within the sound of the chapel bell he prepared himself for the day when he would answer those commanding chimes and enter the university's classes. His resources were slender in the panic-ridden year of 1877, and after his freshman year he dropped out to teach an elementary school in Grayville, Illinois.

Bryan did not receive his Bachelor's degree from Indiana University until 1884, and two years later he was awarded a Master's degree. At the time he finished his baccalaureate work, Lemuel Moss recommended to the trustees that the university should keep its bright young men and mature them into professors. He had in mind William Julian Bryan,* who showed extraordinary promise, and Moss added, "He will come cheap." That year Bryan was elected to the position of assistant in Greek, but the salary was so low that he chose to accept a place as an assistant to James A. Woodburn in the preparatory school. Apparently some kind of financial adjustment was made and the *Indiana Student* announced in December of 1884, "Everyone will be glad to hear of the promotion of Mr. Will Bryan to the position of assistant instructor in the University." The new English teacher would give instruction in elocution and rhetoric. The editor pointed to his brilliant record and predicted from him an ever-broadening reputation in education. On December 20, he sat for the first time with the faculty. The next year David Starr Jordan informed the trustees that he wished William J. Bryan made an associate professor of English

* He was later to become known as William Lowe Bryan, adopting the maiden surname of his wife.

and philosophy. "As to Mr. Bryan," said Jordan, "I need only say that his work ranks with the best I have ever seen done anywhere; I regard him as one of the most gifted teachers in the state."

Though born and reared in the very heart of rural Indiana, William J. Bryan was hardly a provincial in either outlook or formal training. In 1886 he left Bloomington to study in the universities of Berlin; in 1900 he returned to Europe for a year of study in Wurzburg and Paris. In 1892 he was awarded the Doctor of Philosophy degree by Clark University. Thus was launched what promised to be a truly distinguished career in the field of psychology.

Bryan not only took pride in his intellectual accomplishments but also in a lifetime of physical well-being. He was moderately tall and had a roundish face topped by a high, if not protruding, forehead. Sometime in his youth, while playing baseball, he had broken what otherwise would have been an aquiline nose. His mouth was shaped by slightly thin lips, and his eyes had a distinctive brightness and clarity. He was a meticulous dresser in a rigidly moderate style. Bryan at once impressed people with his code of personal rectitude; in fact many thought they detected an unusually strong element of prudery and austerity in him. To friends he revealed an essentially friendly nature but one tempered with social and intellectual conservatism. He was an interesting conversationalist, and he reflected deep religious and intellectual commitments.

When William Lowe Bryan faced his inaugural audience on January 21, 1903, he charted the essential course he would pursue to the future with certainty:

> What people need and demand is that their children shall have a chance—as good as any other children in the world—to make the most of themselves, to rise in any and every occupation, including those occupations which require the most thorough training. What the people want is open paths from every corner of the State, through the schools, to the highest and best things which men can achieve. To make such paths, to make them open to the poorest and lead to the highest is the mission of democracy.

Young President Bryan, vibrant with excitement at having an opportunity to clear new paths to learning for his home people, saw his task as that of opening doors for more people to enter the university. As pioneer Hoosier constitutionalists had outlined so eloquently the mission and objectives of their backwoods university in an educational clause, Bryan stated those of the modern state university in his inaugural address. Seldom have inaugural addresses outlined so succinctly and clearly the aims of a new president. He was still captivated by the abstractions set forth in *Varieties of Religious Experience.*

Personally William Lowe Bryan was a deeply sentimental man who expressed a parental concern about both his public and private responsibilities. In 1885 he was returning to Bloomington from Indianapolis when he met Charlotte Lowe, whom he married in 1889. So much a part of his emotional being did his bride become that he dropped his middle name of Julian for her maiden name Lowe, partly to distinguish himself from the great Commoner William Jennings Bryan. Bryan's sentimental and stern Calvinistic side did not conceal his indefinable quality of natural leadership which inspired respect in his colleagues.

The new president's face reflected a boyish gentility of nature and also an elder man's sternness of character, which at times seemed forbidding and unyielding to associates and students. Critics saw in William Lowe Bryan an uncompromising Calvinism which they believed handicapped him in leading publc Indiana University into the mainstream of the new American learning in an age when old values were being sharply revised. More objective observers saw beneath the armor of conservatism a man capable of genuine educational statesmanship. His scholarship was well on the road to being established, and he had already honored himself in one of the newer disciplinary fields as a "starred" name in *American Men of Science.*

In the 1890's Bryan had lived up to David Starr Jordan's statement that he was an excellent scholar and teacher. Twice that persistent nemesis of Indiana University had tried to lure Bryan away to Stanford University to fill the chair of psychology and philosophy. About the time the second offer reached Bloomington, editors of the *Arbutus* for 1899 expressed their affection for the professor in a merry jingle:

> This is our Dr. Bryan
> But that is not meant
> That he's the B. who's tryin'
> To be the President.

We're glad he's not, for true he
(And that no one will doubt)
's the one man in the Faculty
We couldn't do without.

For the new president, in the stifling June of 1902, satisfying the needs of Indiana University seemed to be beyond his capability. There was no honeymoon; the university's troubles were too well known to him to delay solutions. He reported right off to the board of trustees that there was an enrollment of 748 students, 85 of whom were registered in the law school, and the remainder in liberal arts. This was one of the first fundamental issues he chose to face. Just prior to his elevation to the presidency, Bryan had made a careful study of comparative enrollments in the liberal arts courses in eight top-grade colleges and universities. On November 6, 1903, he informed the trustees that Indiana University was near the top in this area, both numerically and proportionately, but therein lay a fundamental institutional weakness. For the next thirty-five years the president expended much of his energy trying to achieve a professionalization of the curricular organization of the university.

Bryan was resolved to cut the cord which tied the institution so tightly during much of its past to the classical English academy tradition. Indiana University must now concentrate its energies in several of the more broadly applied professional and service fields if it were to compete successfully in the future for public support. Purdue University had a distinct advantage despite its brief existence in being free of either a classics tradition or a "gentlemanly" image. Its faculty was service-oriented; its students demanded "practical" applied education; and the institution could present itself directly to farmers, industrialists, laborers, bankers, and legislators as being keenly interested in their various activities.

In 1902 Indiana University had only three service or applied channels open to its graduates. These were teacher training, the law, and politics. The proud boast that the institution was a training ground for college presidents, professors, and public school teachers—a laudable enough accomplishment—viewed from the perspective of ever-broadening American educational objectives was a disturbing fact, as William Lowe Bryan was repeatedly to remind the board of trustees.

[9]

Bryan had only to make a random examination of the correspondence which flowed in and out of university offices to reach a conclusion as to where historical emphasis of the institution had been placed. Literally thousands of letters requested information about teacher training, requested recommendations for teaching jobs, or pertained to public school problems. For the new president this was an era of stocktaking. Since the graduation of the first class down to date, university graduates had done well in many fields. Among them had been some of Indiana's best lawyers; many had become doctors; scores had turned to politics; and many were successful businessmen, newspaper editors, ministers, and military men. A fair number of Indiana governors had attended Indiana University, and an increasing number of legislators over the years had attended college in Bloomington. This was a pleasant chapter in the history of the school, but Bryan knew it was just that. The modern university had to be brought into closer harmony with an age and a people who demanded application of learning to specific problems and needs.

Time was distressingly short for Indiana University to make its transition after 1902. A new curriculum either had to be created or the old one vastly revised. Any indecision at this point would mean that Purdue would become in fact Indiana's chief university. Indiana University enjoyed in its official mandate the necessary authority to broaden its base at any time it saw fit. There was, however, a very thin line between the objectives of the two state institutions, and any crossing of this line could spell disaster for one or both of them.

If William Lowe Bryan knew intimately any one fact about Indiana University, it was that historically the Indiana legislature had never given the institution more than barely enough support to keep body and soul together. Reflective of this knowledge he had hardly been in office three months before he submitted a report to the trustees which described the economic conditions of the university. On top of the curricular emergency which existed, there was the more immediate problem of maintaining an adequate faculty with severely limited funds. Though the times had advanced, Indiana legislators still thought in mid-nineteenth century terms when making institutional appropriations. Bryan recommended reducing the faculty body, lowering materially the ratio of professors to students, increasing the sizes of introductory courses and advanced classes, frequent quizzing of everybody, and maintaining freshman and sophomore recitations in keeping with traditional procedures in this area. He thought it wise to reappraise small elective courses, or to drop them altogether, and to keep the institution a university instead of a college.

"The thing here proposed," Bryan told the trustees, "is to allow a student to have as his major subject, not only particular sciences, such as chemistry, history, or the like, but also particular groups of sciences each of which leads to some occupation such as law, medicine, journalism, architecture, or business." He was positive that some way had to be found to broaden the base of the university, and this seemed to be the place to start. The president believed a school of architecture could be established by a proper rearrangement of existing courses and curricula. The same thing would apply to the organization of schools of engineering, business, music, journalism, and education. Before 1902 Bryan had expressed the idea that every university should have a college of engineering as an adjunct to its departments of mathematics, physics, chemistry, and government.

For the next three years President Bryan was to demand of the trustees serious consideration for an expanding scientific curriculum. Every university, he said, gave courses which fell within the field of engineering. Indiana University had done so since its beginnings. In 1903 Robert Judson Aley, mathematics; Arthur Lee Foley, physics; and John A. Miller, mechanics and astronomy, had already devised a program for civil and mechanical engineering. Miller believed his courses could be expanded with little added expense to include arches, masonry, and bridge and roof design. Some staff additions would be necessary in the future, but Indiana University, like other state schools, could maintain an engineering college at modest cost.

The president was clear in his statement to the trustees that in its moment of grave needs he saw nothing that would be more meaningful to the university than the organization of professional courses along technical lines. The needs of modern civilization demanded these. To sustain his arguments Bryan cited the experiences of the universities of Michigan, Kansas, Iowa, Mississippi, Colorado, and Washington. In all of these states there were two schools of engineering; the one major exception in his mind was Indiana University.

[11]

However the board of trustees chose to resolve the academic dilemma so far as classes and curricula were concerned, there was an even more vital issue. Bryan told the trustees there was deep dissatisfaction in the faculty with salaries and salary policy—if the board's yearly arbitrary decisions could be called a policy. The time had come to fix a salary scale, re-examine faculty ranks, and adopt more generous rules applying to leaves of absence, retirement, and pensions. To date trustees had arranged salaries largely in keeping with the amount of funds immediately available and had not presented the legislature with more than an overall request for a given amount of money. Examination of the highly simplified budget for the decade prior to 1903 reveals the fact that the salary scale was static. It is now almost impossible to detect any significant change in the scale or to note a consciousness of the exigencies of the new age in America.

The so-called faculty roll for 1902 totaled $88,450, and the next year—the first full one of Bryan's administration—the total remained almost the same. Out of $184,147.59, the trustees provided for faculty salaries and upkeep of the physical plant, met some construction costs, and paid all other university obligations. The average full professor's salary hovered around $2,000, with the maximum being $2,300. For the years 1903 to 1905, the university's annual income for all purposes was slightly over $200,000, an amount which included expenditures for capital outlay, income from interest on endowment, and direct legislative appropriations.

It was in the area of expanding the university's physical plant that the Bryan administration sought an increase in extraordinary expenditure funds. The plant of the university was within itself a limiting factor in university expansion. On January 21, 1903, the new science building was dedicated and was immediately occupied by physics, geology, psychology, philosophy, and education. To the students it was the "Crazy House" because of the experiments conducted by psychologists on rats and monkeys. Nevertheless, the addition of this large building relieved the enormous pressure for space. The old gymnasium was further reduced in efficiency by the addition of the carpenter shop in one end. The old observatory was an eyesore, which was defaced annually by freshmen and sophomores with their adolescent epithets painted on the walls. By September, 1904, the $25,000 power plant was almost completed, and plans were underway for the construction of the student building. The five administrative offices in Owen Hall had been refurbished, and each one of them was equipped with a telephone. This was the extent of plant improvements for the time being.

When Joseph Swain went to the presidency of Swarthmore he left behind in Bloomington many unfinished tasks. For example both town and campus roadways were dirt and gravel. Extended rainy days in the Ohio Valley turned the place into a quagmire. This accounted for the fact that William Lowe Bryan rode to his office on horseback with his trouser legs encased in leggings. In 1903 Bloomington and the university joined forces to improve Indiana Avenue. Dirt was hauled from the sloping side of Jordan Field to fill in the swag on that part of the street north of the River Jordan. On the campus itself plank and gravel walks led up from Kirkwood Avenue to the three main buildings, and other casual paths cut across woods and meadow. Wet weather brought lingering mud and slush, and cold and snow produced ice. No provisions were made for cleaning the walks and for days at a time they remained unsafe for pedestrian use. This incurred the wrath of student editors who pretended to believe the university had little concern for life and limb, and the janitor answered back that he could not scrape away the offending ice.

The driveway leading to Jordan Field was deeply rutted and almost impassable. Many people drove to athletic events and sat in their carriages on the sidelines. As late as May 25, 1904, the *Daily Student* said, "To do so [travel to Jordan Field] at present necessitates going hub deep in mud. It is not customary to attend games in log wagons nor to wear overalls, but nothing better at present can go over the driveway without damage."

Wherever students assembled on college campuses in North America they were trailbreakers, and those in the first decades of this century at Indiana University were no exception. They cut paths across Dunn Meadow to the mouths of three or four streets, and scored the campus woodland with their by-ways. Placards posted about the grounds begged pedestrians to remain on established walkways, and to take an active part in preserving the natural beauty of the university setting.

Conservationists sought in other ways to protect the sylvan glades of the campus. The deciduous woods contained a rich variety of oak, maple, ash, persimmon, black walnut, cherry, and beech. Some of the older trees were estimated to be as much as two centuries old. In April, 1910, when the site for the heating plant tunnel was being prepared for excavation, it became necessary to destroy a two-hundred-year-old tree. This disturbed the campus editor. "None of the natural growth of trees," he said, "are less than 125 years old. Storms and decay are destroying the magnificent trees at a rate of six a year."

The *Daily Student* was grossly mistaken. A majority of the trees were relatively young as is revealed in contemporary photographs. Professor David Myers Mottier, William R. Ogg, and campus workmen had been busy for the past decade planting seedlings from the university nursery's indigenous stock. This gave the appearance that the trees had sprouted from seed where they stood. Despite mud and dirt roads and walks the campus during the early years of the Bryan administration presented a pleasant appearance, but the front portion along Indiana Avenue was only sparsely wooded as late as 1911.

Dense woods on the university's campus made an unusually romantic appeal to strollers but at the same time offered moral affronts to the Victorian in shocking violations of the institution's code of moral decorum. Mottier wrote with righteous indignation in his report of 1911 to William Lowe Bryan, "Certain circumstances which have to do with morals on the campus need attention. On Sunday night, May 28, disgraceful, immoral proceedings were carried out by two couples in plain view of the brick walk, leading from the observatory to Kirkwood Hall." He suggested lighting the campus so "conditions would be much less favorable for the grosser forms of immorality." What Mottier did not tell Bryan was that just such an incident had given Bohannon's Hollow its name.

To give an even more authentic wilderness touch to the campus, hunters and trappers were paid in the summer of 1903, to capture gray and fox squirrels to be turned loose in the woods. These animals were kept in a large wire cage back of the new heating plant until they became "accustomed to the grounds," and until the Bloomington City Council could enact an ordinance forbidding poachers to shoot squirrels on the university grounds.

At the same time university officials concerned themselves with an architectural semicolon which was added to the middle of the campus in the form of a miniature structure which in years became the central landmark of Indiana University folklore, tradition, and microbic exchange. This little building was the impulsive dream of Theodore Frelinghuysen Rose of Fairfield and Muncie, who graduated with the class of 1875. Rose had succeeded as both lawyer and banker, and came to wield broad influence as vice-president and president of the board of trustees. Equally challenging was his service on the building and grounds committee, where he looked upon the campus as his private domain. In a burst of enthusiasm he suggested damming the lower end of Dunn Meadow to create a romantic lake and relieve the drabness of a neglected corner of the raw new campus. His peers, however, were still frightened by ague and malaria and feared the mosquito plague would obliterate every vestige of beauty.

Rose's most acceptable suggestion was the acquisition from the Bloomington City School Trustees of the porticos of the old University Building and mounting them as a monument of the past and a symbol of the future astride the entry way to the campus drive from Kirkwood Avenue. By October, 1904, his plans to acquire the portals were underway. William Lowe Bryan wrote the enthusiastic trustee, "I send you by mail blueprints of the college portals . . . and also measurements showing the width of the sidewalks and the roadway at the Kirkwood entrance to the campus." He explained he had laid the proposition before the Alumni Association and the City School Trustees and would soon have an answer.

Bryan's university was astir for the next three years with plans and problems of greater moment and not much time could be given to purely sentimental objectives. The Student Building was under construction, frantic searches were being made for a dependable water supply, and even campus walks and drives cried for attention. Professors and students sought new library facilities. To help carry out all of these activities Professor Arthur Lee Foley, head of the Physics Department, was made campus construction overseer, and his hands were full with building and departmental details. He had little time to give to the esoteric portico project. It was evident before the first mortar seam was pried loose in the old building at the end of College Street that the narrow gothic arches would only serve further to block entrance to the campus, not even pedestrians could use the side entries with comfort. A less practical use had to be found for this cherished memento.

Obsessed as they were with the subject of water, president and trustees thought instinctively of the blessings of a well house.

[1 5]

Patton and Miller, architects for the Student Building, were already on the grounds, and they were asked to design a fancy edition of this homely Hoosier necessity, a well sheltered by the ancient portals. Also an architect named Mehurin was asked to contribute his ideas. Professor Foley was forthright in his criticism of both sets of plans. To him the architects had drawn plans for a burial vault, a morgue, or an entry to a medieval arsenal. In July, 1907, he wrote Trustee Rose, "I am vain enough to believe that I have a better plan than either of these suggested. I have already worked out the roof features and have been working on the ceiling, and pump itself." In his own plans he undertook to lighten the details so as to fit the structure to the ground and to allow a maximum amount of natural illumination to flood the interior. Tradition has it that Foley's design, at Theodore Rose's suggestion, included a foundation approximating the shape of the Beta Theta Pi fraternity pin, although no such instructions appear in either the official Board of Trustees Minutes, the rather extensive personal correspondence, or the contemporary campus paper.

A. Soupart, a stonebelt craftsman, was placed in charge of removing the portals from the old building and delivering them safely to the new campus. Foley hired Monroe County stonecutters and masons to construct the building. When common laborers threatened to strike because they thought they could earn higher wages working on the new county courthouse, Foley fired them and hired new workmen. Three stonecutter brothers agreed to work on the project during the cold months, dressing the stone so that construction could be carried on quickly at the break of winter.

William Lowe Bryan and local members of the board of trustees located the site of the well house in January, 1908, just off to the side of the north fire cistern in such a manner as to spare some large trees. The main walkway ran due north and south through the portals, and led almost directly to the entry of Wylie Hall. During the spring of 1908 workmen were busy raising the tiny structure. "Never in the history of the University," said the *Daily Student*, "have chisel and pick been so busy; never has work on one of its buildings been so rushed." The rush was caused by a desire to have the well house ready for commencement.

On June 2, 1908, the new building was made a center of the commencement fete. Lemonade was available at a nickel a glass or the frugal ones could pump a free drink of cistern water with the new pump while they admired Professor Foley's two half domes and the central ceiling vault with its arc light. Outside, the roof line gave the general appearance of a Greek orthodox church with a peaked arabesque touch. The bright red Spanish tiles added a further Old World touch. The ancient university inscription adorned one portal while the seal appeared on the other, both of which had been carved by William Stevenson in 1854.

Later that month Theodore Rose, his wife, a grand-daughter of Andrew Wylie, and their son Frederick presented the well house to the university as a memorial to the class of 1875. In response William Lowe Bryan wrote the benefactors that the trustees accepted the gift, and that a friend of his had said, "that the Well House was the diamond stud on the shirt front of the University." More irreverently the *Arbutus* for 1912 announced that the National Order of Tin Cup Bacteria planned its grand convention in the well house. The delegates, said the editor, had the "chained community cup" on their minds, and, perhaps, the ardent midnight kissing which transformed plain innocent college lasses into full fledged co-eds.

Building the Well House was part of the drama of the early Bryan years. Three years after the new president came to the office, the institution found itself once again involved in a second and highly complicated public land drama requiring the drawing of a fine line of distinction between it and the Indiana common schools. This issue was not to be solved for a quarter of a century. The escheated lands of George Donaldson, a Scottish citizen who died in Maidens, Scotland, in 1898, lay east of the waters of the South Fork of the White River in Lawrence County and near the town of Mitchell. They were contained within two irregularly shaped and adjoining tracts of slightly over 182 acres. Flowing through the property was Lost River or a branch which fed through a cavernous area containing two fairly large caverns, Donaldson and Twin Caves. This land was first settled by Sam Jackson, a Canadian who had fought on the American side in the War of 1812. In time this emigré built a mill and opened a farm.

Between 1814 and 1865 the Jackson farm passed through several hands, but the most colorful owner was George Donaldson, a hunter and a traveler. He acquired the lands in 1865 and 1867, and built a quaint house near Lost River, then lived the quiet life of a semi-recluse, allowing the wilderness to reclaim the soil and the streams to remain unmolested.

The Donaldson caves were veritable ichthyological laboratories containing especially interesting specimens of blind fishes. These were known early to David Starr Jordan and Carl Eigenmann. The latter saw in this natural wonderland an especially fruitful source of further study in his specialty. George Donaldson left the White River country about 1883 to live in Alabama, and fourteen years later he returned to Scotland where he became an invalid requiring intensive nursing care. In 1898 he died at Maidens, legally intestate. He had held his Indiana lands for more than five years, and under state statutes of 1861, 1881, and 1883, the failure of an alien to make proper conveyance of title invalidated his heirs' claim to the property. Thus Donaldson's property could not be entailed to his Scottish nephews and nieces; instead the estate escheated to the Indiana common school fund.

Because of the scientific importance of the caves and the surrounding virgin forest to the university's expanding programs, William Lowe Bryan and Carl Eigenmann persuaded the legislature in the spring of 1903 to rest title in the trustees of the institution. From 1903 to 1927, however, this title was placed in constant jeopardy by various contestants. First, Donaldson's heirs undertook to recover title at law. Then there were repeated efforts to reclaim it for the public schools, with strong overtones of personal greed among petty politicians in Lawrence County who hoped to have the land placed on the public market.

In June, 1906, the Indiana Supreme Court handed down a decision in *Donaldson et al.* vs. *State, Ex. Rel. Attorney General* denying the Scottish heirs' claims. Just before the court rendered its verdict the legislature had vested title in the university. It appeared from a facetious remark by Deputy Attorney General, C. C. Hadley, that the assemblymen held the land in low esteem. He suggested that the caves be sliced into small segments and sold for post holes. Carl Eigenmann was decidedly of another opinion. He proceeded to develop what he called "a blind fish study station." This also included a study of the fauna surrounding the caverns. In 1904 he brought specimen of blind fish from Cuban caverns, which he had visited, and deposited them in the Donaldson pools. This blind fish collection in time was to attract icthyologists from all over America.

Annually after 1903 there appeared in the minutes of the board of trustees reports on this off-campus property. In 1906, Eigenmann made an extensive survey in which he recommended the development of a forestry program and broader exploitation of the area's biological resources. Again in 1909 the biologist was back before the board of trustees asking that the over-aged timber be salvaged, and that the deteriorating cottage be restored. He asked for $175 to accomplish this.

Donaldson Farm, however, was to prove over the years more a trouble than a blessing. Lawyers continued to argue over its title. The Supreme Court of Indiana in 1913, in *Donaldson et al.* vs. *State of Indiana Ex. Rel. Honan, Attorney General*, reviewed the title in which it made a detailed review of George Donaldson's life and apparent intent as expressed in his Glasgow will. This time the court reversed itself and remanded the property to the common school fund. It held the legislative act of 1903 invalid because common school lands could not be sold under the terms of a local law. In Bloomington the *Daily Student* said, "This decision means a great loss to the University as it was planned to establish a zoological station on the farm similar to those at Winona Lake and at Mitchell. . . ." Two years later the General Assembly enacted legislation allowing the university to purchase the farm for $4,000 and plans were revived to operate a biological and forestry program there. This latter price was established from the fact that John T. Stout, a speculator, had paid the Scottish heirs this sum for their title claim.

The university was not to occupy the land with security. Within a decade political pressures to incorporate the Donaldson lands in a state park (Spring Mill) became so great that on March 11, 1927, the legislature authorized the board of trustees to instruct William Lowe Bryan to execute a deed of transfer to the Park Commission on the condition the university would receive $9,747.41 in payment. This ended a troubled chapter in the university's history and relieved the trustees of a thorny problem. This had been a pioneer effort on the part of the institution to break the provincial boundaries of its operations to Monroe County and the Bloomington campus. Equally important, the fate of the Donaldson land reflected the blithe disregard with which the development of a scientific program in the university was viewed.

Organizing the academic staff, developing grounds and properties, and looking after the welfare of students were continuing issues before the board of trustees. This was largely true because board members and their executive committee concerned themselves with minute details of university operation, obscuring academic matters of the early decade of William Lowe Bryan's administration. One of the most distinguishing features of the period was the grasp the permanent heads of departments early fastened on the central instructional program. It was a major paradox in the university's history that Bryan was so perceptive from the outset in redesigning the curriculum, in his efforts to liberalize the elective system, and in broadening the academic base of institutional service and yet he seems to have held with unrelenting grip to the permanent departmental headship as an administrative facility.

Whether by deliberate design or acceptance of firmly entrenched tradition, President Bryan made no proposals during his early years of liberalizing departmental leadership. No doubt he fell under the influence of the European head-professorship tradition and retained it at Indiana. Too, the new president was intellectually unprepared to imagine an institution of higher education operating except under tight personal control. There is every reason to believe that as president he was the only one who gave ultimate direction to the institution's academic activities. Heads of departments constituted a kind of university senate or executive committee wherever decisions were to be made by the faculty. Within individual departments the heads were masters of the domain and almost beyond challenge in every phase of the division's operation. With Bryan's tacit consent they made schedules, assigned work loads, recommended new appointees, fired men, regulated their colleagues' personal and scholarly activities within the university, and spoke for their departments on all occasions. Names of department heads were bunched at the top of the lists of professors in the catalogues, at the head of the salary roll, and they were singled out in many other ways.

William Lowe Bryan was from the outset of his administration the personal embodiment of the university. He conducted faculty meetings himself instead of deferring to Dean Horace Addison Hoffman, supervised the curriculum, and influenced all decisions of academic policy. Contemporary critics felt Bryan in fact transacted general university business in liberal arts faculty meetings, without giving an indication that he was doing so. Both faculty and board of trustee minutes confirm this observation.

Because of the determined will of the president to be constantly in control of all university affairs, and in turn encouraging the same willfulness on the part of department heads, there developed in Indiana University after 1902 a certain internal rigidity which no doubt restrained many efforts to expand and diversify course offerings. In no area was this more clearly revealed than in the recurring attempts to review and define the program of elective studies. Another manifestation of headship influence revealed in the records was dissatisfaction of younger men with their subordinate position in the tight hierarchy. It is almost impossible, of course, to document the degree of existing unhappiness, but it is clear the president and heads of departments supervised too closely their underlings' professional lives. If a junior rank professor wished to institute a new course, change a laboratory manual, adopt a textbook, or use modern or different techniques, he might have been prevented from doing so by his superior.

By no means were all the heads of departments narrowly autocratic, and some were men of genuine intellectual leadership. Carl Eigenmann, for instance, was quite conscious of being head of his department but he was an active scholar as well. James A. Woodburn was highly respected both as a scholar and administrator, so were men like John A. Miller, E. R. Cumings, and D. B. Myers. These men set good standards of performance for their departmental colleagues, and they appear in the record to have been humane in their associations, yet they were all parties to the tightly administered university system.

The administrative operation of Indiana University, 1902 to 1915, was not unique. This was an age of strong presidential personalities. William Lowe Bryan had as presidential neighbors the strong men William Rainey Harper, James B. Angell, Charles Van Hise, Cyrus Northrup, and Jacob Gould Schurman. These presidents, with the exception of Harper, were busily engaged in interpreting public universities to the people; they did this while they built new plants, revised curricula, hired and retained staffs, and gave oversight to the proper formulation of accrediting standards. On top of this they were called upon to stand in the forefront in sensing educational needs of the times. None of them, perhaps, faced quite so many physical challenges as William Lowe Bryan. The manner in which he dealt with his daily problems became essential chapters in Indiana University's twentieth century history as did the development of Indiana's educational program.

[2 1]

In the latter area Bryan was to prove himself a highly competent leader, despite his traditional handicaps and failures to liberalize the administrative system. Professors, board members, and legislators all reflected an incipient fear that somehow or other higher education would lead to the undoing of a provincial society which cried out for change and progress but clung to the conservatism of the past with unshakable tenacity. It was within this paradoxical context that Indiana University was to develop into a more aggressive institution in a world of rapidly recurring twentieth century changes. Repeatedly Bryan was to indicate in his well formulated annual reports a clear sense of the expanding sphere of American higher public education without being truly able to assume the role of innovative pioneer.

[I I]

Early Crises

SETTLING THE UNIVERSITY on its new campus and planning for expansion of enrollment and the internal institutional program challenged all the energies the administration and faculty could muster. William Lowe Bryan and his colleagues faced the future, certain that in some way they could overcome baffling handicaps. The rurality of the university's location, as always, pressed upon the administration with its nagging day-to-day problems. Bryan had to spend a disproportionate amount of time looking after affairs which did not arise in other universities, or which modern universities now handle well away from the president's office. For instance, the Bloomington boarding houses were unable to give adequate care to women students in the manner their parents desired. Out in the state, Bryan told trustees there was genuine opposition to coeducation. He believed the university must assume a much closer parental guardianship over its women students, and at least over those whose parents expressed a desire for such watchcare. The only way this could be done was to build dormitories with either public or private funds.

Already President Bryan had a plan in mind which copied the Eastern scheme of supplying dormitory accommodations to students at private cost but under university supervision. He knew first-hand all the pitfalls and snares of the private boarding houses of the town. Open housing for men and women had existed since the 1870's, but as more women entered the university, the system, or lack of it, brought severe public criticism. Boarding house ladies could not assume the disciplinary functions of the home or university, nor could the university alleviate the anxieties of Hoosier parents and deans of women. In 1905 there was formed a corporation which promised to relieve the state of the expense of constructing a women's boarding hall. This body of private investors proposed to construct on the eastern rim of the campus a resident building to be known as Alpha Hall.

On October 15, 1906, the Indiana *Daily Student* said the new women's dormitory was completed and ready for occupancy. Already thirty girls had moved in and were taking their meals in the basement. The new hall contained more than fifty bedrooms, a dining hall for 150 girls, a hospital and dispensary, an assembly-theatrical hall, and a modern laundry. Colonel Theodore J. Louden was the part-owner and general manager, and Mrs. A. B. Foley, a former matron of a women's dormitory in Nashville, Tennessee, was in charge. With more than a spark of jealousy the *Daily Student* lamented, "Oh, Jupiter! would that there was a male dorm also."

Colonel Louden was never one to do things by halves. There was a certain pretentious air about him that matched his title. He held the grand opening for Alpha Hall on Thanksgiving 1906. The university reporter said the Colonel served a "very fancy menu which consisted of raw oysters, roast 'possum, barbecued suckling pig, and decorated buffalo tongue." This sounds more like a menu for a militia muster than the opening of a girl's dormitory, and no doubt there is a generous touch of campus whimsy in the *Daily Student's* account.

There was some ground for local boasting that the new Alpha Hall was the most elegant home for lady students in Indiana. The rooms had two closets, hot and cold running water, single beds with the best felt mattresses, electric and gas lights, twelve bathrooms; all of this for $1.25 a week, or $35 or $40 a term. With justification the *Daily Student* told the girls, "You cannot afford to stay any place else."

As the number of girls increased and the dean of women became more precise in her social demands, it was necessary to make other provisions for women students. In June, 1911, President Bryan told the trustees that the local Episcopal church had bought a large residence on Kirkwood Avenue and proposed to operate a model dormitory for girls. There were still the shabby, inadequately supervised boarding houses, and Miss Louise Ann Goodbody made frequent visits to see that the landladies were enforcing the strict rules which had been devised originally for the sorority houses.

It is doubtful that the vigilant dean got more than a glimmer of all that went on in the "wayward" student houses. The Bloomington *Telephone* spilled the beans in a news story on February 25, 1908, when it disclosed a gambling ring. "The muck rake and the lime-light of public disapproval has come to Bloomington and is probing and exposing a time honored custom of university students. Betting at the boarding clubs is at the mercy of reformers with prospects that it will be speedily stopped." From time immemorial, as the article suggested, students had bet their desserts on any probability from grades to athletic records and scores. With the publicity came the reformers. Notices had gone up in the boarding houses on February 24, 1908, that it was against the principles of morality to foster the wickedness of gambling on the periphery of the campus. "No papal decree of Medieval times," said the *Telephone* reporter, "created more of a stir than this announcement as it is understood to be only the first move of a concerted action on the part of boarding club owners. The latter desire to stop the practice because it is a difficult matter to keep straight just who gets the pie and prunes."

President Bryan and his sober faculty must have looked upon this bit of tomfoolery with real trepidation. That they took some of it seriously was reflected in the fact that in July, 1911, they again sought to devise new standards for boarding houses accommodating both men and women. Professor Augustus Grote Pohlman and William J. Moenkhaus were appointed a committee, under the surveillance of Dr. Fletcher Gardner of the Board of Health, to pass on all boarding house matters. Dining rooms, sewage disposal, and general sanitary conditions concerned them. Too, they were supposed to glance at moral conditions. They had the power to disqualify houses for student use and to recommend others. This committee, however, accomplished little to improve conditions. In 1912 Professor Thurman Brooks Rice suggested

that Indiana University should adopt the eastern plan of constructing dormitory units which would accommodate one hundred men
each.

Before the university administration could turn its full attention
to present physical needs, President Bryan felt he had to deal with
the question of employing a dean of women. In the decade of 1903
to 1913, this was a major issue in the president's mind. Throughout his reports to the board of trustees he gave an insight into
how perplexing the problem was. Yearly the number of women
students attending the university increased while accommodations
for them fell behind.

The construction of Alpha Hall solved only a part of the problem of supplying decent housing and board for female students. In
this highly conservative age university officials felt obliged to assure Hoosier parents that parental overseeing would be exercised
by what President Bryan later was to call a woman of "rock bottom
integrity." Such a woman was Mary Bidwell Breed, a Swain legacy.
Miss Breed was a woman of many talents. She was a social arbiter
of campus and boarding house row, a disciplinarian, a public
health expert, and a teacher. Conditions she admitted were difficult
for the administration of her office. Her charges were scattered
over the town. Their living quarters were often shockingly poor.
Social life was undesirable at best, and menacing at worst.

Before the construction of the Student Building the president
of the university, faculty wives, and Dean Breed were taxed to the
limit of imagination and energy to break the drab monotony of
college girls' lives in Bloomington. Certainly President Bryan
could lay no claim to efficiency in this area beyond admonishing
girls to be good, eat well, take plenty of exercise, and study hard.

Trudging the muddy streets from one boarding house to the
next, Mary B. Breed got a highly realistic notion about the girls
and their college surroundings. On the slightest excuse they danced
the Boston, low dip and all, or any other step that appealed to
them. Many of them were not averse to exploring the countryside
with a male companion on extended buggy rides. Miss Breed had
such possibilities in mind when she told Bryan that she had been
"handicapped by conditions." She felt there was need for a female
physician, more women's dormitories, and more organizations
open to co-eds. Too, more university controlled entertainment
should be provided. This, however, was Miss Breed's valedictory.

William Lowe Bryan was beset by too many other problems

to appreciate fully the blueprint offered him by the departing dean. He still considered the central business of the university to be expanding its academic base, reappraising its curriculum, and seeking additional financial support from the legislature. Fortunately, by November, 1906, he had found a successor to Miss Breed in Louise Ann Goodbody, who was chosen on an emergency and trial basis. Immediately Miss Goodbody surveyed her glebe and reported the presence of 101 sorority girls, 40 in non-sorority groups, and a total enrollment of 385 girls. Sororities and fraternities, she said, controlled social affairs, and in order to change this condition she enlisted the assistance of faculty wives, members of the Women's League, and the girls themselves. She cheered the paternalistic board of trustees with the statement that living conditions had changed for the better in the past five years, but even now the reader of Miss Goodbody's report can hear the echo of Dean Breed's shout, "only in degree"!

Three problems beset the acting dean of women. She discovered, if she had not already known, that Hoosiers of this era liked to do few things more than dance. In her opinion there were too many dances on the campus, although she faced student opposition when she suggested to the girls that they limit dances to Friday and Saturday nights. Only part of the woman problem in Indiana University came from the women themselves. The male student population, Miss Goodbody believed, should feel the parental hand of a dean of men. Finally, she told the trustees, there was the ghastly problem of the everlasting boarding houses and clubs.

Dean of men or not, President Bryan forged ahead with the pressing business of the university. He kept the trustees informed that he was baffled by but not oblivious to the needs of 408 women students, or by the greater number of men. He was not too busy, however, to keep a wary eye on Miss Goodbody and was favorably impressed by her capabilities. On June 19, 1908, he reported to the trustees that he had reached the clear conclusion that she should be made dean of women. He said it was difficult enough to find a fit man to be president of a university, but even more so to find a fit woman to be dean of women. He thought Miss Goodbody did the important things well, but he failed to specify what unimportant things she neglected.

Having quickly worn paths smooth underfoot in her visitations to girls' rooms, the newly made dean felt her position secure enough to make a special request of the university administration.

She informed President Bryan, "The University of Missouri, I am told, keeps a horse and carriage for the use of the Dean of Women and she naturally has found it a great advantage for her work." This was a novel idea for the Indiana president and trustees, and even they had to admit that in the face of local conditions, not an unreasonable one.

Again resorting to the Women's League for assistance, the dean of women planned monthly teas both to entertain her girls and to teach them social grace. She worked hard at democratizing the social lives of all university girls, sorority and non-sorority alike. She invited the famous University of Chicago sociologist, Sophronisba Breckinridge, to speak on the career woman. This daughter of a famous Bluegrass family could not only captivate the Hoosier girls with her own career experiences, but also by her stately personal grace. Less sophisticated was the presentation by home talent of Augusta Stevenson's *Mr. Witt's Widow* in a pallid effort to interrupt the passion for dancing.

With the enunciation of a new set of social rules for 1909, however, Dean Goodbody clamped down on the women, and men as well, with a harsh parental hand. In six mandates she covered her code of social decorum. Men callers, she decreed, could appear only between 2:00 and 10:30 P.M. Sorority houses could have only two calling evenings a week, women should not ride in single buggies at night (the dean had apparently never heard of southern Indiana covered bridges), and when they rode in those virtuous family barouches or surreys they had to be home by 9:00 P.M. Sororities were instructed to keep their porch lights burning during calling nights, women were not to enter fraternity and boarding houses unchaperoned, and above all they were not to appear on "up-town" Bloomington streets after 9:00 P.M. unless chaperoned.

Upon establishing her social code and time schedule, based to a large extent on farm families' hours, Miss Goodbody resigned her position. On March 13, 1911, President Bryan was again before the board of trustees with the well rehearsed lament, "There is no position connected with the University more difficult to fill than that of Dean of Women." His despair was deepened further by the fact that he had no idea where he could find a new dean. The executive committee gave the president a partial stay in his search by appointing Mrs. James A. Woodburn to fill out the year. By June, Bryan had made a diligent search and after endless correspondence had the name of a candidate in hand. Before he revealed her name, however, he listed for the trustees what he conceived to be the qualifications for such a staff member. He again reported, "I regard this position as almost the most difficult one connected with the University." This lady, he repeated, should have *rock-bottom integrity*, sound judgment, tact, courage, and spontaneous sympathy. If she lacked any one of these qualities she would fail. Almost as an afterthought President Bryan said the new dean should have, if at all possible, a fine education, extended social experience, and as many other good qualities as possible. She should be Lydia Pinkham and Whistler's mother draped in a sorority gown and adorned with a master's degree. Bryan located such a saintly character at Iowa Wesleyan College in Carrie Louise DeNise.

Dean DeNise was "rock bottom" in many of the graces. A native of Burlington, Iowa, on the banks of the Mississippi, she was ready to tackle Bloomington, landladies and all. She had been in Indiana less than a year when she held the social mirror before Hoosiers to reveal all their warts and blemishes. In a lofty and slightly angry report to president and trustees, Dean DeNise spared no one. Landladies were irresponsible, the five sorority houses were of poor quality, prices for board were out of line, unhealthy conditions threatened everyone, dusty carpets covered plain dirty floors, double beds sagged under thin mattresses, there was insufficient light and heat, halls were dirty, and in comparison bathrooms were worse. "Forlorn parlors," she wrote, "are sufficient encouragement for the evening stroll rather than the social call." Even Cupid was threatened with malnutrition and dysentery in Miss DeNise's candid opinion.

Although the dean had overwhelmed President Bryan and his colleagues with her accusations, Miss DeNise was not finished. Alpha Hall, which housed sixty-four girls, was as dirty and unhealthful as the boarding houses. She conceded the boarding clubs were trying to achieve improved living conditions, but those landladies were something else. They knew little of correct preparation of nutritious food or of serving it tastefully. They had the oldtime frontier farm notion of a loaded table, but nothing they cooked reflected the art of cuisine. They still patronized country hucksters who specialized in selling cheap and filling produce, desiring only to make a profit. Boarding house tables were overcrowded and boarders had to elbow their way through meals.

The result of all this, said the dean of women, "Is that Indiana young women entrusted to a state school during important years of physical growth can not store up enough reserve energy which is their right, and the *State and Nation must suffer in a future lack of efficiency.*" Not content to lecture the institution's elders, the dean addressed herself over their heads to Hoosiers in general. "Although the foundations of the University are laid firm and true," she told them, "we know that certain phases of its life are justly criticized as being still in the rough." The people of Indiana needed to wake up to the facts of the time. Only in the past half century could Indiana sons and daughters be educated together, and this helped develop for them great social problems. "We insist that some fundamental advantages counterbalance, *but we must also concede the great lack.*" Dormitories were urgently needed, said the dean, and Indiana should do as well by its daughters as Michigan, Miami, and Kansas and build four housing units for fifty girls each.

By June, 1913, President Bryan perhaps admitted to himself that Miss DeNise had many of the qualities which he had so idealistically outlined to the trustees when she was hired, but he surely had doubts that she had "spontaneous sympathy." In her second annual report she was at the Hoosiers again. She had abolished all forms of dancing except the "dipless" Boston. She tried to break up the semi-weekly hops but with limited success. Girls, she felt, tried to maintain some form in their dances, but the Indiana males were still heavy footed militiamen in the modern ballroom. "Several times," she told the trustees, "visiting men from Wisconsin, Northwestern, and other universities have been commended for their good form on the dancing floor." On the other hand, many "Indiana men avoid all that is not good form, but many others are ignorant, or not amenable to incidental suggestion." Clearly Miss DeNise was not mistress of "incidental suggestion."

Dean DeNise departed Indiana in 1914 to continue graduate study in Wisconsin, and subsequently to be secretary of the Y.W.-C.A. in Brooklyn. By this time William Lowe Bryan was certain that Joseph Swain had been right, a university president could not order his administrative affairs by William James' abstract principles. When he gave his annual report to the board of trustees on June 19, 1914, he wasted no ink and paper on the Victorian and motherly qualities of a prospective dean of women. He had found Miss Ruby Mason who was willing to take the job on a one-year appointment at $1800, and if she proved satisfactory her salary would be raised to $2000. Happily Miss Mason was reasonably well satisfied to accept many of the facts of life in Bloomington and to exhibit "spontaneous sympathy" toward students, Hoosiers, president, and trustees in her annual reports.

There is ample documentary evidence in the files of local newspapers and university records to sustain the fact that Bloomington offered problems as well as advantages to the university. Located in a wooded spot as it was, the grounds seem almost to have invited the vagrant and the vandal. On April 30, 1903, Governor Winfield T. Durbin surprised local officials with an ill-tempered message alluding to this problem. He wired Sheriff Thrasher, "Private advice from credible sources received by me this morning indicate that there has been another manifestation of mob law in your community, the second within a brief period, and there has been no serious effort on the part of local officials to prevent it or to bring punishment to those who have thus inflicted disgrace upon Monroe County and the State of Indiana. . . . Permit me to call attention to the fact that there is a growing sentiment among the people of Indiana against the continued location of a state institution of learning in a community where there is either an absence of a predominant public sentiment in favor of the suppression of violent lawlessness, or, what I prefer to believe exists, a chronic callousness on the part of public officials to that predominating sentiment."

Governor Durbin said that helpless women had been set upon by a mob of malicious hill-billies or white-cappers within the shadow of the university. Unless there were an immediate effort to stamp out violent anarchy in Monroe County, he threatened, he would recommend in his message to the legislature that the assembly agree to move the university to another location.

The incident which stirred Governor Durbin's fury occurred on East Eighth Street on the night of April 29, 1903. Mrs. Sarah Stephens and her three daughters were accused of operating a house of prostitution in "Bucktown," and of miscegenation. It was said they were living with Joseph Shively, an elderly Negro. A mob of about fifteen men broke into the Stephens' house at one o'clock on Sunday morning and led the women off to Dunn Meadow where Rebecca and Ida were whipped with barbed wire until their legs and backs were badly lacerated. Joseph Shively received the same treatment and was ordered to remove himself from Bloomington within fifteen days. When police started toward the scene of disturbance, four masked men stopped them. There was more than an implication that it was not difficult to dissuade the officers.

Judge Nathaniel Usher Hill, Sr., as a trustee of the university, replied to Governor Durbin, "It would be as reasonable to remove the Soldier's Monument from Indianapolis because Dr. Alexander has not been convicted of grave-robbing as it would be to remove the State University because some drunken toughs got into a fight in a house of ill-repute."

Once the Indiana press took a second look, and the Governor calmed down enough to view the commotion in Bloomington in the proper perspective, the story seemed less sensational and the university in far less danger than the Governor had supposed. The Indianapolis *Sun* said Governor Durbin's impulsive threat to recommend removal of the university, "is foolish, absolutely foolish. In the first place, nobody will for one minute think that the legislature would take such a step, and without the aid of the legislature the Governor could [do] nothing." The Salem *Democrat* felt if the university should be removed Salem would be the place for it. "Anyhow," said the opportunistic editor, "the farther from Indianapolis the better. Our state capital is a city of vice, iniquity and sin. A murder occurs once a week 'right under the shadow of the monument!'"

All the furore over the white-capping incident no doubt harmed the university a bit before the public. Readers of the newspapers perhaps failed to differentiate between the town and the university. It was not until the following February that the last of the news stories about this incident was printed. In the meantime a menacing outbreak of smallpox was of greater consequence than a disturbance in a house of prostitution and the irresponsible ravings of an impulsive governor.

A lingering problem, as noted elsewhere, was the fact that student health conditions in Bloomington left much room for improvement. Part of this problem originated in a town which had a drastically limited water supply, no sewerage system, and a body of archaic public ordinances. Some of it arose from the habits and ignorance of students and their parents. Many students came from counties where vaccination rules were unenforced, and in Bloomington they fell ready victims of smallpox, scarlet fever, and typhoid. In 1903 there were 195 smallpox and typhoid deaths in

Indiana. That year President Bryan informed the trustees that there had been five cases of smallpox and scarlet fever in the university. Two years later the same situation prevailed. The cost of special care for afflicted students was considered to be high, and really no provisions were made to provide adequate treatment.

A letter to the editor of the *Daily Student* from Ray Sieber on January 13, 1904, said nothing impressed the newly arrived freshmen in Indiana University so much as the "uncouth and unsanitary condition of the community." In that modern age, he thought, "This university has at its disposal a corps of scientific men, whose time could not be occupied to better advantage than by utilizing their knowledge and experience in behalf of the health of the community. When an epidemic breaks out it is almost always due to either contaminated water or infected milk."

There was truth in Ray Sieber's contention. The following year eight students fell victim to scarlet fever. Two more were confined to the pest house with smallpox, and the Delta Gamma house was under quarantine. So prevalent was illness among students that an editorial in the *Daily Student* suggested that a fifty cent assessment be made against each student to raise $1500 as a sick student fund to be spent at the discretion of the faculty.

Criticism of local sanitary conditions brought no detectable change in local health conditions for a decade and a half into the new century. In 1910 twenty students were ill with typhoid, and the state health officer said infection came from several eating places where there were open privy vaults. William Lowe Bryan asked for a careful inspection of student boarding places. So serious had recurring epidemics become that he reported to the trustees that the university's enrollment, "has undoubtedly been affected to a considerable extent by this outbreak." Three university students had died, and as a result Bloomington had received a bad name over the state. A year later Bryan told the board that the university should be made a model of sanitation. It had men on the faculty and in the Indianapolis branch of the Medical School who knew what ideal conditions should be. In his opinion it was not enough to serve the university alone; he said he felt health and sanitary conditions throughout Indiana were bad.

In 1903 the problem of recurring drouths and water shortages was already an ingrained part of Bloomington and university history. The university administration and board of trustees had to spend time, energy, and imagination not just on academic affairs but on the development of a dependable water supply. Ray Sieber was right, contaminated water threatened the successful operation of the university.

At the outset of his administration William Lowe Bryan recognized this threat. None of the makeshifts in the past had succeeded. In fact, Bloomington's population had grown almost as rapidly as the university's student body, each worsening the water problem. Unhappily the school was located atop a porous limestone formation which defied attempts to locate an adequate subsurface vein of water, and to hold it, and there were no lakes or streams with constant level of flow nearby.

Bryan entered the president's office in an especially dry year. The great drouths of 1902 and 1903 dried up the Bloomington water resources, and in the summer of the latter year the university was forced to fall back on its precious reserves. Registrar John Wesley Cravens told a *Daily Student* reporter in December, 1903, "If the city supply gives out we have five cisterns on the campus and every one of them is full. With a little economy in the labs we will have enough to supply our needs until the end of the term." To the suggestion that snow be melted to maintain the levels of the cisterns, Cravens asked where the snow shovelers were. Superintendent David E. Helfrich of the Bloomington waterworks labored day and night to stop leaks in the city reservoir, even so, the water supply from that source promised to hold out for one day only.

By December 12, 1903, the Bloomington water resource was exhausted. The city's pond or lake was dry, and the two feeder springs had failed. Only a protracted rainy season could remedy the situation. The university's heating system could not be operated, and classrooms were frigid. That day workmen began digging out an old spring in the corner of the campus near Eighth Street. This was largely a futile effort to keep the institution functioning. At the same time the board of trustees ordered that a well be punched at a dollar a foot just north of the men's gymnasium in a frantic search for enough water to keep the university open.

Not only did the drouth threaten the disruption of the academic program, it forced an end to the athletic schedule. The final game of the inter-class basketball tournament was canceled because there was no water for players' baths. By the opening of the new term in January, 1904, the water situation had been eased a bit; the wells and springs fed a fresh supply of water into the university, but these were known to be at best only limited and temporary supplies. Bryan's report in March of that year made clear that more positive steps had to be taken to stabilize the water supply so as to alleviate the horrors of the recurring drouths. Behind all this lay the constant threat of removal.

There was at least one realist in Bloomington. Professor Edgar R. Cumings of the Geology Department based his views on something other than the twisting of a forked switch in the hands of a water witch or the frontiersman's sentimentality for a murky hillside spring. He told members of the local Fortnightly Club in February, 1905, that the present Bloomington water supply was hopeless. He suggested that several wells be sunk in the Bean Blossom bottoms four miles east of Bloomington and the water piped into town. This would cost, he estimated, $200,000, and would require a special tax levy. Cumings knew full well that, when rain began to fall, Hoosiers sat tighter on their pocketbooks. He had history on his side. By mid-summer 1908 the drouth had returned, and the university power plant was using $1.50 worth of water a day.

On December 4, 1908, the Bloomington *Telephone* announced the region was the victim of the worst drouth since 1762. "Out at the University," said the paper, " 'Don't waste the water' is the notice pasted in the famous well house on the campus." So bad had the water situation been that fall that the washer women of Bloomington were warned that no more washing was to be done until it rained. In order to keep its medical laboratories open, the pump in the university power house was connected with the main water line which had been checked at the city limits to supply pressure. Rain fell on the last day of November, 1908, and the water which flowed from building roofs into the cisterns was the first since the past March. By the first week in December it was thought necessary to drain the city pipe system to prevent the small amount of water accumulated there from freezing. The city and university were now at the mercy of fire and disease without access to the water system. At this point, said the *Daily Student*, "The water famine has brought the University authorities to the point of seriously considering the construction of a university waterworks pond, in the shape of a campus lake. As it is now talked of, this lake will be located on Dunn Meadow south of Seventh Street and east of Indiana Avenue." The dam would extend from Sixth to Seventh Streets. The only obstacle in the way was the fact Jordan River was used as the university sewer, an obstacle which would be removed when and if the city established a sewer system.

For the next year the story of water shortage and the ineffectual attempts to remedy it became highly repetitious. By the end of 1908 it was clear that if the university was to remain in Bloomington and expand its program it had first to solve its perennial water shortage. The legislature appropriated $20,700 for a project to develop a university reservoir on Griffey Creek. First it was proposed that wells be bored in this area, but more informed engineers and geologists recommended construction of reservoirs to be fed by an ample watershed. In his annual report to the board of trustees, President Bryan upped the estimate of cost to $35,900. He warned board members that the experts said there would surely be another water famine, and the university would be in an even less satisfactory situation to deal with it. Permanent action had to be taken at once, he said, to "escape an intolerable situation."

By April, 1910, plans were underway to develop a reservoir on Griffey Creek on the farm of either W. I. Fee or Ray Rogers. From the promontory above this point water would flow to the campus by gravity. The university bought seventy-five acres of Hinkle farm land for twenty-five dollars an acre, but ran into difficulty in efforts to buy the Rogers land. The owner refused to sell, forcing the university into time consuming legal proceedings to secure the needed watershed area.

Plans for the new water plant and system were drawn by Professor Arthur Lee Foley, and construction bids were invited. On May 12, 1910, the trustees rejected three bids submitted because they exceeded the amount of money available. Preliminary plans suggested a 200 foot dam 30 feet high and an impoundment of water in an 8 acre pool or catchment basin. Rejection of the bids left the university in a desperate situation. It had to spend its appropriation by October 1, or the funds would revert to the state. A month later a contract was signed with Morris N. Defrees and Sons of Indianapolis. The company agreed to construct the dam of concrete, and J. A. Pike was to construct the secondary reservoir or standpipe atop the ridge next to the university. Two and a half miles of pipeline would lead onto the campus to connect with the existing plumbing system.

When builder Pike began laying the pipeline to the campus he ran into serious obstruction from Moses Dunn. A part of the line had to cross the Dunn property, and this the Bedford lawyer forbade. He even refused permission to allow the pipe to be laid above ground. Dunn, a long time friend of the university, had become incensed at the City of Bloomington over annexation and taxation on his property.

Within the year Defrees and Sons completed their work, and J. A. Pike, despite the Dunn pettishness, had tied the university pipeline on to the standpipe. In August, 1911, all that was lacking was the placement of plumbing machinery and a good rain to place the new water supply in use. Cost of the project had escalated to $40,000. At the end of January, 1912, when the pumping plant was finally in operation, there were over 25 million gallons of water in the catch basin, enough to insure a daily bath for every person in the university for the next two years. Water was turned into the university main and all believed an era of famine and disease had come to an end. The shouting, however, was premature; troubles persisted. First, two farmers, one of them Ray Rogers, fed cattle and hogs on the watershed thus polluting the reservoir. Second, was the failure of the new system really to serve the needs of a majority of the university's students because they lived in off-campus boarding houses.

In October 1912, President Bryan expressed a note of disappointment in his report to the trustees on the pollution and impurities which rendered the new reservoir practically useless. Until the university could get full control of its watershed, there was little hope for real improvement, no matter how much liquid water flowed through the pipes. Too, it was already evident that the thirty foot dam would have to be raised another twelve feet before it would be efficient. The original estimate was that the University would consume 80,000 gallons daily, and at this rate it could not hope to go through a drouth unscathed. Only one engine and pump had been installed, and drouth or not this limited equipment promised eventual failure from overwork.

The first head of water had hardly reached the university spigots before the *Daily Student* began a militant campaign against an ancient and honored institution, the public drinking cup. Buildings, said the paper, were inadequately supplied with drinking facilities. The Library had faucets and common cups "by which you may quench your thirst if you are not particular about the 'public drinking cup.' " The *Student* said thirsty freshmen and co-eds could find water nowhere that didn't have a dirty rusty drinking cup. "Checked everywhere to no avail. Solution-drink old rusty cup." The paper did not say where upperclassmen drank water, if that is what they drank.

Actually the university solved only the immediate institutional needs for water by constructing the reservoir. Most of its students remained dependent upon the city's resources because they lived beyond reach of the campus mains. Really the only advantage students enjoyed was access to university shower baths. This fact was underscored in 1913, when another drouth beset the Monroe County area. Bloomington had made no real headway in solving of its water problem. In November it was again confronted with a crippling famine. President Bryan believed that the history of the past decade would repeat itself in predictable annual outbreaks of diseases. In order to protect students the university had to establish water routes and deliver cans of water to boarding houses, ostensibly for student use, a practice which was followed for several years. Actually, not until the late 1950's was Indiana University relieved of its vexatious water problems.

Almost equal to its perpetual water crises was the problem of the university's geographical isolation. There is no way of knowing how many times during its first century university officials apologized to prospective visitors and staff members for the complicated means of reaching Bloomington. This apologetic approach perhaps started with Dr. J. D. Maxwell's first letter to Andrew Wylie in 1828. In 1903, Indiana University was not unique among American colleges because it was isolated geographically from an urban center and a transportation hub. Indianapolis, a historic crossroads of the Middle West, was too far away to have much influence on its country neighbor in Monroe County. The state of Indiana, like the southern states, was just beginning in the first decade of this century to discuss the good roads movement. The plain fact was that student and visitor travel in this era had made remarkably little advance over that of the 1780's. The Monon Railway, up until the first years of the twentieth century, was the sole modern artery of travel, and its accommodations were to be measured in terms of convenience and motion, rather that in comfort and adherence to schedules.

The university and the railway were dependent upon each other, a dependence the railroad recognized in 1903 by granting a fare concession of one and one-third rate for a round trip, provided purchasers were certified students. Just before the holidays the registrar's office was crowded with departing students seeking certificates to show Monon ticket sellers.

Three years later the Western Passenger Association revoked its two-thirds fare concession and granted instead a straight 10 percent reduction in round-trip tickets. The railways took this action, not from an interest in student welfare, but because they feared the legislature would enact a two-cents per mile limitation on all fares. This change angered students, but they looked upon a boycott of the railroads as an exercise in futility, if not an invitation to long distance walking.

By May 21, 1906, the Monon monopoly was broken when the track of the Indianapolis-Southern branch of the Illinois Central was laid into the town. The track laying from the south attracted large crowds of spectators who gathered along the right-of-way less to satisfy their curiosity than to celebrate further reduction of the university's isolation, and the arrival of a competing road.

Floyd MacGriff, a departing senior of 1912, described the realities of trying to flee Bloomington following commencement. He thought few Indiana students had crossed the Rocky Mountains on pack horse, or jolted over a corduroy road in a prairie schooner, "but quite a few of them have had more thrilling experiences on the tramways which connect Bloomington with the homefolks. Transportation is partially attained within the corporate limits of Bloomington by the persistent efforts of six antiquated stage coaches, where motive power is supplied by gravity one half the time & profanity the other. Each outfit is a separate enterprise & an individual annoyance. There is only one class of passengers coming into Bloomington who do not object to the transportation service—those who go into executive session with the medical school upon their arrival."

This author compared a train ride into or out of the town with a country frolic. Cars, he said, were propelled by a "neurasthenic engine, [and] three prehistoric passenger coaches which will stop at the least provocation." For recreation one could, "shoot craps, chew tobacco, smoke, take a swig of whiskey, or play poker in any one of the coaches." As a final fling at the local railroad, young MacGriff noted, "A transportation company generally maintains engines, coaches, shops, freight cars, passenger stations, & a road-bed. It is disputable, whether the transportation companies oper-ating in [to] Bloomington have roadbeds."

William Lowe Bryan had still another view of the failures of the Monon. On June 3, 1908, he wrote E. S. Shumaker, the ram-pant dry crusader of Indianapolis, that he had gone from Bloom-ington to Hammond aboard one of the Monon's parlor cars. When he entered the coach he said, "I found a group of women sitting at a table. They were drinking. When I left the car at Hammond they were still at the same table still drinking. They spent most of the day there in that occupation. They were boisterous at times. The whole affair, as you may imagine, extremely unpleasant to the respectable men and women who were passengers in the same car." Dr. Bryan evidently overlooked telling Shumaker what it was the "ladies" from Tom Taggart's halls of pleasure were drink-ing, but he seemed to infer it was not the well known French Lick concoctions of tomato juice or Pluto waters. He sought of his friend assurance that there would not be a recurrence of the affair. He wanted to know if there were not a law to prevent this kind of conduct, and if none existed he advocated immediate enactment of one. Further, Bryan implied the Monon hauled entirely too many boisterous people between French Lick and Chicago for the moral comfort of either the railroad or its respectable and temperate customers.

Despite all the facetious remarks made about the Monon and the Indianapolis-Southern, these railroads served Bloomington with a fair degree of comfort and convenience. Perhaps they were safer and more adequate than are modern private automobiles which travel over the same knobby country roads between Bloom-ington and the "outside" world in the 1970's. There was a distinct and intimate institutional connection between the university and the railroads, and, despite seemingly angry student jibes, the roads were more butts of their good natured *Arbutus* humor than sub-jects of their fury.

In these years Indiana University broke other and significant isolating barriers. Events of the moment involved it in the new directions the nation itself was taking as a rising world power. A fresh human element was to be introduced into its student body, and old social and political mores were brought under new stresses and demands for tolerance. Nevertheless, Indiana University embarked upon its future with modest but exciting involvement in its first experiences in international education.

While the new Bryan administration dealt with multiple organizational problems in and out of the university, it was called upon to meet a broader challenge. In its efforts to assume the role of protector of the Philippine Islands, the United States embarked upon an educational program whereby young Filipinos were to be brought to colleges and universities in this country for training. Out of the first contingent to arrive in the United States four were assigned to Indiana University.

By 1903 several Japanese and Chinese students had found their way inland to Bloomington. When Bryan became president there was at least one Japanese on the campus, Hiro Ichinomiga. He was enrolled in general courses for the purpose of learning to speak English in the shortest time possible. The next year Masuji Miyakawa was enrolled as a third year student in the Law School, training he was to put to good use when he later opened law offices in San Francisco and Tokyo to enjoy a highly prosperous practice.

An occasional western European found his way to Bloomington, but the student body was predominantly of provincial Hoosier origins. In 1901, Indiana University was to form a direct personal association with the Philippines when Elmer Burritt Bryan, professor of education and psychology, was appointed principal of the insular Normal School. Two years later he became superintendent of education for the islands. He headed a system which employed approximately 800 American teachers, among them many Indiana University graduates. Bryan also encouraged Filipinos to come to Indiana.

At the opening of the fall semester in 1904, the four Filipinos assigned to the university arrived in Bloomington. They had been selected from the 175 students who were sent to American universities. They came as wards of their government, but also as guests of the United States. Not all Hoosiers were pleased with this development, for one, Governor Winfield Durbin, who raised the question of whether foreigners would pay out-of-state fees. Soon other signs of irritation with the presence of foreigners appeared, especially against nonwhite foreigners. As time went

[4 1]

on, an ugly racial attitude was revealed in the state against the Filipinos. Senator Cy Davis introduced into the Indiana General Assembly in 1909 a resolution which was intended to interdict marriages of white women to persons who had more than one-eighth Filipino blood.

Senator Davis' bill set the newspaper reporters going. It was said the proposed legislation grew out of the fact that now there were five island students in Bloomington and they were seen flirting with university co-eds. Senator Davis was quoted as saying, "Parents would as soon leave have their daughter marry a Negro as a Filipino." This bill was actually introduced as an amendment to section 2, of the old racial act of 1852 in which the phrase "or Filipino" was to be added to the phrase, "one-eighth or more of Negro blood."

Quickly the Filipinos defied Senator Davis and the legislature in a letter to the *Daily Student*. They expressed great respect for American women, "Yet, if the Indiana Legislature in its unbounded wisdom, should see fit to pass a law requiring Filipino students not to marry American girls, we certainly, with sorrow, would have to violate that law, because when it comes to such a serious matter as that, we will have our choice to stay within the bounds of our race, *as we still and forever will love our country* for which we will sacrifice anything, self-interest, ambition, affections, and what not." They reminded the racial bigots that all they had to do was to go into Illinois, Ohio, the Philippines, or even Brown County to get married.

The *Daily Student* editor was of the opinion the Filipino marriage issue was a first-rate straw man. It had arisen from the over-zealousness of an unscrupulous Indianapolis newspaper reporter and a jilted Bloomington bachelor. "We wish," said the editor, "to assure the young men that they overestimate the importance of the sensational newspaper stories in question. . . . We want the boys with us and they may feel assured the large percent of the student body gives them sympathy and support."

This incident brought about a visitation from W. A. Sutherland of Washington and the Bureau of Insular Affairs to see if the Filipinos were being treated fairly. He quickly discounted the Davis-newspaper pseudo-scandal. The Filipinos would remain at Indiana University. In fact, the Bureau reported, "In no other colleges and universities in this country have the Filipinos made so satisfactory progress as in Indiana, which means when the next batch of students comes across the Pacific the Hoosier state will get more than its share."

Despite the unfortunate incident of 1905, Indiana University proved itself remarkably successful both in training Filipinos and in its associations with the islands. Not only did Elmer B. Bryan establish a good reputation as head of the Philippine schools, but he was instrumental in hiring many university graduates as teachers. By 1911, this service had become well enough established that a limited number of salaried positions were made available to Indiana graduates for research in the fields of education, political science, natural science, sociology, and the linguistics.

In the latter year Indiana University began a second chapter in dealing with foreign students. Susan Berman of "Northwestern" Germany came to Bloomington at the instigation of William E. Jenkins, the librarian. He had met her in Paris where she told him of her desire to study English literature in America. Almost immediately after she reached the campus she was pledged to the Kappa Kappa Gamma Sorority. This appearance of the German girl came, however, too close to the outbreak of World War I, for Indiana University to expand its European student program, but the pattern was set, and in future years literally thousands of foreigners from every point of the globe followed the pioneers who came in the first decade of this century. The original group of Filipinos became honored graduates who gave good account of themselves as professional men and political leaders. Francisco Afan Delgado, for instance, became Justice of the Supreme Court of the Philippines, ambassador to the United States and to the United Nations, and led resistance forces against the Japanese invasion. Jorge C. Bocobo became professor of law, dean of the law school, and president of the University of the Philippines. Mariano H. de Joya became professor of law, a member of the Attorney General's staff, judge of the Court of the First Instance, and a member of the Philippines cabinet. These accomplishments marked a long span of years and experiences from the day when four homesick Filipino boys arrived in Bloomington to begin educational careers. Few graduates of Indiana University demonstrated more productively the advantages of a college education than did these lads from a beleaguered country. When the university dedicated the wings of the sprawling McNutt Quadrangle on April 28, 1968, it named three of these for its distinguished Filipino graduates who had died.

[4 3]

[III]

Fleshing Out a University

I N EVERY DETAIL of its operation Indiana University after 1900 came close to the workaday world in which it functioned. Its modern history came to be cast more and more against the background of this pragmatic age. Personally William Lowe Bryan formed a human link between the transitional scientific era of the 1880's and the intensively industrial one of the early 1900's. He had many of his faculty colleagues engaged directly in the task of constructing the organizational skeleton by which Indiana would within a decade transform itself from college to university. Jordan, Coulter, and Swain before them had struggled mightily but unsuccessfully to attain this objective. There were, however, the intangibles which mitigated against a full or easy transition. Indiana people and their public officials were at least an academic generation behind in their willingness to support a modern public university or to comprehend its value to the state. Old sectarian rivalries still breathed and writhed and periodically threatened to revive some of the bugaboos of the past. A new threat hove onto the scene in the form of public institutional competition. Hoosiers in 1903 were as tax shy as had been their pioneer ancestors in 1816, and financial support remained constantly a central concern.

There was, however, a basic strength which sustained Indiana

University when it embarked on a new phase of its modern history. The institution had traditionally been able to retain a small core of dedicated teachers. It is true that few of its faculty could be called great by either contemporary or modern standards. Few or no departments had attained a satisfactory degree of scholarly maturity, yet some professors and some departments outshone those of many other American state universities. There were, however, the challenges of Cornell, Michigan, and Wisconsin; and in medicine, The Johns Hopkins, Pennsylvania, and Harvard.

It was fortunate for President Bryan that the central body of his faculty spanned two eras in the university's history. Among them were Carl H. Eigenmann, Horace Addison Hoffman, Robert Judson Aley, Arthur Lee Foley, Robert Edward Lyons, Ulysses Grant Weatherly, Ernest H. Lindley, Amos Shartle Hershey, Guido Hermann Stempel, Edgar Roscoe Cumings, James Albert Woodburn, and others. These men and their younger colleagues comprised a good teaching and promising research faculty. Some were even nationally recognized scholars; among them Carl H. Eigenmann, David Myers Mottier, Arthur Lee Foley, and William Lowe Bryan were starred names in the early editions of *American Men of Science*. In 1904 seven Indiana University professors were listed in *Who's Who in America*, and two years later there were eighteen, thirteen of whom had the doctor of philosophy degree.

These men bore the responsibility of restructuring Indiana University. They conducted no searching self-study, invited no visiting expert for his analysis, or carried out any other such dramatic examination. Occasionally Bryan and some professors sent out limited questionnaires to other universities in seeking comparative notions of Indiana's progress.

What was called for after 1903 was a curriculum and university organization flexible enough to conform quickly to constant changes in Indiana society itself. The editor of the *Arbutus* for 1906 explained that Bryan in an interview said Indiana University should "give courses that will prepare young men and women for any kind of work that has a place in the complex life of the 20th century. [He] believes that education by the state should be as broad as the life of the people and should conform to that life."

Everyday America before the turn of the century had met and solved most of its problems with the help of "self-made men." Only minimal learning was required to comprehend the workings of windmills, hand manipulated looms, locomotives, and sawmills in the American economy. Pure learning was considered to be the precious jewel of the humanists who figured in the shaping of American culture but lived well away from the grime and clamor of the factories. William Lowe Bryan and his colleagues, no doubt, if left to their own desires, would have preferred to continue to live in the humanistic world, but the impact of national and world changes denied them the privilege.

After 1900 professors functioned largely in an age when looms, windmills, and locomotives gave way to more sophisticated machines. Indiana University's records for this period are filled with ample evidence of the searchings for directions in the area of the applied sciences and social studies. Bryan's annual reports and periodic oral communications to the board of trustees were studded with outlines for new schools to be seeded within existing programs and departments. Engineering could grow out of mathematics, physics, chemistry, and astronomy; architecture could stem from the same sources. Trained businessmen could emerge from political science, economics, history, and sociology. Journalism had a ready-made curriculum in English, history, and political science. All that was needed in the beginning to create a school was the addition of one or two specialized courses. A music school, a domain unto itself, could be served in infancy by a single professor and a few semi-private assistants. Medicine, which is treated extensively elsewhere, could in 1903 be sprung from the loins of chemistry, physics, and biology. Thus the skeleton of a university developed by degrees, bone by bone from an existing corpus. Fleshing out the academic and professional program became a monumental task for Indiana for the next half century.

William Lowe Bryan expressed the belief many times that Indiana University could hope to be no stronger than its faculty. A central problem was that of hiring good men and then keeping them. The latter challenge often proved traumatic. President and trustees could never fully persuade legislators to bring the needs of the university into full focus. This was revealed with frightening clarity in the era when Indiana and Purdue were locked in mortal combat over the administration of a medical school in Indianapolis.

A dramatic incident which pointed up the predicament of Indiana University in the first decade of the Bryan administration was the loss of John A. Miller from the headship of the Department of Astronomy. Miller was both an able and a popular man. His widely publicized observations of Halley's Comet and his journey to Spain to observe a total eclipse of the sun had given him a fine reputation. At the time he accepted the headship of astronomy at Swarthmore College he was also serving as a member of the Bloomington City Council. A perceptive editorialist in the *Daily Student* commented that the bitterest reminder "of the most perplexing problem facing the institution [is] the inability to offer financial inducements strong enough to keep wealthier schools from pirating I. U.'s better faculty members. The problem is an old one. No sooner do I. U.'s faculty members achieve distinction than some other school snatches them away." It would have taken twice the resources available in any year prior to 1906, said the *Student*, to halt the injurious raiding of the faculty. The paper expressed the thought that students and faculty members should busy themselves with the election of legislators who could grasp with intelligence what was happening in the state and the university.

The student editor spoke as though he peeped over William Lowe Bryan's shoulder. Repeatedly the president revealed his anxieties to the board of trustees: he found it difficult to hire good men, and doubly frustrating to keep them. Typical of faculty problems of the period were the numerous changes which occurred in 1907 and 1908. Out of a full-time staff of approximately forty-five members Professor John M. Clapp had accepted the headship of the Department of English in Lake Forest College, John Miller had gone to Swarthmore, Mary Breed was watching after the girls at Missouri, Louise DeNise followed Clapp to Lake Forest, Zora G. Clevenger accepted a job in private business in Pittsburgh, and Edward H. Thurston was displeased with Bloomington and returned to the law faculty of George Washington University. Five other staff members were on research and study leaves. The vacancies these professors left necessitated a considerable number of replacements with young and inexperienced instructors, and this proved a serious handicap to planning for the enlargement of the institution's future program.

Changes such as those described above tended to aggravate another traditional university problem. In 1907 ten of the new in-

structors appointed to the staff were Indiana University graduates. Periodically the institution was stalked by this ghost, and
the university was severely criticized for the practice. Burton D.
Myers, in a more objective study of employment practices for the
period, seemed to discount the more caustic accusations, even
though Bryan himself complained in his annual report of 1907 of
the dangers of academic inbreeding.

Added to the problem of inbreeding was the kindred one of
nepotism. Many faculty wives and children sought employment
in the university. As an example Lillian Wilcox Hershey sought
permission in 1902 from Joseph Swain to offer a course in the
history of music. President Swain expressed to the trustees the
opinion that the idea was right, but "The fact that her husband is
a professor in the University is both an objection and a reason for
her employment. As a general proposition, the employment of
wives of the members of the faculty is objectionable." Swain's
Hoosier thrift outweighed his objections however. Mrs. Hershey
would teach for much less money than anyone else, because she
had to stay in Bloomington to look after her absent-minded Amos.

Since 1884, the Indiana University faculty had become conscious of standards. First was the qualification of students presenting themselves for admission to the university and then the
matter of work offered in the university's own classrooms. During
the period when the university was shifting from the narrow curriculum of the past to the broader elective system introduced by
David Starr Jordan, there was constant debate over the standards
of grading and other means of evaluating student performance.
Whatever grading system was adopted it had to be meaningful to
faculty members, students, and, especially, to parents. At the
same time the transfer of credits to other universities had to be
kept in mind. After considerable study, the faculty in February,
1908, recommended the use of letter grades. The new plan instituted in fact six categories which ranged from "A" to "D," and
two professorial options of "conditioned" and "failed" when students fell below "D" in a course.

Except for the "A" grade, each of the descending letters represented a margin of nine digits from 65 to 95. There were several
reasons for adoption of the new grading plan, but primarily the
controversy was over the rating of students for honors and awards.
Past decisions in this area were made largely upon professors'

[4 8]

opinions, instead of objective standards of measurement. Too, other universities were now turning to letter grades, and the increasing external accreditation of colleges and universities forced changes in old individualistic practices.

Students and some professors expressed dissatisfaction with the proposal to give specific grades which meant the opening of student records for inspection by responsible persons. *Daily Student* comments on the issue of whether or not the student himself should be allowed to see his grades took an interesting turn. Strangely, the editors opposed giving students such information. They argued three highly patronizing reasons. First, professors were said to be too busy to spend hours giving out grade information, to make tedious explanations of their conclusions, and then in soothing the disappointed ones; the committee on extraordinary course loads, it was said, would find it trying to explain all but microscopic marginal differentiations between students; and, finally, it would be humanly impossible to make an absolutely fair and definitive estimate of some student grades. The editors thought, perhaps, it would do no harm to show departing seniors their four year cumulative grades, but no one else should be given his grades.

Behind the move to establish qualitative standards was Professor Ernest H. Lindley. As an early professional psychologist and educationist he gave serious attention to tests and measurements. In the first faculty meeting in 1909, Lindley proposed the appointment of a committee to examine grading practices. He thought the generosity of some professors seriously damaged the quality of honors awarded by the faculty.

Between October 27, 1909, and January 13, 1910, the Lindley committee reported its findings. A survey had been made of four universities, Harvard, Missouri, Wisconsin, and Indiana. For all students Indiana gave 29 percent "A's" to Wisconsin's 16, Harvard's 9, and Missouri's 5 percent. The range for "B's" was from Indiana's 42 percent to Missouri's 21 percent. In the lower grade ranges Indiana had the lowest percentage of "C's," "D's," and "F's." Freshman and sophomore grades followed generally the same range, except Indiana had a failure rate of 5 percent as compared to 7 percent for other schools. The faculty expressed concern in a special meeting because one or two colleagues consistently gave high grades. This partly accounted for the university's unfavorable comparative standings, and, again, damaged the honors system. For the first time, perhaps, the term "snap" course came into use on the campus.

The faculty took a second step to insure a rise in standards. The committee on graduation was asked to report evidence of generosity in issuing grades and to seek justification for their decisions from the instructors. Another resolution asked professors to remain in their classrooms during examinations and to keep an eagle eye on students. In the same meeting, May 21, 1910, the faculty adopted the rule that afterwards Indiana University instructors would use the "Harvard blue book" as a way to prevent students from exchanging papers in examinations.

Concern for grades, the division of university sessions, and the need for revised academic standards was not wholly generated in Bloomington. As the university extended its offerings into graduate and professional fields, its faculty and administration became more sensitive to the significance of discriminating standards. At its tenth meeting, held in Ithaca, New York, in April, 1909, the Association of American Universities admitted Indiana University to membership, a high recognition indeed. The next year William Lowe Bryan reported to the trustees that, for the university to hold memberships in the various new accrediting bodies, it had to earn proper respect for the quality of its work. He said that the Association of American Universities had twenty-two members, and that there were at least thirty non-member universities which had larger incomes than Indiana. Indiana had been chosen largely because of the promise of its graduate work.

Indiana University had a fairly long history of graduate work extending back to 1882 when the first earned advanced degree was conferred. Some of the first degrees were conferred somewhat on the European plan. Graduates of the university who had been away from the institution for several years might claim an additional degree based on professional accomplishments plus one year of active residence. Documentary evidence of this practice exists in the numerous letters addressed to William Lowe Bryan from old lawyers, doctors, and teachers asking consideration of their long faithful, temperate, and moral careers.

It was not until 1902 that serious agitation was begun for the formal organization of a graduate school which would develop and conform to rigid curricula and procedures in the preparation of candidates for masters and doctoral degrees.

In this latter year there developed some concern, if not controversy, as to whether Indiana should not leave graduate work to richer and better equipped universities. Part of this opposition stemmed from the fact that a small committee controlled the offerings of advanced studies, and its members were not always politic in their actions. It was not until the committee was expanded to include all heads of departments that much progress was made in developing this function in the university.

Bryan wrote in his annual report for 1908, that in spite of inadequate resources and other difficulties the graduate program had made progress. That year the university would confer three doctoral degrees, and the number of masters candidates had increased. For a full fledged graduate school the university needed to appoint a dean. To accomplish this he recommended Carl H. Eigenmann who he said was a dedicated scientist with an international reputation. Eigenmann had already demonstrated great executive ability. Bryan gave heed to another Eigenmann achievement—he had raised large sums of money for zoology from private sources.

The president explored further the subject of graduate studies with the trustees. He told them there were fifteen members of the Association of American Universities, and in all of these graduate work was emphasized. Further, member universities were not disposed to recognize work done in non-member schools. In his opinion Indiana University was in grave danger of not being recognized as a university anywhere unless it supported a graduate program of good quality. He outlined the procedures for accomplishing this important step: students entering the professional schools would be required to take one year of academic work and in the immediate future would be asked to submit two years, and the existing advanced academic courses would have to be materially strengthened. "We must meet these conditions," said the president, "as a matter of self-preservation."

The trustees accepted Bryan's recommendation and Carl H. Eigenmann was elevated to the graduate deanship in 1908. Eigenmann immediately began one of his famous campaigns to secure money. In March, 1910, he sought $1000 with which to purchase professorial reprints for wide distribution, and he requested $2000 to support ten graduate fellowships to be awarded to graduates of Indiana colleges. The following October Bryan gave the trustees more precise information about graduate work.

Since 1891 the university had awarded 409 advanced degrees, most of them in history, education, and English, in that order. It would require, he thought, $50,000 annually to satisfy requests for research grants alone, a sum equal to income from a million dollar endowment.

Bryan no doubt formed his concepts of graduate work largely from information furnished him by Eigenmann. The dean made an early survey of graduate work in the United States and developed firm notions of what was needed at Indiana. The nature of his findings was reflected in a characteristic Eigenmann homily.

> That research must be a matter of growth which requires some sort of soil however rocky; that while its growth may be accelerated by specially favorable conditions or by tilling or even by hothouse methods the prerequisite for it is the proper seed, and that without this even ideal conditions will fail to give results. If this conviction is correct it follows naturally that those individuals in the University who have in progress specific researches regardless of conditions, deserve to have their patch improved before the soil in general is provided for future seed and inspiration to plant and reap. If no increased appropriation can be secured to develop a general plan of graduate work I would recommend that every effort be made to advance the work of those men who under existing conditions have made and are making contributions to knowledge.

This plea was answered in a modest way. The legislature appropriated $17,500 to support research and graduate studies. There then developed the perplexing issue of how to spend the funds in the most judicious manner, and in areas that would produce the most satisfactory results. Never before had Indiana University professors had such a melon to divide, and they were somewhat overwhelmed. Even so small a sum generated demands for extensive considerations. In the end the money was used to improve some faculty salaries, to establish annual fellowships, and to award special research grants. The president and trustees were asked to screen all requests for these grants.

Hard on the heels of the establishment of the graduate school and resolution of the great dispute over medical education, another old issue was settled. In the fall of 1909, Governor Thomas R. Marshall called a meeting of university and college presidents at his office in Indianapolis. By this time William Lowe Bryan had become so cautious that any gesture from Indianapolis was suspect. He reported to the trustees that he went to the governor's conference, "full of concern, not knowing what the spirit or outcome of the meeting would be. It became evident that the leading Indiana college presidents and most of the members of the conference were determined to show that there was not and should not be any revival of the old school controversy. An extreme illustration to show this determination was shown in their unanimous vote refusing to demand that the State Normal School should cease to give the A.B. degree."

More to the point was the fact the presidents expressed the opinion that there should be only one graduate university in the state, and it should be given the means, if necessary, by special taxation, to become a university in the fullest sense. Truly, said the presidents and the governor, it should be the head of the educational system of the state, and they voted unanimously to accomplish this objective. The presidents found no duplication among the state schools at the moment, now that the medical school issue was settled. They voted for reasonable tuition fees and encouraged Indiana University to emphasize graduate work.

The startled Bryan was almost tempted—not quite—to believe the university had come to the great divide. Bryan was still cautious. He told the trustees, "I am not supposing that we have overcome all of our troubles and that the millennium has arrived. I do believe, however, that there will never be another fight against the state institutions by the non-state schools. I believe further that the attitude of these gentlemen is such that our own responsibility to them has become very great and that we must seek to give them a service in return greater than any they render us."

Even the portraits of Andrew Wylie, Cyrus Nutt, of Lemuel Moss, and of David Starr Jordan must have registered amazement at this favorable turn of events. So long had the rivalry among the colleges persisted and now, in one conference in Tom Marshall's office, it showed signs of ending. Fortunately, the Indiana college presidents asked no conditions that the university was not ready and anxious to fulfill.

Having conceived the idea of establishing schools of medicine, music, architecture, engineering, and graduate work in the first year of his administration, William Lowe Bryan turned to other fields where professional programs could be organized with the least possible expenditure of money, and the greatest of existing staff and facilities. None offered an easier transition than the creation of a school of commerce or business, largely within the context of liberal arts courses. Since 1889, with the appointment of Jeremiah W. Jenks to the staff, Indiana University had nurtured a strong tradition in the field of economics. Jenks took advantage of curriculum revisions of the Jordan revolution to establish his subject firmly in the university program. During his three year stay in Bloomington, he advanced the cause of economics, but he too heeded the siren call of Ithaca.

Jenks left behind the ambitious sociologist-economist Edward A. Ross to carry forward the cause of economics. Ross, like Jenks, helped to make it a popular subject. Constantly in the *Daily Student* and *Arbutus* references to the field appeared. Ross, however, followed Jenks to Cornell to begin a distinguished national career in the new area of sociology. Ernest L. Bogart succeeded him in Indiana and quickly rectified the loss, but as he succeeded outsiders stood ready to toll him away. Bryan, with limited funds, had to watch this fine scholar go off to Princeton. Added to this galaxy of rising young stars in the field of economics and social science must be added the name of John R. Commons, who began his career at Indiana.

With all the records in on these famous scholars who pioneered the field of economics at Indiana University one can only speculate what glory the institution might have enjoyed had it retained these youthful front runners. It is doubtful that any American university in its history has had so many promising young men interested in the social sciences on its staff, and who later achieved such high scholarly recognition. Even one at a time and in succession they added luster. If for no other reason, William Lowe Bryan had eloquent reason to bemoan the stinginess of a state which left its university economically strapped to the point that it could not stave off repeated raids. Obviously promising men were enticed away by more attractive salaries and career prospects.

In 1903, despite losses of so many able scholars, Bryan was blessed that he could continue to call upon Ulysses Grant Weatherly and William A. Rawles to further the economics tradition and expand the curriculum of their department into the field of applied business. In this year there appeared in the university's curriculum special courses as offshoots of the economics department which indicated that with little fanfare Indiana University had embarked upon the organization of a business school—a move in keeping with the demands of the age.

Like the doctors the businessmen drew heavily upon the established resources of the liberal arts. Business listed courses in mathematics, physics, political science and history, and sociology. Within a year it was necessary to add the assistant registrar U. H. Smith and Walter Myers as associate instructors in accounting and economics. There were thirty-six students enrolled in the special course and the infant school was under way. While law and medicine were largely set apart in a major portion of their work, the business school functioned as a closely integrated part of the general university program, and because of this it attracted a minimum amount of attention. Business education required no special library, laboratories, or classrooms. Significant differences lay in the addition of a few specialized courses to the curriculum. Some of the practical or vocational courses were very similar to those offered in the popular proprietary business colleges which turned out bank clerks and ardent disciples of Spencerian penmanship.

By 1908 it was an established fact that women were rapidly taking their places in the business world. Their entry into this masculine field was made at first timidly as a step through the side door of service. Miss Jesse M. Little was encouraged to move her Bloomington Shorthand and Training School to the basement of Maxwell Hall and to conduct what the registrar euphemistically called a "Stenographic Practical Training School." Under this impressive title Miss Little drilled her charges in phonography, piano typewriting, and practical English and spelling. By 1911, however, it could hardly be said that the "professor" of the piano typewriter was threatening the superstructure of Maxwell Hall with vibrations from her machines. Four students had their choice of five Remington "new improved" typewriters and under Miss Little's watch and care they mastered the art of the keys and prepared to help generate new mountains of typed records of Hoosier commerce.

At the outset of his administration William Lowe Bryan undertook to create an agency of public relations, and at the same time to add a new professional dimension to the university's academic program. On September 25, 1903, he made provisions for the establishment of a press bureau to be located in two rooms in Kirkwood Hall. The *Daily Student* saw this as the first step toward the creation of a professional school of journalism. Bryan had responded in part to a statement that a press bureau would greatly facilitate the gathering of campus news for the city dailies. The editorial headquarters of the *Daily Student* were to be located in the rooms of the Press Bureau, and the city reporters and student journalists believed this would be profitable. This bureau was placed under the professional overseeing of Ulysses Weatherly, John M. Clapp, and Fred B. Johnson. Bryan became so enthusiastic about this new arrangement that he contributed $25 to be awarded for the best student news story that year.

In November members of the Press Club felt even more ambitious and petitioned the board of trustees to establish a college of journalism, using the basic liberal arts curriculum in history, economics, and English as foundation courses. President Bryan agreed, telling the trustees the school could be started for as little as $500 a year. The *Daily Student* saw as an impelling reason for the establishment of a school of journalism that "learning of the difference between an editorial and a news item would teach [students] to draw finer distinctions between personal & public interests."

All the youthful arguments were little short of fine-spun dreams of members of the Press Club playing professionals. Not enough students registered for the special journalism course in the spring of 1904 to justify its being offered, and the *Student* suggested fledgling journalists take instead courses in English and economics. Despite a lack of interest in the specialized field the Press Club and university were said to be well represented among the political reporters of the Indianapolis dailies.

Two years later, and after a bit of a crisis in campus newspaper publishing, the evergreen vine of professional journalism sprouted anew. William Lowe Bryan accepted an invitation to speak to the Press Club on the subject, and Professor Fred Poulton Hall of public speaking and government joined students in promoting their cause. It was Professor Hall's opinion that a school of journalism in Indiana University "would be unique in this country." In this burst of enthusiasm the professor demonstrated a will to make a modest beginning.

Victory came close for the journalists in 1907 when Bryan recommended to the board of trustees a special curriculum which would lead to the granting of a bachelor of arts degree with professional implication in its content. He suggested W. D. Howe, Samuel B. Harding, and U. G. Weatherly as professors. The technical course work would be under the direction of Fred B. Johnson, formerly of the Indianapolis *News*. This time there were students, but organization of the school of journalism still had to wait.

In the great effort to enlarge the university's program and to create new colleges, the subject of music was very much an active concern. Interest in music in some form had been a part of the entire tradition of the institution. Earlier interests were expressed in the singing of sacred songs, the playing of a limited number of instruments in chapel services, offering musical programs at commencement time, and in patronizing professional concerts and renditions arranged by the Concert and Lecture Committee.

Contemporary with the Jordan period in the 1880's glee club singing in American universities was even more popular than participation in athletics. Indiana University students proved no exception in their fascination with this form of group singing. The university Glee Club grew in importance in the 1890's, and constituted not only a pleasing aesthetic part of the university's instructional program but also one of its most effective goodwill instruments. The Glee Club on tour was fine advertisement for the institution, especially when it visited the hometowns of its members.

Because of obvious benefits Indiana University had already garnered from its severely limited musical program, William Bryan's activity in developing new colleges extended well beyond the applied fields of science and commerce. He now turned to those areas which he believed would soften the twentieth century's spirit of crass commercialism.

As athletic rivalries grew more intense and college spirit became as much a fact in university life as roll books and deans of women, all sorts of nostalgic sentiments were expressed in songs. For this reason the subject of a new college song was re-opened by the *Daily Student*. On October 21, 1904, the paper carried a picture of the handsome Joseph T. Giles, author of "Hail to Old I. U." and beneath it gave a biographical sketch of the author. At that time he was teaching school in Marion and far away from the scene of college razzle-dazzle in both time and memory. There were in his life no more Monon trains loaded with carefree students on their way to shout the "Big Red" team to victory in Lafayette. Giles said that he got the idea for his song in 1892 while on the way to play Purdue. There was at the time a popular demand for an Indiana song but so far no lyricist in search of immortality had composed one. Giles and his companions on that day to Purdue had in mind Indiana and Gloriana, but they felt need for a third rhyming word. Ernest H. Lindley recalled that a new shipment of soap and perfume, bearing the trade name "frangipana," had just been placed on display in his father's Bloomington drugstore. This name was derived from the sweet aromatic scent of the bloom of an *apocynaceus* tropical American tree, the red jasmine, and a member of the dogbane family. With "frangipana" in mind it took Giles only a few hours to write "Hail to Old I. U." The first public rendition of the song was in 1893 by the Indiana Glee Club in the Plymouth Church in Indianapolis on the occasion of the state forensic contest.

A decade later Frances Morgan Swain, that irrepressible mother figure of Indiana University, sent back from Swarthmore a new song of three lengthy stanzas in which she paid nostalgic tribute to Indiana in the name of the lovely mayflower. At least her song had the virtue of locating the botanical allusion nearer home, and at last removing Giles' seeming implication that Indiana might possibly have been pronounced by some "Indiany" in 1893.

The *Arbutus* in 1894 published the first version of "Gloriana," which interestingly contained the word frangipana but removed Indiana from the rhythmic trilogy. The next year Thomas E. Sanders of the class of 1895, and in reminiscent mood, paid an over-affectionate tribute to "Dear Old I. U." set to the tune of "Maryland, My Maryland." Unlike "Gloriana," Sanders so overworked the "Old I. U." theme that his love offering failed to elevate alumni blood pressure and pride at athletic games.

Far away from the banks of the Jordan and safely behind the shuttered ramparts of his Paris publisher's office, the priggish French traveler Paul Bourget commented on the raw, blustering mauve decade in America. With a pen dipped in gall and safely out of rifle range he passed judgment on many things, one of which was higher education. In his two volumes entitled *Outré-*

Mer he cited an example of what he called, "crudeness, savagery, and even education"—the Indiana song which he said began "Gloriana, frangipana."

Despite Bourget's scornful comments the Hoosier songwriters were unstoppable. Russell P. Harker of the law class of 1912 sought to wrest fame from Joe T. Giles with a new song. Inspired in a burst of a football victory, and while directing the band after the DePauw game he went home to Bloomington to write "Indiana! Our Indiana!" This song was first played late in November, 1912, at the Northwestern game.

The veritable cacophony of rousing college songs and Glee Club practices in the years 1904 to 1914 must have been traumatic for William Lowe Bryan. Maybe partly out of self-defense on June 18, 1904, he made an oral plea to the board of trustees to approve the establishment of a school of music. Joseph Hooker Shea moved that the president be instructed to begin at once a search for a professor or dean, and to begin the organization of courses anticipating a mature music program.

Frantic correspondence followed on the subject of locating the right person to administer a school of academic music. As was true every time he sought a new staff member, Bryan wanted an individual who was proficient in his subject, of high moral character, and who promised to deliver more than his salary would indicate. In this particular case his letters also reflect the anxiety he suffered because of a lack of knowledge and experience with the field. He was forced to rely largely on someone else's judgment. Professor N. J. Corey of Detroit was invited to Bloomington to lecture and to inspect the university in the fall of 1904. A week later, October 20, Bryan wrote A. L. Manchester of Wellesley Hills, Massachusetts, cautiously inquiring whether he would be interested in coming to Indiana.

By mid-November the president was back before the trustees with the discouraging report, "It is extremely difficult to find a man whose musical training is quite first-rate and who has also the good sense and executive ability required." One questions at this point whether Bryan sought to employ an artist-teacher, or an entrepreneurial professor with some musical talent.

Behind William Lowe Bryan's vigorous effort to establish a music school was hardly personal enthusiasm for the subject itself. The Lecture and Concert Committee had been successful over the

years in bringing some genuinely good music groups to Bloomington. The list for the decade prior to 1910 is impressive. By 1904
it could be said without exaggeration that local taste had been
vastly refined and there was growing appreciation for competent
musical performances. At least there were now many persons in
the locality who could distinguish between the amateur efforts of
a church choir or a dance carousal and a formal orchestral rendition. The Thomas Orchestra Company of Chicago which had appeared for the first time in 1899 contributed materially to the
cultivation of this interest in its annual visits. During these same
years the concert pianist Edward Ebert-Buchheim of the Danville,
Illinois, Normal Institute, enjoyed a popular following, and in the
eyes of many he became the local personification of Mozart, Schubert, and Beethoven. His sonatas stirred the aesthetic spirit along
the Jordan and gave the piano an artistic masculinity which it had
not enjoyed before.

On the evening of May 25, 1905, a sophisticated concert performance by local talent was said to have "stamped Bloomington
as a musical city." The Lecture Association had arranged a May
Day festival under the direction of Franz Bellinger of Indianapolis. The *Daily Student* reviewer said,

> The distinctly new thing was a large chorus (though it might
> have been three times as large) with competent soloists, supported
> by an orchestra of highly trained musicians, the whole directed
> by a master in the high mystery of music. The technical imperfec-
> tions, which it would be fatuous blindness to ignore, were offset
> by the pioneering aspect of the venture and were negligible in the
> face of the favor found with the audience. . . . The rhythms were
> regular, the harmonies free-flowing, the emotional quality uni-
> form; but there was also the grand climax at the end.

In short the chorus did both itself and Director Bellinger
proud.

While Franz Bellinger's rhythms flowed at regular beat,
William Lowe Bryan continued his lonely hunt for that
practical man who could raise an audience's emotions, win
the registrar's respect, and give music a safe berth in the university curriculum. Aside from aesthetic reasons, there were others
which drove him onward in his relentless search. The president
was obsessed with the subject of enrollment. Perhaps because he

had lived through a period when professors watched anxiously to see if there would be enough returning students each fall to open classes, he never got over a lingering fear of failure. Repeatedly Bryan greeted his correspondents with the statement that all was well in Indiana University because the enrollment was constantly increasing. In his mind he believed the most meaningful measure of success which Hoosiers would apply to the university was whether it attracted a growing number of students. Clearly a major source for enrollment was the daughters of Indiana. To attract them to Bloomington, however, the university was compelled to offer courses, music of major importance among them, which would be inviting.

Beginning in 1905, rumors ran through the campus that the university was on the verge of establishing a music school. The *Daily Student* suggested on October 6 that when the Student Building was completed Mitchell Hall would be available for the music school of the university. Within a year this prediction came true in part when the band and Glee Club were housed in Mitchell Hall.

The campus newspaper's rumor and optimism were premature. Three years passed and Bryan had made no progress in finding a music school professor. As a temporary arrangement he proposed the appointment of Professor Charles Divin Campbell of the German Department as professor-in-charge of music. Professor Campbell had a rich German university background and had developed more than a casual knowledge and appreciation for the subject. He had taken full advantage of his opportunities while abroad to cultivate a critical understanding of musical history and appreciation. Too, he was a highly vocal supporter of formal musical training. He told a *Student* reporter, "To have merely a school of applied music might have a tendency to draw a class of students who merely wished to dabble a little in the fine arts." For university purposes he suggested more choral and orchestral drill.

That same year, 1907, the university arranged with the popular Ebert-Buchheim to move to Bloomington where he could offer regular instruction in piano on what seems to have been a contingent basis. The Bloomington *Telephone* announced at the opening of the fall semester that the Professor was established in Mitchell Hall and "prospects [are] excellent for a large number of students." More than this, the paper thought within a year the university would have a new building and a conservatory of music. "Practically nothing," it said, "has been given out from the University in regard to the new department. It has been recognized for some time that if Indiana were to hold her own as a co-educational institution she must have a first-class music department. DePauw has at present a musical department which is recognized as one of the best in the west." As a result there were almost twice as many girls as boys in Greencastle.

The *Telephone* was engaged in wishful thinking. Prospects were unlikely that Campbell, Ebert-Buchheim, and the old worn out choirmaster Lucius Matlac Hiatt would develop a superior school. There were twenty-three students enrolled in piano, and Mitchell Hall reverberated to Professor Ebert-Buchheim's rendition of Schubert, Grieg, Schumann, Liszt, and Chopin as he prepared for his semi-weekly soirees. Bryan knew the truth. He told the trustees in June 1910, "We have had a very unsatisfactory and inadequate provision for music and we have delayed making a change for lack of means."

Charles D. Campbell agreed to serve as director of music on a year-to-year basis until a competent professor could be found. He would direct the university orchestra, chorus, and soloists in a performance of *Robin Hood* on commencement eve. During the coming year, 1910–11, he would also offer a limited amount of classroom instruction in music, but this would not constitute a curriculum for a full departmental offering. Campbell, however, had introduced ten new courses in history, elements, forms, singing, orchestra, and band by the fall of 1910. Ebert-Buchheim and Hiatt offered instruction in vocal and choral music. Hiatt seems to have lacked both physical and intellectual stamina, or the professional ability to carry institutional music instruction beyond the elementary church choir director level. He had directed a high school band, and for the past decade had charge of choral music in the university. This latter assignment seems to have been no more than directing the chapel choir. In 1910 President Bryan told the trustees that Hiatt was not equal to the demands of director of a music school, and besides he wanted to retire, and did so that year. Further, said Bryan, "I may say that it became apparent years ago that Mr. Hiatt was not equal to the demands of this place."

When the university opened in the fall of 1911 the music field seemed to be at its lowest ebb. More trouble, however, was to come. The president was informed that the faithful old tuba which had boomed through so many athletic forays was worn beyond repair, and there were insufficient funds to buy a new one. It would be impossible for the band that fall to lift the melody of "Hail to Old I. U." in proper martial style, and as a result the college spirit would wither. There were other needs. The band needed new music pads and this required an outlay of $150. A year later university musicians made a purchase, strange for a department of performing arts, of a player piano and $150 worth of rolls and records. This was a far cry from the late Ebert-Buchheim's swallow-tailed evening performances at the piano.

Even the purist Charles D. Campbell was forced by circumstances to surrender to expediency. He signed a purchase order for a victrola and a generous supply of records. Campbell, however, was selective in the causes to which he would succumb and eased his troubled conscience with a strong lecture to professors and trustees on the civilized aspects of music. There were, he said, 136 students enrolled in university courses in music, 120 of whom were bandsmen—nevertheless they had an interest. Colleges and universities in the United States spent $600,000 annually on music instruction. Unless Indiana heeded the example its concerts and recitals would be prostituted by inexperienced students who had low moral standards and over-developed desires to make money. These spoilers would "put on real live up-to-date stuff"—such stuff being "nigger minstrels and cheap vaudeville of the day." Opera, Campbell contended, was the best means of cultivating musical appreciation, and he countered the minstrel menace by organizing and directing several operatic performances.

In a more philosophical vein, Campbell told the administration and trustees, "The average American youth is brought up to consider himself a highly important individual with little regard for constituted authority, with supreme contempt for those whose opinions differ from his own, and with the firm belief that it is all times his duty to put forth his own personality. Naturally then he makes a poor team player." And, he added, a poor musician. Too often Indiana lads revealed a desire to play to the benches. On the other extreme some students submitted too completely to devotion to music and neglected their other studies. A music teacher made a heavy investment in time and patience in training student musicians and if they misbehaved or failed their work then there was great waste. This long lecture was provoked by the antics of some members of the Glee Club on tour which landed them before the faculty disciplinary committee. Expulsion, Campbell, said, would result in extraordinary loss to the institution.

Thus it was that William Lowe Bryan was still in the field hunting for the proper man to develop a music school when the first guns of World War I brought the end of an era. Actually he had nothing to show thus far for his diligence but a stern lecture from Professor Campbell and a thick folder of fruitless letters. The dream of establishing a music school awaited the future for fulfillment, but by its efforts Indiana University had pre-empted the field of public school music.

The organization of the Music School could wait until a proper dean could be hired, and necessary funds were available. Bryan and faculty were too occupied with the challenges of the new university to frustrate themselves with disappointment over a single setback. During the past decade the whole burden of restructuring the university had presented as many challenges as there were areas of academic interest in the institution. The mountain was only partially scaled. Indiana University was still in a vigorous struggle to keep pace with its neighboring universities, and with a cultural and educational age which in many areas had a significant head start.

[IV]

The Long Step
into Professionalization

BROADENING INDIANA UNIVERSITY's professional curriculum involved complexities which no one in 1903 could fully contemplate. It was one thing to plan a modest beginning for a professional school but an altogether different thing to reckon with the professional men and the politicians. No doubt William Lowe Bryan and his faculty thought in 1903 that all they needed to do was develop a two-year medical program at Bloomington as a rib from the side of the university and then advance their students to four years of training either by merging with a clinical school in Indianapolis or by organizing an independent medical school. This proved to be an entirely false premise.

At no time in its whole history did Indiana University come nearer the brink of political chaos, if not actual self-destruction of the university itself, than when it began the serious business of organizing a medical school. In this adventure it found itself in a damaging public rivalry with Purdue University and a group of willful doctors in Indianapolis. Controversy over medical schools has been a common phenomenon in American education, but it is doubtful that many controversies involved more cross currents and institutional snares than did that in the first decade of this century in Indiana.

The legislative act of February 15, 1838, which changed Indiana's status from college to university, contained in section (I) a statement of the purposes of the institution, which were "for the education of youth in the American, learned and foreign languages, the useful arts, sciences (including law and medicine), and literature. . . ." Parenthetically legislators included the two major professions. As a matter of fact most of the lawmakers left no doubt that they thought doctors and lawyers were trained in the offices of practitioners and not at public expense in colleges and universities. Little could the semi-frontier legislators know that almost a century later their casual phraseology would cause such an emotional storm in the General Assembly.

There is a vague statement in Indiana University history that a medical school existed from 1870 to 1873, and again in the 1890's there was talk of addition of medical training to the institution's curriculum, but nothing came of this. In March, 1903, the board of trustees authorized President Bryan to make necessary plans for a two-year medical program which would lead in time to a more extended offering. That same year Bryan described for the trustees a four-year curriculum which would lead to a combined bachelor of arts degree in preparatory medicine. By September, he said, classrooms had been set aside on the top floor of the newly dedicated Science Hall, and anatomy had been added to the curriculum. Emphasis was to be placed on mammalian anatomy, and the *Daily Student*, September 19, 1903, thought the university had now opened a flourishing market for cats and dogs, and maybe even human bodies. It hastened to explain, however, that there would be no offensive odors from the laboratories to upset Latin scholars and prospective lawyers. The medical subjects required separate laboratories, and better equipment would have to be purchased than that used in the past with the traditional sciences.

Dr. Burton Dorr Myers, formerly of The Johns Hopkins Medical School, was employed as head of the medical department. Dr. Robert E. Lyons, head of the Chemistry Department, was given responsibility for courses in his field. In fact Lyons was already teaching chemistry in two of the proprietary medical schools in Indianapolis. President Bryan assured the trustees that in establishing a two-year school in Bloomington they should consider an ultimate merger with a medical college in Indianapolis a distinct possibility, otherwise the university would have to take steps to

[6 6]

assure that its students were admitted to out-of-state schools. Since the two medical colleges in Indianapolis had failed to unite, the university hastened into the field of medical education. Further, Bryan noted a pronounced questioning in Bloomington of the professional seriousness of medical professors in the capital city.

In addition to laboratories and equipment there was now a need for human and animal cadavers from a dependable source. President Bryan thought the university had a legal right to demand of the State Anatomical Board a fair share of laboratory materials. The thought of having cadavers in a university classroom excited the *Daily Student* reporters. An unknown man was murdered by a contractor named Spiegel at the railroad camp northeast of Bloomington in December, 1903, and coroner Weir turned his body over to Dr. B. D. Myers and his students. The campus paper described its physical condition in nauseating detail. A few days later the body of a nameless tramp was found near Nashville and it, too, was sent to the university. This time the news story became even more gruesome in its descriptive minutiae.

There were more pressing needs of the infant medical school than the mere procurement of anatomical materials. In March, 1904, President Bryan informed the trustees he would be ready to submit full plans for the medical school in June, and that he would recommend a much sounder program for the school. Already he had suggested that the location of the advanced part of the course be in Indianapolis. Although sincere in proposing a possible merger with any one of the existing schools, he declared that the board of trustees should retain full control over every department of the institution. "I am firmly convinced," he told the trustees, "that it would be fatally bad policy to make such arrangement [accepting a separate board of doctor trustees] even if it were legal." He saw no reason against having a joint executive advisory committee to make recommendations to the board, but ultimate responsibility for medical education should finally remain with the university.

Bryan had anxieties about favoring two years of work in Bloomington and two in an Indianapolis medical college even though he had stated Bloomington could not supply the clinical support the school must have. He felt practitioner-professors already had given too little attention to classes and laboratories, and the university should not perpetuate this failure. The Indianapolis proprietary institutions were known to doctors and university officials alike to be inferior in every respect. While good schools in the United

States were lavishing funds on their medical schools to establish and maintain clinics, the doctor-proprietors in Indianapolis were starving their already antiquated colleges. "Do what we will," said Bryan, "it may be that within the next ten years, the Indianapolis schools under whatever management will die. Two causes in active operation make for their death. The low grade medical students are going to states and schools where the standards are lower and the high grade students are going to schools where the facilities are far better. We cannot avert this outcome simply by organizing in some new way, by giving our name to a school in Indianapolis, leaving the school meanwhile in character substantially what it is at present."

The university's president was emphatic, that, as severely limited in financial resources as the university was, only a medical school properly organized and managed by the highest standards could really survive poverty and inferior reputation. In practical terms this meant a school staffed by more than self-seeking practitioners, with adequate clinics, and a research hospital. If Indiana should organize a medical school in Indianapolis then Bryan expressed himself as wanting a good one, not a self-serving makeshift. Fortunately, for political reasons, Bryan's sharp remarks were made in the privacy of board meetings. The trustees reacted favorably to his suggestions and appointed a committee composed of James William Fesler, Nathaniel Usher Hill, and William Lowe Bryan to consider further negotiations for an advanced medical school connection in Indianapolis.

Within a month after William Lowe Bryan reported to the trustees, a committee of doctors led by Dr. W. V. Gott of the State Board of Examiners and Medical Registration visited the university for the second time. The Daily Student said the doctors were well pleased this time with the medical instruction in both classroom and laboratory.

In the Student's opinion the medical school was off to a flying start in its antiseptic quarters. It described the wonders of microscopic technique, the thoroughness of classroom lectures, and the expertness of laboratory technicians. This pride and confidence seemed to be justified by the promptness of the certification of the school by the state board. The state board's favorable action was construed by the Bloomington Telephone to be a victory for the medical faculty of the university and eased the animosity which had arisen between it and the state because of a former rejection.

By the time the first two-year medical class was almost ready to graduate from the university, plans were underway for affiliation with a school in Indianapolis. This move, however, was to be fraught with troubles. The Indianapolis *Sentinel*, on September 26, 1905, said fourteen of the twenty-five members of the board of trustees of the Central College of Physicians and Surgeons had in a meeting on the previous day adopted resolutions to consolidate their school with the Medical College of Indiana (organized in 1869), and with Purdue University.

In Lafayette the *Purdue Exponent* hailed the news of the new medical college of Purdue with joy. The consolidation it said gave "Purdue the largest school of medicine in the state and one of the largest in the West. The addition of the two medical colleges is only in line with the progressive strides of the University within the past few years. That Purdue should have a School of Medicine is obvious. She has, for years, maintained an excellent school of pharmacy and offered a pre-medical course intended to prepare students for a more intelligent study of medicine after graduating. Medicine, too, is recognized as a scientific study, and the study of science is one of Purdue's strongholds."

The physicians planned to consolidate not only the two Indianapolis schools but also the Fort Wayne College of Medicine. The meeting of the trustees was called so hurriedly that members were summoned by telegraph. The haste with which the merger was effected caused considerable resistance on the part of many interested doctors, and even from the students of the three schools. Later it was revealed that the plan for merger had been quietly discussed for a year and Purdue was a party to much of the discussion. An attempt had even been made, said the newspapers, to merge with Indiana University. This was true, but the doctors wanted to use the name of the university only and refused to surrender their control of the medical schools.

This action in September plus the previous agreement between Indiana and Purdue and the Indiana College of Medicine opened one of the stormiest chapters in Indiana University history. Immediately friends of the university protested that the merger would duplicate work offered in Bloomington. In order to prevent this they promised a battle royal in the forthcoming meeting of the General Assembly. Thus a three-way controversy was provoked by consolidation of the schools, and what appeared to be a violation of the unwritten understanding between the two state universities, and between staffs and stockholders of the medical schools, and among the state legislators.

The *Purdue Exponent* took a sober look at the new school. "What benefit is this to Purdue?" it asked, "Probably the material benefit is offset by the burdens and responsibilities accompanying the gift of the new institutions. It must be borne in mind that Purdue is not a personality which can benefit by anything. It is a state institution, an agent for doing in education what needs to be done, and what is best to. . . ."

The history of this troubled era began when the Indiana College of Medicine undertook to make an agreement with Indiana University by which it would consolidate its program with the institution, but would either be controlled by a separate board of trustees or by a strong representation on the Indiana Board. Both propositions violated William Lowe Bryan's positive admonition that the university trustees make no agreement which would relax their authority. The agreement was never signed and it was at this point Purdue University entered the story. The latter institution offered to take over the Indiana Medical College on the latter's terms. Indiana University then turned to the Central School of Physicians and Surgeons (organized in 1878), but the Central board decided its best interests would be served in merging with the Indiana College, the Fort Wayne Medical School, and Purdue University.

Immediately following the Central College decision there erupted an angry protest from both medical school students and Indiana University. Purdue was accused of exceeding both its declared charter purpose and its legal authority. Some critics believed the terms of the John Purdue will would be an insuperable obstacle to Purdue's entry into the medical field. Partisans of Indiana contended that the Lafayette school was organized as an institution of mechanic arts and agriculture. The authority "to embrace the professions" was reserved to Indiana University by law. The university cited the hazy fact that it had operated a medical school from 1870 to 1873. At that point only one hopeful fact emerged, consolidation of the two Indianapolis medical schools, and addition of the school from Fort Wayne did strengthen the institutional core for the future. At that time approximately 300 students were enrolled in the three schools, but the standards and methods of instruction were said by critics to be far behind those being set by the new medical school accrediting agency.

President Winthrop E. Stone of Purdue told the Indiana newspapers that he viewed the consolidation as a matter of hope rather than as a source of conflict and controversy. The matter had been under discussion for three or four years, but he did not say by whom. "The present union," he thought, "is not a triumph for either college, but a witness of the generosity and sacrifice of many good men. What the colleges have wasted in fighting each other," he believed, "will now go to the improvement and advancement of the new institution, which will be a credit to the city and state." Most of the original medical school faculties, the president said, would be retained, and a necessary transfer of equipment would be started at once. A dean would be chosen, and the medical program would take on the semblance, at least, of the organization of Purdue's other academic courses.

Central College's agreement to the merger of the medical schools with Purdue was both a genuine disappointment and danger signal for Indiana University. Dissatisfaction of the Central faculty and student body was short-lived indeed. Mass meetings were held in the two colleges which turned into cheering matches. President Stone adroitly allayed Central College members' anxiety in a speech in the school on September 28, 1905, in which he explained the advantages to future doctors in attending the larger institution. Following this speech the Indianapolis *Sentinel* expressed the belief that all of the medical students in Indianapolis would enroll in the new medical school of Indiana. To confirm this fact members of the faculty and students from the Indiana Medical College led their Central colleagues and fellows to their new academic home where they participated in a second love feast. That night the bond of fellowship was drawn even tighter in smokers "arranged for the entertainment of the students" at several Indianapolis hotels.

There were no smokers and love feasts in Bloomington. Gloom hung heavily over the Jordan. Only three courses were now open to Indiana University. First was to brag about the strength of its two-year courses which made up the Indiana curriculum. The *Daily Student* described the university's scientific courses, and took solid comfort from the opinion of a visiting medical stu-

dent from The Johns Hopkins University who declared that Indiana's courses were as good as any in the country. Dr. Burton
Dorr Myers spoke with more maturity and scientific certainty
when he assured friends of the university that the medical course
had "advanced greatly, considering the fact that it was so recently
organized, and that it now stands on an equal basis with all the
medical schools of its kind in the country." A second course was
to fight the Purdue merger in and out of the legislature. To do this
required organizing a four-year school, and this the trustees determined to do as quickly as possible. "The policy of the board has
been," said the *Student*, "to proceed conservatively and in harmony
with the methods of the best medical schools in the United States."

By January, 1906, the university began to reveal its approach
to the medical school controversy. The law of 1838 said the administration and trustees were authorized as soon as financially
feasible to organize a school of medicine. President Bryan, at once
assuring the public and implying the illegality of the Purdue plan,
said, "We have taken each step in strict accordance with the law
and in harmony with the methods and spirit of the best medical
schools in the United States. Our work has been legally recognized in this and other states and has been accepted without discount in the best medical schools of the country. I know no reason
why we should turn aside from the programme which has been
made our duty by the law of the state." One of the Indianapolis
newspapers, said the *Daily Student*, quickly sensed in this statement the making of a sensational fight between the two state
universities.

Indiana University further revealed its tactics, observed the
Indianapolis *News* on January 29, 1906, when its friends purchased the Central College of Physicians and Surgeons at 214
North Senate Avenue. Bryan refused to comment on this story.
Nevertheless it was made clear that the university was planning to
move its last two years of medical training closer to the clinical
resources of the larger city. The building for this college was purchased at a cost of approximately $75,000 by Bloomington sup-
porters of the university who held an organizational and subscription meeting in the Grand Hotel. Present at this time were William
Lowe Bryan; F. H. Gentry of circus fame; J. D. Showers, furniture
manufacturer; Walter S. Bradfute; and several Indianapolis doctors who had formerly been connected with Central College. The

News informed the public that a four-year medical school affiliated with Indiana University would be organized, but in order to side-step the law confining university operations to Monroe County, Bloomington citizens would be the active operators of the branch. This latter question of location was the only valid one standing in the university's way of conducting a full scale medical school with access to ample clinical material.

The Bloomington *Telephone*, on February 2, answered a query as to why Bloomington interests would want to establish a medical school with the challenge, "If Indiana University's medical department is to be captured by Purdue, and friends of the institution lay down, how many years will it be until some other department here goes the same way? In other words, Purdue has made the first radical assault upon Indiana by not only attempting to take over a department, but has tried to shut out the most important field—Indianapolis. Important because it is the capital city, but equally so because it is there, or in a like city, that a medical student must go to get the clinic work to complete such a course."

From this date, February 2, on, the medical school controversy grew much more complex, and partisans became angrier in their charges and counter-charges. Attorneys W. H. Miller and Ferdinand Winter were employed by the Indiana trustees to give legal and political advice on future action. Dr. Allison Maxwell, recently an Indiana Medical College professor, was a leader in soliciting professional support in Indianapolis. President Bryan, said the Indianapolis *Star*, was acquainted with all the details and had said that the policy of Indiana University would be to follow the law and to see that other schools (Purdue) did likewise. No doubt much of the basic story of the political maneuvering is implied in the large volume of correspondence between William Lowe Bryan and the trustees and Indiana doctors, and between the trustees and the doctors. Of even meatier substance were the private agreements and subtle political and social pressures. Unfortunately these cannot be recovered by a historian.

On one of his periodic visits to Indiana, the omnificent David Starr Jordan, in April, 1906, was asked his views on the rising medical school argument. In a ponderous and irritating answer he straddled the issue by saying he felt there was room in Indiana for two medical schools. Jordan knew full well it would be difficult indeed to secure sufficient support for one. His answer, however, was framed within the context of information which had been presented to him. The State College of Physicians and Surgeons, as an affiliate of Indiana University, was soon to begin classes, and he was told the local doctors generally favored this school.

By May 3, papers of incorporation for the State College of Physicians and Surgeons were ready for execution. Ten incorporators representing various sections of Indiana were made corporate trustees. In the same month the Indiana Superior Court rendered a decision in the case of *Doctors Scherrer and Souders* vs. *Purdue University, the Indiana Medical School et al.* The plaintiffs argued that as stockholders of Central Medical College their property rights were violated. The merger, they contended, also violated the terms of John Purdue's will, and the terms of Dr. Lomax's will by which the Indiana Medical College was endowed with a large sum. By the terms of the latter will, said the plaintiffs, the school could merge with Indiana University, Wabash College, or DePauw University, but not with Purdue. Judge McMaster said in his refusal to grant the defendants a demurrer that his decision was made along the lines taken by the friends of Indiana University. He felt Purdue was going outside its legitimate field in attempting to operate a medical school, and he cited its charter to sustain his opinion. He said Indiana farmers were already complaining that Purdue neglected their interest, and the university had only used them to secure appropriations for non-agricultural purposes.

By September the newly organized State College of Physicians and Surgeons was ready to begin classes in a building which was 60 by 100 feet and which contained two wards, each having a capacity of ten or twelve beds. There were also several small laboratories and classrooms. On his way home from a Michigan vacation, President Bryan stopped by Indianapolis to inspect the school. "I am more than pleased with the opening of the new institution," he told a reporter, "and especially the remarkable attendance; and from what I can hear, the medical department down here is going to be so crowded that we are to have all we can care for." The hospital proved to be popular. When it opened on September 13, it had thirteen patients, and ten days later the place overflowed with forty patients and there were no beds to accommodate them, and twenty patients were turned away.

Bryan's cheerful report was soon clouded by the fact that both the Bloomington and Indianapolis branches needed more professors, classrooms, equipment, laboratory materials, and funds than could possibly be made available. The president told the trustees that it was possible to shift such equipment as microscopes around from department to department. Some other laboratory materials could be shared in the same way. Dr. Myers was far less certain this arrangement could be made to work. He suggested that medical students be charged special fees. He told the President and trustees that Cornell and Chicago charged $150 and $120 respectively, and Indiana University should charge from $56 to $67. Not only would fees produce desperately needed funds, but would also save the university from needless criticism and embarrassment from other medical schools. There were sixty-one medical registrants in 1906–1907, or, according to B. D. Myers' confusing annual report, 93 students in medicine.

Woes over a lack of funds and the need for support of the fledgling State College of Physicians and Surgeons in Indianapolis did not in any way obscure the much greater struggle with Purdue in the fall of 1906. A special bulletin was issued at that time which outlined Indiana University's future plans. It would ask the General Assembly early in 1907 first to allow the institution to rectify the law to allow it to offer two years of its program in Indianapolis, and to recognize medical education as a vital part of the institution's early mandate.

In submitting its future plans to the legislators, the university's administration undertook to analyze the causes of the prevailing controversy. It was thought to have resulted from efforts of a half dozen Indianapolis physicians who wished to dominate medical education in the state by exercising trustee control from within either Indiana or Purdue universities. This same group said the university refused to recognize on a basis of equality the Central College faculty, or the long established legal right of Indiana University to establish and operate a medical school.

Perhaps at no time in his career as president of Indiana University did William Lowe Bryan meet a truly troublesome problem with more determination and coolness than he did that of the medical school. In December, 1906, his letter-writing talent proved to be an extremely useful and persuasive asset. The Indianapolis *News* reported the president's integrity had been brought under question by certain physicians. He prepared two letters describing the condition of medical education in Indiana, one of which detailed work already being done, and the other was a persuasive brief as to the university's right under the law to proceed with the larger scope of training. Bryan cited the fact that twenty-six states supported medical schools, and that all of these were connected with state universities, and never, in any case, with agricultural and mechanical colleges. He believed it unfair to call upon the people of Indiana to support two medical schools doing precisely the same work at double the cost, when there were insufficient funds to support one school. One of these letters was directly to the point. On October 24, 1906, Bryan wrote President Winthrop E. Stone of Purdue, "The present situation has many difficult complications, involving on our side questions which we regard as fundamental to the whole future of the University and involving certain obligations of honor." He then offered to talk with Stone at any time.

Bryan further touched upon a sensitive point in his letters when he denied that the Purdue merger brought harmony among the state and proprietary colleges. Without its ever being stated, the records seem to reveal that turmoil and jealousies among the doctors and their colleges were the basic troubles. "But in fact," said Bryan, "the whole affair was carried through in complete secrecy from the only medical school already established and conducted in the state." The latter school he declared to have antedated the Purdue merger by several years. He offered the people two plans, either of which Indiana University would accept and operate by. First, that there be the least possible duplication between Purdue and Indiana. Second, each institution be permitted without restrictions to offer any work it desired, thus giving the state two complete universities. This meant Purdue would offer medicine, and Indiana would establish courses in engineering and agriculture. These letters were sent to university alumni, physicians, and legislators.

To the people of Indiana President Bryan offered additional assurance that never at any time did the university propose moving the latter two years of clinical work in medicine away from Indianapolis. "We propose instead," he wrote, "to bind ourselves to maintain the clinical work at Indianapolis for all time, to use all the resources of the Medical College of Indiana toward the clinical work in Indianapolis and to labor to secure further funds for the same purpose." He also took occasion to say that Doctors Henry Jameson (Dean of Indiana Medical College), George Kahlo, and Christian B. Stemen had abandoned their story that Indiana University would merge with the Indiana College of Medicine if it were moved to Bloomington. The truth of this issue was that the university would not surrender any part of the authority of its board of trustees. He said the story of the friends of Purdue would fall to pieces in the face of revealed evidence.

Thus the scene was set for a highly dramatic public controversy and fight between the state's two universities when the General Assembly met in regular session on January 10, 1907. No one could see clearly at the outset what tragic results to Indiana public higher education this contest promised. Friends of Indiana University, in and out of the legislature, were alerted. The *Daily Student* said, "It has been their ambition to establish and maintain a course equal to that of the best schools in the United States, namely, Johns Hopkins University, Harvard, Western Reserve, and the University of Michigan. Their trials, worries, and disappointments have been many, but now it seems that success must crown their efforts." This was indeed a time of decision.

Precisely, Indiana University asked the legislature to recognize its arrangements with the State College of Physicians and Surgeons to offer clinical courses and to maintain instructional and hospital services outside Monroe County, and for sufficient financial support for the school. Purdue made almost the same requests, that is, the legislature was asked to sanction its merger with the three medical schools. With the introduction of these proposals lines of opposition were drawn not only between political friends of the two institutions, but between doctors and between newspaper editors. As the Bloomington *Telephone* said, "The medical school contest gives various state papers an opportunity to strike," and strike they did. As a sample, "The Greencastle *Banner*," said the *Telephone*, "speaks out plainly against the plan of the State University to establish a medical college at the expense of all tax-payers of Indiana and to the detriment of every non-state college in the state. The fact is the people of Indiana who must pay the bill through increased taxation if the legislature enables the State University to carry out its scheme, are not advocating the establishment of such an institution. There is no need therefore, no demand for a medical school conducted at public expense. Medical students have been well taught in private schools. What the legislature needs to do is to give the proper consideration to the common schools of the state for in the common schools all the people have direct interest."

[7 7]

This ill-tempered editorial proposed to re-open one of the hoary arguments used at the outset against the establishment of the university, and which some people still believed in the twentieth century to be a valid reason for abandoning university education.

On January 10, 1907, the *Purdue Exponent* reported a speech by President Winthrop E. Stone to the faculty and students of Purdue, in which he repeated the argument that for many years the Indianapolis medical schools had sought to unite with one of the state universities. Indiana University had its chance and passed it by. Purdue was only profiting from this mistake. It planned to organize the three medical schools into an efficient public school of medicine and to operate it on the same plane with the school of agriculture and engineering. The conflict which had arisen between Indiana and Purdue, Dr. Stone explained, was an honest difference of opinion. He deplored the unfortunate newspaper publicity. He assured his audience the two schools were not quarreling or fighting each other. He then expressed a paradoxical hope that the two universities would soon resume athletic relations which were broken in 1905, but "for the present," he said, "Purdue is quite right in not playing since the relations of the large bodies of students are so strained." He commended the Purdue students for their attitude, and thanked the *Exponent* for handling the issue with delicacy and wisdom, independent of faculty advice.

The issue of the Purdue Medical School was placed before both houses of the legislature in the form of a bill and a resolution. These sought authorization for Purdue to conduct a medical school, to accept in the name of the state the gift of the three medical colleges in accord with the agreement made in 1905. On the same day a bill was introduced in the legislature by Indiana partisans seeking authorization for the university to maintain the latter two years of a medical school outside of Monroe County. This bill received a quick and overwhelmingly favorable approval before the house judiciary committee, but President Stone insisted that he be heard, thus delaying the committee's report back to the house.

Before the proposed legislative medical school measures advanced out of committee hearings the doctors entered the discussions and helped to charge the issue emotionally. Legislators had hardly begun debate of the issue on January 29, 1907, before the *Exponent* quoted an extensive article from the South Bend *Times* which accused Indiana University of mismanaging the whole question of medical education. Said the *Times*, it had proposed to lower standards by granting bachelor of arts and doctor of medicine degrees for only six years' work, while other good medical schools required eight years. "Students," said the editor, "who intend to study medicine will flock to the Bloomington school instead of going as hitherto to such institutions as Notre Dame, DePauw, or Wabash for the course in arts." Indiana in the eyes of the editor proposed to mutilate college education. Since the university proposed to throw away two years of training, it would be reasonable to assume a faker in Bird Center would give an arts degree for no work at all. Then the South Bend editor ridiculed clinical work being done in Indianapolis, away from the microscopes and laboratories in Bloomington.

Ten days earlier the Indianapolis *Star* proclaimed on January 17, 1907, "War is on now between the factions of the medicine men and scalpels are out. The person on the fence cheerfully remarks, 'Go it, Purdue! Go it, I. U., and may the best crowd win!' " President Bryan and his colleagues realized war indeed had begun. Bloomington citizens had raised $75,000 to purchase the old Central College building to present to the state. Every Indiana alumnus in the legislature was placed on the firing line, and friends of the university worked back home in the counties where legislators had no ties with the school. Doctors were prevailed upon to go to Indianapolis to lobby. "Never has Indiana University mixed in such a terrific fight before the legislature," said the Bloomington *Telephone*, "and every resource is being called into play. Many citizens of Bloomington are called upon and respond readily regardless of other things that may demand their attention." Telegrams were sent all over the state to friends; no avenue was overlooked.

The Indiana University bill was scheduled to come before the House of Representatives on January 25. An amendment was submitted by John H. Edwards to the effect that all branches of medicine be represented in the curriculum and staff personnel. This was accepted unanimously by the committee, and the Indiana supporters waited with assured confidence that their forces were strong and the next day the bill would be passed, ending half of the fight in the legislature. So assured were they that some of the Bloomington delegation came home to spend Sunday and to attend church. Others, including President Bryan, John W. Cravens, Major Theodore Louden, Walter Bradfute, Edwin Corr, and Joseph Henley remained behind to patrol the capitol corridors and hotel lobbies.

At this stage the excitement of the drama in Indianapolis had spread across Indiana. Prominent citizens supporting one side or the other had gathered in the capital. Purdue had its line-up of doctors along with its political friends. Indiana had someone from almost every county, said the *Telephone*, and all of the trustees were on hand. Nathaniel Usher Hill, Sr., state treasurer, was a skillful strategist, and his treasury office was an excellent headquarters. It was the scene of many hurried conferences led by J. W. Fesler of the board of trustees.

In the Senate committee, as in that of the House, the battle lines were drawn and the skirmishing grew hot. The *Telephone* called it "a battle royal—a contest of giants, and the masterly presentation of President Bryan will be always remembered. It was clear as a bell, and in comparison with President Stone of Purdue he indeed measured like a giant." Trustee Benjamin Franklin Shively made the Purdue partisans groan with his tight argument. He accused the Lafayette school of engaging in a trial marriage. President Stone, said Charles L. Henry, "the well known electric line man", in the Purdue argument made a manful effort to conceal the fact that sooner or later Purdue would ask the state for money to support the medical school which it proposed to operate free of cost. A major part of his concealment was the act of dangling a gift of $100,000 worth of property before the legislators as coming from the three medical colleges.

The show-down argument before the Senate committee was provoked when Senator Will R. Wood of Lafayette introduced a joint resolution on January 16, 1907, authorizing the trustees of Purdue University to accept the gift of the medical school property. Such authorization by the legislature at that time would have been in fact a ratification of the Purdue agreement drawn in 1905.

At the same time that the Wood resolutions were pending before the Senate committee, Senator Oscar E. Bland of Owen and Monroe counties introduced a bill to permit Indiana University to conduct a medical school in Marion County. Later, in August, 1907, the Indiana Board of Trustees meeting in Indianapolis accepted Judge Vinson Carter's recommendation that Indiana University and the State College of Physicians and Surgeons should form a tighter union to conduct a four-year medical school under the "style and name of Indiana University School of Medicine." President Bryan, Dr. B. D. Myers, and Mr. Fesler were appointed a committee to prepare a petition to be submitted to the State Board of Registration and Examination which would set forth detailed terms on which the school would be merged and operated. Specifically the course of study would be prescribed by the university faculty and board of trustees, and degrees would be granted by the same bodies.

In the forefront of the medical school controversy was Dean Henry Jameson of the Indiana Medical College. It was he who had been the leader in the consolidation of the three schools in 1905, and in the formulation of the Purdue agreement. In January 1907, he was present in the legislative halls and was ever-ready to comment to the public press or to corner a legislator. He was an important personal force behind President Stone and prompted the plea for a full discussion of the Indiana bill because it was felt the Senate committee was ready to report in favor of the Indiana Medical School. At this point the only hope Purdue supporters really had was to hold up and confuse the committee report.

Across the way in the House of Representatives the legislative skirmish lines continued to be tightly drawn. Indiana University supporters stood off an attempt to recommit their bill to the education committee, instead it went to the combined Senate Judiciary-Education Committees in which much political pulling and hauling took place. There was never any doubt, however, but that the Indiana partisans had firm control of the bill's fate. Again on January 22, a sharp debate occurred in the committee where the hearing room was filled with spectators consisting largely of Indianapolis physicians, medical students, and members of the Indiana and Purdue faculties. Tension was high. Thomas T. Moore, chairman of the educational-judicial committee ruled there would be no applause, and if his instructions were violated the body would adjourn and the hall would be emptied. Both President Bryan and Stone gave for the second or third time histories of their schools' involvement in organizing a medical school, and each asserted stoutly his institution's legal right to operate such a program.

Before the legislative committees, the presidents approached their arguments from different premises. Following the presidential presentations, attorneys Benjamin F. Shively of South Bend and

C. L. Henry of Indianapolis argued the case for Indiana University, and Daniel W. Sims of Lafayette and Addison C. Harris of Indianapolis interceded for Purdue. President Stone again repeated Purdue's request for permission to carry out its 1905 agreement with the three medical schools and emphasized the size of the gift proffered the state. The Indianapolis *News* said, "The trustees of Purdue declare that the Medical College of Indiana will be a gift to the state, absolutely without condition, and assert that as it is self-supporting it [Purdue] will ask no appropriations from the General Assembly for maintenance. The value of the property Purdue has acquired and which it proposes to give to the State is declared to be $100,000."

President Stone was careful, however, to describe the Purdue agreement as tentative, and he realized it could not be put into effect until it was approved by the legislature. Plans, he said, had proceeded amicably among the schools so far. "We deny that in establishing a medical college Purdue has, in the slightest degree, infringed on the rights of Indiana or has overstepped its own province. If there is any logic in the fitness of a college to teach medicine, I should say that Purdue University is eminently equipped and that she has clearly vested rights, conferred by an act of Congress, by which Purdue was founded." He then attacked Indiana University by saying its friends asked the legislature to approve its medical school in Indianapolis without saying how it would be supported. In answering a question from a committee member President Stone repeated the naïve proposition, "that the institution (Purdue) should not in the future ask financial aid from the General Assembly. The funds of Purdue cannot be diverted to the Medical College of Indiana and there is every reason to believe that the medical college will continue to be self-supporting."

Again, Bryan stated Indiana's request in the simplest terms. It asked the privilege of offering two years of medical work in Indianapolis in collaboration with the State College of Physicians and Surgeons. President Bryan told the committee the question boiled down to how far legislators wished to go in encouraging duplication of instruction in the two state universities. He believed better judgment would not dictate wasteful duplication. There was no reservation in his mind; Indiana had the clear legal right under law to operate a school of medicine. Furthermore, it had a school of medicine already in operation. Interestingly, he had dated the beginning of the school back to 1890 when David Starr Jordan had taught a course in comparative anatomy.

When Bryan finished speaking, Senator Thomas Moore of Putnam, Morgan, and Marion counties asked how much appropriation Indiana would need for its medical program. Bryan replied, "None this year; none next year. I am unable to say or to estimate what appropriations will be needed in the future. Unlike Purdue we can not see how a medical college can be made absolutely self-supporting."

Dean Henry Jameson attacked the divided program of Indiana. He felt a clinical atmosphere should prevail throughout a medical student's training, an impossibility in Bloomington. Benjamin F. Shively then did real damage to the Purdue cause when he asserted the proposed gift of the combined Indiana Medical College property was illegal from the outset. The schools had a complex financial history. The Indiana College was especially involved. It was largely a gift from Dr. Lomax and his wife of Grant County, who had invested their savings with the understanding that at sometime in the future the college might be merged with Indiana University, DePauw, or Wabash College. He also contended that under the contract with John Purdue, that university could not legally establish a medical school in Indianapolis. Daniel Sims disputed this fact.

Lawyers in and out of Indianapolis sided largely with the Shively contention, said the Bloomington *Telephone*. Bloomington supporters claimed they could almost match the vaunted Purdue gift of $100,000 in the value of the old Central College building, and this offer was free of all legal entanglements. During the week of the great debate both Lafayette and Bloomington poured their leading citizens into Indianapolis. The *Telephone* said, "During the last two weeks Purdue has come to look upon the Bloomington contingent as a bunch of 'fighters' that have not one semblance of a yellow streak in their make-up. The faithfulness with which they worked day and night and their great loyalty to Indiana has excited the wonder and admiration of the members of the legislature." The paper spoke of the Bloomington supporters almost in terms of earlier militiamen going off to the Wabash Valley to fight Indians.

Before the Senate the sponsor of the Indiana bill amended it to require a chair of *materia medica*, and that the law should not

[83]

become effective until the property of the State School of Physicians and Surgeons had actually been transferred to the state.

On January 29, 1907, Indiana University's hopes to establish a medical school in Indianapolis were suddenly and without prior warning dashed to the ground by the unexpected House vote of 51 to 44. This result was a surprise to friend and opponent alike. The Lafayette *Journal* admitted that in counting noses the night before the vote was taken the Tippecanoe representative believed his friends had lost. In fact they asked for an additional day to cool things off, but the Indiana partisans refused to listen. The defeat was indeed a setback for the university. It became clear to Purdue supporters, however, that they were in for the same fate. The *Journal* said, "It may imply that the sentiment of the House is opposed to the state's embarking in the medical school business." The perceptive editor also judged correctly, "the issue is more than an incident with the friends of the University. One would conclude that they are fighting for the right to live."

An even more perceptive legislator who claimed to be neutral on the issue said, "Indiana sees more in the medical school move of Purdue than the establishment of a medical department. . . . At some future day there will be but one State university. If Purdue is allowed to establish a medical department there is no reason why she shouldn't have a department of law, and by all means she should have a scholastic course. You see then that the medical school project is an attack on Indiana's prestige—it threatens to establish a precedent."

Purdue's test was to come in the House of Representatives. Its partisans were frightened as to what might happen there, and, like Indiana, assembled its forces. Not only were Indiana supporters angry about their defeat, but they demonstrated strength by defeating a bill to create agricultural high schools in each county in the state. On February 1, 1907, the House committee made two reports—one favored the Purdue proposal, the other asked that the bill be indefinitely postponed. In an open house vote the minority report for postponement was defeated by almost the identical vote of Indiana's defeat in the Senate. It now seemed clear that a medical bill could not be passed that year.

What was even clearer was the fact that the embittered controversy in the legislature had involved the two universities in a dispute which if continued would be disastrous to both of them.

Purdue especially stood to lose because the great furore and newspaper publicity had angered the Indiana farmers. Purdue partisans were politically astute enough to realize that the Senate defeat of the Indiana resolution was for them a pyrrhic victory. There was lightning in John H. Edwards' statement, "We knew the time was ripe to kill this [Purdue] bill, and we determined to bring things to an issue. We knew just what our strength was when we demanded that the Committee on Education report the Purdue resolution to the House."

What emerged clearly from the legislative maneuvering was an indication of sufficient anti-public higher education sentiment to be a sobering consideration. Many legislators were said to believe the state had limited any responsibilities of the two universities to maintain medical schools. Such a sentiment was voiced by Thomas Carr Howe in the House of Representatives, "The thing for us to do is to stand up here like men, and vote as we think right. It's clear that the medical school proposed can not be maintained unless the expense is saddled on the State, and with our eyes open to the fact, we can only vote to indefinitely postpone the resolution." Some legislators saw in the private colleges a calmer and less expensive system of schools.

In assessing the defeat President W. E. Stone told the Purdue *Exponent*, "My regret is that the fair prospects for a progressive educational step have been so obstructed, and indefinitely postponed." He thought the people of Indiana had an unusual opportunity to give medical training its proper place in the educational system of the state. The legislature had thought differently and the universities had to abide by the decision. Paradoxically the Purdue president still expressed hope that a Purdue medical school could be organized.

Pragmatic politicians and sideline observers said the reason for defeat was that angry supporters of Indiana were driven by an insane desire for vengeance. A commentator said, "to use a football expression, the sidelines were crowded." This no doubt was a justifiable belief. Indiana University friends were stung to the quick by their defeat, and they were furiously determined not to remain defeated. The Lafayette *Morning Journal* February 2, 1907, charged, and perhaps correctly so, that John H. Edwards was the master villain. Said the editor, "Mr. Edwards bellowed forth defiance to the foes of the Bloomington institution and demanded recognition of Indiana's rights, pleading the great demand for medical school education. Today [February 1, 1907] he talked beseechingly as if in quest of lost souls, saying that the people of the state are sick of the whole controversy, that the question should be decisively settled in order that 'the business of importance' could proceed. . . . Mr. Edwards was shortly followed by some bushwhacker with a big mustache [sic] who represents a southern county. He waved his arms and screamed economy, scaring the timid into the belief that the recognition of the Purdue medical school would mean bankruptcy for the state." The editor said the results of the House vote reflected astute political leadership and organization. This latter must have been a fair appraisal.

Back of the political organization effected by the university was the fact that a large number of the state's doctors had less than an enthusiastic attitude toward Dr. Jameson and the Indiana College, or Dr. Jameson and the proposed merger. Indiana University, though it failed to get approval for operating the latter two years of its medical school in Indianapolis, had hope for a more favorable hearing in the future. The Bloomington *Telephone* chortled, "There is evidently no truth in the report that Senator Will Wood [of Lafayette] will ask an appropriation from the state in order to place a statue of Nat U. Hill on the Purdue University campus."

In the post mortems of the House vote all sorts of things were said. One rumor, however, had a high charge of fright in it. Word went around that the state, independent of the universities, would take over the State College of Physicians and Surgeons and operate a medical school. In this case pre-medical courses would be continued at both schools as feeders to the central college. The Lafayette *Morning Journal* said some doctors thought such a school would serve to stop the exodus of good medical students out of Indiana.

The Indiana *Daily Student*, February 6, 1907, quoted Dr. Burton D. Myers as saying only the first battle had been fought really without victory for either side. If Purdue had won the right to maintain a medical school, then "Indiana could have 'whistled' for her funds this year and in the future." Supporters of both schools almost too late were shocked into the realization that they had brought their institutions dangerously near the brink of serious political injury. Stories began to appear in newspapers to the effect that supporters of both schools now sought some form of amicable agreement between them. The Bloomington *Telephone* of February 12 said, "doubtless they realize fully by this time that if they do not live together in unity they will die separately." Purdue quickly learned the truth of this. It had asked for an increase in its budget, but the visiting legislative budget committee ignored the school's administration and listened to farmers who complained that money raised for agriculture was not spent on it. The committee recommended $100,000 for the building of an unsolicited experiment station. Indiana University was awarded an equal amount but happily the funds went directly to support the institution.

In all the roar of debate Governor Frank Hanley undertook to catch the university administration and trustees off-guard. He slipped a bill into the Senate hopper on February 24, which, if passed, would empower him to appoint five out of eight trustees. The educational committee reported the bill favorably. Again Nat U. Hill's yeomen went into action and made clear that they wanted Governor Hanley to have nothing to do with the appointment of the university's trustees—most of all they did not want the institution to fall under his control. President Bryan, John W. Cravens, Professor Ernest Holland, and Nat U. Hill actually went onto the Senate floor during the debate, and no doubt directed the bill's defeat.

Near the end of the legislative session of 1907, Indiana University partisans forced a new medical school bill onto the floor of the Senate but it failed in a tie vote. The university supporters themselves no doubt produced the tie because in the process of debate four highly questionable amendments were tacked on to it, the most damaging of which was the one offered by Senator Edgar Allen Poe Kling of Miami and Howard counties. His amendment proposed that Indiana University be required to maintain a four-year medical school in Indianapolis, the last thing the university wanted to do. Although this bill was defeated by a tie vote the debate on it revealed the thinking of some legislators. Senator T. T. Moore of Putnam, Morgan, and Marion counties reflected this fact when he said, "I don't believe that the state should be burdened with any more appropriations. The non-state schools are doing just as good work as the state schools, and yet we are appropriating $700,000 each year to the state schools."

For a year following the adjournment of the legislature the rumor mill worked overtime as to the ultimate resolution of the medical issue. Numerous newspaper stories were published on the subject, some of which President Stone denounced as "street rumors." In March, 1907, Dr. W. N. Wishard announced to Purdue students, in President Stone's behalf, that Purdue would continue its affiliation with the Medical College of Indiana, and hinted the fight for acceptance of the agreement would likewise be continued. As the year advanced, however, Indiana expanded its medical program in Indianapolis, by providing more teaching and hospital facilities.

Early in 1908 news leaked out that Bryan and Stone were carrying on a series of conversations about a possible solution. No one knew the precise subjects discussed or what progress the two presidents were making. On March 27, 1908, the Indianapolis *News* expressed the opinion that within a few weeks there would be a decision, and that Purdue would entirely abandon the field of medicine. Governor Hanley was said to be trying to find a solution that would save everybody's face. He had brought Bryan and Stone together in the first place. The man who had caused much of the controversy, Henry Jameson, Dean of the Purdue School of Medicine, denied on March 27, 1908, that any progress had been made in solving the issues between the two schools. He told the Indianapolis *News* reporter, "It is true that President Stone of Purdue, and President Bryan of Indiana University, have had several conferences on the proposition but nothing has been done, and it is not likely that anything either way will be decided on for several months. No one knows whether such a consolidation will be brought about or not. All the parties recognize the fact that any plan that might be decided on would have to safeguard carefully the interests of all parties and we do not know whether a satisfactory plan can be worked out. At any rate, it is certain that nothing has been done thus far." Maybe Jameson was right, but the voluminous correspondence indicates otherwise. The Dean was doing a bit of wishful thinking.

Ultimately President Stone prepared a proposal by which both universities would withdraw completely from the medical school business. Later he said Indiana University would have the sole privilege of organizing and operating the clinical schools in Indianapolis, and without prejudice to Purdue. Stone gave as his reasons, said the *News*, an unexpected growth in the "regular line" of Purdue's program. This work had already been planned and now it demanded extraordinary attention and support. He further proposed that Indiana and Purdue would in the future work together harmoniously, "each taking special care to work along in its own line and going before the people of the State, asking the necessary appropriations to carry on successfully its educational functions."

Bryan proved himself a shrewd and determined man in these months. He was thoroughly conscious of the fact that he was engaged in a life and death struggle to save, not a medical school for Indiana University, but Indiana University itself. At the two-year medical school's first commencement he was speaker. He told the graduates Indiana had been confronted by great obstacles but it was determined to succeed. "It is written," he said, "that when the Jews under Nehemiah were rebuilding the walls of Jerusalem in the face of a circle of enemies . . . 'everyone, with one of his hands wrought in the work and with the other held a weapon'!

"We have been forced unhappily at times to the same necessity, but with us as with Nehemiah the walls continue to go up and are each day more solidly established." Bryan told the seniors that Indiana University was right to the core, and it intended to develop a first-rate medical school. "We are not done. We are building the Wall," he concluded.

How faithfully Indiana's supporters had worked at the wall was revealed in a meeting of the board of trustees in the Claypool Hotel on April 3, 1908. They rejected outright President Stone's proposal that special medical school trustees be appointed. They then indicated their own terms. The Medical College of Indiana would be united with the university, and directly under the administration of the university board. The faculties of the Indianapolis schools should nominate from their membership those doctors who would form the new faculty. These would be appointed by the university trustees in the same manner as all other professors. Two years of work was to be maintained in Bloomington, and the latter two years, of the four-year course, would be offered in Indianapolis. Doctors Jameson, Wishard, and Graham were present at this meeting. They said they would recommend that Purdue accept Indiana's tentative proposition, provided "that Indiana University trustees will undertake in good faith to secure legislative approval of an act providing for a complete school of medicine, as defined by the laws of the State of Indiana, at Indianapolis." The trustees refused this suggestion.

Purdue, acting through John H. Edwards, suggested almost the same proposition as the doctors and the Indiana trustees delayed further action. In the meantime President Bryan gave President Stone a carefully planned memorandum which set forth in terse fashion what the university would agree to. "The two state universities," he said, "while organically distinct, should and do maintain a certain relation and interdependence, their curricula supplement each other in that they together comprise a general scope administered in certain universities in a single institution. There is no prospect of future consolidation. Therefore we should eliminate as many sources of conflict and friction as possible." The controversy of the last three years had antagonized friends of both universities, and had shaken the faith of Indiana's citizens. Bryan now believed the schools should dismiss all legal questions, and suppress the idea that one or the other university was gaining. He did not favor the two schools abandoning the idea of a medical school in Indianapolis and withdrawing to their pre-1905 positions. There is full implication that the Indiana president saw the delusion in this proposition.

On March 14, at another conference, Bryan and Stone were able to agree that Purdue would withdraw without condition from the medical school field. Jameson, however, was still insisting on a four-year school in Indianapolis, and that several trustees should be elected from the Medical Society. A fortnight later Stone pleaded by letter with Bryan and the Indiana trustees to act quickly before public agitation could produce serious consequences. Bryan was away in Cleveland, Ohio. When he returned he was highly irritated that the contents of his private conversations with Stone were being used to oppose a solution of the problem. At the same time the Purdue trustees adopted resolutions approving a four-year medical school for Indianapolis under the supervision of a board of directors representing Indiana University and the State Medical Society. In a memorandum to the Indiana trustees Bryan rejected nearly all of the Purdue proposal. He said, however, he was willing to reach the earliest possible decision. This meant he would make a concession on duplication of elementary work done in Bloomington and Lafayette. In his opinion it was up to the Purdue faculty and trustees to decide what elementary courses that university would offer.

In the end the Purdue trustees capitulated. They asked the Indiana board to act in good faith and to sign a compact agreeing with the contents of President Stone's letter. The trustees of the university refused to sign such a compact, believing the law to be a sufficient guarantee.

On April 6, 1908, the Lafayette *Daily Courier* defended the position of Purdue saying that the school only wanted to serve Indiana as fully as possible. Medicine had never been regarded as an essential part of the institution's program, and now it was believed that such instruction could be done as well or better elsewhere. The Purdue *Exponent* the next day carried the copy of the signed Bryan-Stone agreement. It was brief and pointed, "Indiana University believes that it has been especially charged with the responsibility for such instruction [medicine], the latter institution has been selected to proceed in the matter and the trustees of the two universities have this day mutually agreed to the following conditions to which the faculty of their respective medical schools assent, namely: to a union of the two medical schools under the direction [of the university] with due regards to members of the present faculties; and to the maintenance of a complete medical course in Indianapolis as well as the two-year course in medicine at Bloomington."

In bold headlines, the Bloomington *Telephone* hailed the agreement as a glorious victory for Indiana University. The agreement brought to an end a long and bitter controversy which never should have occurred in the first place. This was a classic chapter in American higher education of a conflict arising between two fundamental philosophies of public university purposes and functions. The land-grant college undertook to broaden its base at the expense of the older liberal arts and professionally oriented university. Neither school had taken a close look at the outset at the accompanying partisan political horse-trading and in-fighting.

Standing in the wings during the Purdue-Indiana contest was Governor Frank J. Hanley. At times it was difficult to determine either his views or his motives, but in the end he seems to have sensed the grave dangers involved for the two schools. On April 9, 1908, two days after an agreement had been reached, Bryan gave some sense of the Governor's role when in a personal note he wrote, "I remember that you spoke to me a good while ago urging in the kindest way that the difficulties between Purdue and Indiana should be, if possible, harmoniously settled. Efforts were made repeatedly by friends of both institutions in that direction, but, as you know, we did not escape a severe contest. I trust it will be a satisfaction to you that we have now reached a harmonious agreement, and that this has taken place in your administration and in harmony with your sentiments."

Without concrete evidence to the contrary it must be assumed that both schools suffered. Certainly the controversy polarized the legislature on the issue, and the ever-present ghost of opposition to state universities was ominously present in House and Senate chambers, committee rooms, hotel lobbies, and editorial offices. The modern historian has only the official record, the news stories, and what President Stone called street rumor on which to base much of his interpretation, but behind all of this is the strong suggestion that the heart of the story lay in the lobbying, hurried conferences in Nat U. Hill's office, hotel rooms, and in the councils of the Indianapolis doctors. This was an incident which dragged the two universities down from their pinnacles of virtue to the ground level of horse-trading politics. The huddled foyer conferences, the frantic messages which flew over the state, the whispered directives on the legislative floor, and the other tactics could hardly help but generate rumors—most of which were damaging. Nathaniel Usher Hill, Sr., U. H. Smith, John W. Cravens, Benjamin Franklin Shively, Will Wood, John Edwards, and even William Lowe Bryan took to their graves the intimate details of what happened. So did many doctors from Indianapolis. To William Lowe Bryan and the friends of Indiana University, April 7, 1908, was in effect a second foundation date. Had Indiana lost its battle to establish a medical school it would have dropped the key out of the arch of its university structure. No longer could it have claimed with much justification to be the state university, and no doubt it would have been demoted to the role of a secondary college.

The university trustees received and accepted what amounted to the Purdue board's capitulation on April 14, 1908. This was a masterpiece of face-saving strategy. The Purdue trustees said, "In furtherance of medical education and in consideration of the action of the Board of Trustees of Indiana University of this date, agreeing to unite the two existing regular schools of medicine now in operation in Indianapolis; to conduct a complete course in medicine in Indianapolis in accordance with the requirement of the law, in addition to the two years work in medicine provided in Bloomington; and providing for the same, the undersigned with the authority of the Board of Trustees of Purdue University and full consent of the faculty of the Purdue School of Medicine agree that: whenever a contract embodying the above provisions shall have been executed between the Indiana University and the Trustees of the Indiana Medical College, the School of Medicine of Purdue University, that Purdue will relinquish its interest in said school." Back of this were the deft hands of Henry Jameson and Dr. W. N. Wishard. The university board showed considerable reluctance to sign a formal contract. The General Assembly concluded the controversy in 1908 when it enacted an enabling law authorizing the Board of Trustees of Indiana University to conduct a medical school in Marion County.

With the medical college issue decided, the university entered a new phase of its history, and its needs and responsibilities were greatly enlarged. First, with the addition of the medical school, Indiana was ceasing to be an isolated provincial university. It now had to conform with accrediting standards for professional schools set well beyond the reach of political legislators and partisans in Bloomington and Indianapolis. Not only was this true, but the whole area of American professional education was being markedly upgraded, demanding of Indiana an even higher standard of performance than would have been required a decade earlier. For both university and state the time had come by 1908 when no longer could Bryan and his faculty draw instructional and professional talent from within the university's existing personnel resources. The accrediting boards stopped this.

Almost a year later, March 25, 1909, William Lowe Bryan informed the board of trustees that the university and the State of Indiana had undertaken to form a medical school in one of the most important eras in both local and national educational history. The trained doctor had become a most important figure in society. As for the university Bryan said, "This university differs from all other universities of standing, whether state or non-state, in the meagerness for professional education. A fundamental and permanent need of the State on the one hand and a fundamental condition of making this institution a university in fact as well as in name compelled us to enter this new field. We have had together six years of arduous labor."

An interesting sidelight on the Indiana-Purdue controversy was the fact that the public supporters of both who were either indifferent or ignorant of the medical school issue demanded the resumption of athletic rivalry. Between 1905 and 1908 the relations between the two schools had been suspended. Coaches Sheldon and Nichols of Indiana and Purdue were able to agree on renewing the games, a step which no doubt lessened tensions which otherwise might have smoldered dangerously.

State- and nationwide attention greeted the final settling of the medical school issue. Dr. Arthur Dean Bevan of Chicago, chairman of the committee on medical education of the American Medical Association, wired: "I want to congratulate the profession of Indiana upon the settlement of the medical college situation. It will mean that within a few years the great commonwealth of Indiana will have one of the great medical departments of the United States." Other messages carried the same theme. The key to interest in the Indiana situation rested as much with anxiety over the possible revision of the American university-land grant college structure as with medical education itself.

Within a month after the settlement President Bryan and a committee of seven Bloomington and Indianapolis doctors set out for the East to visit several medical schools, among them The Johns Hopkins Medical School, Jefferson Medical School, the Medico-Chirugical Medical School, Columbia, Cornell, and Harvard. They had their eyes opened by both the new methodology and the administrative and instructional organization of these institutions. Most of these schools had new and expensive equipment, were alert to changing concepts of medical education, and had access to an abundance of clinical materials.

In the first year of the existence of the Indiana University Medical School, President Bryan and his faculty learned that they were beginning a four-year medical program in one of the most important transitional periods in modern medical educational history. They soon discovered that most of their arguments and discussions at Bloomington and in that great scientific body, the Indiana legislature, had been little more than idle chatter. First the Indiana curriculum had to be completely reorganized and realigned to fit the requirements of the Association of American Medical Schools. On top of this, the powerful American Medical Association had already concerned itself with such matters as professors' time devoted to courses, course sequence, and the nature of electives. An even more startling discovery was that all but two medical schools in the United States were now requiring five years of work.

At the next meeting of the board of trustees, President Bryan took considerable pains to make clear to the trustees the demands of the times. He admonished them to maintain close supervision of the entire medical program so as to impress upon it the university's stamp of quality rather than that of a doctor-run proprietary school. At the beginning of the session in 1909 the faculty of the School of Medicine began the process of change. It voted to require a full year of collegiate work before a student would be admitted to medical classes, and after 1912 two years' preliminary preparation would be required. To further emphasize Bryan's plea to imprint medical training at Indiana with the university mark the Indianapolis faculty voted to send the seniors to Bloomington for commencement ceremonies.

By early fall, 1909, the university began to reveal some concern about outside inspection of the medical school. It was necessary to organize hurriedly a teaching and research hospital in order to ward off failure of inspection. This meant the purchase of a building and the procurement of equipment. Both faculty and administration were keenly aware that if the Carnegie Foundation failed to recognize Indiana's school it would be for lack of a hospital. Bryan was even more pessimistic when he told the trustees on November 8, 1909, the time was approaching when Indiana would either have to establish a hospital or give up attempts to offer medical training. Too, the time was overdue when a dean had to be employed who would give most of his time to the medical program.

To the relief of everybody, perhaps including Dr. Henry Jameson, the Dean of the Indiana College resigned in 1908 and later the administration of the medical school was placed in the hands of Doctors William Niles Wishard, John Finch Barnhill, Edmund Dougan Clark, Burton Dorr Myers, and Frank B. Wynn. This proved, however, an unsuccessful stopgap arrangement, although the committee did cut through the tangled underbrush of personnel of the medical school to produce a list of names for faculty appointments. It was here that the university came to face its most trying faculty situation. Scores of names of doctors appeared on the medical school roster who had little or nothing to do with the institution. They had allowed their names to appear for vanity's sake. President Bryan suggested a greatly reduced list with emphasis on teaching and laboratory direction, and none on personal pride.

In the meantime Bryan began talks with Dr. Pritchett of the Carnegie Endowment about a prospective gift from that foundation. In 1913, however, he was to suffer sharp disappointment. After an extended courtship by Indiana, Andrew Carnegie decided to give Vanderbilt University a million dollars because the South had no first-class medical school. It was cold comfort indeed to be told that there was no other place where the Carnegie Foundation was more disposed to spend $500,000 than Indiana.

Early in 1911 Bryan recommended that the board of trustees make arrangements to sell much of the scattered medical school property in Indianapolis to provide funds for the construction of a new plant, especially classrooms for anatomy and pathology. Equally important as laboratories, equipment, and classrooms was hiring a small group of professors who would give full time to classes. Such men could be found only if they were allowed to carry on a private practice in the hospital to supplement their professorial incomes.

These were urgent needs, but the most urgent of all was the appointment of a strong dean. Doctors Henry S. Pritchett, Abraham Flexner, and William Henry Welch recommended Dr. Long Cope of the University of Pennsylvania. Nothing came of this and the search was continued. Dr. Allison Maxwell had acted as interim dean. In June, 1911, Dr. B. D. Myers was sent east to conduct a personal hunt for a likely candidate. He returned to Bloomington with the name of Dr. Charles Phillips Emerson, of the The Johns Hopkins University, who was highly recommended and seemed to Myers to be an excellent prospect.

Unable to attend the board meeting in Indianapolis on July 1, 1911, because of the illness of Mrs. Bryan, the president wrote that Dr. Emerson should be employed. He reiterated that if Indiana were to have a first rate medical school it must have a good dean. By September Dr. Emerson was in Indianapolis, and on November 28, the *Daily Student* crowed that Eastern medical authorities were said to believe conditions in Indiana were headed toward the establishment of a great medical school. Perhaps the paper's "Eastern authority" was Dr. Willis D. Gatch who had just been made head of the department of operative surgery. Dr. Gatch quickly revealed himself an outspoken critic. He thought the division of medical classes between two years in Bloomington and two years in Indianapolis was needlessly confusing.

Contrary to what President Stone and even President Bryan had said in the legislative fight, the medical school not only needed money, but, comparatively speaking, big money. At its meeting of October 30, 1912, Bryan told the trustees the particular need of the medical school was a larger income. At that time the state contributed $25,000, when the minimum should have been $75,-000. Now that a hospital was at the school's command, it needed to get on with the organization of a first class institution. Substantiating the president's request was the frantic note from the head of the department of anatomy reiterating his urgent need for a skeleton. At last the school had installed an incinerator to dispose of the remains of cadavers. The medical school in Bloomington and Indianapolis had been the target of some vicious shots because of the desecration of human bodies by denying them decent earth burials.

In his first annual report Dr. Charles P. Emerson lifted the curtain on backstairs medical politics in Indiana. He gave the board of trustees a graphic summary of conditions. The hospital was at last underway and this would prove a vital asset to teaching. Of the men on the faculty, Dr. Louis Burckhardt was one of the strongest, but unfortunately he was an obstetrician who had to spend much of his time waiting for the tide of motherhood to favor him. Dr. O. G. Pfaff was a strong man in gynecology. Not all were of this caliber, however. A Dr. Thrasher, who took blood samples for Wasserman tests, gave the school not an hour a day, but used orderlies, nurses, and guinea pigs to further his private interest.

As the medical school educated new practitioners with higher standards, the Dean saw hope for distinct improvement in the medical school. "The standard of medical practice in the city in the past has been such that it could not inspire much confidence, for a very powerful medical ring gave the people just what it wanted to, and was able by pure medical politics, even to [favoring] the position of consultant, a man with minimum training."

Emerson was certain that the "managers" were beginning to realize, and a Dr. Morrison in particular, that they could not use the medical school as an advertising medium. Their patients, he thought, were discovering "how low their ideals were and in some cases were unwilling to trust further the men who held these ideals." Still, there was, said Dr. Emerson, a considerable amount of hostility among staff members, especially among the surgeons. Two men, especially, Morrison and Hutchins, were doing their best to foment trouble. So far they had failed. Nevertheless they had interfered with the operation of the school by exerting influence at city hall, thus shutting off certain services and supplies from Indianapolis. One of them had written opposing the appropriation of $6000 to the city dispensary on the Indiana Medical School letterhead, indicating thereby that he was a faculty member.

Like these doctors or not, Dean Emerson faced the reality that they technically were still members of the medical school faculty. He asked the trustees to drop them because, "from their position in the school they can hurt us terribly. If they could be dropped before the legislature meets their influence certainly would be much less since we could then show that they [part time doctor professors] had sufficient motive for their opposition."

The Bloomington *Telephone* reported on January 27, 1911, that Governor Thomas R. Marshall had gone before the House of Representatives and announced that Dr. and Mrs. Robert W. Long of Indianapolis had made a gift of $200,000, largely in the form of real estate, for the building and equipping of a hospital to be known as the Robert W. Long Hospital. The Longs wished $160,000 to be spent on the building, and $40,000 for equipment. They made a somewhat vague promise that ultimately their gift would total a half million dollars. In fact they quickly erased the vagueness when Dr. Long asked for a legislative act to guarantee that the terms of his will would be fully honored.

It was not until March, 1911, that President Bryan announced the Long gift to the regular meeting of the board of trustees. By this time, his announcement was news to no literate Hoosier, even though the fight over the location of a site for the Long Hospital was. Dr. Long had made a proviso that the St. Clair Park adjacent to the State Blind Asylum in Indianapolis would be a highly satisfactory site. This partially reopened the old Purdue feud. Senator Will Wood of Lafayette led the debate in the Senate against the St. Clair Park location. Finally it was decided to shift the hospital location to the largely abandoned south end of Military Park, a memorial to veterans of the Civil War, or possibly to land being set aside for the state library and historical building on Senate Avenue.

Mention of Military Park brought the Grand Army of the Republic hobbling out of retirement. To many of the boys in blue that soil was as sacred as the blood-stained heights of Cemetery Ridge or the loess banks of Vicksburg. William A. Ketchum, a former student at Indiana University, and at one time state attorney general, begged the trustees to build the hospital in the park because he believed this would be a means of keeping the spot sacred to the memory of the veterans.

Before any further headway could be made with site location for the hospital a dispute between the state and the city reached a mild boiling point. Mayor Shank and his city hall supporters were opposed to both the St. Clair and Military Park sites and favored a sixteen acre location in the western part of the city bounded by Hiawatha Street on the east, and Porter and Elmwood on the west. Governor Marshall approved the shift and said he would ask the legislature in 1913 for the $40,000 purchase price provided the mayor and city council failed to provide the funds. He told the city officials that if they did fail to provide funds the state would resort to a pro rata admission of patients from over the state. As it was expected that 90 percent of the patients seeking admission to the hospital would come from Indianapolis this could prove a costly arrangement for city and citizen alike. If, however, the city purchased a hospital site then the state would give it a quit claim to Military Park to be used as a "breathing spot."

By November, 1912, the university trustees were anxious to begin construction of the hospital. R. F. Daggett and Company of Indianapolis had been employed in February to prepare plans for the building. The conflict between city and state was delaying and costly, but most threatening of all was the possibility of further public involvement. This was indicated by the fact the State Centennial Commission, the City Park Board, the Civic Improvement Commission of the Commercial Club, and other organizations were inching their way into the argument. Mayor Shank aroused the people with handbills, called meetings of the West End Merchants' Association, and the West Side Civic League. He threatened to hire legal counsel and go to court. Like Barbara Frietchie of old he stood figuratively at the gate of Military Park and shouted, "The plan to spoil the park as a breathing spot is one of great outrage. If I can't stop it as mayor I am willing to contribute to a fund to file suit in the courts to see if the plan can be defeated." Bryan retorted, "The title to this land is in the name of the State of Indiana, and not the City of Indianapolis."

Thus the argument went. Despite all the frantic pleas for haste it was not until October 7, 1912, that a contract for construction of the hospital building was awarded the Bedford Stone Company of Indianapolis for approximately $162,000. Optimists believed the building would be ready in a very short time. Finally the site at 1076 Washington Street was purchased and the second battle of Indianapolis was ended. A hospital was being built which would contain eighty-eight ward beds, fourteen private rooms, laboratories, operating rooms, and a training school for nurses. By 1914 this plant was in operation. After eleven years of battling self-serving Indianapolis doctors, Purdue University's president and trustees, Indiana politicians, and Mayor Shank and the city government of Indianapolis, William Lowe Bryan and the board of trustees might well have been excused if they had shucked off their dignity and their coats at the hospital dedication and stepped forth to release their emotions by giving the Indiana University Medical Society yell:

> Doctors! Doctors! herb concocters!
> Honest we are doctors! Wow! Wow! Wow!

[V]

A University in Fact

THOUGH GOVERNOR THOMAS MARSHALL and the presidents of the Indiana colleges gave their blessings to Indiana University and its drive to develop graduate education to the highest possible level, they reminded the institution of its original mission of serving the public education system of the state. As important as doctors and lawyers were teachers trained in the modern techniques of their craft. The accrediting agencies also gave emphasis to this point in their inspections and reports. This was an area in which the university's administration and staff felt most comfortable.

In 1910 when President Henry S. Pritchett of the Carnegie Foundation discussed reasons why Indiana and Purdue Universities were finally accepted to membership in the pension group he gave as the first reason better relations with the public schools. He perhaps was inadequately informed about the university's long history in this field. The institution had been in the business of training teachers from the outset. It supplied instructors not only to Indiana, but its graduates had gone as far afield as the new omnibus states of the Northwest. In the 1880's and 1890's it had set standards of work for the schools, and classified their standings. It would be reasonable to assume, in the absence of precise

statistical knowledge, that 50 percent of the university correspondence from 1903 to 1914 pertained to public school matters. There
was a constant flow of requests into the president's office seeking
assistance in the employment of public school teachers, or letters
from teachers seeking additional training. Indiana University had
been a dependable source for teachers from 1828 on, but its teachers were trained with the philosophy that if they had mastered the
contents of severely proscribed liberal arts courses they could
learn the techniques of teaching by active practice.

In 1904 a teacher's agency was established in the administration building. Over 300 prospective teachers registered for jobs
the first year, and of the first 175 registered all had found employment. That year John A. Bergstrom was employed as professor of
pedagogy and head of the Department of Education. His report
in October, 1906, indicated education courses were now underway. Two manual training students and a psychology laboratory
assistant had been hired to help with the new courses. Bergstrom
had enrolled twenty-eight students and told the trustees he was
ready to take the next step in preparing professional teachers. He
reported that schools of education had already been established at
Illinois, Minnesota, and Missouri. He felt Indiana could well
profit from a co-ordinate college program to meet the same challenge as that of neighboring universities. Both Bryan and Bergstrom told the trustees it had become the fashion among state
universities to expand this major phase of their service function,
and they outlined areas where Indiana could best meet its public
obligations. In his second annual report, Bergstrom materially
strengthened his argument by citing the histories of Columbia,
Chicago, and Minnesota in the field of teacher training.

The demands for teacher training after 1900 reflected several
important social and educational changes in Indiana. Since the
1870's the university had attempted to discontinue its own involvement in preparatory training. By establishing its list of commissioned high schools it had ushered into Indiana a standardized educational organization which forced local communities to revise
their attitudes toward teachers and schools. Eggleston's Hoosier
Schoolmaster was as outmoded as the muzzle-loading rifle. Liberal
arts presidents and professors were forced to submerge their opposition to the normal school and to permit it to award the A. B.
degree. As head of the Indiana educational system the university
could not falter in the area of teacher training. Finally the organi-

zation of a college of education opened the doors of the university
even more fully to women. It was now an established fact that
women constituted an enormously important source of teachers,
and to cost-conscious legislators and local boards of trustees, the
cost of their hire was much lower.

The establishment of a school of education in Indiana would
also sanction the view that teaching shared a dignity with the
other professions. Bergstrom stated succinctly his philosophy of
teacher training in his report. "Differences between actual teaching and what would be best for the preparation of teachers," he
said, "is often so great that some believe that intending teachers
should be taught by a special faculty such as they have in part in
Columbia, Chicago, and certain other institutions." He urged
that professors in the regular literary and scientific departments
be used in the training of Indiana teachers. Utilization of present
university facilities, he said, seemed a better plan than that of dup-
licating many services in a separate teacher's college staff.

Bergstrom requested library facilities for the study of history
and science of education, funds to support observation of model
teaching, the study of special methods, and to make provisions for
practice teaching. Bryan agreed with Bergstrom. Indiana University had a greater demand for teachers than it could meet, and it
needed more professors to help train them than it could afford. In
June, 1908, at the same time the President was urging so strongly
the establishment of a graduate school, he told the trustees that
Indiana University confronted no greater difficulty than the establishment of a school of education. Under new Indiana education
laws pertaining to teacher certification the university was now
forced to make ample provisions for training of better instructors.
Where the training of high school teachers was concerned he said,
"We have no choice—we must provide for their professional training and that in a first-rate way." The university had in large
measure set the standards.

Before the school of education could be established, Edward
Cubberly and David Starr Jordan had enticed Bergstrom to Stanford. Bryan's task was now enlarged, he had to find a dean who
could organize the new school. He wrote a friend in Michigan that
Indiana University wished to hire a much better man to head its
educational program than it had money to pay him. Despite personnel and financial handicaps the School of Education had entered
its first year by November, 1908, with an enrollment of 195 stu-

dents and an elephantine need for staff, supplies, physical facilities, library, and teaching aides. Its immediate needs were necessary literature to facilitate teaching industrial training, domestic science, nature study, and agriculture. Besides this it was urgent that a practice school be established which would better suit the School of Education than the arrangement with the Bloomington city schools. All of these expanded new programs presupposed the construction of a special building to house them, and this had to be considered more than a remote possibility.

The idea of establishing a practice school in connection with the university conformed with William Lowe Bryan's concept of teacher training. Being a psychologist he had given considerable thought to the processes of learning. There is ample evidence that he placed great stock in the experienced teacher, and he felt the fledgling classroom instructor had much to learn just from the observation of a mature professor's classroom procedures.

Bryan wrote C. N. Kendall, Superintendent of the Indianapolis schools on May 10, 1905,

> I have thought for years that the best method of making a real advance in education in the United States would be through the establishment of a real model school; that is to say, a school whose aim should not be the exploitation of this or that educational theory and not the training of inexperienced teachers, but the development of the best school possible. If we could once show what could be accomplished under the most perfect conditions; above all things, under the conditions that all of the teachers should be first rate, the things accomplished would serve as models for the entire country. I have long wished to establish such a school in connection with this university but have been unable to do so for lack of money. I shall not be jealous of you if you succeed in establishing the ideal school at Indianapolis. Indianapolis deserves to have the honor for no city in the country has done more to advance our modern democratic school system.

Lack of money and personnel continued to deny Bryan the realization of his dream to place the university truly at the head of Indiana's public school system and in the forefront of national teacher training, but with such resources as the institution could attain it made progress. The appointment of Walter Albert Jessup as the first dean of the School of Education was a long step in this direction.

Walter A. Jessup of Richmond was chosen dean in the spring of 1912. He had a Master's degree from Hanover and a doctorate from Columbia Teachers College. By 1912 a development had taken place which neither Bryan nor Eigenmann had envisioned. There was a rapid increase in the number of high school superintendents who came to the university seeking Master's degrees in education. Too, the new rule of the State Board of Education required that all teachers who had not taught prior to 1908 would have to secure teaching certificates by taking special teacher training courses. So heavy was the demand resulting from this rule that there were now three professors and three assistants in the School of Education, and Jessup warned Bryan he would have to employ more staff members for the spring term of 1913. By the outbreak of World War I, Indiana University had embarked upon a broad program of teacher training, an area in which in time it was to gain a favorable reputation.

Closely related to the organization of the history of professional education training in the university was the organization of university classroom extension and correspondence work. Beginning in 1890, and at the suggestion of James Albert Woodburn, lectures were offered in centers like Indianapolis and Chicago. The concept of this type of extension work became popular in this region. It is difficult at times to distinguish between formal course and series of lectures offered in summer normals and special institutes. The latter were to come under frowning scrutiny. In 1908 or thereabouts a mimeographed communication signed by William Lowe Bryan, Winthrop E. Stone, and E. E. Robey was distributed over the state which said,

> The State Board of Education has learned with regret that a considerable number of those recently employed as instructors in the county institutes of the state seek mainly to give entertainment, and that often of a trivial character, rather than to give instruction of real value. There is doubtless a legitimate place for entertainment of a proper character in connection with the institute as in connection with any school. . . . Everyone knows, however, the instant demoralization of a school whose teacher devotes himself largely to the entertainment of his pupils, even when the kind of entertainment is in itself unobjectionable. . . .

The three presidents expressed belief there was a place for genuinely worthwhile instruction in institutes and classes outside the universities, but it should be of the extension-correspondence type and should be given under institutional supervision.

Both Bryan and his colleagues were invited to give lectures, singly or in series, to all sorts of groups about Indiana. Bryan had a popular reputation as a speaker and nearly every mail seems to have brought a lecture invitation, most of which he answered by saying he could not accept but he could send a professor. No doubt off-campus extension courses were offered in Indianapolis with some regularity by individual professors, but this fact is difficult to determine. The period from 1900 to 1908 appears to have been a gray one so far as records of this sort are concerned. In the latter year the Reverend James A. Brown, pastor of the First Baptist Church of Bloomington persuaded President Bryan to consent to the offering of a lecture course by extension to townspeople who were unable to enroll in the university. The minister revealed he had made a special study of university extension work as offered in Chicago, Wisconsin, and Columbia. He told Bryan, "The object of the university extension is to bring, in a measure, the advantages of the university to the man and woman not in the university."

The *Daily Student* reported, "President Bryan is distinctly in favor of the new extension course. He likens it to the university correspondence courses in its primary purposes, which he says, is to give the poor laboring man a chance to advance himself in society." He told the reporter, "we don't wish to do anything we can't do well, so we are going at this thing on a small scale." The president felt that to do extension work well required the services of able full-time men.

Once there was newspaper publicity about the extension, the Federation of Women's Clubs of Indiana asked for a correspondence course in literature, a request which was granted. In the following October there were more than 200 applicants for the newly organized English Literature extension course.

By 1911 extension work was fairly well established. The number of courses made available in this program was increased. Lantern slides illustrating several subjects were collected and distributed. Materials on debate themes were made available to high school debaters, and other materials were assembled for widespread use. Nevertheless, Bryan frankly admitted that a student could not derive the benefits from a correspondence or extension course which he could from a resident class. "But," he said, "a half a loaf is better than none. Since the University exists for the people, and more people can be reached through a correspondence course, it is the duty of the University to supply such a course."

Indiana University was not only definitely committed to extension work in 1912, it was actively seeking to expand it. W. A. Rawles, an imaginative promoter, sought to insure the firm establishment of extension. Rawles used as an argument the pioneering experience of Columbia University, and cited a survey by Professor Louis E. Reber in which sixty-five universities had been queried on the subject. Fifty-four of those offered extension work, and of these, thirty-two were state institutions, of which twenty-three supported extension programs. Rawles used strong arguments to secure favorable consideration of his division. He was persuasive in the contention, "The alternative is not whether Indiana shall do this work or whether it shall be left undone. It is a question whether Indiana shall do it or leave it to Purdue University. The field is going to be occupied." By this time the agricultural college had acquired fairly broad experience in the fields of home economics, drama, and agricultural extension.

Rawles actually proposed an extension program to the president and trustees of Indiana which would rival the agricultural extension service in the fields of civic and social services, including an offering of information pertaining to food preparation, personal hygiene and sanitation, civic improvements, the geological survey and its services, and a lawyer's conference. Indiana needed to act immediately if it were to avoid a recurrence of the horrendous medical school debacle.

The university did act. By the fall of 1912 it was ready to offer a fairly complete program of lectures in various Indiana cities, to give courses by mail, to supply general services of an informational nature, and to give material guidance to debate teams. Four departments, including English, history, German, and philosophy, had full correspondence programs in progress. Rawles was made director of extension and by October of that year he was ready to offer courses from twelve departments. Enrollment increased immediately and annual director's reports in the future vindicated Rawles' ambitious promotion of both services.

Rawles was not satisfied to cite mere enrollment statistics. He justified both extension and correspondence courses by saying students found the work harder than if they had taken it in the classroom. Language students especially missed opportunities to converse in the languages which they studied, but even so there was almost unanimous agreement that extension work was successful, and the program should be expanded to include some specialized professional fields. One-fifth of Wisconsin's extra-class enrollment was said to be in the field of business education. Requests were made for the same offerings in Indiana, and Rawles was anxious to favor the business community. Also, clergymen, teachers, and social workers needed instruction and guidance in social problems, and the Extension Division of the university was best equipped to offer this service to Indiana society.

By 1915 the extension division was fully established, and during World War I it proved a valuable asset in serving the various war activities of the state and federal government.

An inseparable part of the great struggle to create several schools within the university, was the necessity to develop a library of mature university caliber. Maxwell Hall in 1903 was crowded beyond toleration. Housing as it did the Law School, some professorial offices, a few classrooms, and the library, there was no room to promote growth. At the head of the list of new buildings needed in the year of Bryan's formal inauguration as president was a new library. There was an enrollment of 790 students and a maximum seating capacity in the Maxwell Hall reading rooms for only 125 students. The *Daily Student* described the seriousness of conditions by saying that "providing there [are seats for] the 500 out of 800 who wish to study in the library during chapel or before exams there will be 375 left out in the cold."

Agreeing with the student newspaper, William Albert Alexander, assistant librarian, acknowledged a shameful lack of space, and expressed anxiety for a new and adequate building. "But," he said, "it is out of the question to talk of a new library unless someone induces the legislature to make an appropriation, and this is a difficult task." A "prominent student" asked, "does that mean the state of Indiana cannot keep up with the increased attendance at her institutions? Do not our smallest cities build new schools, when the old ones become over-crowded? It seems that the legislators could be induced to take care of her students down here. It is their duty & by no means too much for them to accede to the reasonable demands of the state institution."

As shown earlier there were other and demanding pressures

on the university's library resources. More professors were actively engaging in scholarly research. As head of the Department of History and a graduate of The Johns Hopkins University history seminar, James A. Woodburn recommended in March, 1903, that the board of trustees approve purchase of a file of the Indianapolis *Journal*. Already other materials were being collected, and the annual book purchases overflowed shelves and stack rooms. The annual appropriations from 1898 to 1902 averaged about $7,000, and President Bryan asked that this amount be increased.

If shelf and seating space was limited, so was staff assistance. Louise Maxwell was acting librarian and she had three assistants including W. A. Alexander who would later become head librarian. Annual staff salaries ranged from $600 to $1100, and there was little hope that these would be improved at any time within the predictable future.

So severely was the library limited in its facilities and services that professors and students alike were handicapped to the extent that the depository was almost useless to them. In April, 1905, William A. Alexander reported that despite handicaps, however, Indiana students somehow or other made good use of the library. For the first time use statistics were being kept, and so far the assistant librarian estimated that daily between 200 and 300 volumes were being used in the reading room, and this did not include borrowing from departmental libraries. Some days the entire library staff was engaged in serving calls at the loan desk, and to serve the excess borrowers faculty reading rooms and the stacks were opened to them. Alexander was careful to say that the librarians had no notion of instituting open stack privileges. "When the new library is opened year after next," he said, "there will be ample room for all. This is little more than Job's comfort to Juniors and Seniors; the other half of the student body, however, may sit out on the steps of the various buildings and dream of better days to come."

A slight glimmer of hope appeared in the academic firmament of Indiana University in 1905, when the legislative budget committee at last recommended the appropriation of $100,000 to construct a library and to release the cramped Maxwell Hall quarters to other uses. The library rooms in this building were planned in 1890 to accommodate a top enrollment of 300 students. The Bloomington *Telephone* said the legislative decision was largely the result of the visit of committeemen to Bloomington who saw first-hand the urgent needs of the university.

When legislators had departed Indianapolis and the library appropriation was beyond revocation, the trustees in April began discussing the location of the new building. William E. Jenkins, who had become librarian in 1904, had general plans ready and a board committee was instructed to employ an architect. In mid-June 1905, the trustees announced the employment of Patton and Mills of Chicago as architects, and early in November construction bids were requested.

In the meantime Jenkins had examined many of the good libraries of the country, and had returned to Bloomington with information on what not to do as well as how to plan the perfect building. Patton and Mills were experienced library architects. They had built many of the Carnegie libraries, and the college library at Oberlin. Before they were awarded the contract J. W. Fesler extracted the promise that the partners would give close personal attention to the Indiana structure. Albert Frederick Kuersteiner, professor of Romance Languages, protested to President Bryan that more consideration should be involved in the location of the library than selection of a mere plot of ground. It should be considered as only one of several buildings which would be constructed across the west end of the campus. Bryan and the trustees were sympathetic to Kuersteiner's contention and explained a long-range concept to erect an administration building and one or two other harmonious structures along Indiana Avenue.

The successful bidder for construction of the new library would be asked to agree that the building would be ready for occupancy by September 1, 1907. Stack rooms were to have a capacity for 200,000 volumes, and room to seat 400 readers. Unhappily bids submitted exceeded the amount of funds in hand, and this delayed beginning of construction, and certainly nullified the opening date for the building. More disappointing, however, was the necessity to reduce the projected stack area by almost half in the drafting of new plans.

While architects and trustees struggled with problems of revising plans, reconciling bids with funds in hand, and settling upon a location, the library itself had to remain a functional institution under the most difficult circumstances. In December, 1905, there were five staff members, most of whom were untrained. There were 55,149 volumes on the shelves, 4,944 of which had been acquired the past year. Bryan reported to the trustees that the librarian had circulated 61,716 books, 6,567 in excess of the library's holdings. This had been done under the most difficult conditions. Card catalogue cases were falling apart, reading rooms were more crowded than ever, lighting was poor, and shelving defective. On top of these handicaps William A. Alexander, reference librarian, resigned.

Early in January 1906, bids still had not been completed for the new building, and Bryan was worried for fear the unexpended funds would revert to the state. Happily this issue was quickly resolved, and the *Daily Student* said a contract had been awarded W. F. Stillwell of Lafayette for $91,630, and subsidiary contracts for heating, plumbing, and wiring had been awarded to sub-contractors with the stipulations that work would be finished by April 1, 1907.

While the administration waited for the contractors to complete the new building, President Bryan and his colleagues were called upon to deal with several perennial library problems. First was theft of personal possessions left lying unguarded in the reading rooms. The *Daily Student* thought, "serious measures [should] be taken to stop the depredations, or rid the University of the offenders." A second problem was that of students hiding reference books for their exclusive private use. Possibly of greater concern, but no less insidious, was the constant argument which went on between professors and librarians as to who owned the books. Professors contended that books bought with departmental funds belonged to them to use as freely as they chose. Bryan sided against the professors saying this practice involved duplicate expenditures for equipment, confused mail orders, and if carried to an extreme would result in the dissolution of the central library collection and administration. The nub of this problem was stated in more picturesque terms by a student reporter who said, "By ginger, if th' profs wuz required t' pay like the rest uv us poor wretches, there'd be some Jaundee Rockebilts in the faculty. This is more than one way uv gittin' well soaked nowdays, fellers."

At last it became apparent in mid-March, 1906, that the new library would become a reality. The contractor had assembled a field full of material in the lower end of Jordan Meadow, and on April 14, the *Daily Student* was jubilant in its announcement,

"Workmen began breaking ground this morning for the new library building. Several carloads of stone have been hauled and placed on the site of the new building, and it is said the excavating work will be pushed rapidly."

Later William E. Jenkins outlined for the trustees the cost of three floors of shelving, tables, cabinets, and file cases. He estimated the stack space would care for 100,000 instead of 200,000 volumes mentioned originally, and the cost would be almost $61,000. At the same time he publicized new rules for library use which would permit students to check out two books for two weeks of home use, and permitted the privilege of a single renewal if the request was made in writing. If a student asked for more than two books he had to confront the librarian in person to explain such extraordinary rashness.

After publishing what seemed a liberalization of library rules over the past, the librarian excepted more than half the books in the library as being unavailable to home borrowers. It was said that out of the 63,000 volumes in the library, 2,500 were classified as reference works and could be used only in the building. Others were parts of standard sets, or were classified as rare, and there may even have been some that were too risqué to be loaned indiscriminately.

In planning the move from Maxwell Hall to the new building Jenkins informed President Bryan that it would require six days' work, and the staff and students could perform the task. This latter note hardly reached Owen Hall before it was discovered the contractor was making almost imperceptible progress, and the trustees appointed Professor Arthur Lee Foley and President Bryan an overseers' committee to determine the reason. The *Daily Student* indicated on October 17, 1907, that the committee had a wholesome effect on the builder, and that the library building would be ready by December, a delay of nine months from the original date for its completion. The actual removal of books from Maxwell Hall was accomplished in two hours by students and professors on February 8, 1908. This was too late for dedication of the building on Founders' Day that year.

David Starr Jordan came back to Bloomington to deliver the commencement address and he was on hand to see the new library dedicated on June 22, 1908. At ten o'clock that morning alumni, faculty, and students gathered around the new building to hear

John Vance Cheney of the Newberry Library extoll the cultural advantages of a well-stocked library. He was assisted in his dedicatory responsibilities by Winthrop E. Stone of Purdue. This within itself was an interesting fact because at that date Indiana and Purdue were still warring, publicly at least, over the medical school in Indianapolis.

In less than a month after the new library opened W. E. Jenkins proposed offering work leading to a Bachelor's degree in library science. He, like all the other promoters of new professional offerings, selected courses from the general liberal arts curriculum and suggested a limited supplementation with specialized instruction in the techniques of library operation and management. This was not a displeasing suggestion because by this time there began to appear in the inflow of university mail requests for library advice, and even for trained personnel for the state's public school libraries.

The administration was highly pleased with the bright response students made to improved library facilities. Bryan told the trustees there was a genuine thirst for knowledge on the Indiana campus. Students, he said, had made repeated requests that the library remain open until 11:00 P.M. on Saturdays. He had submitted one of his famous brief questionnaires to other universities about opening the library on Sunday, and a majority of the respondents said their collections were opened throughout the week. Bryan no doubt was taken aback by the answers and was left little choice but to grant Indiana's student requests. In his report to the trustees the president softened his decision by using highly apologetic phraseology: "Not of course for the purpose of encouraging students to work at that time, but to afford an opportunity for recreational reading." The reason for all this student zeal about keeping the library open on Saturday night and Sunday may well not have been of purely scholarly origin. On February 12, 1912, a killjoy student editor wrote, "lovemaking is an art to be encouraged but not in the library. Our advice is use the lobbies."

After 1908, use statistics were encouraging, and in 1911, the library collection contained 82,121 volumes; withdrawals numbered 113,280 volumes. Now that most of the kinks had been straightened out in the new building and most of the rules were established, the institution could settle down in its new home and give attention to the nagging problems of vandalism and noise. The librarian threatened to close the newspaper files to general use

[1 1 3]

because vandals were clipping them into a state of uselessness. Other predators marked and scribbled in some of the rarest books. This promised to be a serious situation in that the library in 1912 had purchased the complete publications of the Shakespearean Society, the Huth *Library*, the Elizabethan *Dramatists*, Nicholls *Anecdotes*, and the Ballad Society *Publications*.

Late in 1913, the library had a staff of six salaried members including W. E. Jenkins and Louise Maxwell. In his report to President Bryan, Jenkins said the library had an "evenness" of quality, but intimated this was not a virtue. It lacked distinction in any one area. "It is this [strength in a given area] rather than size that spreads the fame of a library and of the institution to which it belongs." Logan Esarey of the Department of History and editor of the *Indiana Magazine of History* had learned that the McClellan Collection could possibly be acquired by the university. Bryan argued that such an acquisition "would result not alone in a great stimulation to the growing interest in western history in Indiana but in promoting the library to a higher rank." He proposed as an inducement to the McClellan family that the librarian promise to keep the collection as a unit, give it any suitable title the family would approve, and keep up subscriptions to periodicals to the extent of $400. Esarey believed the collection to be worth $16,000. This was the beginning of a new phase of scholarly library management in the university, broadening the foundation for the graduate program and setting a course for a much more scholarly future for the institution.

The university in this decade was to gain recognition from two prestigious organizations. By the turn of the century Bloomington had been recognized as a center for scientific study in several fields. Bryan in psychology, Eigenmann in biology, Cumings in geology, Mottier in botany, and Lyons and Foley in mathematics and physics gave the institution a highly respected staff in these areas. This fact was established nationally when a chapter of the Sigma Xi scientific honor society was installed on the campus on November 30, 1904. Eleven faculty members were listed either as initiates or as members. R. E. Cumings kept meticulous minutes as to membership affairs, but he gave little indication of what if any ceremony took place on this occasion. William Lowe Bryan was made president of the chapter, a position which he resigned almost immediately, although the minutes do not indicate he was a member.

Six years after the installation of Sigma Xi, President Bryan was approached by Professor Edwin A. Grosvenor of Amherst College, national president of Phi Beta Kappa, with the suggestion that Indiana University should have a chapter of the society. A petition was prepared under the supervision of Warner Fite who had carried on an extensive correspondence trying to determine what the petitioners should do to prepare a proper statement about the school. Fite and James A. Woodburn took the petition to New York in September, 1910, to present it to the triennial meeting of the Phi Beta Kappa Society. This request was approved unanimously, Bryan reported to the trustees on October 18, 1910, an honor accorded no other university at the New York meeting.

The Bloomington *Telephone* said on January 20, 1911, "Tomorrow the 91st Foundation day of Indiana University, promises one of the most interesting events in the history of the institution." There was to be a full day of exercises followed by the installation of the Phi Beta Kappa chapter that evening. Dr. Grosvenor was the speaker. He said the university might have had a chapter much earlier if only it had applied for one. He told the audience that the university met the standards required for high level scholarship and liberal culture. It is strange that Grosvenor had to encourage the submission of a petition because there were already eleven members of Phi Beta Kappa on the faculty.

Following the informal installation of the chapter several faculty members were initiated, and a search was begun through university records for qualified persons who had graduated from the university within the past forty years. Their records while students and their achievements in their professions were used as criteria for membership.

Installation of a chapter of Phi Beta Kappa established in the university another obligation for the institution to maintain good scholarly standards. It also removed another bit of the independence which Bryan so often proclaimed because the society became in a way another accrediting agency.

These were indeed formative years and the university community was constantly being stirred out of its complacency by the tremendous pressures of the Bryan administration to create a university of respectable standards. Yet, from the minutes of the faculty and from student newspaper columns, it appears that some professors were reluctant to abandon the simplicity of the past. On the eve of the great excitement over the formal organization of the graduate school and the admission of the university to membership in the Association of American Universities, the professors spent considerable time debating the official university spelling and pronunciation of "program." With august solemnity they concluded to spell it "pro-gram" and to pronounce it accordingly. The faculty was reluctant to depart the worn ruts of the past, and the dominating hand of the president was indelibly clear. Bryan presided over the meetings when he was on the campus, which was most of the time, and he usually determined the subjects to be discussed. Indicative of how jealously he guarded his prerogatives was his appearance on one occasion in the midst of a faculty meeting over which Dean Horace A. Hoffman was presiding; Bryan immediately assumed the chair. Professors were thoroughly conscious of his presence in the meetings, and of his personal likes and dislikes. On one occasion a professor stepped over a row of chairs to get from one seat to another, and instantly lost presidential favor.

Bryan appears to have had no liaison body between himself and the faculty. Standing committees dealt with specific problems, but there was no senate, council, or executive-faculty committee. On several occasions the president took pains, however, to inform the faculty about the problems of finances, the medical school, the hopes and aspirations of the University, and, sometimes, about student affairs. In his private correspondence he once expressed pride in the faculty reception of his reports.

It is abundantly clear in the record that Bryan leaned heavily on U. H. Smith, John Wesley Cravens, and several townsmen for advice and counsel in political and fiscal areas, but there is almost no hint that he enjoyed such counseling in academic matters. Perhaps Cravens, Eigenmann, Hoffman, and Woodburn were influential with the president, but the records seem to indicate that all of them deferred to him. As time advanced and the university program grew more complex, outside influences and increasing numbers of administrative pressures played a greater role in shaping academic policies, but Bryan never ceased to be the central and decision-making figure.

While professors often dawdled with inconsequential matters in monthly meetings, the students demonstrated a comparably casual interest in university affairs. They stood on the sideline and watched the faculty, seldom comprehending fully what was happening. There is evidence that an occasional underground paper was published which made adolescent appraisals of professors, some of which were witty and others barbarous. On October 30, 1906, the *Daily Student* reported the results of a survey in which it had attempted to determine what to call members of the staff. Everybody was indiscriminately called "professor," whether he merited the title or not. Harold Whetstone Johnstone told the youthful interviewer that in the classroom he preferred "professor" but elsewhere he would settle for "mister." "Daddy" Woodburn had no preference, "mister" was good enough for him. The dapper Lewis "Chappy" Chase tucked another carnation in his lapel and left the matter to the students, a view shared by Henry Thew Stephenson and Horace Addison Hoffman. Enoch George Hogate wanted to be called "Judge," and the medical professors pre-empted the title "doctor." Thus it went, and the students were as thoroughly confused after the survey as before. They devised their own nicknames of "Eigie" for the ubiquitous dean of the graduate school, "Grandma" for the great Hershey, "Dudey" for Alfred Mansfield Brooks, head of the Art Department, "Daddy" for Woodburn, and other names both affectionate and derisive for the rest of their instructors.

If professors dawdled away precious time debating the obvious in faculty meetings, most of them demonstrated an unusual amount of well directed energy elsewhere. In 1906, Hershey had two books underway, and the changing world of diplomacy stimulated his imagination. Woodburn whittled away at a biography of that strange but powerful Reconstruction political figure Thaddeus Stevens, Henry Thew Stephenson promised a volume on the life and manners of the Elizabethans, Nollen was ready to publish a study of Schiller's *Maria Stuart*, and Joshua William Beede had a major paper underway on the "Red Bed" Rocks. Carl H. Eigenmann, Samuel Bannister Harding, and Will David Howe were engaged in serious research. Primarily, however, the faculty was most concerned with the day-to-day responsibilities of teaching, giving only a minimum amount of attention to research and writing.

While professors debated various internal issues in the crucial years 1907 to 1910, they discussed a highly controversial subject— that of division of the school year. Like the discussion of the grading system, no one in the history of American public higher education has ever been able to settle on a happy division of the academic year. Traditionally Indiana University had used the three term plan, but not without periodic modifications, and a healthy amount of discussion. At its December meeting in 1911, the faculty had before it a proposal that the university discontinue the term program and adopt the two semester division. Under the term arrangement, which had last been revised in 1903, the fall session was begun on the Tuesday nearest September 21, and ended thirteen class weeks later. The winter term was several days shorter to allow for holidays, and the spring term ended on a Friday in June, which rounded out thirty-six weeks in all. Dropping this cherished system in 1911 strained many sentimental cords in the faculty, but contentions that the new arrangement simplified making of the university calendar, especially in light of staggering holiday vacations, were convincing. Too, the semester system was becoming nationally popular.

With all of his other chores Bryan busied himself in the area of the faculty fringe benefits, with perhaps as much hope to solve some of his personnel problems as a desire to benefit the staff. Again outside pressures were forcing a consideration of instituting a retirement and pension program. From the days of Andrew Wylie down to the opening of the second decade of this century the question of retirement with a pension was one which had at times seriously hindered the maintenance of an effective faculty. This was especially true when competition for good professors had been intensified nationally. Early in 1907, President Bryan attended the fourth annual conference of the Midwest universities. While in Madison he discussed with other presidents the prospects of state universities receiving aid from the Carnegie Foundation. Wisconsin had already adopted the Cornell plan of giving aged professors emeritus status with reduced pay and duties. It seemed to Bryan that there was a remote chance that Indiana might secure comparable support—at least it should take the necessary steps to seek assistance.

Bryan was right in his assumption that state schools might be aided. In the spring of 1908 the Carnegie Foundation announced it would extend aid to public institutions and that the first group of schools would be admitted to the foundation's roll as beneficiaries. At that moment Indiana University had five professors who were believed to be either eligible or soon to become eligible because of age or length of service to the university. These were Amzi Atwater, Harold Whetstone Johnstone, James A. Woodburn, Horace

A. Hoffman, and William Lowe Bryan. Before these men could receive such a pension, however, the Indiana Legislature had to approve the foundation's plan. The Carnegie Foundation required that the recipient professor have twenty-five years of service as instructor in a good college, before he could be retired on half pay, or a maximum of $2000 per year, and that a state university professor have a service record of fifteen years and be sixty-five years of age.

The *Daily Student* reported on April 9, 1909, that John Gabbert Bowman, seretary of the Carnegie Foundation for Teaching, had visited the campus the day before inspecting the university for possible inclusion in the retirement program. Precisely a year later the paper said that two secretaries were preparing a report for the Carnegie Foundation giving many details about the university and its student body. As always the reporter was optimistic. "There is a rumor," he said, "that Indiana University will be approved by the Carnegie trustees to receive the big fund for pensioning retiring professors. . . ." His prediction was correct. In June it was announced that Indiana had been placed on the list of Carnegie Foundation schools.

The first published report after Indiana and Purdue universities had been admitted to membership of the Carnegie Foundation contained an interesting note by Henry Smith Pritchett, president of the foundation. "Indiana University and Purdue University," he wrote, "taken together constitute today the culmination of the education system in Indiana and form in effect a single strong state university. Each now articulates with the high schools of the state, and each offers a group of related courses which are not duplicated in the other. Liberal arts, education, law and medicine are taught at Indiana University; applied science, engineering, agriculture and pharmacy are taught at Purdue." Pritchett gave an interesting sidelight on why the two schools had not been admitted to the Foundation in 1909 with the first group of universities. First, it was not then evident that the Indiana schools were "coordinating" parts of the state system of education. Second was the backward state of medical education and the unseemly fight of 1905 to 1909 that had taken place between the two schools. Now that the schools were again cooperating with their programs they were declared eligible for admission in June, 1910.

In 1910 William Lowe Bryan, along with Charles Van Hise of

Wisconsin, was elected a trustee of the Carnegie Foundation, a position which gave him a first-hand insight into the various activities and plans of that body. Primarily Bryan hoped he could persuade Andrew Carnegie to make a half million dollar grant to the medical school. He was adamant, however, in his insistence that the university enter into no arrangement which would threaten its independence of operation. In his opinion neither retirement aid nor a special grant would be worth a sacrifice of freedom in this area.

This chapter covers only a part of the stirring changes which took place in Indiana University in the years 1903 to 1914. No other decade had seen the school advance so rapidly toward university status. The basic structure was completed by 1914 and the rest of the history of the university was to center around the schools and colleges established in this period. To say that this was the work of one man would be ridiculous, but one man did stand at the vortex of the swirl of change and maintained the momentum. It was William Lowe Bryan's vision, bulldog determination, and loyalty to standards that projected the new university into the future. It would not be at all rash to compare him with Charles Van Hise, William Rainey Harper, Edwin A. Alderman, and Jacob Gould Schurman.

Bryan's history of Indiana University is badly clouded by legend and folklore. He suffered on both sides, from those who idolized him and placed him on a pedestal, and from those who saw him only as an unbending puritan who could instantly be repelled by a profane word, a glass of beer, or an uncouth personal act. On one occasion he wrote Seumas MacManus, the Irish author-poet, that he had thoroughly enjoyed his book, and that the Irish heart of his ancestors had welled up in him. He invited MacManus to come to lecture at Indiana University. There is no evidence that the Irishman accepted. It is just as well the two never met because they were sustained by Irish hearts of different rhythms. Nevertheless Bryan was an affable man, impressive in personal demeanor, and inspiring in action. He was a shrewd patrician functioning in a Babylon of Hoosier politics. On campus and safely enthroned behind his acre-square desk he was an educational statesman.

As an administrator Bryan was at times unreasonably brusque, always a benevolent autocrat, genuinely democratic at heart and in theory, a dreamer in spirit, and an unswerving moralist. Many of his character traits are left undescribed in formal university records.

His marriage to Charlotte Lowe of Pendleton was perhaps as much idyllic as conjugal, and this in itself became a part of Indiana University folklore. Whatever the truth may have been about this union it was obviously a love affair of Victorian gentility and attentiveness. Mrs. Bryan was an educated woman who, so long as health permitted her to do so, pursued her interest in the fields of poetry and classical literature.

Glimpses one gets of Charlotte Lowe Bryan are those of a beautiful, fragile woman who might well have stepped bodily out of an Elsie Dinsmore book or a Dresden china shop without so much as a bobble or an apology. She had rigidly conservative social views which no doubt re-enforced many of Bryan's personal convictions, a thing which apparently shaped his reactions to rising issues on the campus and abroad. Unlike Mrs. Joseph Swain, Mrs. Bryan crusaded for almost no causes, nor did she become a mother figure on the campus. Indications are that she cultivated few friendships with faculty wives.

The Bryans entertained fairly frequently with little publicity of the occasions. Mention is sometimes made of presidential receptions during the commencement week. Mrs. Bryan did travel on many occasions with her husband, and she was on the train with him to Indianapolis when the Purdue train wreck occurred. Once, as a matter of record, she took an active hand in the drive to secure a pipe organ for the Student Building. She wrote Andrew Carnegie on September 1, 1908, on the president's office stationery, asking whether he would entertain a request for such a gift. This letter bears a notation in Bryan's hand, "Written by Mrs. W. L. Bryan— There was no answer." But in this case one must conclude that clearly the hands were those of Esau, but the voice was unmistakably that of Jacob.

The only certain thing that can be said is that Charlotte Lowe Bryan's husband shared time about equally between living room and office. In the early days the president rode horseback from his residence on North College Street, and hitched behind Owen Hall, and at noon he mounted and rode away from the campus for the day. He spent afternoons and evenings reading to his wife, or keeping her company. As a result he must have been the best read university president of his day. What he read is unknown, but he had a good classics library which is still largely intact in Chancellor

Herman B Wells' office. A trustee at a later date described a trip he made with Bryan when they shared the same hotel room. He was much impressed when the president settled down for an evening of relaxation to read a book in original Greek text.

Long before he reached the office of President, Bryan had gained a reputation as an excellent public speaker. He was not a noisy barnstormer like the "Great Commoner" of the same name, nor did he possess the eloquence of Daniel Voorhees or the great Albert J. Beveridge. Rather he was a calm, logical reasoner before an audience who had the capacity to capture and hold attention. He once quoted George Ade to a friend by saying the downfall of a man began when it was discovered he was a good after-dinner speaker. Bryan used great care in the preparation of his speeches, often writing several drafts before he achieved just the right mood and expression. There is ample documentary proof of this in his letter files. Many documents in his hand were edited almost beyond original form and purpose. More often than not his audiences assumed he spoke extemporaneously, and he intended that they think so. President Bryan once told a friend that he had a recurring dream that he was the last man on a long program and when he got up to speak his auditors were walking out on him. He shouted to them to wait and hear him, he would be brief. Because of this haunting dream he learned to be brief and pointed in his speeches. He could have spent full time away from Bloomington on the lecture circuit, and if there were time to spare it would have been absorbed in refusing invitations.

Bryan's Indiana University colleagues treated him with great deference. An example was his election to the presidency of Sigma Xi on the occasion of the installation of the chapter in the university. Professors respected him for his integrity and his dedication to the institution, even if he was aloof toward them. When some of them at least conferred with him they knew they had not much more than five minutes in which to state their business. The wise ones learned to ask his secretary Nellie Green what mood he was in before they entered his office. Later Miss Ruth McNutt confirmed this fact to the author. They took with them two propositions, one for testing, and one for serious consideration. If the trial one was rejected they never stated the other. There was one among them, however, who spoke his mind. Bryan prepared a long confidential memorandum on January 10, 1913, for Dr. Charles P. Emerson in which he appraised individually the members of the medical staff. He commented on the crusty old Dean of the Campus Medical School. "Myers," he said, "rubs the fur the wrong way. Besides this, he has a German way of telling the truth. Moreover, he can not be worked, nor frightened. For all these reasons he is unpopular. I can understand it. No other man has withstood me to my face. But I very greatly prize him for just this." There is ample evidence that Bryan kept university affairs rather closely to himself, and could be gruff if a professor, less bold than Dean Myers, tried to pry into them. He was truly *in loco parentis* to everyone.

In no part of his administration was Bryan more successful than in preventing himself from becoming directly involved in Indiana political infighting. He had trusted friends who did this job for him, and he relied on them for advice and political muscle. His confidential correspondence reveals this fact. At no time is there even a hint that Bryan was willing to make an opportunistic political horse trade, or in any way jeopardize the university's standards. Repeatedly there appear in his letters and reports two phrases which almost became trite, "rock bottomed" and "quite well."

That Bryan enjoyed the affections of most of his colleagues and masses of students is well established. In an undated letter, perhaps in the fall of 1908, Ernest H. Lindley wrote, "Not long ago Dr. Ferris, now Governor of Michigan, said to me. 'you have a remarkable state of affairs at Indiana University. I have talked with several of your faculty and I discover that you have a President who is *loved by his Faculty*.' These words were essentially true then: they are true now! For sometime I have feared that you were *not* in position to *understand* nor to interpret to yourself nor to these men, the persistent loyalty of these men who have often crude ways but honesty of expressing their convictions that you are the greatest and best one among us." Lindley tried to persuade Bryan to go to Europe on an extended leave. He owed himself the relaxation. Lindley assured Bryan that he had recently had an opportunity to sense the current of thought on the campus and he could assure him with confidence that he enjoyed faculty loyalty.

There was more implied than said in Lindley's letter. Bryan was emotionally upset in the latter part of his first decade as president and he had every reason to be. He had fought politicians, self-serving doctors, chiseling stone companies, drouths, disease, and institutional poverty. In May, 1913, he was exhausted. In this state of body and mind he submitted his resignation to J. W. Fesler, a member of the board of trustees. In Fesler he found a sympathetic friend, but one who refused to contemplate Indiana University without Bryan. On May 15, he asked the president to grant permission to have his letter returned by J. W. Rose of Anderson. "I know," he wrote, "the strain for practically every month of your presidency has been enough to discourage, and break, and kill any but the rarest of men. And I know your devotion to the University has been deeper grounded than any desire for successful administration." Fesler explained the university had no right to demand the fulfillment of another obligation of Bryan. Those persons who loved the school had come also to love its president. "You are tired," said Fesler, "you have all but exhausted your strength; you have given it for the University." Like Lindley, Fesler suggested that Bryan take a year's leave to travel in Europe where he could get some rest and clear his mind of accumulated worries.

Bryan did allow Rose to return the letter but he refused the trip to Europe. Fesler was right, he was exhausted. He was the first Indiana president to learn that administering a twentieth century American state university was as much a test of human physical and emotional strength as of intellectual stamina. This was an age in which a university could not hesitate if it expected, in one of Bryan's favorite phrases, to do "quite well."

[VI]

The Other Half of
the University

UNIVERSITY ELDERS joined the chase in the medical school fight with such complete devotion that they and the state officials all but lost sight of the fact that in Bloomington there were students and particular problems of social relationships which required the fullest attention of a responsible university administration. Correspondence and other contemporary sources reflect the importance of this half of the university's relationships. The basic course offerings, revision of the university's academic base, and the contest with Purdue over medical training were life and death matters of structure and operation, but student welfare and decorum were even more important. For almost a century the university had made little actual headway in lifting its student body out of an unhappy involvement with the town of Bloomington and its closeknit small town society. That students sometimes proved unruly and difficult of management was as much a reflection of failures of the university to provide for them as it was a state of lingering adolescent willfulness.

There was no place on the campus where students could gather for relaxation and recreation, and no place outside classrooms and the chapel in which to conduct their various organizational affairs. Thrown upon the meager resources of the town they had to create their own social life without much positive guidance from anyone including the university and local churches.

Frances Morgan Swain had recognized this fact during her husband's presidency and started a move to centralize women's activities within the confines of the campus. When Joseph Swain accepted the presidency of Swarthmore, his wife had to leave behind the legacy of the idea for a central student building.

On March 29, 1901, Mrs. Swain appeared before the board of trustees to suggest that a women's building be constructed on the campus. She was certain that social life for university women existed only under dismal conditions or in facilities that lay beyond the control of the university administration making parents reluctant to send their daughters to Bloomington. Between March and July, 1901, her idea was expanded to include a building for everybody in the university. Before any plans could be made, however, it was necessary to conduct an extensive fund raising campaign, the first of its nature in which the institution was to become involved. Before this date students and alumni had raised only minimal funds to finance tree plantings, installation of commemorative plaques, and to erect other small memorials. Now they were asked to subscribe generously to a large and utilitarian project.

William T. Hicks and Ulysses H. Smith were appointed "secretaries" to conduct the student building fund drive. Canvassers were assigned to each of the ninety-four Indiana counties to solicit financial support. In the meantime the secretary of the board of trustees corresponded with university presidents about the country where there were student centers. He sought not only information about such projects, but also the names of architects who could plan such a building. This latter chore proved frustrating. Several architects who were consulted refused to consider such a project without competitive bids. They reasoned that such a procedure would commit the university to carrying out the construction of the building once it had gone so far as publicly to seek bids, and before sufficient funds to finance the building had been accumulated. In the meantime C. E. Richards of Columbus, Ohio, visited the campus to investigate the situation regarding the proposed building.

Following Richards' visit President Bryan either acceded to local pressures or acted on the architect's advice and suggested that a joint student building was cheaper, even though he personally favored separate buildings for men and women. The new building would answer a longstanding student complaint by providing a gymnasium, parlors, offices for student functions, and rooms for social and religious meetings.

Joseph Hooker Shea of Jackson County proposed to the board of trustees on November 7, 1902, that two buildings be constructed. He suggested that the women's building be located on the site of Mitchell Hall, and the men's structure on the site of the old gymnasium. By January, 1903, however, it was clear that even one building seemed little more than a pipe dream. Canvassers had returned only $6,398.01 in cash and $29,199.92 in pledges. This was indeed a disappointing amount of money. By this time there was more than the construction of a student building involved. The *Daily Student* on December 7, 1902, reported the more cheerful note that John D. Rockefeller had pledged $30,000 to the building fund provided the university could produce a like sum. In the following March President Bryan informed the trustees that he had received a letter from John D. Rockefeller, Jr., saying his father would match every dollar raised prior to July 1, 1904, to the extent of $50,000. The June report in 1904, revealed that the fund drive was still $13,300 short of having the necessary $50,000 to claim the full amount of the Rockefeller gift, and to accept less might be both costly and humiliating.

With $80,000 in sight by October, 1903, the trustees announced that a decision had been reached, and on June 23, it was revealed that Vonnegut and Bohn of Indianapolis, instead of Gibson and Company, as announced earlier, had made plans for a single building. Any funds collected over the estimated $80,000 would be used to buy equipment and furniture. Location of the building was again discussed, and this time James W. Fesler moved that the new location be fifty feet northwest of Maxwell Hall, and on a spot where no trees would have to be removed. The south line of the structure was to be lined up with the middle window in the Maxwell Hall West bay. There would be two wings, one for men and the other for women. Thus everyone's concept of the student building had to be sharply revised because of a lack of money.

A contract had been awarded William F. Stillwell of Lafayette. This builder was thoroughly familiar with the campus because he had constructed Kirkwood Hall and had rebuilt Wylie Hall following the fire. Stillwell agreed to erect a three-story fireproof building to contain a chimes tower, an auditorium seating 500 persons, two swimming pools, a women's gymnasium, and social parlors, the structure to be ready for occupation by May 20, 1905.

Central feature of the building was to be an imposing tower to house a set of electrical chimes. It was to be no less than ten feet square and would extend fourteen feet above the peak of the roof of the building. The four classes then enrolled in the university began a campaign to raise $3000 with which to purchase ten or eleven bells. By securing a pledge of a substantial amount of stone, and by making a grant from public funds, the trustees were able in April, 1904, to award a contract in the amount of $71,570 to W. F. Stillwell of Lafayette.

By June 16, 1904, enough progress had been made on the new building to permit the laying of the cornerstone. President Bryan told the trustees that on the twenty-first, Frances Morgan Swain would be present to take a chief part in the ceremonies. The university had won a major victory, and the Bloomington *Telephone* said, on July 5, that a certified check had been prepared and was being sent to John D. Rockefeller as an assurance of good faith. He was also informed as additional testimony of good faith that the building itself was well underway. It was discovered after the certification of the check, however, that pledges of the Monarch, Diamond, Chicago, and Bloomington, Monroe County Oolitic, National and the United States Quarries were believed to be faithless. In a letter to the various companies, dated October 10, 1904, President Bryan detailed the university's complaints. First, the stone pledged was either not delivered, or that which was delivered was of such inferior quality that it was useless. He described for the companies the fund raising campaign, and said that the university had pledged its integrity and word to John D. Rockefeller, and now the companies had failed the university. "We are prouder," he wrote, "of nothing than of the gifts of our local contributors. The students gave four thousand. The women's clubs gave one thousand. Many citizens gave generous amounts to the common cause and among these were some of those who also subscribed stone." When it came to the stone pledges, however, William Lowe Bryan had considerable reservations. Listing five complaints ranging from failure to meet pledges to downright cheating on materials he was specific in his disappointments. The university stood to lose from 20 to 100 percent on these gifts, plus the expenses for labor it had incurred in loading and transporting the materials. In a stern, moral tone Bryan shamed the company officials for their shoddy behavior. "But if these men [who had always supported the university] come to believe that while their subscriptions have been paid in cash and in full some of ours have shrunk to nothing—what are they going to say to us when we next call upon them for any kind of support? I do not wish to exaggerate the dangers of the present situation, but in my opinion, if the situation is not cured, Indiana University will suffer one of the most serious calamities which it has met in a quarter of a century. Presidents, professors, and trustees may come and go, but if the University loses its friends, where will it turn for help?"

Bryan sought, although never fully received, an answer from the companies which he could present with moral assurance to the next meeting of the board of trustees. There followed an extensive correspondence between A. Soupart, construction superintendent, and President Bryan, the kernel of which was the worthlessness of the stone that had been shipped to the building site. Because of the unhappy failure to secure suitable building stone the masons halted their work on August 27, 1904, and construction of the Student Building came to a standstill. In November the president told the trustees that Vonnegut and Bohn had rejected lot after lot of stone as unusable. There was no further use in trying to get the companies to rectify their failures to honor their pledges. No more donated stone was to be accepted, and the contractor was authorized to purchase stone of his own choosing.

At this date it is next to impossible to determine the facts of the stone contributions. For the only time in his presidential career William Lowe Bryan truly angered men who talked back to him. A sheaf of angry letters from the stone companies deny that there was anything irregular about their gifts. Several of them said stone sent to the university was exactly the same quality as they supplied their best customers. There was even hint of a feud between the builder and the suppliers.

In other ways the progress of construction of the Student Building was beset by troubles. John L. Nichols resigned as general superintendent, and in the emergency Professor Arthur L. Foley, head of the Physics Department, assumed the duties of superintendent. On June 16, 1905, the trustees authorized the builder to make what amounted to new plans for the tower. The footing had to be redesigned and materially strengthened. Together the bells and clockworks weighed four and a half tons. The newly designed tower would extend upward over a hundred feet from foundation level, and well above the peak roof level. Contracts were awarded the Seth Thomas Clock Company for a clock to cost $1,490, and the McShaw Bell Company of Baltimore was awarded the $3,650 contract for a set of electrically operated bells.

Other delays in completing the building brought both disappointment and human tragedy. First, some heavy timbers needed for the auditorium superstructure did not arrive in Bloomington until October 3, 1905. Apparently they had been drifting from one railway assembly yard to another with no one able to locate them. These timbers seemed to be jinxed. When they were being put in place a scaffolding near the top of the building gave way and six men were dumped in amongst falling timbers and were left maimed and bleeding, requiring the services of a dozen physicians to save their lives. There were other accidents and delays.

In spite of the gloom, the *Daily Student* of November 21, 1905, was overjoyed with the prospects that the Student Building would be ready for dedication early in the next year. The paper reported that a modern lunch counter would be located in the basement, and an auditorium 52 by 90 feet exclusive of the stage seating 800 people was to be included in the building. Just before students left for Christmas holidays the chimes were expected to arrive in Bloomington and prospects were they would be in place in time for John Foley, "chimes musician," to ring in the new year.

While the *Student* was too optimistic, President Bryan did not allow Christmas cheer to blur his perspective. He firmly believed that there was no chance of dedicating the new building on Founder's Day in January because of a necessary revision of plans. It would be April at least before the structure would be finished. Like the heavy timbers, the chimes got lost in transit and not until two days after Founder's Day on January 20, did the Monon drag them into town. John Foley had to welcome the new year with nothing louder than a rapping on his xylophone. Late or not, the *Student*'s ardor remained undampened. Indiana's chimes, when and if they were ever placed in the tower, said the paper, would rival those of Cornell.

Two days after the bells were finally hoisted into place there were grim doubts that the bells would rival even the cow bells of Monroe County. Professor John Foley had tested the chimes and learned that, although the lower notes were clear, not so the higher ones. People more than four blocks away could not hear them. It was believed the bells had been improperly hung. The clock was also undergoing infuriating regulatory tests. The wood grill was removed from the apertures of the tower to free the sound. By April 21, 1906, the bells and clock were adjusted and campus spirits rose. It was announced that the tower bell system would announce class changes. At the same time a professorial committee tested the bells individually and assured President Bryan that their tones were perfect.

In his report to the trustees in 1908, President Bryan was relieved that the Student Building was at last finished. Only one more incident was to mar its early history. In September, 1912, the Bloomington *Telephone* reported that forty-seven local barbers had become involved in a hot verbal war with the Student Union shop. So hot did this controversy become that the trustees had to take cognizance of it in their next Indianapolis meeting. The Bloomington barbers proclaimed a sort of bill of rights by saying that public competition to their trade had no right to exist in a state institution. They presented a petition signed by 600 "enraged Bloomington citizens" opposing the university shop. The town barbers threatened further to secure a court injunction against the university barbers, and they even laid their case before United States Senator Benjamin Franklin Shively, a man who had long and seasoned experience with disputes involving the university. This was a contingency which Frances Morgan Swain, William James, and William Lowe Bryan had not foreseen. Certainly Joseph Swain, however, had meant to cover such a case in his admonition that university adminisration deal with day-to-day emergencies on the terms under which they arose.

Construction of the Student Building obviously was only one aspect of student-university relationships. This was an age of change in which institutions became more conscious of students as maturing human beings who fitted into an intermediate society between childhood and maturity in their university experiences. Those of Indiana University reflected almost all the strands of Indiana life itself. However much William Lowe Bryan and his professor-colleagues may have wished to maintain the status quo and to fit students into preconceived plans for curriculum expansion, they had to reckon with the realities of the times, and in terms of the social conditions of the Indiana home and society.

Class status in the first quarter of the twentieth century in Indiana University assumed what now seems to have had a childish meaning. A great deal of student time and energy was expended on class symbols and modes of dress. In 1905, the juniors decided both boys and girls would wear old gold golf jerseys. Seniors chose sombreros which they ordered from a Chicago house at $2.75 each. To show off their new hats the graduating class agreed to sit together at the Wabash football game. "There seemed to be a prevalent feeling among students that students at I. U. should wear distinctive dress like seniors at Wisconsin and Purdue universities," said the *Student*; "the Purpose would be to promote class unity and to put seniors on a higher plane to promote leadership."

Over the years the selection of class dress added excitement to school opening in the fall. Sophomores were positive that freshmen should wear close fitting green caps with three inch bills, adorned on top with an inch diameter red patch. Some of the classes selected curious garments such as the senior corduroy britches of 1912, which could both be heard and seen. Sophomores in 1911 selected steel grey felt hats with purple bands. A traditions committee was formed in 1911 to enforce freshmen to wear green caps and to encourage all classes to observe their customs.

Although the history of Indiana University was of a highly masculine nature during the first seventy-five years of its existence, radical changes emerged after the turn of this century. Bryan wrote in 1903 that, "The problems arising out of the question of co-education are growing increasingly difficult with the increase in the university's population and with the general tendency toward more strenuous social life. There is reaction against co-education. I believe the University must assume a closer guardianship over the women students." There was a further plea for girls' dormitories to get women out of Bloomington rooming houses. Out of 1,469 students in 1903, 560 were women, or slightly more than a third of the total enrollment, but the numbers were yearly creeping toward a balance.

The girls in the student body at Indiana seemed to have presented a mixed social and academic image. First, they were forced to find living quarters on their own and in town. In their searches they were often victimized by landladies' preferences for male roomers. Co-eds had to protect their maidenly image as best they could in conformity with a strict moral standard of the pre-world war years, yet they often lived in what both parents and deans of women viewed as unsatisfactory proximity to male students.

[1 3 2]

Women in the university had limited voice in expressing opinions about either their welfare or campus matters. Instead they had to depend upon the Women's League and Dean of Women to speak for them in many matters.

There is ample evidence that women students had a refining influence on Indiana University in days when student behavior tended to be rowdy and uninhibited. They may have even soothed the savage hearts of "scrappers" and sophomoric barbers who felt as much dedication to shearing freshmen as to attending classes. Girls from the outset offered scholastic competition, they insisted on participating in various contests, they possibly influenced curriculum revision, even if the university "fathers" did not support the inclusion of a course on bread-making. In the field of athletics there was a girl's basketball team which sometimes played in the privacy of feminine gymnastic folds.

As the number of co-eds increased, Greek letter sororities became more significant social enclaves. The sisters were devotees of the dance, so much so they would have danced seven nights a week if it had not been for dean's rules which suggested they give token attention to studies and sleep. In curbing the girls the dean of women reached out and took the men also under her guidance. From 1905 to the entry of the United States into World War I, dancing became a campus mania. Many students learned all the popular steps and music. At least it could be said for this campus craze that it absorbed energy which might otherwise have been expended in carousing.

With increasing numbers of social functions on the campus there appeared a more refined courtesy and grace. In February, 1907, the *Daily Student* editor observed that men should be polite and open doors for girls, especially the heavy ones at Kirkwood Hall. Fraternities were lectured from time to time on the protocol of entertaining girls in their rooms. All of this took place with somewhat less fanfare as the university registered a near parity in numbers of men and women. There was an area, however, in which it was difficult for men to be chivalrous, and that was in the competition to find rooms within short walking distances of the campus.

Bloomington may have been a "sleepy county seat town," but it was not entirely safe for co-eds to walk unaccompanied on its streets. Four girls returning to their rooms at the end of the

Thanksgiving holidays in 1906 were assaulted by a man, and Pearl Stover was dragged screaming down an alley and robbed. These same girls had been attacked a month earlier on Kirkwood. Later Edith Flood of Terre Haute and Bertha Hanges of Scottsburg were returning to the campus when they were assailed at Fifth and Lincoln Streets by a robber who snatched Edith Flood's pocketbook. Two weeks later there occurred what the Bloomington *Telephone* called, "The most sensational hold-up ever known to Bloomington." Two co-eds were held up and searched by a lone male robber. When the bandit demanded the girls' money and was told they were penniless he said he knew where women hid things. The girls were so embarrassed by the thoroughness of the search that they refused to report the incident to the police. The townspeople were horrified, said the paper, but the robber still remained at large.

Not all invasion of co-ed privacy was maliciously planned and inspired. In August, 1909, four demure scholars sought to escape the summer heat by taking a dip in the nude in Griffey Creek. They had hardly taken to the waters before a buck-toothed lad appeared on the creek bank and refused to go away until he was bribed by payment of eighty-five cents to not tell on the girls. He went away all right, but he took both their clothes and money.

On campus, girls asserted their femininity by holding an annual banquet called by the ungodly name Panthygatric. This was likely no more than a mild annual social event, but it piqued masculine curiosity. One dean of women said later, Panthygatric was an annual feast of cold beans, ham, and pumpkin pie. In 1908, several boys crashed their way into the banquet hall and claimed at least to have viewed some informal girlish antics if nothing friskier. In some way the Indianapolis *Star* got material for a full story of the crashing, the activities of the girls, and pictures of co-eds clothed in pajamas and parts of pajamas. Dean Louise A. Goodbody undertook unsuccessfully to prevent the publication of the story. Her word had always been law, but in this case she pursued a losing cause and admitted it in a letter. "I have nothing to say about this article," she wrote the *Star*. "After trying all week to keep it from appearing I am not going to worry now that it has been published in spite of me. However, I will say, and that most emphatically that never again shall a photographer be admitted to Panthygatric." Dean Goodbody had presidential support to back up her ultimatum.

Panthygatric, swimming in the nude in Griffey Creek, and breaking the dean of women's rules were the ephemera of co-education in Indiana University. Perhaps there were neither means nor demand for any radical reshaping of the curriculum. The faculty remained predominantly male, and it stuck steadfastly to traditional courses and fields so far as possible in the years of profound academic change in the university. The fact that a majority of women graduates who accepted employment in education and business brought new standards of worth to these professions enabled the university to have a marked impact in these areas. Female teachers especially sent to the university freshmen much better prepared than had been true of their predecessors. The institution also made a considerable contribution to the quality of Indiana homes. There was no doubt that in another area Indiana University-trained women made their influence felt in their vocal and active campaigns to secure the vote for women and the adoption of the Nineteenth Amendment.

Throughout the post-Civil War and World War I years, a very difficult adjustment Indiana University had to make was in the field of human relations. The institution not only had actively to enlarge the area of feminine participation in its program, it also had to recognize the new status—economic and social—of the Negro. Indiana had some of the same problems in this area as did the former slave states. The Negro population in Indiana in 1900 was 57,505 and in 1910, 60,320. It is almost impossible to determine precisely from university records when the first Negro students were admitted into the institution. On November 1, 1890, David Starr Jordan told the trustees that three Negroes along with a Japanese student had been admitted to classes. One of these, James Williams, a graduate of the Indianapolis High School, entered the sophomore class with a highly creditable record. Frank Beck, in *Some Aspects of Race Relations at Indiana University*, quoted William Lowe Bryan as saying there was not a single Negro student in the university from 1877 to 1884. The president's memory in this case was faulty, there was a Negro student in the university in 1882, but whether he was a regular student or enrolled in the preparatory school is impossible to determine.

During the first years of the Bryan administration there was some degree of excitement about the Negro and higher education. Professor Ulysses Grant Weatherly spoke on race relations to students in a chapel ceremony in January, 1903. He took an optimistic view, saying he believed the question of race relations remained acute and should be seriously considered. He held the view that free suffrage was a mistake. "During the period of Reconstruction," he said, "the North made mistakes that can never be wholly rectified. Chief among these mistakes . . . were [sic] the granting of ignorant slaves suffrage and the disastrous education experiments." Weatherly had high praise for Booker T. Washington. "In my eyes," he told the chapel audience, "Booker T. Washington is the greatest statesman and civilizer of the age."

There persisted, in southern Indiana at least, a pronounced racial prejudice outside the university. Occasionally an unhappy incident occurred involving the institution. The Northwestern University baseball team in 1904 had a Negro shortstop. The manager of the hotel where Northwestern's team was to stay in Bloomington refused to house the Negro because it would displease his white guests. Finally he offered the boy a cubbyhole unfit for sleeping. The Negro athlete had not wanted to come to Bloomington in the first place, and now he was trapped in an unhappy and discriminatory racial incident. A local critic wrote the *Daily Student*, saying, "And to what a sorry end! An intelligent young man, a leader in his classes, and an equal to his fellow players on the diamond, a student whose attainments far outshine his persecutor, and whose only misfortune is the possession of a dark skin, has been maltreated, turned out of doors and humiliated at the seat of Indiana's learning." There is evidence that much of the campus population lived ahead of the community in racial attitudes.

Already in 1904 there was a Negro fraternity. The Alpha Kappa Nu fraternity was organized at Indiana, and, in the year following its founding, the *Daily Student* reported it had "been growing steadily ever since." On October 2, 1911, the Bloomington *Telephone* reported the fraternity had bought a house on West Kirkwood, and the campus paper boasted that this was the first Negro fraternity chapter in the country to "occupy its own home." Later on the fraternity moved to 721 Hunter Avenue. Sometime in the early 1920's a Negro sorority was organized on the campus. By 1914, the Kappa Alpha Nu fraternity had established chapters at Illinois and Iowa, where it was considered to be a strong organization. The name of this fraternity was changed to Kappa Alpha Psi on April 15, 1915, and was the only Greek letter fraternity founded at Indiana University.

Doubts as to whether or not the Negro could compete in higher education was reduced when Samuel Dargan, as a junior in 1906, won first honors in a discussion contest of the "Tariff in the United States." Perhaps the most dramatic achievement of a Negro student was that of L. A. Lewis, who appeared as a medical licensee before the State Medical Board in 1911 and made the commendable record of 947 out of a possible 1000 points. Lewis also led his class earlier in the entrance examination as an intern seeking to practice in the Indianapolis City Hospital.

In 1915 the university medical school in Bloomington was upset by an incident involving Robert Shelton, a senior, who was sued by a local Negro girl in a paternity suit. Bloomington Negroes expressed strong opinions that Shelton was being made a "goat" in the suit and sided with him. Dean Myers and President Bryan, however, were stern puritans in matters involving morals and they expelled the boy. The Negroes of the town then threatened court action unless Shelton were reinstated. They failed to budge the university's administration, however, and the dismissal remained in force.

On the eve of World War I there were enough Negro male students enrolled at Indiana to form a Negro football team. On Saturday, November 14, 1914, the Indiana team met the Indianapolis Royal Athletic Club team on Jordan Field and won by a score of 16 to 13. A week later the university team engaged in a foot race rather than a football game with the Muncie Athletic Club, winning by a score of 76 to 0, thus assuring the university the Negro state championship in football.

Much of the history of the Negro in Indiana University before 1925 was centered about the well-known barber and nurse, Halson V. Eagelson. Eagelson seems to have enjoyed the respect of both blacks and whites. Earlier his son Preston had played on the Indiana team, and he had been involved in a case of discrimination in Crawfordsville when the Indiana football team had gone there to play Wabash College.

Halson Eagelson, Jr., entered Indiana University in 1921, and became a member of the university band, to the irritation of some whites. Just before the Purdue football game in November, three white students—Clarence Ullum, Hugh Shields, and Guy Owsley —kidnapped Eagelson and hauled him off to Spencer. While they were enroute Sheriff Nealy McCartney received a call from a man named "Moore" who said he was an Indianapolis detective and wanted Eagelson arrested. "Moore" gave the sheriff no reason for the arrest. The Negro, said "Moore," was traveling with three white companions in a Ford coupe. Sheriff McCartney, apparently more a man of action than of judgment dashed off and took the Negro into custody on unspecified charges. After Eagelson had been placed in jail and held long enough to prevent his going to Lafayette, "Moore" called the sheriff to say a mistake had been made, the man he wanted had been arrested in Bedford. When confronted with accusations, the white students said the whole thing was a "coincidence."

On November 29, 1922, President Bryan announced a faculty committee would investigate the Eagelson case thoroughly and would take steps to punish those students found guilty of the kidnapping.

The Eagelsons, however, felt the injury deeply, and filed a suit in Monroe County Court. The case stirred the university community for more than a year. A vigorous attempt was made by both campus officials and townspeople to bring about either a withdrawal of the suit or have it postponed indefinitely. The newspapers entered into the general effort to quiet the suit, but Mary Eagelson, a sister, was adamant. She assured the public that her family would not compromise the issue. She blamed the white community for rising racial tensions, saying she had been threatened often with violence from townsmen unless she consented to the withdrawal of the suit. Town officials said they feared violence would occur if the case came to trial. They attributed the racial tension to the fact that Negroes were allowed to eat in the Indiana University cafeteria.

Five "prominent" Bloomington businessmen expressed eagerness to become security for the white students' bonds of $1000 each. Among these were Wood Wiles, H. Coombs, and Dr. Robert Rogers. The Eagelson case was finally tried on November 30 and 31, 1923, and on December 1, the jury reported a split decision of 9 for acquittal and 3 for conviction. On December 4, the state said it would re-try the case, but in March the next year Judge Randall dismissed it for lack of evidence. There is little doubt from the record that the university's image suffered from this incident.

Nevertheless, active efforts were made soon after 1920 to lower racial barriers and tensions. The Inter-Racial Commission came into existence in November, 1925, and had for its central purpose the promotion of the culture of the two races. One of its approaches to this understanding was the reading of Negro novels by Dunbar, Toomer, Maran, Chesnutt, Tancent, and DuBois. As time advanced more Negro portraits appeared in the *Arbutus*, and there were fewer racial incidents on the campus. Occasionally irresponsible people injured relations by name-calling, especially during athletic games. At the Michigan State-Indiana football game in November, 1927, the Indiana *Daily Student* reported that such an incident had occurred when Indiana fans uttered unseemly outcries of prejudice. A Negro player named Smith had entered the game for Michigan State and some fans made insulting remarks. The student paper chided those responsible and remarked that they had let the university down.

In the depths of the depression President Bryan wrote the trustees, "I call attention to a communication from Mrs. Katherine Bailey of the National Association for the Advancement of Colored People in which the Association asks that colored students be permitted to practice in the Long and Coleman hospitals and that colored patients be admitted to those hospitals."

In all areas of student life Indiana University was forced to accept changes thrust upon it by evolving social mores in America after the opening of the twentieth century. These were made in the context of gradual departures from the social conditions of the frontier itself, but also in light of the rapid advances of industrial and urban society. The student decorum of the Indiana campus resembled that of other comparable institutions. Thomas Jefferson learned in the first quarter of the nineteenth century that student behavior was perhaps an even more important fact in American university operation than curriculum and staff building. Indiana University had long years of learning the same facts.

[VII]

The Spirit of Youth

A T THE TURN of the twentieth century the average American state university student reflected a rural-small town background and attitude. He had little urban sophistication and demonstrated a remarkable lack of independence in asserting his will and his views. This is not to say, however, that he was incapable of expressing himself in his rowdy pranks, head-breaking class contests, resistance to parental university rules, and various other forms of sinning. The years 1900 to 1915 were transitional ones, from the rowdiness of the early years to the more adaptable and permissive years after World War I. While the president and professors struggled during the early Bryan years to reorganize the university students continued to act like academy boys. Indiana students reflected the conditions of society in the state; in fact the university's student body was a microcosm of much of the Roosevelt era's midwestern life itself.

In 1908 the registrar published an analysis of Indiana student ages. Freshmen ranged from sixteen to thirty years and averaged twenty; sophomores were a year older; seniors ranged from 18 to 35 and averaged twenty-four years. In nearly every category girls were a year younger.

A troublesome legacy of the academy was the annual burning of Homer or Horace by the sophomores on or near Abraham Lin-

coln's birthday. For Bryan and his colleagues this affair proved
an annual horror; for students it threatened tragedy. In 1902 the
faculty tried to tame the "scrap" by diverting it into what they
thought would be a gentler "color rush." This was to be an indoor
form of track meet concluded by a dignified bonfire. But the color
rush actually promised more tenacious rivalry and fist-and-skull
fighting than had the former free-for-all burning debacles. This
new contest required that the green colors of the freshman class,
designated with the proper numerals, be nailed high up in a tree,
and that the sophomores would maneuver to capture them. Extensive rules were drafted and trustworthy judges were appointed,
and everybody agreed to a gentlemanly rush, but the old instinct
of fist-and-skull asserted itself in the heat of battle.

In 1902 three thousand persons braved February cold to watch
sixty-five enraged sophomores assault freshmen in pioneer Ohio
valley Indian style. In ten minutes the one hundred and ten freshmen had the sophomores pinned to the ground and were pummeling them into a bloody pulp. The battered sophomores retaliated
in the evening in traditional style by burning "Dear Horace." They
were successful because they started a series of false bonfires
which divided freshman ranks.

Student scraps at Indiana University went on longer than the
Trojan Wars, did injury no doubt to the study of the classics, and
threatened the physical welfare of a lot of stalwart Hoosiers. Burning books finally proved a less satisfying release of energy for the
"barbarians" gathered up from the Indiana countryside than college sports.

There were also other forms of primitive physical expression.
The practice of "scalping" freshmen had its day at Indiana. In
1903, Karl Wellhausen, a sophomore, held fifty freshmen at bay
with a shotgun when they attempted to enter his room on Atwater
Avenue. Wellhausen was angry because he had been partially
shorn the week before, and now the vandals were back before his
door. Reminiscent of the Shawnees, and maybe the Kickapoos,
the Indiana sophomores were scalp collectors, and they ranged
boarding houses and campus paths in search of locks to add to
their trophy strings. In October, 1903, sophomores John Ogden
and Camden McAtee were called away from their rooms and then
were set upon by a band of unfeeling freshmen who stripped them
of hair and hide, but worst of all their pride. So fierce did the scalp
hunts become at times that a board of arbitration had to intervene.

Many students, it was said, had become afraid to walk along the streets, or to attend classes or visit the library for fear they would expose themselves to rowdy assault. "Hair cutting," said the *Daily Student*, on October 14, 1903, "loses all traces of fun & becomes a deterrent, not only to the classes involved, but to the University at large" and the student with a clipped head looked ridiculous.

Hazing in at least one incident led to an unpleasant off-campus commotion. A story originating in the Logansport *Journal* in October, 1903, said that freshman Charles Ballard, an Indiana University student, had been lured into a Bloomington dance hall by a beautiful Logansport siren and had been terribly beaten by upper classmen. Young Ballard's bleeding carcass was left on the dance floor unattended. His mother started for Bloomington at once, but at Lafayette she learned the story was a hoax. Dr. Ballard and his brother called on *Journal* editor Arthur Keesling and administered him a severe pummeling while his staff retreated for safety behind a barricade of type cases. After the fighting was over and emotions had cooled it was learned that Joseph Kardes, a former Indiana student, had given editor Keesling the story as a joke.

There were other undesirable results from inter-class rowdiness. Faculty minutes for October 12, 1904, describe an incident which could have had fatal consequences. One lad became a bit over-enthusiastic and squirted formaldehyde through the old gymnasium floor in an attempt to break up a freshman assembly. He then climbed to the balcony and attempted to swath the audience with the fluid. This grave offense was brought before an angry court of professors who declared the lad guilty on every count and recommended that he be sent home. Students protested this stern treatment, but William Lowe Bryan, final arbiter of university affairs, wrote the boy's father about the sophomoric frivolities, saying that, "On October 8th he undertook, in company with a number of members of his class, to break up a meeting of the freshman class in the Gymnasium." After describing the offense, Bryan continued,

There seems to be an indestructible tendency upon the part of college students to engage in scraps of one kind or another. We have for many years followed the policy of mitigation, seeking to prevent any serious injury and in the main we have been successful in this policy. My constant fear is that some one will thought-

WILLIAM LOWE BRYAN, *President, 1902–1937.*

THIS PICTURE SECTION selected from the archives gives some of the flavor of Indiana University in mid-passage. Included are names, sights, scenes, and groups that helped shape the university.

SAMUEL BANNISTER HARDING, *Department of History, 1894–1918.*

JAMES A. WOODBURN, *Department of History, 1883–1925.*

LOUISE ANN GOODBODY, *Dean of Women, 1906–1911.*

WILLIAM A. RAWLES, *Professor, then Dean of the School of Business, 1886–1935.*

The new University Library, 1909.

Burton Dorr Myers, *School of Medicine, Bloomington, 1903–1940.*

David Myers Mottier, *Department of Botany, 1890–1937.*

Amos Shartle Hershey, *History, then Department of Political Science, 1895–1932.*

Ulysses Grant Weatherly, *Department of Economics and School of Business, 1899–1937.*

Wylie Hall, one of the three original buildings on the present campus.

HOAGY CARMICHAEL, *student, 1920–1924, Bachelor of Law degree, 1926.*

Indiana University co-eds, 1927.

WENDELL L. WILLKIE, *student, 1909–1913, Bachelor of Law degree, 1915.*

PAUL VORIES McNUTT, *student, 1909–1913; professor, then Dean of the Law School, 1917–1932.*

The Well House, with portals of the old college building, 1914. Here Indiana University girls were converted into full-fledged co-eds.

Indiana University baseball team, 1910.

Indiana University football team, 1912. Season record 2–5.
Coach James H. Sheldon, second row, left.

Indiana University basketball team, 1910.

Women's varsity swimming team, about 1928.

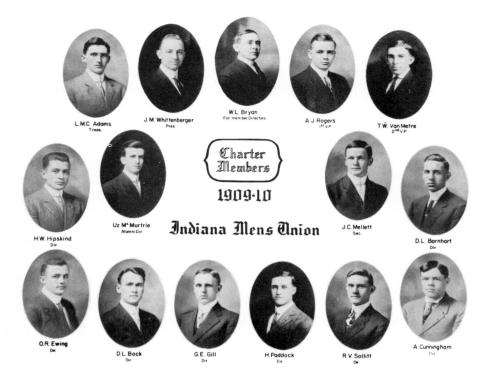

Charter members, Indiana Men's Union, 1909–1910.

Indiana University Women's League, 1910.

Cast of the Jordan River Revue, 1926.

The Book Nook commencement, 1928. Peter Costas at the rostrum.

New recruits on their way to the campus, 1918.

Alpha Hall, the women's dormitory, with military occupants, 1918.

Indiana University School of Medicine, Indianapolis, 1910.

Robert W. Long Hospital, Indianapolis, 1938.

William Lowe Bryan breaking ground for the new Administration Building, 1937. The opening of the WPA building era on the campus.

He'll Be President-Emeritus July 1

Dr. William Lowe Bryan, who has resigned from the presidency of the University, a post he held for 35 years, is pictured above at work at his desk in the new Administration building.

"He'll be President-Emeritus July 1." The Indiana Daily Student, *June 14, 1937.*

President Wells' inaugural dinner, 1938.

Herman B Wells and the Board of Trustees, 1938.

The Indiana Memorial Union Building.

lessly or recklessly do something which will be dangerous. The attempt to break up a meeting by means of chemicals is plainly a thing of this class. I have partial evidence of the fact that a bottle of tri-chloride of phosphorous was taken from the chemical laboratory here at the time of this scrap. If it had been used the results would have been, as you know, disastrous.

He told the father his son was too ignorant to be left running around the university.

No case in Indiana University disciplinary history illustrated more clearly the fact that president and faculty could be unreasonably severe in disciplinary matters where class rivalries were concerned. The student involved in the formaldehyde incident transferred to Western Reserve University, and in time became one of America's truly outstanding psychiatrists and author of several standard works in the fields of psychology and psychiatry. Perhaps one of his most distinctive works is a monumental three-volume study entitled *Abraham Lincoln's Philosophy of Common Sense* (New York Academy of Science, 1965).

It was said, partly in jest, that Indiana University had no rules governing the personal behavior of its students. This was only partially true. The word of William Lowe Bryan and his appointed faculty committees made the rules as need for discipline arose. Bryan felt generally that the student was an adult in the face of the law and so should conduct himself while registered in the university. If he ran afoul of the law, like every other citizen, he should face the charges like a man.

One of the bitterest scraps in university history occurred in February, 1906. George Washington's birthday was marred by a general fight followed by a run-in with the Bloomington police. Freshmen and sophomores had squared off in a battle royal. "No one was seriously injured," said the *Student*, "It is claimed that 50 freshmen 'turkeyed' just before the scrap began." Following the fight the victorious sophomores sent up a bloodcurdling scalp yell from the steps of Maxwell Hall, and then led most of the student body on a rampage around the town square.

On the day following the big disturbance William Lowe Bryan gave his views of law and order to the Bloomington *Telephone*. "I wish to state," he said, "1. that I stand with the officers in their attitude toward students who carry their fun to a point where it becomes a nuisance. I am sorry if innocent students are involved and made to suffer. But when the rights of citizens are violated, they have a right to call upon the city for protection and the city has the duty to afford them protection. 2. The University has scarcely any rules except to ask its students to be good citizens. . . ." Bryan then explained that students no longer were children who could enjoy the liberty of men without being held accountable for their acts. Then in stern language he informed his charges that if they ran afoul of the law the university would also take an interest in their cases.

Both faculty and student memories of the spring melee remained green during the summer of 1906. President Bryan had appointed a committee on student affairs to try to get the "scrap" problem in hand. School opened in September with three cases of hair cutting, followed immediately by what was called a "furniture scrap" which centered around the location and furnishing of dining rooms. Four students were suspended four days for fighting over boarding house advantages, a thing which again set off freshmen and sophomore warriors, and resulted in the shattering of both furniture and landladies' peace of mind. This resulted in an agreement to stop hair cutting and raised hopes that "furniture scrapping" would cease. Hopefully the Bloomington Courthouse Square could be turned back in peace to the whittlers, horses, and pigeons.

Such was not to be. In late November as a result of a clash between students and police two students were jailed. The "celebration" honored the end of an unusually successful football season. Students in all states of dress and undress flocked into the square in the evening, built a bonfire, made inflammatory speeches about nothing, and otherwise held the cottagers at bay. They rushed the southside theater sending the actor-villain to the wings in fright where he demanded police protection. The theater manager rushed into the street and demanded immediate silence. For an instant there was silence, and then came an unsettling yell urging these self-appointed warriors to charge four men in blue. The policemen clubbed down a boy, two students were jailed, and the night ended with Bloomington nerves frayed.

The favorite student beachhead for bonfires and scraps was the Harris Grand Theater. In October, 1908, the students set off a bonfire which resulted in a commotion with firemen and police.

In the confusion the large plate glass front of the theater was broken. Manager Dill threatened students that if they did not replace his glass he would begin criminal prosecutions. Both the faculty committee on student affairs, and students themselves went to work to establish fault for the breaking of the theater glass. After an extended investigation the faculty committee decided that eight identifiable student leaders of the riot would have to make restitution to the theater owner by a given deadline, or bear the criminal consequences. On the campus there was quickly organized the "Innocents Club" composed of the eight accused culprits who sought to raise money by popular student subscription to pay for the damaged theater front. Manager Dill estimated his damage at $40.00, and the ingenious students began at once a bidding contest among the Bloomington hardware merchants to get the glass for a lesser price. Von Behren's store agreed to replace the glass in a manner satisfactory to Manager Dill for $22.00.

The Harris Grand, which, ironically, depended upon student patronage was not to see the last of student misbehavior. In May, 1911, 300 students entered the theater to see a performance of "The Flirting Princess." They began to make uncomplimentary noises and the manager called the police. When the noise continued several boys were arrested and hauled off to jail. This started a street riot which wound up with several boys getting knocked down, and some of the rioters losing teeth by being hit on the head with police clubs.

The university administration became aware that the rowdiness on the campus hurt the institution's image. In June, 1909, Professor Ernest H. Lindley, at a "Love Feast for Law Enforcement" banquet, boasted of the "unique" relations which existed between students and the town of Bloomington. He said as he traveled over Indiana a great many old graduates asked affectionately of the town and the university. He assured his audience that students were not antagonistic toward Bloomington. Too, many Bloomington people had "fathered and mothered" boys and girls during their years as students. As a result Professor Lindley felt the streets of the town should be made as free to students as possible. "It has been said," observed the professor with considerable truth, "that what happens between 6 o'clock in the evening and 6 o'clock in the morning have more influence over a student's life than anything that happens in the classroom so you people of the town have as much to do with shaping the future lives of students as we instructors at the University do."

Maybe Mrs. Frank Clampitt would not have been quite so enthusiastic about the idea of "mothering" homeless students as was Ernest Lindley. She reported to the faculty in February, 1909, that Frank Kimball, Clarence Compton Taylor, and Harry Goldberg uttered "curses and swore habitually, using vulgar and indecent language, sufficiently loud to be heard all over the house; threatened her with violence if she informed on them and to burn the house [407 North College Avenue]; threw heavy boxes down the stairs, also the bed clothing and made so much noise day and night in the house that it was impossible to sleep and study, and the noises were kept up at times, until after midnight." Judge Enoch H. Hogate, stern barrister of the Law School, headed a committee to gather evidence. The committee sustained Mrs. Clampitt's charges and the three lads were suspended from the university.

The memory of these years burned deeply in the minds of some old graduates. In 1924, an alumna came back to Bloomington with her husband and daughter. She had sworn earlier that she would "never send my daughter to Indiana." Things were quiet, however, on the campus in the 1920's. The old fires had smoldered, and if there were rowdiness of the earlier sort it was well concealed. The woman reminisced that when she was a student in the university, "Men and women students roomed in the same house. A landlady had no more right to dictate what time co-eds in her house should return at night than does the renter in metropolitan centers. New students were thrown upon their own responsibility in finding rooms."

Students in the first decade of Bryan's administration developed a sensitivity about persons and institutions in Bloomington. They were perhaps more conscious of political and social issues than the town's citizens, sometimes to the consternation of local politicians. Local and state politics appealed to them, and each presidential campaign brought out hosts of partisans who affiliated themselves with political clubs. Harshly critical views of local candidates sometimes ruffled feelings. Occasionally students' voting in town and county elections may have decided choices of officers. Clubs like the traditional Jackson organization was a training ground for many of the men who later would dominate Indiana politics.

In almost every other area of life in Bloomington student influence was important. All the students wanted was a cause and a leader and they were ready to support a movement with zeal. The Bloomington *Daily Telephone* lamented in 1914, "Today is not like the 'good old days' when on each Washington's anniversary the I. U. students had a pitched battle that was carried on in all parts of the town. Ten years ago on Washington's birthday, the city schools were not dismissed, and the students having a brotherly feeling for the 'kids' marched down town and compelled the city teachers to dismiss their classes for the day. In those days February 22 was a knock-out and drag-out party for the college boys, but no one was severely injured."

On another occasion students joined townspeople in a fight against the local telephone corporation. In February, 1908, the phone company upped its rates and about two hundred students and their clubs and fraternities voted to disconnect their phones and join the local boycott. The student president of the boycott spoke to citizens assembled in the Harris Grand Theater and was greeted enthusiastically by the town's "telephone fighters." He said over three-fourths of the organizations in the university supported the reinstatement of the earlier rate structure.

There were mixed feelings, however, on the local rum question. The evils of drink were vividly demonstrated on October 8, 1909, when a student parade around the town square was disrupted by a drunken Monroe County bully who drove his horse and rig at full gallop through the parade lines. Maybe he was father of that summer school student who "fell off the water cart" in July of that year after consuming a good part of a quart of "medicinal spirits." He "fell" in fact out of a Monon boxcar into the Bloomington jail.

Such incidents were shocking to William Lowe Bryan, who looked upon drinking and smoking as the filthy work of the devil. He no doubt bespoke a majority opinion in Bloomington. Bryan expressed satisfaction to President Winthrop E. Stone of Purdue,

Bloomington has been dry by remonstrance for several years. I have been surprised to find how generally our people are pleased with the results. We have had blind tigers, some very bad ones with attendant evils (some of the keepers are now in jail) I am told, and believe, that a considerable amount of liquor has come in legally and illegally. On the other hand conditions have been very greatly improved in a number of ways. The public budget is better on the whole by the reduction of court and jail expenses. The businessmen around the Square report better conditions. . . . The money that was going for liquor is paying the grocery bills and buying shoes for the children. . . . We didn't have one case of discipline for drunkenness at the University last year or this."

Bryan spoke too soon, the storm was soon upon him. The next year the police raided "Mother" Sarah Anderson's popular "boarding house" and the "Red Onion." In the first place they found plenty of university and high school students, and a liberal supply of beer and liquor. They found in a bedroom a man in bed and a frightened girl underneath. At the police station the brazen Sarah peeled off $450 from a roll of greenbacks for her bond, even astonishing the officers with her liquid wealth. This raid aroused anew the anti-saloon forces on the campus. Bloomington's precincts were not so dry as President Bryan had described, and the call once again went out to hoist the banner for sobriety.

Temperance had long been an issue in the university, and President Bryan kept active watch over his charges. The editor of the 1904 *Arbutus* learned this fact the hard way. He had published an advertisement of the Indianapolis Brewing Company. The happy brewers told departing seniors that its "Progress" brand beer had won a Paris gold medal in 1900, and that if they could not obtain its "goods" in Bloomington the company would ship them in barrels containing six dozen quarts. The barrels would bear no identifying markings to stir the gossips and excite the nosey. It would appear on the surface that students were going into the chinaware business. This indiscretion resulted in most of the graduating seniors signing an apology to the president for allowing the advertisement to appear in their yearbook.

The Prohibition Club in 1904 was said to have become extinct for lack of a cause. All the saloons were thought to be closed. Two years later, however, the club was back in business under the name of the Intercollegiate Prohibition Association studying questions arising from the liquor traffic. This time there was no illusion about the death of John Barleycorn. Four hundred and thirty students petitioned the Monroe County Commissioners in 1912 to close all saloons for a period of two years. They no doubt had in mind a close watch on student traffic in and out of Bedford where there was no Intercollegiate Prohibition Association to interfere with the sale of the products of Louisville, St. Louis, Cincinnati, and Milwaukee. In this stonebelt town erring students could load their suitcases against the ravages of the Bloomington desert.

In spite of the demoralizing impact of World War I, in January, 1917, collegians promoted the signing of a fifty-four foot petition against alcohol bearing the signatures of 1,300 students representing all of the organizations in the university. This document was hauled off to Indianapolis by Dr. Burton Dorr Myers and a student delegation, to be added to petitions from Purdue, DePauw, and other colleges. The legislators were in the process of considering a statewide prohibition bill, and when news of the law's enactment reached Bloomington on the evening of February 2, 1917, the Student Building chimes rang out in its honor.

Smoking was regarded by President Bryan as embodying all the evils of drink. In June, 1907, he was approached by Joseph Knox Barclay for possible employment as an assistant gymnastic coach. That afternoon the president saw Barclay smoking a cigarette on the steps of Maxwell Hall and wrote him, "This morning you asked me to consider you as a coach. This afternoon I have seen you smoking a cigarette on the steps of the Law Building. I do not understand why you expect me to trust you in an important position when you ignore a request I have many times made." Evidently peace was made between the two because Barclay was listed in the catalogue as a gymnasium assistant.

Professor Robert Judson Aley earlier conducted services in the Bloomington Christian Church in which he spoke on life's handicaps. He said, "If you smoke cigarettes don't worry about your future—you haven't any!" On the campus of the University anti-smoking notices were posted on bulletin boards, frequent sermonettes against the evil were delivered in chapel, and the *Student* carried anti-tobacco stories. President Bryan stopped students on the walks and lectured them on the evils of smoking and asked them not to give in to the habit while enrolled in the university. "Needless to say," said the *Student*, "his requests have been complied with." Bryan said smoking was repulsive to young women and their presence and wishes should be respected. He was supported in his anti-tobacco stand by Janitor Delmer Hannah of the Student Building. Hannah denounced tobacco as a "vile and filthy weed," with ample provocation. The anti-smoking campaign was futile. In 1911, the junior class chose pipe smoking as the distinctive symbol of its academic status in the university.

Other forms of the vice met faculty disapproval. S. W. Schaefer and J. W. Douglas were found guilty of spitting tobacco juice on the Gymnasium floor during the Indiana-Illinois basketball game in February, 1911. For this offense they were barred from attending other athletic games during the rest of the semester and were required to apologize to Dr. C. P. Hutchins, the faculty member of the Boosters Club. Whether or not the conduct of Schaefer and Douglas had any bearings on student morals is an open question. Something, however, in 1911 and 1912 caused marked apprehension on the part of President Bryan and his colleagues on this issue. They were engaged in a crusade to morally sanitize the university, but without specifying what immoralities prevailed. They investigated fraternities, sororities, and clubs. There were numerous conferences on the subject, and the president told the trustees he considered the question of utmost importance.

In 1912 the Bloomington *Telephone* reported the campus in an uproar over the embezzlement of class dance funds. "The biggest scandal which has occupied the attention of the University people for some years has been on for the past few days...," said the paper. Someone has filched $40 to $50 from the class till by charging on paper higher prices for supplies than were actually paid out. Student marshals were asked to make closed-door investigations of the charges and counter-charges. Deep secrecy prevailed, and everybody connected with the dance was under suspicion.

A movement for student self-government was begun in February, 1912. The *Daily Student* announced that a campus council was proposed which would be composed of representatives from every organization in the university. That fall a first step was taken in the organization of the governing council when the faculty athletic committee, at a meeting in the home of Dr. Hutchins, endorsed the idea of instituting a corps of student marshals to police public assemblies and athletic events, and maybe to corral the tobacco chewers. The first proposal was that the student body should be represented by four men who would be entitled to vote on questions of athletic management and student behavior.

Interest in the area of student affairs was divided. The Boosters Club concerned itself largely with promoting athletic fortunes by stirring up support for teams, raising money, and bettering university athletic standings. In 1890, another group of students and professors had organized a cooperative bookstore and had distributed shares to patrons entitling them to reduced book prices and year-end dividends. This organization was granted a twenty-year franchise by the trustees, 1890 to 1910. It angered Bloomington storeowners who felt they should have student patronage free of competition. At times local merchants sought to destroy the cooperative. In March, 1910, William Lowe Bryan raised the question with the trustees as to whether or not the student bookstore should be re-chartered. He told them that the excuses for its existence were to lower prices, to maintain adequate textbook stock to supply all the courses in the curriculum, and to make available unprofitable books of a specialized nature. In town, Claude Steele's bookstore had maintained vigorous competition. Its owners had been able to skim off much of the profit from the higher yield trade, and ignored the need for low profit materials, and in 1910 offered to purchase the university store. Instead Dean Enoch Hogate of the Law School faculty bought the debt-burdened store for $3300 to continue its operation in faculty-student hands. The store had begun with no capital, in the latter year had an inventory of $3,745.21, and had never cost the university anything. Unhappily at that moment it had a deficit of approximately $3000. In its twenty years of existence it was said to have saved Indiana University students $40,000. Dean Hogate and his colleagues proposed to carry on the business under a new charter, with Nicholas O. Pittenger as manager. In fact this was the beginning of the modern bookstore.

After 1908 college student organizations underwent important changes. This may have been reason for a part of the restlessness and desire for more active student participation in both campus and social affairs. Too, there was a wave of concern with national issues which drew students into state and national political campaigns and imbued them with a progressive sense of reform. On the Indiana University campus the new Student Building was a tremendous asset, but it failed in uniting the student body in a common interest and loyalty. Because of the ever-widening division between fraternity and sorority and non-organized students the campus was being pulled apart. There was need for a centralizing force and incentive which a mere physical building could not supply.

In 1907 a freshman named John Whittenberger, a country

farm boy from Miami County near Peru, entered the university. He came from a substantial but unusually frugal farm family who believed the lad should pay his own university expenses. Whittenberger's stay at the university was interrupted by periods of absence when he taught country schools in Miami County or traveled in Michigan for a commercial firm. In Michigan he visited that state's university and became interested in its new Student Union. In the fall of 1909 he was back in Bloomington sweating through a period of conditioning as a football player and making new friends on the campus. He was almost obsessed with the idea that a union would draw Indiana University students into closer bonds of friendship and purpose. During that year he promoted the idea, and his papers revealed later that he had spent considerable time drawing plans for a building to house an organization comparable to that at Michigan. The organization of a union board was begun in the fall of 1909, and its members first consisted largely of class and club presidents. By early spring, 1910, the Union Board had been organized with John Whittenberger as president. In September, and in the midst of one of Bloomington's famous water shortages, Whittenberger contracted typhoid fever and died. Thus his dream was left to others to be realized in the future.

William Lowe Bryan favored the idea of organizing a student union, and had the support of Dean Enoch Hogate and Ernest H. Lindley. Students also had the cooperation of other faculty members. By December 6, 1909, the newly formed Union had recruited 115 male members and the roll grew until it reached 500 in June of the next year. Under John Whittenberger's presidency temporary reading, pipe-smoking, and billiard rooms were set aside for union members in the still unfinished Student Building. Installation of a billiard parlor again stirred the wrath of Bloomington proprietors, and there was also some criticism within the university family on moral grounds. To console the pious, the *Daily Student* said the billiard parlor on the campus was the only place where students were not permitted to swear.

So enthusiastic were students and President Bryan for the new club that plans were made to approach John D. Rockefeller once again for a substantial gift, and President Bryan asked an architect to draw plans for completion of the Student Building. It was felt the stated purpose of the union would appeal to the Standard Oil baron. The *Daily Student*, January 1, 1910, in reporting the organization of the student group, editorialized, "One of the most promising movements that has been started for years at a state institution is the formation of the Indiana Union; which is to take the place of a University club. . . . The club proposes to become a network, which will draw students of the state institution into a closer web of friendship, giving them a place to spend their leisure time with their fellows, and form a bond of unity, which will keep the interests of Indiana graduates riveted to their alma mater after leaving college."

Professors donated money with which to purchase periodical subscriptions, and there was a promising stirring among alumni indicating financial support. By mid-January, 1910, there was a membership of 203, and 400 students had crowded into the auditorium to hear a discussion of the establishing of recreation rooms. Almost immediately these rooms became the most popular of any on the campus. Later a committee of professors was to complain in a formal report that the Union was too popular. They, like the local billiard parlor keepers and barbers of Bloomington eyed this competition with jaundiced eyes.

In the organization of the Union Board, William Lowe Bryan was made an active director. Dean Barnhart filled out John Whittenberger's unexpired term, but there was already on the scene an ambitious young student politician, Paul Vories McNutt, who became president in 1911, and the *Daily Student* proclaimed it "The one great organization at Indiana which welds the love of each individual for the institution into the great school spirit." For a dollar a year students reaped lush dividends in recreation and brotherly love. Paul V. McNutt was almost as vigorous in his labors as Whittenberger had been, and by fall, 1912, the club had become so successful the membership had climbed to 500, and the student president was buoyed by William Lowe Bryan's statement, "I would like to see every man in the University in the Union. It exists for all and should be supported by all." There were even bigger plans. A hospital fund would be started to care for student health, and a committee would be appointed to determine whether or not an ailing member should be sent to a hospital for treatment. To support the drive for broadening the Union's activities, students invited Governors Judson Harmon of Ohio, Woodrow Wilson of New Jersey, and Augustus E. Willson of Kentucky, to speak on the campus.

Ambitions grew with each meeting. Plans were made to launch a building campaign to house the Union in its own quarters. It was contemplated that the Union Board would take over the long-time popular Athletic Minstrel and produce shows and divide funds between the Union and the athletic teams. Ralph Richmond, speaking for the Union Board in October, 1912, proposed that the nine university clubs then in existence be drawn into a national federation of university organizations, and Whittenberger's idea of close harmony be given wide application.

The spring semester of 1912 was a stirring one for the Union. On January 4 the new barber chair was in place, and for fifty cents a student could purchase a punch card which entitled him to several haircuts at drastically reduced rates. This started the fight with the Bloomington barbers that was to cause William Lowe Bryan so much difficulty. Thinking well beyond personal services, student officers began a move to purchase a building and proposed to raise from $150,000 to $250,000 for this. In May the directors met with Colonel Louden and discussed the possibility of purchasing Alpha Hall as a union building, provided an expert could advise them that the building could be reconditioned at reasonable cost. Colonel Louden, however, did not have full control of his building, and the directors of the First National Bank of Bloomington vetoed the idea. Besides, Alpha Hall was too good a revenue producer as a girl's dormitory to be sold to the non-profit Union Board.

Undaunted by failure to purchase the Louden building, the Union Board proceeded to organize minstrels and concerts to raise money. It worked out an agreement with the Harris Grand Theater for use of its stage on which to produce its entertainment. A dispute with a Chicago minstrel compay arose because it claimed Indiana students had infringed copyrights by using three currently popular songs. Nevertheless the Harris Grand was filled with customers and the students produced entertainment in the form of a girl burlesque, acrobatics, skits, and a dramatic play. The times favored the Board, and in 1914, President Bryan was recommending to the board of trustees that the Indiana Union be allowed to set up moving picture apparatus in the Student Building and collect admissions for its showings. A year later it was announced that the Union would operate an open air movie nightly during the summer and profits would be added to the building fund.

World War I interfered seriously with the drives to promote

the construction of a union building. Despite all of the war activity, however, and the almost calamitous reduction in masculine activity in the university, the Union Board held the organization together and even made progress. For instance, in 1916 it brought to the campus a concert and lecture series that included H. G. Wells. The famous English historian, for a fee of $300, predicted for his audience a certain end of all mankind unless men changed their behavior.

Because of the shifting demands on the university from the war and the nature of American higher education itself, the Board of Trustees in 1916 instructed President Bryan and N. O. Pittinger, the bookstore manager, to purchase the equipment of the Indianapolis Cafeteria Company for $3600 to be installed in the Student Building to supply a campus food service. Miss Nola Treat, an expert in cafeteria management and an instructor in home economics, was given responsibility for running the new dining room, while President Bryan fought off angry Bloomington boarding house keepers who felt they were being put out of business.

Early the next year Bryan reported an encouraging income from the bookstore, and from this date on the store was to make substantial gains. Out of this and other income from student projects there was created a student loan fund in 1913, which in 1916 amounted to approximately $2000, and from which fifty-eight small loans had been granted to needy students. Membership in the Union was severely limited because of the spartan regulations of the Student Army Training Corps, and there were losses in the latter war years from the movies, but the other activities showed profits. These funds enabled the Union Board to sustain many activities which came clearly within the objectives that John Whittenberger had outlined. Immediately after the war in 1919 a new drive for membership was begun and in the fall of that year the Union Board announced that it proposed even to enlarge the activities of the organization. Bryan told the trustees that Kentucky, Purdue, Kansas, Ohio State, and Iowa A. & M. College all had drives under way to memorialize their state's sacrifices in World War I. He proposed that Indiana University alumni embark upon a similar campaign to raise a million dollars to build a girls' dormitory, and an outdoor athletic stadium.

During the summer of 1921, much campus energy went into the organization of the Memorial Drive, and on October 20, 1921, the *Daily Student* said William Lowe Bryan and William A. Alexander had been appointed co-chairmen of the drive. Fittingly the first pledge to the fund was made by Joseph and Frances Swain in the form of a $200 check. There followed a vigorous campaign which at times developed the fervor of a camp meeting. All sorts of campus and public organizations became involved in the solicitation for funds. President Bryan told men students: "I call upon you to marshal yourselves and march to the million dollar goal as you marched thru Argonne. I call upon you to build here a great memorial in honor of those who have fought in all our wars. When you build that you are building a greater thing, a thing whose price is supreme sacrifice, the victorious Indiana spirit." W. A. Alexander took the same message to women students. The *Daily Student* admonished everybody to "Let the folk at home know that for the first time in the history of Indiana University they have an opportunity to provide three greatly needed structures for students and alumni."

In November James A. Woodburn, on the eve of retirement after thirty-two years of service on the faculty, pledged a thousand dollars. A month later William and Charlotte Lowe Bryan subscribed $2500. In Palo Alto Jordan proved longer on oratory than on cash. He told Hoosiers, "Some thirty years ago, I went over the state of Indiana to tell the people the great truth that of all the state's possessions the University at Bloomingon was relatively the least appreciated but actually the most important, not altogether from what it was but for what it was destined to be. Not many believed my words at that time but those who did were young men. ..." He listed among these "Will" Bryan, and he assured the people that Indiana University under Bryan's leadership was coming into its own, and the Memorial Drive would establish this fact.

So enthusiastic was the response to the fund drive that by January, 1922, when subscriptions had reached $104,605.25, Dean Agnes Wells announced to the press that arrangements had been made with Lowe and Bollenbacher of Chicago to plan a girls' dormitory of gothic design to be constructed along Third Street. There were to be four memorial towers to symbolize Indiana University's participation in four American wars. A union building with club rooms, a swimming pool, and a theater would be built along Indiana Avenue, taking the whole block opposite Fourth Street to Kirkwood. Business was booming. Day by day the *Daily Student* announced pledges were pouring into the memorial fund offices. John Whittenberger's dream shone brighter almost by the hour.

So encouraging was the Memorial Fund Campaign that it was decided the commencement ceremonies in 1922 should center about Indiana's war sacrifices. Preparations would be made to present to all alumni clubs a moving picture of life on the modern campus. At the same time it was hoped alumni hearts would be cheered by the fact that Indiana University's badge of poverty would be removed in the demolition of Assembly Hall, or the "Pine Barn called 'Old Faithful.' " The student paper condemned the hall, saying it was in such "bad unsatisfactory and overcrowded condition as to be a positive menace to student health." It was characterized as an old worn-out flimsy, versatile shack, a detriment to scholarship and a disgrace to the university. It was said that "the 1913 groundhog was scared by the sight of it before he saw his own shadow."

On March 9, 1922, the campus goal of $400,000 had been exceeded. John Simpson Hastings and U. Z. McMurtrie, two golden orators, had all but unsettled their listeners and made them give until it hurt. The rule limiting the number of dances to three a semester in the men's gymnasium was relaxed and Hoosiers danced in celebrating the bright prospects for a union building. In a shout of joy President Bryan took the stage to tell students, "In April 1917, I saw the boys of Indiana leap forward to enlist for the great war, and I saw the girls as eager to enlist for their part in the fight. Today I see my boys and girls in another glorious fight for a cause which is to run not for two years, but forever. I laugh all the pessimists to scorn for I know these wonderful sons and daughters of Indiana can do anything. Thank God I was born to work with them!"

It was said Indiana University was a pioneer in obtaining financial support from its students and alumni for campus buildings. No other university was said to have made such successful appeals as those for the Student Building and the memorial buildings. In the latter campaign the general response from students was phenomenally high, $200 per capita. There were many examples of sacrifice. Members of the Kappa Alpha Psi fraternity for Negro students, members who for the most part worked their way through school, were especially commended for their liberal subscriptions. Juanita Schardt, a blind junior who was paying her way through school crocheting pieces of table linen pledged a hundred dollars. Forest M. (Pop) Hall sacrificed his flowing beard on the altar of memorial flame as part of the celebration of the $400,000 victory.

By April, 1922, enthusiasm for the three memorial buildings was at fever pitch. James A. Woodburn wrote that relationships between town and gown were so cordial that many people referred to the school as the "University of Bloomington." Perhaps the first automobile bumper stickers to appear in the university were the 3000 which bore the legends, "We Are for the Memorial," and "Make it More than a Million." Children were encouraged to donate $25 to be paid in five annual installments from money they earned during the summers. Monroe County had passed the $100,-000 mark on April 21, and Bloomington promised to exceed $200,000 in pledges by commencement time.

William Lowe Bryan wrote his neighbors an open letter in which he said,

> On May 1st I am to speak from the Government Radio Station at Washington to alumni and friends of Indiana University as far as my voice will go over the United States.
>
> I am to tell people over thousands of square miles what the students did in their wonderful 31 hour fight for four hundred thousand dollars.
>
> I want to tell them that the people of my town and my county have won their fight for two hundred thousand dollars. Neighbors let me go and tell the United States that Bloomington and old Monroe County have won their part of the battle.

On this trip east Dr. and Mrs. Bryan and the "flying squadron" were guests of Warren G. and Mrs. Harding. Then they were to go on to Philadelphia, New York, Boston, and Cleveland. The Washington visit resulted in a moment of glory on the White House lawn when the Bryans and their party and President Harding were photographed. One can only wonder what the Bryans thought later when they read about the scandals of the Harding administration. Had Harding been a professor Bryan no doubt would have fired him.

Success of the memorial fund was assured by the tireless labors of many canvassers. Edward Von Tress, alumni secretary, was one of these. He worked along the West Coast with marked success, renewing communication with Indiana alumni who were all but forgotten back in Bloomington. While in San Francisco Von Tress called on David Starr Jordan, then in retirement at Palo Alto. He attended one of Jordan's famous meetings with students in the scientist's home, and when the discussion was concluded the old president agreed to make a donation to Indiana University. He took the subscription card and seemed to write interminably as though he were signing away the Stanford fortune, but when Von Tress had an opportunity to see the amount of money Jordan had agreed to donate it was a token five-dollar gift plus a characteristic Jordan message.

While President Bryan led the "Flying Squadron" to the east, Von Tress worked the South and the Florida peninsula. The cause of Indiana University in creating a World War I memorial had now become a national crusade which centered partly around actual campus needs, but largely it symbolized an expression of gratitude of Americans everywhere.

Back in Bloomington everybody on the campus was working to create a big university exhibit to show commencement visitors. Uz McMurtrie, president of the senior class, devised the slogan "Let I.U. and Its Welfare Be Your Hobby!"

When June arrived the canvassers raised their sights to $1.6 million, and an auditorium, dance hall, dining and sleeping rooms, and a tap room heightened student and faculty visions of Armageddon. Again the Monroe County stone companies came through with $21,000 worth of stone. All the old scars opened in the construction of the Student Building seemed to have been healed. At last the great day arrived in March, 1923, when ground was to be broken for the construction of the stadium and the girls' dormitory. March 6, however, was too rainy to be outside and the ceremony was delayed. The cornerstone for Memorial Hall, the women's dormitory, was laid on October 24, 1924, and on November 15 that of the stadium was put in place.

There seems to have been no dispute over placement of the dormitory and stadium, but the location site for the Memorial Building became a hot issue. So much had been said about this building that it had come to seem like a precious dream too sacred to be landbound in a prosaic place. T. C. Steele, the famous Brown County landscape artist, was in residence at the university. It was his opinion that the Indiana Avenue location would impair the natural beauty of the campus. He thought a location just east of

Owen Hall a most desirable site. This artist was drawn into the memorial drive partly by Dr. Bryan who admired him, and the Bloomington *Daily Telephone* announced his canvases would be placed in the building. There were differences of views between Steele and outspoken co-eds who wished the Union to be located away from the center of the campus.

Whatever happened over the location, the *Daily Student* emphasized students should participate in the final decision and said the building should be accessible, have a pleasant entrance, and not mar the beauty of existing buildings. Generally it was said the Union Board favored the Indiana Avenue-Kirkwood site. This plot seemed to be of such a nature that it could accommodate the $500,-000 basic structure and leave ample room for the later addition of a million dollar wing to contain hotel rooms, a dance floor, theater, offices, service units, and a recreational area.

In June, 1923, Lowe and Bollenbacher presented both a map of the campus and drawings of what was called a "middle ages gothic citadel" on the site of Owen Hall. This historic structure would be removed, and an entrance to the campus on the southeast would be made through a romanesque arch embellished with gothic pillars. President Bryan appointed Paul Vories McNutt as chairman of a special committee to consider all possible locations for the Union. In the midst of all this excitement 150 students submitted a petition to the board of trustees asking that the River Jordan, just north of Owen Hall, be bridged. Several persons they said had been injured in trying to cross the stream. Three years before the trustees had refused such a request.

While the memorial campaign was at its peak, the Fort Wayne *News-Sentinel* took the sword of malevolence in hand, said the *Daily Student*, and broke it on the "grasping" university. "Of all the flagitious instances of narrow-mindedness," scoffed the campus paper, "and misinformed sensationalism in journalism," the worst had come out of Fort Wayne. The up-state editor had written, "Down at I.U. in benighted Bloomington, they are preparing to put up a new $250,000 steel stadium. This will tend to cement the fortunes of the school with the town of its unfortunate location. By the way, just where did the $250,000 come from, anyhow? Every time the legislature meets, we hear a dolorous yap from the school to the effect that it's hard up and poverty-stricken—that it hasn't enough money to pay the professors living salaries." The editorial

[1 6 0]

drew the hot retort that the *News-Sentinel* editor was absurd; that he was barbarian in literally trampling on the hearts of thousands of grateful people.

Almost before the last bitter comma was in place in the northern Indiana editorial office, jubilant campaign workers announced that $1.4 million had been pledged to the memorial fund, and the goal was in sight. Now began a period of collecting the pledges. In November, 1925, the trustees were informed that only 5 percent of the $1,453,000 in pledges were in arrears as much as a year. Already the women's dormitory, with its proud arch and medieval towers was up and in service. The stadium also was in use.

The issue of location of the Union Building had not finally been settled in February, 1925, and a new selection committee headed by George W. Purcell of Vincennes was appointed. For the next four years his committee debated among themselves and with the university community over the issue. Not only was the matter of location at stake, the broader question of the full purpose of the Union was now to be considered. The university's public program was being enlarged and reviewed. On September 2, 1929, the board of trustees concluded that the auditorium should be separated from the Union and built as a more adequate and independent structure financed from the Indiana Building Tax Fund if necessary. This helped considerably to clarify the Union location problem, and a month later a site north of Owen Hall along the River Jordan was chosen, and J. C. Bollenbacher was appointed architect.

Construction on the Union Building had advanced sufficiently that it was possible to make plans to lay the cornerstone on the homecoming weekend of October 31, 1931. President Bryan was given the honor of symbolically setting the stone in place which enclosed a copper box. W. A. Alexander, chairman of the fund drive, chose campaign literature, a copy of the *Daily Student*, the *Alumni Quarterly*, portraits of President and Mrs. Bryan, a snapshot of the campus, and a list of bookstore and commons employees to be encased in the building. The formal opening of the Union occurred on Founder's Day, May 4, 1932, and the dedication was held at commencement time on June 13. Special guests were veterans who had fought in the Civil War. Thus John Whittenberger's dream of a student union with its own building came to fruition within little more than twenty years. By 1932 the gothic monolith rising above the trees along the Jordan had become a monument, not only to young Whittenberger and his nine pioneer colleagues of the student union movement, but also to thousands of people who worked so enthusiastically to help Indiana University to assume leadership in this area of student-university relationships.

The construction of the three memorial buildings, all of which were located outside the angular plan of 1885, inaugurated a period of physical expansion which was to see Indiana University in the next quarter of a century outgrow the bounds of the old Dunn Farm itself. The advent of the New Deal the year after the dedication of the Union Building was to bring emergency legislation in the area of public works. This enabled the university to embark upon a greatly expanded building program, including a much more commodious auditorium than anyone even in 1932 could have conceived.

[V I I I]

In Search of Glory

INTIMATELY INTERWOVEN with the academic history of Indiana University is the troubled story of athletics. The fabric of this history is comprised of mixed strands of achievement and disappointment. To some alumni looking at the school's accomplishments season after season there has been dissatisfaction with failure many years to compete successfully with the athletic front runners in the "Big Nine," later the "Big Ten." Athletic fortunes at Indiana have risen and ebbed for more than half a century. Like every other university in the Middle West, Indiana has been indecisive about the primary objectives of collegiate spectator sports; whether they constituted a necessary part of the university's concern with the physical man or were sports for the entertainment of students, alumni, and townsmen.

Since 1883 athletics at Bloomington gradually evolved from informal grass lot beginnings when students, and subsequently faculty committees, exercised casual supervision. In these decades William Lowe Bryan played baseball, so did Charles J. Sembower, Harold Whetstone Johnstone, and other members of the faculty. Even the dignified James Albert Woodburn was proud of his sports record. In Indiana the private schools had perhaps advanced more rapidly in this area of college life than had the university and

Purdue. Elsewhere in the Old Northwest athletics rapidly became an integral part of university programs. At Michigan football had advanced to the stage that James B. Angell gave serious thought to its role in the university. William Rainey Harper at Chicago was faced with the perplexing problem of keeping sports from over-shadowing the academic institution.

While educational statesmen at the head of more prestigious universities cogitated the issue of increasing emphasis on athletics, President James H. Smart of Purdue was able to foresee the chaos which might come to exist unless universities combined their energies in this field and developed controls to keep sports in line. He proposed at the opening of January, 1895, that seven north-western regional university presidents meet in the Palmer House in Chicago to draft regulatory rules and to form an intercollegiate association. The presidents of Purdue, Wisconsin, Chicago, Min-nesota, Northwestern, and Michigan met on the eleventh and or-ganized what was later to be called the "Big Nine Conference." It was not until 1899, however, that Joseph Swain and the Indiana board of trustees joined the University of Iowa to complete the roster of the Big Nine Conference. At that time they subscribed to the twelve-point set of rules adopted in 1895. These covered a wide range of subjects from the appointment of responsible and university controlled athletic committees to revising game rules to reduce physical injuries.

Even with the new rules, football by 1905 was under serious fire as being too brutal a game for the American campus. Had President Theodore Roosevelt not intervened, the sport might even have been abolished. In the latter year President James B. Angell of Michigan proposed encouragement of intramural games to re-duce public pressure, to shorten the playing season, to reduce the number of games to be scheduled, in some way to aid brains to triumph over brawn, and to control the amount of money spent on football players.

At Bloomington the Indiana University administration faced all the problems described by President Angell plus some of strictly local origin. President Swain was thoroughly conscious of the po-litical infighting on the campus in the repeated attempts to elect a football captain in February, 1902. The selection of a captain may have stirred adolescent competitiveness between fraternity and non-fraternity team members, but there were more pressing problems. Coach James Horne promised to be a satisfactory enough coach but he received woefully little financial support to equip his team. Supporters and coach faced this dilemma during the first year of William Lowe Bryan's presidency, and the university suffered its share of public and alumni nagging. The football team in the fall of 1903 was most unpromising. After the opening of the season Coach Horne was soliciting the student body to supplement his thin 170-pound line. The *Daily Student* translated the coach's appeal into the succinct statement that what he wanted was more beef on Jordan Field. He could not recruit from the student body experience, but he was said to have had plenty of courage and energy among his players.

The season's opening games confirmed Coach Horne's pessimism. Up to the date of the Wabash game early in October no first team had been chosen, and following the game the coach seemed to be of the opinion that any choice of players was largely an exercise in futility. "I have never seen such poor playing by an Indiana team" was his resigned judgment. With stouter heart the *Daily Student* thought, "Disgraces may be outlived. The practice game is not the whole season. There are many good men on the football squad. They will scour the tarnish from the fair name of old I.U." Far from being certain of this fact, the coach locked the Jordan Field gates and set his escutcheon polishers to work in earnest. Possibly some hidden talent would emerge for the forthcoming game with the University of Chicago. Chicago, however, had other ideas and trounced the Hoosiers 34 to 0.

A soberer student editor took a serious look at the football team following the second disaster. He thought maybe the football players should take to heart the claims of Professor Shinkiski Hatai, a member of the Department of Neurology at the Chicago University Medical School. This scientific genius claimed to have discovered a miracle substance called lecithin, which produced extraordinary and instant growth. The *Daily Student* writer volunteered the information to Coach Horne that the professor's address could be obtained at the newspaper's office.

On Jordan Field coaches worked again with the team, this time in preparation for the state championship game with Purdue to be played in Indianapolis on the last day of October. This game was to take place in Washington Park on a Saturday afternoon. Promoters in Lafayette, Bloomington, and Indianapolis saw in the meeting of the rival teams an opportunity to give a social and cultural twist to a contest which begged for extra brawn and athletic talent. What they said they hoped to do was stir up a rivalry which grew ivy leaves in imitation of the eastern colleges. In more practical terms, it was hoped the game would raise an appreciable amount of money for athletic purposes. General admission was seventy-five cents for the privilege of walking through the gate of the park, and the more affluent could reserve boxes for a dollar and a dollar and a half. *Exponent* and *Daily Student* editors promoted the game. The Bloomington paper predicted a thousand Indiana students would go to Indianapolis, and it hoped for even more. The editor almost shouted that finances should keep no one away. It might be a genuine sacrifice for some to spend two or three dollars, "but who is there who would not spend double that amount to see Purdue defeated?" asked the paper. If a student was broke and had no friend to lend him the money, then the *Daily Student* stood ready to advance funds. Bloomington businessmen had raised $250 to make sure the town made a good showing on Saturday, and the student editor promised to turn every bank vault in Bloomington inside out for more.

Indianapolis papers were hardly more temperate. They reported a high pitch of interest by local supporters of both Indiana and Purdue. "The Indiana-Purdue game will be somewhat in the nature of an innovation in the way of football in Indianapolis," said a special to the *Student*, "as those in charge are going to add interest by making this struggle a sort of society event with all the significance of an eastern game." Governor Winfield T. Durbin and his staff, Mayor John W. Holtzman and other city officials, students from the high schools and representative citizens of the city would be in attendance. Four excursion trains hauling about 1,000 students from each university would converge on Indianapolis. Bands from Indiana and Purdue would add to the noise and confusion, and it was hoped everybody would be waving pennants. Opinion was divided between the partisans of each team as to the outcome of the game, but the local gamblers remained on neutral ground and bet "even-stephen."

In Lafayette the *Courier* of October 21 raised a discordant note of defeat and doom. It had little confidence in the Purdue players. The editor thought the team should be organized to win or be disbanded altogether. He did not approve of maintaining a team for any other purpose, and certainly not to satisfy the ego of Indiana University. "The businessmen of Lafayette," said the editor, "have rendered substantial aid to Purdue athletics and the people generally have generously assisted on all occasions, so there can be no well-grounded complaint of lack of public appreciation."

Another discordant howl was heard in Lafayette. The Purdue team had played Beloit College of Wisconsin that fall. The visiting team had a Negro member, and angry shouts had gone up, "Kill the nigger!" The *Exponent* took up this unseemly incident and speculated, "Does a Negro belong on the football team of any white man's school? No! Football is a white man's game and let us play it, as Purdue does, with white men." This outburst of racial bigotry stirred a bit of a tempest in college papers and editors elsewhere expressed their views on the subject.

In Bloomington Coach Horne and his assistants honed the Hoosiers to a fine playing edge. On October 21 they stopped heavy scrimmage because they wanted no one injured. The coaches were not alone in their preparations for the big day. Students organized a rooters' club of "seventy lusty-lunged" cheerleaders equipped with megaphones. This mob called itself the "Howling Hundred" and promised to jar Indianapolis off its pinnings with its mighty vibrations. So high did excitement run along the Jordan that President Bryan, that imperturbable Irishman, was snatched into its swell. He agreed to forego a chapel meeting and turn the hour over to students to practice their yells.

Things were indeed moving. "Indiana rooters are mad with enthusiasm," said the *Daily Student*. "Ever since chapel this morning they have been unable to contain themselves & volley after volley of exultant yells of confidence, are re-echoing from all points of the campus & city." When the band struck up *Gloriana* in the chapel, the old place fell apart. Dunn's Woods reverberated with wild cries of:

> Gloriana, Frangipana, Indiana!
> Ka-Zoo! Ka-zah! Ka-zah! Ka-zuh!
> U-Hurra! U-Hurra!
> Hoopla! Hoopla!
> State University! Rah! Rah! Rah!

and then:

> Poor P.U.! They're easy to do,
> They never were in it;
> Not even a minute.
> Poor P. U.!

The Hoosiers had other cries, all of them designed to make a maximum amount of noise. Never before had so many Indiana University students demonstrated in unison, and in what G. Stanley Hall in 1904 called, "psychic infantilism" or "babyism." Campus and town were in a turmoil of mad adolescent excitement. The *Daily Student* said in the morning more than a thousand persons would be on their way to Indianapolis aboard two special trains. The Monon promised room for everyone and timely arrival in the capital city. Long streamers with the legend, "Indiana," in red block letters were tacked to the side of the coaches. President and Mrs. Bryan would be aboard in a sedate compartment, and as soon as the trains reached Indianapolis a long parade would form and make its way to the Claypool Hotel. From there street cars would transport the crowd to Washington Park in time for the 2:45 P.M. kick-off.

The special trains left Bloomington on time and excitement begun in chapel two days before reached a rising crescendo aboard the cars. Everyone seemed to cooperate by waving a pennant or waving something red. "Commonsense and composure" had been left on the banks of the Jordan, and near insanity possessed the crowd. Thus William Lowe Bryan led his army, Ka-zuhing-Ka-zahing, up through the cornfields of the White River bottoms to the battleground in Washington Park.

As the train pulled into the station an uninformed stranger might have gotten the notion that the railroad was hauling train loads of neurotic guineas with their monotonous cry, "Ka-zuh, Ka-zah." Then there fell a deathly silence. James William Fesler, a member of the board of trustees, met the train to tell the Indiana rooters of the tragedy which had befallen the Purdue team at 18th Street. He had an automobile waiting and took President Bryan immediately to the scene of the train wreck on the Big Four.

Like the Monon, the Big Four Railroad Company had provided two special trains to bring Purdue fans and their team from Lafayette. Instead of organizing trains of its better coaches the railroad supplied inferior cars and locomotives. Some of these were of wood construction. Unluckily the Purdue team rode in a decrepit old wood coach on the front end of the first train. As was later determined, the railway dispatchers on this lazy fall Saturday morning were negligent in transmitting proper instructions along the line. A result was that the first special train plowed headlong into a string of coal cars which a switch crew had pushed onto the main line. Fourteen players, their trainer, Patrick McClaire, and one fan were killed almost instantly, and forty-one others were injured. Chaos prevailed at the scene of the wreck, and the usual exaggerations spread as to the extent of the tragedy. One of the first persons to reach the splintered wooden coaches said he had been riding farther back in the train and scarcely felt the impact. At the front end of the train he saw boys dead or dying among the shattered timbers of the antique cars, while others screamed in pain.

What had been planned as a day of gay parades and football pyrotechnics turned into one of somber processions. Every ambulance, fire wagon, police vehicle, and dozens of private conveyances were commandeered as ambulances. Hospitals and morgues were crowded with the injured and dead. Telegraph facilities were practically paralyzed by an overload of frantic messages. President Bryan found President Stone at St. Vincent's Hospital and they went together to the Denison House where they conferred on what action to take. Athletic Director and Coach James Horne told an Indianapolis *News* reporter, "The thing is so terrible, so lamentable, it came to me with double force because most of those Purdue boys were my personal friends. . . . Purdue and Indiana are athletic rivals, but they are friends, & every Indiana man is heart-stricken."

Indiana rooters, in funereal mood, returned to Bloomington. The full extent of the tragedy at 18th Street was still unrevealed. A story in the Indianapolis *News* did heighten the excitement. It said that an air of catastrophe was noticeable in Bloomington at departure time from the Monon station because railway officials had to go through three crews of trainmen before they could find one to take the special trains to Indianapolis. It was said they had a premonition of tragedy. When finally the first train was underway, none of the 1,200 passengers were aware of a dangerously close call at Limedale. It was said the trucks of the front coach jumped the rails and plowed along the ties for some distance before hopping back on the track. The engineer was quoted as saying he sensed trouble but did not stop. A headlong plunge at that point would have sent two thirds of Indiana's student body and faculty into eternity. This folk story insulted the Monon officials. They said there was no trouble about a train crew, and there was ample physical evidence to disprove the leaping coach story.

The Purdue tragedy added another woe to the already gloomy fall of 1903. On November 2 the *Daily Student* carried a long dirge entitled *The Dying Heroes*. Members of the Indiana football team prepared an extensive memorial in the form of a letter of condolence, an original of which reposes in the University Archives. Official memorial services were held in chapel, and a campaign to raise a memorial fund was begun. Representatives from the university, including President Bryan, went to Lafayette to attend special services there.

In the meantime in Indianapolis, Coroner Harry Tutewiler opened what became a fantastic series of hearings to fix the blame for the wreck. At the outset officials of the Big Four undertook to pin the blame on W. H. Shumaker and L. Irvan, engineer and fireman. Shumaker, it was revealed, had actually jumped from the locomotive after setting the brakes on the light engine, and fireman Irvan had crawled up on top of the coal tender. After interminable hearings in which the newspapers published one sensational story after another, the coroner finally fixed the blame on H. C. Byers, the dispatcher at the central station in Kankakee, Illinois. He had failed, said Tutewiler, to notify switchmen in the Indianapolis yards of the approach of the Purdue special.

One of the reasons Indiana University officials had agreed to the football game in Indianapolis in the first place was to rescue its athletic program from bankruptcy. In the midst of public mourning, the treasurers of the two athletic associations met in Indianapolis to try to determine the depths of their financial disaster. They agreed to present themselves at Huder's Drug Store on two specified days to redeem tickets. The Indianapolis *News* made clear to the public that students and members of the two alumni associations should not ask for refunds. Purdue had unsecured expenses of $600, and James H. Horne said Indiana could not meet its obligations at once. Failure to play the game threw the Indiana Athletic Association into hopeless indebtedness. There was not money enough to pay a $500 advance to a valuable assistant coach who was considering another job. There was even doubt that the football team could afford to play the rest of the schedule. One of the remaining games was with Illinois, which was certain to cost $500 and which Indiana had no hope of raising.

On November 4, 1903, the *Daily Student* said, "The statements of Coach Horne this morning on the financial outlook of athletics at Indiana should make it clear to everyone connected with the University that our athletic finances are in such a shape that it will be a long time before they can be put on a basis of solvency.

According to Mr. Horne we are $2,000 in debt with absolutely no assets, except the football outfits & a small amount of other paraphernalia. Plainly speaking we are almost bankrupt." Lack of funds brought about immediate discontinuance of the players' training table. In addition students were asked to donate money with which to purchase football sweaters. The team had made it clear that its members would not be satisfied with lettered caps.

This incident in Indiana University history revealed to everyone how thin was the margin of support for subsidiary programs. For William Lowe Bryan it was clearly another bit of evidence that the administration could not adhere to any set idealistic formula for the future advancement of a basic university or intellectual program of higher education. The university and its people were too vulnerable to the mishaps of the workaday world about it, and the ivory tower could not be isolated from the normal forces of the society in which it flourished. An Indianapolis coroner searching for the cause of a train wreck, treasurers of athletic associations trying frantically to placate disappointed purchasers of tickets, and the discontinuance of the football training table bore little if any direct relationship to new programs in architecture, engineering, business, and music, but they were necessary parts of the bigger overall affairs of a public university.

Only in degree were the Indiana baseball and basketball teams more successful. It was amazing really that teams in these sports were able to gather any equipment or find coaching. Financing athletics was left largely to students who could make personal contributions, solicit aid from Bloomington merchants, or take part in minstrel shows to raise money. None of these sources proved highly productive. James Horne felt neither public nor students comprehended the cost of equipping the university teams. He estimated that it would necessitate the expenditure of $2000 to buy uniforms and footballs and to pay traveling expenses, or $20 to $25 per man. After a heartbreaking humiliating season of 1903, Horne suggested that the time had come to charge students fifty cents admission fee to each game; most other schools he said charged seventy-five cents.

The rules of the Big Nine Conference were thought to work a hardship on Indiana University by requiring that players come to the campus untouched by professionalism. This was a difficult rule to observe because southern Indiana boys especially earned modest summer incomes by playing sandlot baseball for hire. For years after 1899 there were embarrassing moments caused by discovery that a boy was ineligible either having failed to report his employment, or being ignorant of the fact that it counted against him. Such a case was that of Frank Wade, a football player, who had been out of school a year before his re-entry into the university, and Coach Horne pleaded this was not a violation of the rules.

While worrying about eligibility problems in October, 1903, the football coach was confronted by breach of morals of another sort. Earlham College sought to cancel its game with Indiana on the grounds that too many of its players were injured for the college to field a team. Horne learned that the true reason was that Earlham preferred to play Hanover on that date. Once the wrangle was resolved Indiana had the satisfaction of smashing the Quakers 39 to 0.

During his first year as president William Lowe Bryan was to learn intimately what agitated his colleagues in the Big Nine. He had outlined for him in clear examples the nature of the problems he would face for the next thirty-five years. There was a demand that football players especially be fed at a special training table, and the *Daily Student* suggested that keeping player plates filled with beefsteak and potatoes would result in faster and longer end runs in the dining room than would occur later on Jordan Field.

Perhaps the great end run around the training table was caused partly by "Cupid" Walter Railsback, the star of the team. This behemoth had come from Ohio and possessed enough tact to flatter his Hoosier colleagues by saying Indiana air agreed mightily with him, except it caused him to lose his hair. "Many of the fair young eyes long to count the hairs beneath 'Cupid's' headgear," said the *Daily Student*. The big test, however, was not counting hair, but came on a Friday afternoon, November 6, 1903, when Illinois came to Jordan Field. Students persuaded Bloomington merchants to close shop for this occasion, and made jubilant predictions that henceforth the town and campus would enjoy a common bond in loyalty to the "Crimson and Cream." The Hoosiers beat Illinois 17 to 0, and the campus was thrown into turmoil. A mob of 1200 students and townsmen trailed the band to the Square for an orgy of yelling and speechifying. They did not forget, however, to be frugal, and before the mob disbanded for supper they had raised only $20.00 with which to thank Coach Horne. Orders were given for everybody to return after supper, and following James Whitcomb Riley's lecture, to take up the yelling all over.

The next day the Bloomington *Telephone* reported that the crowd had exploded anvils and fireworks, and men and boys cavorted around dressed in nightshirts. "If anyone has a doubt," it said, "of the hold football has upon the people it would have been a revelation to have been on Jordan Field. . . . Even old men seemed wild with joy and seemed to forget their senses in their enthusiasm."

The howling mob may have been happy over the season, despite the grim Purdue tragedy, but the football players and U. H. Smith were less than enthusiastic. Cash was almost nonexistent. Apparently there was confusion about the awarding of letters, and the players appeared with "I's" turned upside down on their sweaters. In fact they were wearing the letters before they had actually been awarded, or the letters had been sent players with the instruction that they were to wear them concealed on their backs. The team had incurred costs of $5,100.06 and had created a deficit of $1,543.06, toward payment of which students had contributed $79.95.

So limited were athletic facilities for other sports, said the *Student*, that the university could not have both a basketball and indoor track team. Neither team, declared the paper, was a moneymaker—quite to the contrary, it lost money faster than the football team. Coach Horne found himself in the dilemma of developing very good track talent, or of disbanding a mediocre basketball team. This was the year that the first Negro was to take part in track sports. Some arrangement finally must have been made for basketball because the team opened the season in a game with Salem High School, and went on to win victories over five college teams, including Purdue.

In track the following spring Ted Shideler won second place in the 110 meter Olympic trials. So limited were funds, however, that it was decided in 1904 to hire no professor-coach and to leave the training of track athletes and baseball players to the teams' captains. Apparently Captain James Boyle had some success with baseball except for the rhubarb which developed in the seventh inning of the DePauw game when an Indiana player was removed from the field for an infraction. Indiana was ahead 5 to 3, and refused to continue the game.

No real progress had been made during President Bryan's first years to improve financial support for athletics. No real understanding had been reached as to whether athletics was a part of the educational program or simply an entertainment adjunct of student life. The grandstand on Jordan Field was inadequate, unsafe, and unsightly. It gave a bad impression, said critics, to visitors in the university. The low-lying field itself needed raising and draining. Funds to finance this work had to come from most reluctant private sources, and President Bryan in September, 1905, called for the organization of an athletic association to raise money. At times the young president must have felt that he was doubly burdened with both university and athletic financial worries.

While Bryan pleaded for assistance in raising money to field a football team, Chicago newspapers supplied a touch of humor. They accused halfback Willis Coval of trying to steal the University of Chicago's signals and trick plays just prior to the Indiana game. Coval admitted he was in the city to attend a wedding but he was innocent of the charges of thievery. Coach Horne scoffed at the story. If Willis did steal Chicago's signals and trick plays they must have been Alonzo Stagg's discards because the score was 56 to 0 against the Hoosiers.

Perhaps Indiana felt another sting in the fall meeting of the Big Nine Conference when delegates undertook to hold onto a glimmer of academic respectability by requiring athletes to remain in school a full semester and pass all their courses before becoming eligible to participate in games. Claude Elmer Price, a student of Ernest H. Lindley, made an extended study of "The Relation of Athletics to Scholarship at Indiana University." After comparing athletes and nonathletes over a period of four years he found no appreciable differences.

William Lowe Bryan, along with his Big Nine colleagues, was not only concerned about meeting standards of scholarship, but he foresaw a real difficulty for the future over the issue of recruiting athletes, football players especially. On October 15, 1904, he wrote President Charles Van Hise of Wisconsin,

On returning from Columbia, I discussed the one year rule with our Professor [Martin Wright] Sampson, who represents this University upon the Big Nine Committee. I shall ask Professor

Sampson to make a statement as to the discussions and conclusions of that Committee. For my own part, there is no question connected with athletics which concerns me so deeply as the apparent toleration by those in authority of improper methods of securing athletes. I regret to say that I have practically first-hand knowledge of cases where those in the highest authority have done something more than wink at what is practically the purchase of foot ball material. This sort of thing makes me heart sick. I am most willing to join with you and with all others of like mind to fight this sort of corruption out of the Universities. If the one year rule would help the business, and I judge that it would do so, at least, in some measure, I shall be heartily for it. It seems to me that the best method of securing this rule is its official adoption by the Big Nine Association.

No doubt President Bryan's feelings at the moment were agitated by a letter he received from John M. Heenan of Heenan's Smoke House in Terre Haute. Splashed across the letterhead was the proclamation that this neighboring institution sold cigars, pipes, tobacco, and, it was implied, beer. Mr. Heenan addressed his request to the "president of I.U. College," and requested permission to use Jordan Field as a training ground for the Grand Rapids Michigan Baseball Club. He said the weather in the northern city was so fierce that the club was badly handicapped in its spring training. Mr. Heenan thought the presence on the campus of the Grand Rapids nine would prove a great advantage to the university boys because they could observe experts in action. For this privilege Heenan only asked board and room, ample use of the gymnasium, division of all gate receipts, and use of all other university facilities. His team would be in Bloomington from April 6 to 26. In a bold hand stimulated no doubt by livid anger Bryan scrawled across the letter, "What do you think of this? W. L. B."

W. L. B. should have sent Mr. Heenan the minutes of the reconstructed Athletic Association which began functioning in April of that year, or, better still, the baseball scores for Indiana's 6 to 5 eleven game season. The Athletic Association was the outgrowth of dire need for money, a new coach, and more student control of athletics. Forty students and ten faculty members met in Bowles Hotel on February 3, 1905, and discussed plans to form the new body. Actually the movement was begun in 1904, but the illness of Coach James Horne had delayed action. Both faculty and student leaders shared the President's views of athletics, "The athletic interests of Indiana need funds. To provide sufficient amounts the Association is a necessity. Students who have watched athletic developments here for several years express themselves as confident that the thing in which Indiana is deficient is the lack of organized support given the teams." Bryan believed a new approach had been made to the solution of the nagging problem of developing self-sustaining and successful teams.

At the moment the Athletic Association was being formed, a bright ray of cheer broke through the haze of uncertainty. Leroy Perry Samse of Kokomo broke the world's indoor pole vault record in a meet with Wabash College when he cleared the bars at 11 feet 5¼ inches. Samse became one of Indiana's greatest athletes. At Cincinnati on January 27, 1906, he demonstrated that his feat against Wabash was no fluke by bettering his mark by a quarter inch. On June 2, in a meeting with Northwestern, Samse pushed the new world outdoor pole vault record to 12 feet 4⅞ inches. Unfortunately this boy did not continue in Indiana University to graduate.

Otherwise the athletic program of the university was in jeopardy. The fall season opened in 1905 with no coach. Captain Chester Harmeson drilled the basketball team seven days a week, holding a practice hour just before church time on Sundays. Under the leadership of G. H. Ritterskamp and Carl Carr the tentative Athletic Association became most active. President Bryan requested that the association be run like a business. "Be sure," he wrote, "that the head of such an association backed by those he represents may be able to meet all obligations. The University cannot pay debts not contracted by it. . . . I do not mean as president of the University, but as an individual for I have no authority from the board of trustees to employ a football coach."

Bryan had stated only one problem relating to athletic management. In October that year and for about the fourth time students reconstituted the Athletic Association. In doing so the ugly head of petty campus politics had raised its grisly head. Provisions were made in the latest constitutional revision for the president and one board of control member to be of one political faith, and the other two members to represent an opposite party. Finally the constitution was ratified by the first 100 members to join the new association and pay their $2 fee. It was understood that upon ratification of the new document the Athletic Association would have charge of athletics in the university. The *Daily Student* said, "Every effort has been made to minimize politics in the affairs of the association, and to eliminate every loop-hole which would give the least possible chance for graft." This constitution was ratified on the evening of October 16, 1905, when enthusiasm ran high, and more than the initial quota of students joined. The completed and revised constitution was printed the first time in the *Daily Student* the next day. G. H. Ritterskamp, a senior from Freelandsville, was elected president, and sometime early that fall the association determined the fact that the popular and long-suffering James H. Horne was physically incapable of returning as coach, and they approached James H. Sheldon, a young Chicago lawyer of the firm of Manning, Sheldon, and Keehn, and a pupil of Alonzo Stagg, to take his place. Sheldon came to the Indiana campus under the serious handicap of the newly adopted Big Nine freshman-one year rule. The ranks of upperclassmen on the Jordan were thin. In his first season Sheldon tied Purdue 11 to 11, a good start. That game, played in Indianapolis, left emotional scars. The two schools had to pay local promoters $923 for use of the private playing field, and two-thirds of the cost for erecting bleachers. Despite the angry charge of extortion the two universities netted $3,100 apiece.

Within a fortnight of the Purdue meeting, Indiana defeated Notre Dame 22 to 5. A short time later the local circus magnate, Henry Gentry, hauled his bleachers onto Jordan Field in order to seat a thousand fans for the Wabash game. The Hoosiers were set wild by the 40 to 0 crushing they gave their ancient rival. There was, however, a note of nostalgia in the celebration because Indiana would be forced to drop Wabash from its next schedule because of the Big Nine's freshman-one year rule. Sheldon capped his first season with an 11 to 0 victory over rough and undisciplined Ohio State. Several Indiana players suffered broken bones, and charges of dirty playing by the Buckeyes were more numerous than center rushes.

The Ohio State slaughter only aggravated further an agonizing and growing nationwide opposition to football. In both Indiana and across the country there was a threat of taking legal and moral action to abolish the game from American life. President Bryan declared, "I shall be glad to join in any substantial movement for the betterment of football. The evils which must be made odious and which must be eliminated are: (1), current methods of securing players; and (2), the intentional injury of men. Clean and manly football has my hearty approval." In the football season of 1905, eighteen players nationally were killed and 150 seriously injured; the next year 11 were killed and 104 injured.

For Indiana the 1905 football season was a booming success. The university won eight games, tied one, and lost to Chicago, earning 240 points to its opponents' 38. On December 10, the Intercollegiate Rules Committee met in Philadelphia to discuss new regulations. Walter Camp of Yale presided, and the committee decided to create a central body of referees who would be given individual field control of games, and stiff penalties were established for official evasion of rules. This was the beginning of a long process of trying to civilize the game of football.

Back in Bloomington a pall of frustration hovered over the playing season despite the success of the football team. The seniors failed to receive their class sombreros from the supplier in time for the Wabash game. Even more frustrating, seventeen freshmen players had journeyed to Vincennes to play that school's nonexistent football team. When they arrived in the historic town they discovered they were victims of a hoax perpetrated by a lad named John Hopkins who posed as manager of the self-styled Vincennes University Athletic Association. He said he was promoting a match between his private team and the Indiana University freshmen for publicity's sake. The penniless Indiana Athletic Association had to pay expenses, and "Everyone," said the campus paper, "was very angry." Freshmen were arbitrarily assessed fifty cents each to bail out their fellows.

In the first flush of success in October against Purdue the exuberant Ritterskamp instructed Coach Sheldon to inform the football players that if they had a good season the Athletic Association would give each of them a gold watch fob in the shape of a football. The players delivered but Ritterskamp could not. Sheldon told him in March, 1906, the delivery of the fobs had now become a matter of principle, and the players threatened to strike if they were not rewarded. With even so careful and frugal a bookkeeper as Zora Clevenger, however, the athletic budget was incapable of meeting any unnecessary expenditures. Clevenger had paid all debts, except the watch fobs, paid the coach's salary, and was well nigh in the black.

"Jimmy" Sheldon enjoyed President Bryan's favor from the start. Bryan was a vigorous supporter of the university's athletic teams. Frequently he was on the playing fields or in the gymnasium. Sometimes he opened football practice by kicking out the ball. In December, 1905, he and Mrs. Bryan gave a dinner in their home for thirteen lettermen and members of the Athletic Association Board of Control. He was determined, however, that the university would assume no fiscal responsibilities for sports.

Before James H. Sheldon returned to his Chicago law office in the spring of 1906, he had promised to return to Indiana the next fall. He at first refused because he did not wish to coach a "green" squad, but finally accepted the $1000 salary to be paid out of association funds. In the meantime James B. Angell called for a meeting of Big Nine university presidents to adopt the rule that the employment of coaches would be subject to the approval of boards of trustees. In April, for the first time in the university's history, Bryan asked that the Indiana board approve the employment of Sheldon as coach. Sheldon was to remain until 1913, the longest period any Indiana football coach was to serve with the exception of Alvin N. (Bo) McMillin, whose term lasted from 1934 to 1947.

In time the greatest emphasis at Indiana came to be placed upon football. Organized boosters supported it and enough excitement was generated to permit chartering special trains to haul fans at low rates to Lafayette, Indianapolis, and Chicago. President and professors spoke to students frequently on the values of a broadly based sports program, but when the headcount was taken and the books were audited, it was football that had drawn the crowds and made the money. It was football that became the center of collegiate pageantry. On Friday afternoons cheerleaders helped to release the primitive killer instincts of crowds. On Jordan Field almost every scrimmage promised grim tragedy in the form of a broken neck, bones, or serious internal injury. Yet a fleet halfback could break away for a run from one end of a modest cornfield to the other to score and send fans into paroxysms of joy. For the duration of the games the clumsy old bleachers of Jordan Field, supplemented by those from Frank Gentry's main tent, were democratizers. A man waving a crimson and cream banner was for the moment the equal of his seatmate, be he banker or saloon loafer.

Jimmy Sheldon, rather than that nameless hero who coached

the girls' basketball teams and led the balloon-clad seniors to a thumping 8 to 5 victory over the juniors, was campus hero. In a more modest way the track team recruited Jack O'Brien from its ranks as coach, and the rooters took serious notice of this sport only when Leroy Samse cleared the bars in his fabulous leaps. Three tennis courts were opened in 1906, and Professor James A. Woodburn promoted the first tournament in this sport in university history. Tennis, however, teetered somewhere between being too fast and skillful a game or being too effeminate to draw attention from football. Basketball and baseball were much more popular. One of these sports was emerging into popularity and the other was waning. In the winter season, 1905–1906, the basketball team had achieved sufficient success to cause the *Daily Student* to agitate giving its members the big "I."

As predicted in the spring of 1904, Jimmy Sheldon's second year lacked the glitter of his first. Purdue broke off athletic relations with the university because of the medical school controversy. Indiana rooters moralized, "Since our old rival, Purdue 'turkeyed' in athletic relations with Indiana, because she knew the State team would wipe the earth with the Old Gold and Black this year, we now call the attention of the editor of the Purdue *Exponent* to the fact that he has nothing to say about how we do things at Indiana. If the only way he can fill up his sheet is by scandalous misrepresentation of Indiana spirit, he has our consent, for [i]n journalism as in football, Indiana has Purdue beat a city block. . . ." To make up for the loss of the Purdue game three hundred Indiana rooters went off to Chicago aboard a special train to see Stagg's men smash the sagging Hoosiers 33 to 8. There was slight solace a week later when the "Big Red" demolished DePauw by a score of 55 to 0, in the first game after the two schools had resumed athletic relations. The Hoosiers closed the home schedule with a 12 to 0 victory over Notre Dame, and won the state championship. In the closing game of the season with Minnesota an innovation was made. The progress of the game was reported by telegraph in the Student Building, and a roar of angry protest, well out of earshot of Minneapolis, went up when the referee admitted he had made a too hasty decision which gave the Gophers the game 8 to 6.

Hardly had the Gophers and Hoosiers left the field before the Big Nine Conference adopted further major rule changes. No more than seven games could be played in a year by a conference team, and two of these had to be designated "minor." Players were allowed to participate only three years, and the "one-year" rule was removed from minor sports. The new three-year rule was said to have eliminated six of Indiana's best football players in one lick. These caused some local supporters to suggest that Indiana withdraw from the Big Nine.

A sobering fact in the resulting turmoil over conference rules was the proposal that Chicago, Michigan, Wisconsin, and Minnesota form a Big Four conference. At Bloomington, however, calmer heads, led by Professor Ulysses Grant Weatherly, chairman of the faculty athletics committee, insisted that organization of the Big Four conference would not be the end of all things athletic, and that Indiana should remain in the conference. Jimmy Sheldon also opposed Indiana's withdrawal from the Big Nine. "I can see no reason," he said, "why Indiana should withdraw from the Big Nine and I think such a step taken now would be unwise, to say the least. By remaining in the Big Nine we can still be the 'big guns' in the state, despite the fact that Wabash is now claiming the all-around state championship, and then, too, we will continue to be recognized as one of the big athletic colleges of the West. If Indiana should withdraw she would be classed as a State college, and not a Western university." Students, however, wished to withdraw. They argued Indiana could still play Chicago, and without Indiana the Big Nine Conference would fall apart, but in it the Hoosiers would have to submit to the obnoxious eligibility rules.

While football fans fumed over Big Nine rule changes, baseball supporters took heart for the 1907 campaign. Fred Beebe, the star St. Louis National League pitcher, came to Bloomington to coach the Hoosiers until March. Further help arrived when "Johnny" Fisher of the Indianapolis League enrolled as a student. The next year "Doc" Hillerbrand arrived on the campus and Indiana scheduled nineteen games, winning ten of them. Whether or not it was the injection of a certain element of professionalism into baseball by the appearances of big league players, there was a great deal of swearing and vulgarity that could be heard above the roar of the fans. The *Daily Student* editor commented there "is the foulest practice in vogue about the university and one that should be frowned upon on every occasion. . . ." The editor thought the offenders had no business associating with decent people, even on Jordan Field.

Indiana and Purdue resumed athletic relationships in January, 1908. Both university administrations thought that the bitter furore over medicine had calmed enough that it would be safe to sign contracts to compete in all sports during the coming year. The first game played following the renewal of competition was in basketball on February 7, 1908, in which Indiana won 26 to 21.

Although the Bloomington-Lafayette rivalry again added luster to athletic affairs in both schools, Indiana rooters had almost a phobia about playing the University of Chicago, even though they had little hope of defeating a Stagg-coached team. On March 3, 1908, Jimmy Sheldon wrote Amos Alonzo Stagg, who was vacationing in Miami, Florida, asking his old coach to favor him with a later and more favorable date than the one early in October. Sheldon told Stagg, "As you know, I have a comparatively green bunch of material to work with and they get better as the season advances. A bad defeat early in the season sets them back, as you know. I have a particularly good lot of material this year and I am confident that I can have a very good team. I should like very much to make a creditable showing against you this year and I know you are glad to have me do that every year. . . . Of course, I am dependent upon this game with you and if you cannot give me any other date, than the 10th, I shall have to accept that." Stagg was obstinate and refused a later date.

Sheldon told Stagg he was happy about the resumption of athletic relations with Purdue. By that time each school had defeated the other in home games in basketball, and Indiana had defeated Purdue decisively in a track meet, so the pot of state rivalry once again boiled furiously. The big moment, however, came on November 23, when the football teams met in Lafayette. Fans were insistent with their bets. It was said the Lahr House in Lafayette resembled a betting exchange. Bets went 10 to 6 that Purdue would win, or even money it would win by 6 points. One fan was said to have wagered a $1000, another $400. Most students bet five or ten dollars. Indiana broke a seven year losing streak with a 10 to 4 score. Before the game Coach Sheldon had played on the emotions of his players in a pep talk. With tears streaming down his cheeks he said, "Boys, I've done everything I could for you; now, go in and win this my last game!" Cunningham had run 70 yards for a touchdown, and this was supplemented by a four-point drop kick.

There was happiness all the way around. The fans were elated. Gamblers chugged back to Bloomington with thousands of dollars of Purdue money in their pockets, and when the accounts were cleared the Athletic Association had collected $1750 from approximately 7000 fans. The song of victory, however, was short. Lawyer Sheldon announced the tug of clients in Chicago was stronger than that of the gridiron and he planned to resign.

Another sour note greeted the happy warriors at home. President Bryan and his faculty athletic committee awaited the return of student plungers with the wrath of an irate mother who awaited the coming of a wayward son. They expressed strong disapproval of wagering on athletic events, and threatened application of a stringent university rule against such moral lapses.

In 1909, Indiana went in search of a new coach. Sheldon invited John Koehler of the University of Colorado to take the place, but he refused. Perhaps he was somewhat influenced by Coach "Skel" Roach's criticism that, "there is too much 'lovey-dovey' business at I. U. for the good of the athletic teams. . . . I attribute the lack of spirit to the presence of the girls in the University." Sheldon, in spite of his tearful plea to the team in Lafayette and the public announcement of his resignation, remained in Bloomington until 1913.

Sheldon not only coached the football team, he controlled the use of Jordan Field, did his best to maintain rickety old bleachers, and tried to stay on the good side of Frank Gentry so as to use his supplementary seats at the end of the circus seasons. In 1909 he assumed charge of ticket sales, and fans were now issued annual season passes to all athletic events at $5.00 apiece. This was a shock to many Indiana fans. By October only 100 tickets had been sold in Bloomington in comparison with 1600 at Purdue. Despite the fact the Athletic Association had fared well the past fall in Lafayette it was still a thousand dollars in debt, and desperately needed income from season ticket sales.

Before time arrived for the next big Purdue conflict Bloomington tempers had flared. T. F. Moran, chairman of the Purdue Athletic Committee filed affidavits with the Big Eight Conference—by then Michigan had withdrawn—charging professionalism against Clarence Earl Cartwright of New Harmony, the star

Indiana player. This complaint, thought the Indiana fans, was filed unsportingly just before the Indiana-Purdue game, at a time when it would cause the greatest possible injury. Cartwright was charged with and admitted playing summer baseball for pay for Mount Vernon and Rockport. This charge backfired against Purdue, however. R. S. Shade, its star fullback, confessed he was a professional and had been ineligible under Big Eight rules for the whole season. Indiana had further revenge in the fact that it beat the Boilermakers 36 to 3. Receipts from that game finally erased its athletic fund deficit.

Indiana athletics by 1910 had become a matter of deep administrative concern and of increasing complexity within the university's organization. At the moment the academic program was undergoing radical changes, intercollegiate athletics were expanding far beyond anything anyone ever dreamed of happening. What had once been regarded as a loosely organized student activity had now become a major public relations vehicle which promised to have more bearing upon shaping the university's public façade than did the academic revolution.

Too, President Bryan became concerned about three aspects of the athletic program. First, gambling, especially on the Indiana-Purdue game, had become a public issue. Charges of professionalism, proved in the cases of Clarence E. Cartwright and R. S. Shade, had long been a menacing evil. Finally the indifferent performances of Indiana in the so-called minor sports did not conform with Bryan's formula of excellence for university endeavors. Equally disconcerting was the fact that only a small number of students was actually involved in any part of the athletic program.

In January, 1910, the faculty adopted a rule to combat professionalism by saying no student would be permitted to participate in intercollegiate contests for three consecutive semesters without special faculty permission. No student was permitted to earn more than three "I's" in a single year without special dispensation. Further, academic control of athletics was effected through the appointment of Dr. Charles P. Hutchins, former coach at the University of Wisconsin, as director of physical training. It was said that henceforth athletic management in Indiana University would resemble that of the English universities. This program now would be viewed as both internal and external and Dr. Hutchins would try to involve the entire student body in some kind of sports.

It was easy to plan a grandiose program but extremely difficult to execute it because of a lack of funds. After paying all expenses for the 1909–1910 season the Athletic Association was left with a balance of only $150. At the same time "Skel" Roach, baseball coach, demanded a substantial increase in salary. This caused Professor Harold Whetstone Johnstone to declare he would coach baseball himself before he would allow the committee to make such a commitment. In the meantime the dispute caused Indiana to fall behind the other Big Eight schools in spring practice. Roach gave in and returned to his job. In basketball the season ended in a slump, and there was a plea for the enlargement of Jordan Field.

In November, 1911, Indiana cleared $3,097 from the Purdue game, and brought away from Madison, Wisconsin, another $4,000. That year, too, Indiana celebrated the twenty-fifth year of football on the campus by listing some distinguished alumni of the game. A few of these were Attorney-General Thomas Honan, lawyers Harry McMullen and Albert Rabb, librarian W. E. Jenkins, and legislators Dick Miller and Frank A. Gause. That year 1200 tickets were sold for the homecoming game against Illinois, the largest number ever sold by that date. A fortnight later such a large crowd was expected in Bloomington for the Purdue game that the churches prepared to fatten their coffers by serving dinners to the visitors.

David Starr Jordan, in one of his denunciations of football, had proposed the substitution of rugby, and Dr. Hutchins introduced this game to Indiana in the American form of soccer in 1911–12 as an interclass sport. Erick Wilson, called by the *Daily Student*, "a real Johnny Bull," was employed as coach. A letter was to be awarded soccer players, even though the sport lacked intercollegiate status. Minor sports at Indiana, however, suffered from lack of patronage and fanfare. During the winter that year it was said fifteen sports were open to students. A new physical education curriculum had been instituted by the faculty and Dr. Hutchins. Worn facilities, including the sweaty old gymnasium, were refurbished, but still there was urgent need for a new and bigger structure. By this year student enrollment had increased to 1241, and student physical needs had grown even faster.

National intercollegiate athletic interest centered on football, and in February, 1912, representatives of the Big Eight Conference met in Chicago and voted for even more fundamental rule changes. The playing field was reduced to 100 yards, and a ten yard post zone was established. Downs were increased to four for ten yards, the on-side kick was eliminated, and the touchdown was made worth six points. In the same meeting Ohio State University was admitted to conference membership, making it once again the Big Nine. Indiana had served much of the time as the low team in the conference ratings, but now it would have company. That year there was gloom in all the sports. The basketball team did not win a single conference game, the football team had won only from DePauw and Earlham, and U. H. Smith reported the Athletic Association had ended the year $207.17 in debt, a condition which was not to improve the next year, even though the association cleared $2200 from the Purdue game.

The football team repeated in 1912 its dismal showing of the year before. Soccer was discontinued because of unbearably cold weather and lack of student interest. Rumor was again abroad that Jimmy Sheldon was discouraged and was again going back to Chicago for good. The Bloomington *Telephone* was quick to say, "Sheldon is the idol of the undergraduate at Indiana, and although the state school players have not won a conference game in two years, he has never once lost their confidence." Sheldon was "greatly disappointed at the showing made by the team," said the *Daily Student*, "and furthermore was greatly hurt by the 'knocks' which appeared in some places in regard to the coaching." On December 10, 1912, President Bryan spiked the rumor about Sheldon by announcing "Mr. Sheldon is to return next fall. Mr. Berndt is to become director of intercollegiate athletics, a position which has been for some time vacant. I believe thoroughly in both these men. They are men who in every kind of battle win a fair share of victories, but what is far more important, their coaching is a strenuous education of boys toward persistence, loyalty and courage, and other fundamental virtues of the will which go to make a man." Despite Dr. Bryan's brave words about character building, Dr. C. P. Hutchins said athletic endeavor in Indiana University was at a standstill because of inadequate funds and training quarters.

By this time, any victory would have been considered a major achievement. On April 24, 1913, the baseball team played the University of Wisconsin in Madison and won 9 to 3. The *Daily Student* said, "Three minutes after word came through 'the wire' a crowd of several hundred gathered, and marched through the Library, along by-ways of the campus, through 'sorority alley,' and down third street." The crowd finally reached Kirkwood where it rushed the Harris Grand Theater and then set upon the Rex. At the latter place the manager had summoned the police to protect his women and children patrons. The thwarted mob started a bonfire, using the theater's signs as tinder. Bloomington had an ordinance against building fires on the brick pavements, and police charged the fire and recovered the signs. A second fire was started on an opposite corner and officers then attacked students with telling effects. They drew revolvers, arrested students, hit some with their night sticks, and held many others at bay in the hallway of the First National Bank. One student was charged directly with inciting to riot and could not readily deposit a hundred dollar bond for his release.

In all the rock-throwing and commotion the front window of the sheriff's office was smashed and the temple of justice itself was threatened. Bands of citizens turned vigilantes and took the law in their own hands. All through the night there were incidents. The campus paper said all this was the work of a handful of hotheads who disgraced the university.

By this time President Bryan was a veteran at dealing with such incidents. A faculty committee was assigned the task of spying out the guilty, healing the wounds, and restoring order. The Business and City Council declared it had no objections to demonstrations so long as property remained undamaged. The manager of the Rex Theater agreed to allow students to "rush" his house provided they notified him in time for him to clear it of patrons. Other theater and restaurant operators agreed to rushing on the same basis. City officials asked that student marshals be appointed to assist police in quelling such spontaneous upheavals. By the time the baseball team returned to town both students and citizens were too exhausted to welcome them. In fact victory had almost been forgotten in the discussion of issues in settling the "Kickapoo War" it had touched off.

The end of the 1913 football season, in which Indiana won 3 and lost 4 games, saw the end of Jimmy Sheldon's coaching career. He at last returned to the practice of law, and Indiana University hired Clarence C. Childs of Yale as his successor. Childs arrived in Bloomington in time to see the touring Chinese baseball team go down to defeat and Indiana defeat Illinois 13 to 2 in a heartwarming contest. The next week, however, Purdue ended the jubilation on Jordan Field with an 11 to 7 defeat in an eleven-inning game.

In the first week in September, 1914, the new coach led his charges out to a sylvan dale near Helmsburg in Brown County where he got acquainted with his lads. Later he returned to Jordan Field with them, and hopes were high for the new coach and the new season. Childs was enthusiastic about his team after the Helmsburg session, undaunted by the ominous sounds being made by DePauw rooters. Beyond that game, however, lay the acid tests with Chicago and Illinois on succeeding weekends. These materialized into 34 to 0 and 51 to 0 riots. So it now seemed Jimmy Sheldon's coaching was definitely not the trouble. Hoosier honor was a bit brightened by triumphs over Northwestern and Miami. These were fleeting moments because Ohio State and Purdue quickly put the Hoosiers back in their "place," leaving Childs with 3 wins and 4 losses.

From time to time after 1904, pressure groups of businessmen, alumni, ex-"I men", and students all exerted themselves. As an example, at the end of the football season in 1914 Clarence Childs refused to grant quarterback Frank Whitaker a letter. He claimed Whitaker had not obeyed coaching instructions because he preferred to play the "society game," and furthermore he had sassed the coach. Immediately campus clubs and social cliques took up Whitaker's cause and the recalcitrant boy was awarded his letter over the coach's advice. Following this incident a committee of lettermen was formed in Indianapolis to call upon President Bryan to seek alumni representation on the athletic committee. A month later President Bryan proposed a conference of faculty, students, and alumni to meet in Bloomington during the spring to discuss the university's athletic situation.

By the time of Bryan's appeal athletics, and especially football, had become an integral part of the very fabric of the university. There were now external pressures to be stemmed. Indiana University had not made, generally speaking, the kind of showing in competition with comparable schools that met Bryan's standards of excellence. It had become evident that the sharp state athletic rivalries influenced public attitudes toward the university. Indiana's poor showing within the Big Nine Conference placed the school in an uncomfortable position in dealing with other academic matters. The skilled athlete was definitely in demand and became the object of intense student interest as well as the bearer of the university's athletic fortunes.

When President Bryan's conference met in Bloomington in 1914 it seemed imperative that an investment of public funds be made in improving the university's physical plant. In no other way could the athletic or physical education programs be made to serve the student body and alumni. Definitely Indiana had outgrown the shabby old frame gymnasium and Jordan Field and its patched and sagging bleachers were growing unsafe.

The outbreak of World War I in Europe proved a highly disruptive force in intercollegiate athletics, and for those four years it was often difficult to separate interests between the playing field and war activities. Clarence Childs' search for victory and glory was short and Indiana turned to the Wisconsin star Ewald O. Stiehm for wartime leadership. In the meantime students took advantage of the exigencies of war to campaign for a new gymnasium under the guise of securing a building which could also be used as a national guard armory. By spring, 1915, Indiana University had outgrown all of its earlier concepts of the relationship of athletics to its academic program, and a new place was made for athletics in the university's domain. Also, the myth that a good athletic record in a public university was a significant boost in securing appropriations was disproved. Purdue's athletic teams were generally victorious, yet there was no perceptible difference in legislative attitudes in the biannual appropriations.

[IX]

The Hand of Mars

LIKE EVERY other university in the land in 1914, Indiana was caught in the vise of finding new intellectual directions. For a decade and a half its president, trustees, and faculty had worked at restructuring the institution. They labored in America's sophomoric age of national innocence, looking to the day when their labors would level out on the plains of accomplishment and realization. Boys came to college dressed as dandies, wearing button shoes, sailor straw hats, fancy clocked socks, blazers, loud ties, oversized fraternity pins, and looking forward with more zeal to the next dance than to the first class. Just to the north in Indianapolis, on the surface the political situation may have appeared innocent enough, but the quakes of readjusting political levels to new views had left the Republican Party divided between progressives and regulars. By division into factions the GOP camps virtually canceled each other out. The Democrats' star was rising. Under the leadership of Thomas R. Marshall, shrewd liberal lawyer, and Tom Taggart, political activist, the Democrats were able to identify opportunity when it presented itself, and in 1912 the call to action was as distinct as the roar of a rampant bull elephant. Thomas R. Marshall, succeeding the fairly liberal Republican Hanley, helped materially to modify some of the traditional educational directions in Indiana. At home, Marshall earned the respect he received as a practical minded progressive. In the history of the university he deserves a niche for having been the first governor to secure support for it commensurate with its new destiny. Too, with the help of several Indiana private college presidents he quietly resolved the jealousies and rivalries which had handicapped the state's educational system for almost a century. However, when Governor Woodrow Wilson swept Indiana by a majority of 120,000 votes over the Bull Moose Party, and 130,000 votes over the regular Republicans, a political breach opened which has yet spots of sensitivity.

Another publicly held misconception was outsiders' view of the state as being safely buried in midwestern complacency, if not political and geographical isolation. Its people were thought by some to be hardly conscious of the great world in the initial phases of the turmoil which threatened free men. This was indeed a mistaken notion. The university community, containing such men as Bert John Vos, Amos Shartle Hershey, Albert L. Kohlmeier, James A. Woodburn, Samuel Bannister Harding, Will D. Howe, and others, could hardly be charged with being oblivious to world conditions.

The first rift in the age of innocence or peaceful existence came in 1911–12, when Francisco Madero and his followers deposed Porfirio Díaz in a revolt looking to reform. There was distinct reaction on the banks of the Jordan to this conflict which promised conflict with Mexico.

This incident occurred just at the moment when William Lowe Bryan's administration had fairly well stabilized the medical school, had established several new colleges in Bloomington, and Dean Ruby Mason had brought dancing under a semblance of control. With one eye on students and another on the faculty, Bryan labored to keep his staff intact and to add new talent. In 1913, President Woodrow Wilson had embarked upon two years of sweeping reforms of government and its domestic relationships to the people. On a national scale Wilson was to attack public objectives with about the same degree of fervor that Bryan had exhibited in forming Indiana into a more complete university. Generally American public universities were entering the first stages of academic maturity with the advent of the new progressivism.

In the first year of the Wilsonian reforms, Bryan had attempted to resign the Indiana presidency but was persuaded to remain on the job. Little did he foresee what great adventure lay immediately ahead. Wilson's "New Freedom" had brought the force of the federal government closer home to the people as revealed in several areas of American life. This was especially true in areas involving social justice and the moral overtones in the administration of domestic and international affairs.

The conflict with Mexico which had brewed between General Victoriano Huerta and Francisco Madero within the next three years was to involve the Wilson administration deeply in Mexican affairs. As this dispute increased in tempo, and more American property rights in that country were threatened, the jingoist spirit in the United States asserted itself. William Randolph Hearst and his shrill editors and reporters all but screamed for war, a cry that was heard in southern Indiana. An even clearer voice was that of Theodore Roosevelt who over the years had developed friendships with Jordan and Eigenmann, and who was personally popular with other members of the faculty. He had also given his moth eaten ornithological collection to the university. When he accused Woodrow Wilson of kissing the blood stained hand that slapped his face he made an impression. It was even repeated locally that the president danced the Wilson Tango of one step forward and two steps backwards, a slide step, and a moment of hesitation. This was the only dance in a decade which failed to catch on in the university.

Huerta was charged by Hearst, American oil men, bankers, Senator A. B. Fall, Theodore Roosevelt, and others with being a stubborn, bloodthirsty bandit. Admiral Mayo on April 21, 1914, helped mightily to bring the Mexican disturbance to a dramatic head when he cut off a German merchantman loaded with arms and captured Vera Cruz.

Commencement that year was disturbed by jingoist talk. Students responded to the call for volunteers to become members of a company of the Indiana Infantry of the National Guard commanded by Colonel Theodore J. Louden. Hoosier students were to be trained as mounted scouts and would be supported by the Indiana band and a volunteer hospital company. Almost immediately the freshly recruited heroes were accompanied in a march through town by 50 of their fellow students. To lift their spirits even higher the parade passed Colonel Louden's door where he addressed them in clipped military style. The Bloomington Daily *Telephone* reported, "The student boys were wild with enthusiasm for conquest with Mexico and many signified their intention of enlisting in

President Wilson's call for volunteers." One student wrote the War Department, if it commissioned him a colonel he could enlist 500 volunteers from the student body, an offer which went unheeded.

This excitement in mid-April, 1914, disrupted the tranquility of the campus for almost a decade to come, and for the university it ended an era. This undramatic conclusion to the first great crusade to attain full university status by the school was misleading. Colonel Louden's martial oratory was hardly a clarion call to intellectual advancement.

From his porch reviewing stand, Bloomington's man of war gloated that he had secured uniforms for sixty band members, a thing which would convert that organization into a spectacular advertisement for the university, if it needed advertising in the mesquite flats along the Rio Grande. By May 25, the university's band was mustered into service with the state guard. This change in status was celebrated by another heroic march down Kirkwood Avenue, where bandsmen, volunteer guardsmen, soldiers, and students gave the occasion the flavor of a razzle-dazzle football victory parade. Before the volunteers could do more than take Fort Benjamin Harrison, the first war with Mexico was called off by intervention of the ABC Powers, and in July Victoriano Huerta went off into voluntary exile. Colonel Louden's braves came home with little more than blistered feet and soiled band uniforms to show for their service.

The border peace, however, was an uneasy one. Venustiano Carranza was incapable of controlling dissident forces within his country, and revolutionaries, or border bandits as they were called, under the leadership of the audacious Pancho Villa, disturbed the tenor of life along the southwest border of the United States. Once again the Hearst headlines screamed for vengeance against the marauders of the south, and war fever was on the rise. In Indiana University student volunteers formed Company I and prepared a second time to go away to war. The *Alumni Quarterly* virtually held the press open in order to get in a last minute story about the departure of the band and the hospital company. Almost hourly volunteers filled the ranks of Company I, and the Reverend T. R. White of the First Presbyterian Church was made captain, Professor Kenneth P. Williams of the mathematics department was second lieutenant. The new company was spic and span in fresh uniforms, and even Villa and his ragamuffin border marauders would have been impressed with the precise drill maneuvers which the men executed along Kirkwood Avenue before the Seventh Army inspector Captain John R. Toffe. On June 20, the company drilled in several places on the campus, and downtown business houses displayed the flag in their honor. The click of heel and rifle butt again disturbed the lazy summer mood of campus and town as warriors raised the dust on the march to Coutrhouse Square. Sober onlookers dourly observed that six almost certain members of the 1916 football squad were in the ranks.

Hardly had the Monon hauled the volunteers out of sight before a move was begun to collect funds to support them. U. H. Smith, the Bursar, was appointed treasurer, and R. V. Sollitt, Alumni Secretary, solicited alumni for a dollar each. The moment was made even more dramatic by the fact of Villa's firing on El Paso and President Wilson's order for the immediate departure of the guard from Fort Benjamin Harrison. The day before Company I left for Texas a private was sent back to the campus to recruit additional volunteers and he succeeded in finding eight new men.

The moment the militiamen departed Benjamin Harrison a move was begun for them to come home for school opening in September. This created some jealousy in the national guard units. There were fathers and businessmen who felt they should be the first to be released. For college boys, soldier life on the Texas border in August proved to be about as miserable as human beings could endure. Members of Company I wrote their friends to intercede in their behalf. They wrote there were many athletes in the company, and unless they mustered out soon prospects were dim for a football team that fall.

The War Department heeded student pleas, and what in mid-April were such cheerful warriors were to return in October homesick lads with many a woeful yarn to spin. In order to produce proof they were students they flooded the registrar's office with requests for affidavits that members of Company I were enrolled in the university. In the release of Company I a public versus private school argument occurred. Company I also contained Purdue boys, and volunteers from the private colleges contended they were being discriminated against because they were enrolled in other national guard units which did not come under War Department orders for release. This caused several Indiana Congressmen and Senator

John W. Kern to intervene with demands that all students be brought home. To complicate matters further there was an impending railroad strike which threatened delay. The *Telephone* said there was danger the War Department would use the private school and labor disputes as excuses to send no one home.

The squabble about returning the boys went on. The "impractical" Wilson administration was charged with indecision. It was not until September 7 that orders were finally issued to return Company I to the university. In Bloomington the people demonstrated that they had not forgotten the border veterans. The campus Boosters Club gave a rousing welcome when the Monon troop train rolled into the station at 7:30 P.M. October 2. Ten days later William Lowe Bryan and Ralph V. Sollitt met with both Company I and band members to discuss disposition of the alumni funds, and the next day the Company performed a last gallant military act before packing away its war gear. When the company had marched away in June it was accompanied to the train by Moses Sinclair, the last surviving veteran of the old Mexican War. Now Moses was dead, and Company I's summer veterans consigned his body to earth under cover of a proper gun fire salute.

Not all Indiana students returned to the campus with Company I. Still to come were thirty-four volunteers in the Second Indiana Hospital Corps. Dean Hepburn's son Sam was among them, and he wrote his parents the soldiers felt so thwarted by not confronting Villa that they fought a battle of their own making. This was what Sam called "The Battle of Brownsville," an engagement so fierce it was called the "greatest mimic battle on American soil." Sam had never heard of those other great sham battles of Resaca de la Palma and Matamoros fought on the same spot almost a century earlier.

"The Army of the Rio Grande," as the *Arbutus* called the Mexican border volunteers, came home with little if any military glory, but the annual said they stocked up on enough snake yarns and yarns of other sorts to last many a fireside evening. A merciless Texas sun and a sea of mesquite scorched the lads by day, and snakes, spiders, and tarantulas kept them company at night. The volunteers failed to glimpse Pancho and his "greasers," but their perspectives were broadened indeed by the leaden Texas horizon.

Mexico was but a prelude to the big war which almost immediately swept Indiana University into a vortex of emotion and disruption. Many faculty members and students seemed to realize that the incident in the Southwest was no more than a weak sideshow compared with the conflict which threatened in Europe. Hershey, Woodburn, Harding, and Kohlmeier concerned themselves deeply with issues rising abroad and with the foreign policies of the Wilson administration. Fundamentally it appears most of the professors were pro-Wilsonian in policy views if not in politics, and they were pronounced nationalists. There was no mythological midwestern isolationist myopia about their views and expressions.

At the outbreak of the European war Indiana staff members, who sensed its seriousness, regarded it as a dangerous play in power politics and undertook to explain it in these terms. Students who became aware of the struggle viewed it in a different light. In the excitement over the Mexican border troubles, the organization of a national guard company, and possible American involvement in the European struggle, they circulated a petition in January, 1915, asking that a permanent company of the Indiana National Guard be located on campus. Truthfully they had national preparedness less in mind than the possibility that such a maneuver would secure for them a gymnasium in the form of an armory. In this they were opposed by the faculty because the professors felt such a move would take unfair advantage of the public.

Agitation for the gymnasium was instigated largely by the active and vocal Boosters Club. Before any progress could be made, however, it was necessary to convince the faculty that it should also support the proposition. Boasts were made in the campus paper that 500 students had signed the national guard petition, and by February 8, there appeared to be a great deal of enthusiasm for the proposal. The *Student* explained, "Many things about the battalion appeal to the men of the University. The attractiveness & discipline of the drill practice, the benefit coming directly to the University from a financial standpoint & the chance for a ten day's outing at full pay are only a few of the features that impress the students."

Numbers of students signing the petition for the stationing of a permanent company of the national guard in the university were doubtless overstated in every case. Perhaps there were no more than 300 signers, if that many. It was obvious that supporters of the petition were a noisy minority. A backlash set in. The International Polity Club, composed largely of history and political science students, declared the move to bring the national guard onto the campus was "a militaristic measure and contrary to the best interests of the University." Following a lecture by Dr. George Nasmith of Harvard University on international peace, social sciences students circulated an anti-guard petition on March 11, 1915. Charles Crampton, chairman of the Boosters Club, and his followers undertook a countermove by seeking volunteers for guard duty. It was feared that delay would result in the loss of federal drill pay. Crampton was encouraged in his haste by several faculty members.

Thus the faculty entered its March meetings with strong contentions of two student groups to be considered. A claim was made that only certain members of the Polity Club subscribed to anti-guard views. With characteristic indecision the faculty voted to delay action on the issue. It was said that the faculty body as a whole was not in favor of the immediate establishment of the national guard on the campus, but it wanted more time to consider the matter.

Professors expressed the belief that recent action of the board of trustees would insure construction of a gymnasium without involving students in plans to organize at least two military units, these to have no official status in the university. Martially minded students in this move gained support from an unexpected source when James F. Archibald, a war correspondent and a pro-German propagandist, spoke on the campus on March 19, 1915. He deplored the idea that the Indiana faculty was so shortsighted as not to allow the formation of a guard unit because he felt national defense demanded that young men should have an opportunity to secure military training. He also expressed a critical view of the Western allies, and this is not surprising, because at that moment the American press virtually screamed vituperation at Germany because of its naval activities about the British Isles. The sinking of the *Falaba* in March, and the subsequent sinking of the *Gullflight* in May, the *Lusitania* on May 7, and the *Arabic* on August 19, created a tremendous amount of excitement in Bloomington. By now both faculty and student attitudes toward the European conflict were substantially changed.

The summer following the sinking of the *Lusitania* gave the university administration time in which to make decisions. September saw the issue of war and local concern with it revised. An announcement was made at the opening of the fall semester that enlistment of students in the national guard would be started in a few days, and that an armory would be located on the campus. By this time the whole country was agitated on the subject of approaching war. More faculty members had come to believe that Indiana University should organize a cadet corps comparable with those maintained in the land-grant colleges, and that students should have the opportunity to train to be commissioned officers.

Captain T. R. White, veteran of the Texas summer campaign, pressed for military training, favoring, of course, the organization of a national guard on the grounds that such an organization would make students available to the state on short notice. Too, students would be almost altogether subject to the will of the state rather than to the rules of the university. There was now some regret that the institution had not retained its post-Civil War cadet corps.

William Lowe Bryan remained uncertain as to what course the university should take. He told the trustees in October they should consider the wisdom of offering some form of military training. He seemed torn between favoring such a move and heeding the opposition of the International Polity Club and cautious faculty members of the history and political science departments.

Throughout the fall of 1915, the opposing forces within the university kept up an emotional clamor. Captain White sought to enlist 100 men in his national guard company and had succeeded in enrolling twenty-five by late November. Eighty more boys had declared their intention to join. When the *Alumni Quarterly* went to press early in 1916 the issue was still unresolved. The three-year enlistment, the superiority of military authority over university rules, the fallacious belief that the university would gain a gymnasium-armory were lingering objections.

The faculty also thought it would be an act of bad faith to disrupt the financial schedule of the state at a time when the university was receiving the most generous fiscal support in its history. It did not, however, negate the idea of military training. The Committee on the Promotion of University Interests began a survey of military training programs in the land-grant colleges, and correspondence on this subject was opened with the War Department. The universities were asked, Is military drill popular with the students; what are its effects on the moral and physical welfare

[198]

of the students; what is the attitude of the faculty toward it; has there been any difficulty in securing the detail of a satisfactory commandant? Answers to the questionnaire revealed the unpopularity of drill, but the other answers favored military training. The faculty still wanted information. The Boosters Club took a straw vote of student opinion on military training which resulted in overwhelming student approval of establishment of a reserve corps.

By late May, 1916, the faculty was convinced that some form of military training must be provided. At its June meeting the board of trustees, aware of a possible draft of men 18 to 45, concurred with faculty recommendations to make drill compulsory for freshmen and optional for other classes. The university was instructed to request the War Department to detail an army officer to the institution as professor of military science and tactics. It was also asked to establish a training corps for reserve officers under terms of recently enacted Hays-Chamberlain Act of June 3, 1916. Unfamiliar with regulations under which a reserve corps would be established, President Bryan submitted to the trustees a detailed but useless prescription of hours and terms under which the military would conduct its program, these to be applicable after September 1, 1916.

The president opened correspondence with the War Department at once seeking a department of military science for Indiana University. By that time, however, the exigencies of war had overwhelmed the department. It staggered under the task of enlarging, staffing, equipping, and dispersing what at the moment was little better than a third-rate army. The generals had neither time nor talent to spare for the organization of a university corps, and President Bryan was told that nothing could be done until early in 1917. In January of that year Captain C. A. Trott, a Mexican border veteran, visited Bloomington to confer with university officials. He sought information about the school's facilities and tried to sense campus opinion toward military training. On completion of his inspection he recommended that a course be installed, but the problem of staffing and equipping the corps still remained. Prospects were that it would be fall before any action could be taken.

Within a fortnight after Captain Trott's visitation, the Indiana University community, like others across the nation, was thrown into a rage by Germany's announcement on January 31, 1917, that it would resume unrestricted submarine warfare. On February 3, Woodrow Wilson appeared before Congress and said steps were being taken to break off diplomatic relations with Germany. This announcement brought war hysteria to the campus. On March 5, the *Daily Student* said a military mass meeting would be held in the Old Gymnasium, "It will be a pro-American meeting with patriotism as its dominant note," said the paper. "What the University can do immediately toward preparedness will be the urgent business of the gathering." There were to be speakers and band music, and students and faculty would be present. The *Student* indicated the campus had fanned into blaze the long smoldering demand for immediate military training. Something had to be done at once. It was said President Bryan was now convinced that the time for decision had come. Over 2000 people attended the meeting and the Old Gymnasium rang with the cheers of patriots. Hardly had the crowd seated itself before a tottering party of GAR veterans paraded down the aisle waving a Civil War battle flag. The old boys were invited to the stage and given seats of honor. President Bryan presided and Lieutenant Kenneth P. Williams and James A. Woodburn offered war resolutions which said America's cause was now virtually a holy one.

In between the playing and singing of *Dixie*, *Marching Through Georgia*, *America*, *Hymn to Indiana*, and the *Star Spangled Banner* by the Band and Glee Club, James A. Woodburn spoke on "The Spirit of America." Girls sat in the galleries wearing red, white, and blue costumes. Professor "Dudey" Brooks and Elizabeth Sage were in charge of flags and patriotic souvenirs, and forty girls in the Home Economics Department had worked nearly a whole afternoon making patriotic bows to be given each person in the audience. "President William Lowe Bryan," said the *Daily Student*, "with a few words brought the real meaning of military training closer to the hearts of the audience." Joanna Peterson placed the Woman's League squarely behind the military, and Raymond A. Naugle said 200 professional men of the University Medical School were ready to organize a medical corps. Every girl in the audience hopped to her feet when Alvina Wolf, representing the Red Cross, asked them to volunteer to do their bit. Lieutenant Williams was greeted with wild cheering when he announced to the audience that the faculty had approved military training.

By March, 1917, students were unanimous in their wish for

some form of military organization. The only way they could now correct the situation in the university was to organize the Indiana Military Corps and staff it as best they could with local talent such as Lieutenant Williams and Captain White. This corps was not financed by either state or federal government, and its members had to buy their own uniforms. The fount of all military wisdom, Colonel Louden, was asked for his views on the situation. At that moment he was serving as major of national guard Company H, which was composed of Bloomington and Indiana University volunteers. The Colonel told a *Student* reporter, "You ask me for my views on military training at I. U. I might say that I have endeavored for ten or twelve years to get a military unit at the University. After six years the University Band became a regimental band & I later endeavored to organize a battalion in the University having a member of the faculty as a member of the company command. . . . I believed that it would instill loyalty to the University & state & nation which I am sorry to say, is not of as high standard as it might be. Military training will develop the physique & inculcate loyalty & love of country. . . ."

While the pompous Colonel orated on physique building and love of country, students began taking the university pledge to support the Military Corps. At the same time the faculty adopted a set of rules governing the military program. There would be two basic courses plus five hours of drill, and an advanced course in tactics. Military discipline would prevail in the courses, but the professors were vague as to who would teach the military science courses. Captain T. R. White was to have temporary charge, and Company I was finally dispersed and its equipment turned over to the University Corps. Thus in the second week of March, 1917, Indiana University entered the field of military training with its own curriculum and staff. An editorial in the *Student* said: "To the men who have been most interested a picture arises in their mind's eye of a long line of well-trained, physically perfect college cadets marching up Kirkwood Drive, a sight to make proud the heart & create a deeper love for the Alma Mater. It means a greater University for Indiana & a better army for the U. S." This was, thought the editor, the laying of the first board to better things.

Not all were so enthusiastic as the *Student*'s editor. Some thought the program cost too much, and drill took too much time. Some students had not attended the grand convocation and remained largely ignorant of what it was all about. It was disheartening to fervent militarists that it took some exhortation to fill up four companies planned at the outset. The reporter pulled out all the stops: "What do you sacrifice?" he asked fellow students, "A little time, an afternoon date, a picture show & an hr's sleep. What did the Grand Old Army sacrifice?" Then a postscript, "By the way, the co-eds must not think much of the men around here, since they assert they need physical training & need it badly."

Perhaps the *Student*'s prodding paid off. Lieutenant Williams had recruited 215 men by the second day the rolls were opened, and he expressed satisfaction with both the number and quality of men enlisted. There were still no uniforms and no equipment. Again aid was sought in Washington. It now seemed likely the $300 of Company I funds would have to be spent for materials, and a new public subscription list opened.

Plans were made to convert the south end of the Old Gymnasium into a rifle range, and Hoosier boys would be taught once again to handle a rifle and draw a true bead. The band would be placed on a military status, and Dr. Burton D. Myers agreed to organize a hospital corps—thus the glory and the tragedy of war would be served in a self-contained Indiana University cadre.

By March 16, Lieutenant Williams had his troops in ranks at least, and he marched them off the campus for their first public appearance. Establishing a spartan regimen he drilled his first companies at 6:15 A. M. , and the second companies at 4:00 P. M. The spirit was present that day as his boys marched along Kirkwood, even if they gave the appearance of a cornstalk frontier militia muster. Professor Williams learned he could purchase uniform suits for $6.60 apiece, and at least dress his boys alike. This "uniform" consisted of a cotton shirt, pants, and a hat. Just as this arrangement was being made President Bryan was notified by the War Department that it had approved establishment of a senior Reserve Officers Training Corps in Indiana University, and that infantry captain Campbell King would become professor of Military Science and Tactics. For some reason, however, the Captain could not report, and President Bryan now sought to employ a retired officer to take charge of reserve training. There were more than 400 students enrolled in the military cadre and it was impossible for Lieutenant Williams to conduct any sort of an effective program. Foot soldiers under his command slogged through chilly

March weather and on muddy Jordan Field. On March 24, the field became too slippery for the grand review by President Bryan and the board of trustees, and the drill was moved into the Old Gymnasium where only close order inspection was possible.

Still unable to spare an officer, the War Department sent instead 500 Springfield rifles and 30,000 rounds of ammunition. At last, and after much uncertainty, Captain Campbell King arrived in Bloomington. His first act was to encourage every student to enroll for military training, and to issue strict orders concerning drill. The *Daily Student* backed the Captain, saying, "It is the duty of every red-blooded man to take the drill work." The editor thought those who made excuses should be termed shirkers.

By the time the university began in earnest to establish the reserve officer corps on the campus, the Indiana National Guard began recruiting men for field artillery Battery F. There followed extensive activity by this unit, and the press was filled with stories of the recruitment and equipping of this company. At the same time the university hospital corps had finished its basic training and awaited orders to move into active service in France. News of the war abroad was grim, and this served to increase to feverish pitch war activities in Bloomington. Artillery Battery F was organized quickly and its men were anxious to be on their way to the battle front. Joseph F. Dailey, ex-president of the Senior Class, asked, "Shall we wait until the Germans shoot down the Statue of Liberty before we fight?" He was fed up with churning mud and dust on Jordan Field, and at the ungodly hours which students had to be astir in playing soldier. April 15, 1917, was a peak day of excitement. News was passed quickly in Bloomington that the day before the United States Senate had adopted a resolution declaring a state of war now existed between this country and Germany. Two days later the House of Representatives adopted a similar resolution. The nation was now embarked upon a stirring new chapter of its history, and one with profound bearing on the university. A month later Congress passed the Selective Service Act, an act that threatened to decimate student enrollment. After April that year students hastened to enlist for military duty. A special call was made for boys who had a working knowledge of the gasoline engine to enlist in the new aviation branch of the service for special training. Naval recruiters came to the campus seeking volunteers and to locate a training center in the university.

In town Colonel Louden continued to fight his own brand of war. He sought volunteers for a new artillery band. The Colonel gave the impression at least that successful wars were fought to the sound of martial music.

By May, 1917, the campus had virtually become a military camp. Companies of all but leaderless boys marched up and down the drill field morning and evening. Kirkwood Avenue had become a parade stand, and Courthouse Square a military objective. So excited and disoriented did students become that both General Leonard Wood and President Bryan pleaded with those yet uncommitted to give serious attention to their studies. As volunteering and the threat of the draft increased, classes were threatened by lack of enrollment. Curiously the total university enrollment showed no appreciable reduction, it is impossible to separate military numbers from those of regular students.

By mid-May 1917, it seemed certain that some Indiana students would be among the first to arrive in France. They would be among the 1400 Americans detailed for ambulance service. Volunteers for this assignment flocked into the Student Intelligence Bureau of the Alumni office seeking to be among the thirty-six men chosen. By commencement time 307 students had departed the university to fill military ranks in the various training camps. With them went Captain King, and once again Captain Kenneth P. Williams was left the ranking officer on the campus.

As the summer wore on the selective draft and volunteering made inroads into both university staff and student body. Six young professors and a number of students were among the first men called up by the Monroe County Draft Board. During these weeks Battery F had completed its training and left Bloomington early in August.

Departure of draftees, ambulance company volunteers, and Battery F became tangible proof that war for Indiana University was a grim reality. On August 4, Battery F was drawn up in a final parade formation preparatory to marching to the Central Indiana and Louisville railway station. They were given a farewell, said the *Student*, "that the boys might well carry in their memories on the battlefields of Europe." John W. Cravens, university Registrar, made them a farewell speech in which he said, "The sword has been drawn & we believe that this contest will continue until freedom, justice, & democracy have been firmly established in all the world for all the years to come. We hope every one of you will live to see the day when you will carry the Stars and Stripes down the streets of Old Berlin, & sing the 'Star Spangled Banner' & 'Gloriana Frangipana' at the Kaiser's front door...."

The march to the railway station and the boarding of Battery F was a highly emotional affair. There was a great bustle of hand-shaking, and crowds of people surged up to the coaches for a last word. When the train pulled out of the station the *Telephone* said there was a waving of a veritable canopy of tearstained handker-chiefs. In many ways the departure of Battery F left an emotional void in Indiana University. President Bryan continued a diligent search for a commandant. To date his efforts had been as fruitless as his earlier attempts to hire a professor of music. In desperation he called a mass meeting of faculty and students who had received any kind of military training in the past with hopes he could find temporary instructors for the reserve corps classes. The War Department assigned Captain Edwin J. Nowlen, then stationed at Fort Thomas in Kentucky, to be commandant, but Captain Nowlen could not report promptly. President Bryan felt that drill had to be started at once and tried to make plans to do so, even though the instruction was of a highly unmilitary nature.

From all sides the war crowded in upon the university. In October eighty-one naval reserve cadets from the Great Lakes Naval Training Station were sent to Bloomington and they had to be housed and fed. The fact the institution had only one dormitory greatly handicapped it as compared with its neighbors' more favorable housing conditions. Finally the new gymnasium was converted into a barracks and the sailors were bedded down on rows of cots.

It was now difficult to distinguish the university campus from an armed camp. All freshmen and sophomores physically able to do so were required to take military training. President Bryan assumed temporary command of the corps in stipulating this rule. Again in the new semester students were divided into two companies and were drilled early in the mornings and late afternoons. There were only half enough guns to go around and no uniforms; this military activity at times was little more than an organized walking club with which to improve the physical condition of students.

Professors, student instructors, and a captain all worked with the raw recruits. Captain Mitchell had been granted permission by Purdue University to visit the Indiana University campus every Thursday to hold drills and give other military instruction. At last Captain Nowlen reached the campus on November 5, 1917, and took command of all military training. By this time his predecessor, Captain King, was on the battle front in France. Nowlen, however, had scarcely unsheathed his baton of authority before he, too, was ordered to active duty on the European front. Again the university cadre was left leaderless, and President Bryan for at least a fourth time searched for an officer. Not all was impenetrable gloom, however—the War Department was finally able to deliver a sufficient number of rifles for drill.

Six students were chosen from the university corps in December, 1917, to receive special reserve officer training at Camp Taylor near Louisville. They joined ninety other Indiana University cadets who had been selected earlier in the year. Among them were Professors Paul V. McNutt, Matthew Winters, and C. W. Snow. The new reservists were placed in a company composed of students from Ohio and Kentucky.

Early in January, 1918, the War Department validated President Bryan's earlier order that all freshmen and sophomores should be enrolled in military classes. This, lamented the campus newspaper, would play havoc with the band because members would now have no time to practice. Pettibone and Company of Cincinnati sent agents to the university to take measurements for new uniforms which they contracted to supply for $23.50 apiece. Students were required to pay for these clothes out of the semester military allowance.

Sometime during early January the War Department assigned a third commandant, Arthur T. Dalton, to assume charge of military instruction. That spring the Captain had his charges marching up and down Jordan Field and Dunn Meadow, and by the end of March they were considered sufficiently well trained to present some semblance of military order. A grand parade before President Bryan and the faculty was held on the day the new uniforms arrived from Cincinnati. Now the campus took on an olive drab shade, and nearly everybody was engaged in strengthening the war machine.

On April 17, the Reserve Officer Training Corps, the band, and the university staff lined up around Jordan Field for a panoramic photograph. Students were now under full military discipline.

The only time they were permitted to appear out of uniform was in the shower bath, in bed, and from Friday noon until Sunday morning in the barracks when they cleaned and repaired their clothes. They could also engage in athletic sports out of uniform.

Not all college spirit was dampened by the excitement of war events in 1917. Purdue still loomed large in the eyes of students, and depleted though athletic manpower was they still whooped up excitement over approaching games. On October 18, a party of students with the Drum Corps invaded Kirkwood Hall and attempted to disband classes. A faculty committee with Dean Burton D. Myers as chairman looked upon this Indiana war dance with about the same tolerance they would have welcomed Pancho Villa and his roughnecks. They informed students such activity was against the best ethics of the college spirit, and President Bryan agreed with the professors. "I believe," he wrote, "that the poison which has infected our athletics for several years is nowhere more manifest than in such examples of the wrong college spirit. We do not deserve to win and shall not win until the best soldierly spirit is prevalent among us all. A good soldier never does anything to bring reproach upon his regiment." Thus college life stood suspended between the anxieties of war, and the expectations of athletic victory, both of which shattered normal academic life.

Establishment of the Reserve Officer Training Corps on the campus in March, 1917, did not halt student volunteering for active service in the army. In May, 1918, it was evident at a glimpse that blue stars on the 12 by 12 foot university service flag had increased weekly during the past year. Forty men withdrew during the first semester of 1917–18. The *Daily Student* reported, "Every day takes away some student, and before the close of the school year the number should be swelled to a full one hundred." Even the ranks of the Reserve Officer Training Corps were depleted by enlistment. University enrollment for the fall semester of 1918 was said to be 1652, but enrollment data for the war years are confusing because the registrar apparently counted students along with military personnel. Most male students were now highly oriented toward active military service. They appeared impatient to become involved in active battlefield duty. When it was announced late in May that a limited number of reservists would be given special summer training at Fort Sheridan there were 100 volunteers for the fifty-four openings. Members of the reserve corps were ever conscious that they were fully subject to active duty at the will of the War Department.

Indiana University's responsibility for military training was broadened in July, 1918, when 200 men were sent to the campus for eight weeks of special training in the new science of radio communication. The government had negotiated a contract with the institution for this work and by September a contingent of 900 more would be sent to Bloomington. This new challenge necessitated an almost wholesale physical shifting of university departments. The men were housed in the Old Gymnasium or Assembly Hall and were bedded down on military cots until September 28, when they were moved into Alpha Hall. They took their meals in the cafeteria. The Physics Department was placed in charge of radio instruction. Dean Woolworth of the United States Department of Education said that Indiana University was as well equipped for this specialized work in communications as any university in the country.

While university officials struggled with problems of housing and feeding too many men for available facilities, a freight train was wrecked on the Monon just south of Bloomington and this blocked a troop train carrying 420 Wisconsin soldiers who were delayed in the town for three days, and they had to be entertained and fed. They used the swimming pool and athletic fields and were fed by Bloomington ladies. It was with a justifiable sigh of relief that the *Student*'s editor wrote, "The close of the summer session had ended a year full of achievement in the line of military training at Indiana University. The movement began toward the end of the spring semester two years ago. At that time the course was optional, and offered as an opportunity for the students to get instruction of their own free will." Since that time the Reserve Officer Training Corps and compulsory campus drill had been established, and there was more to come.

The announcement was made in Bloomington on September 16 that the university had entered a contract with the United States Government to establish a Student Army Training Corps to train 2000 men. By October 1, said the *Student*, the university would become one of the most active military centers in the state. John Wesley Cravens reported on September 26 that 1224 men had signed up for the specially shortened two-year war course and were waiting to take physical examinations. After the first of

October all fraternity houses were converted into military barracks bearing locational numbers instead of names. Arrangements were also made to convert the new Christian Church into a barracks hall.

While arrangements were being made to accommodate the newly organized Student Corps, the university also had to find living and teaching facilities for those volunteers who preferred naval duties. The *Student* said, "With all the various branches of military instruction that is provided this year for the men of the University, and with a large number of drafted men to be sent here by the War Department for instruction in radio the chief atmosphere of the school will be militaristic. As soon as all have been issued suits, the most popular dress of the campus will be that of khaki."

Movement of five hundred radio men into the university necessitated almost complete occupation of Science Hall, requiring the removal of the departments of physics, chemistry, and biology from the building. This was a "ten pin" movement, forcing most other departments to be moved into most constricted quarters or relocated altogether. In the latter week of September eight newly commissioned lieutenants arrived on the campus and plans were made to administer the military oath to the Student Army Training Corps at precisely 11:00 A.M. on October 1, 1918.

The student corps of 1200 men was formed into companies, and at the appointed time these companies assembled on Jordan Field to take the national oath. This pageant had been carefully organized across the country so that more than 200,000 college men stood at attention and repeated the oath symbolically in unison. While Indiana students took the oath at 11:00 A.M., those at Cornell went through the same ceremony at noon eastern time, and those in Colorado at 10:00 A.M.

On the occasion of the oath-taking ceremony, which had all the color and sanctity of a profoundly religious exercise, townspeople ringed the field. President Bryan told the fledgling soldiers that they were being given a privilege which no other nation had ever extended to its people. No government in all history had been so generous with its youth. The boys, he said, had the power to crush the Prussian theory of might, and so subjugate it that never again would it cause the world such widespread suffering and sorrow.

Following the speech soldiers and spectators sang *America*

with thunderous enthusiasm. In less than half an hour Indiana University had almost ticked to a standstill as an academic institution. The raising of the University Service flag behind the student corps as they repeated the oath revealed how deeply involved in war the educational institution had become. The flag bore 1300 blue stars and ten golden ones. The scene was one of the most dramatic ever witnessed on the campus. The *Student* said, "It is as if a wizard had waved a magic wand and transformed the whole place overnight." The editor was right, and the same wizardry was being worked on 400 other college campuses in a veritable outpouring of American spirit and determination. The swearing in of so many college youths was little short of a national sacrificial offering of the choicest youths on the altar of Mars. The nation had now committed its full academic force to winning the war. Everywhere classrooms, dormitories, and professors were involved with military and specialized war tasks. In Indiana students like their pioneer Hoosier forbears viewed their efforts as those of citizen soldiers ensnared in a world crisis.

Approximately four hundred commissions had been issued to university graduates and students by the last month of the war. Boys enrolled in the student corps had every reason to hope that they might be chosen for special officer training. It was heartening to hear that some of the earlier university volunteers had now been raised to the rank of major, and the army said that college trained boys made excellent officers. Becoming a soldier, however, had its traumatic moments. Boys were not used to being called out at 5:45 A.M. on frosty October and November mornings and getting ready to begin drill within ten minutes after leaving the bed. All the rest of the day was divided into precise periods. Captain Dalton ran a "tight" campus from 5:00 A.M. to 10:00 P.M.; the rest of the time belonged to the footweary soldier. Never before had the fraternity house barracks known such devotion to punctuality. The twelve weeks of basic training before the boys were to be shipped off to regular army training was supposed to convert callow youths to field-ready men. This plan disrupted the traditional university academic program so far as men students were concerned. Had the war continued another six months classes in the traditional sense might well have been discontinued in many areas for lack of both instructors and students.

The university catalogue for 1918 contained the outline of the condensed two-year course opened to military personnel. The university announced, "since students physically fit, entering college at an average of nineteen years of age, can expect to get only two years of collegiate work before being called by the selective service act, it is to the interest both of the student and of our government that this time be devoted to learning something so well that it may constitute the foundation for some special type of training for military service." The soldier was told that courses in several specialized areas had been organized for his benefit. In all, nine areas of interest were listed. Besides the specialized curricula comprising the two-year offering, general war courses were given in history and political science. Woodburn, Kohlmeier, Harding, and McDonald taught "Causes of the Great War" and "Balkan Problems." Hershey offered a course entitled "America and the European War." There were other special courses which dealt with foreign trade, conservation of natural resources, modern Russia, airplane mechanics, wireless telegraphy, European governments, international law, several European languages, and a host of emergency courses pertaining to Red Cross relief, first aid, hygiene, food preparation, social services, and surgical dressing. Much of the remaining university instructional personnel was occupied teaching special work, and oftentimes outside the fields of their specialty.

Smallpox and influenza in the fall of 1918 all but closed what classes the new military regimen did not disrupt. The outbreak of these diseases created a crisis in both civilian and military population. The epidemics were made even more frightening because of the presence of so many soldiers in such crowded housing conditions and because of a shortage of medical and hospital aid.

The first contingent of student soldiers was in the midst of basic training on November 11, 1918, when the armistice was signed in Europe between Germany and the Allied Powers. The end of the war launched numerous rumors as to the fate of the Student Army Training Corps. Would training be continued? Some said the corps would be continued but they could not explain for what purpose. There was a pronounced tone of regret that so dramatic an undertaking would be halted, although some wanted to see training ended. Even the War Department appeared to be caught in a state of indecision as to the fate of the student army. Soon, however, U. H. Smith, Bursar, received a telegram instructing the university to carry on the program at full tilt. Captain A. T. Dalton informed the student trainees that more of them would be sent to officer training camps, and that already Indiana University reservist students previously assigned to the camps had been commissioned and started abroad.

In another area university training plans were on schedule. The weekly sabbath classes had begun in the barracks. The institution had received a few copies of the spiritual guidance book entitled *The Master's Way*, and appropriately, no doubt, the first topic to be discussed was "The Soldier's Attitude Toward Women." Unhappily for Chaplain Floyd Lee not all the books arrived on time, but he set up that new instrument of modern warfare, the mimeograph machine, to make sure every soldier had the lesson in hand. Throughout the war President Bryan had emphasized religion. In September of that year, he lectured soldiers on the subject "Let Us Not Forget." He told them, "Let us devote ourselves to sacrifice by abstinence and by gifts of money and labor. . . . Let us hold fast our faith in God, who is within and above traditions and creeds, who through the ages has created the worlds, who from age to age of peace and of war had made His dwelling in ascending forms of life, who now through us fights to establish in the world a society of justice. Let us cherish the most ancient King of Jerusalem, Melchizedek, type of the Messiah, of whom it is written: He was 'first, King of righteousness and after that King of Salem which is King of Peace.' " Bryan viewed the war as a holy crusade and periodically gave his communications the ring of evangelism. The campus paper ran his brief sermonettes in a front page box.

Excitement and confusion of victory lessened within a fortnight and Captain Dalton received orders to induct no more men into the student army ranks. He, however, continued drilling the awkward troops indoors and out. The *Student* said clumsy lads pushed holes in walls with rifle barrels, smashed toes on "order Arms," pinched fingers in rifle breeches, and played havoc with windows and light bulbs, but they were determined. Sergeants fumed up and down field and floor shouting epithets which they had neither read between the covers of *The Master's Way* nor heard from the president, and which in other circumstances would have caused them to be hustled away from the banks of the Jordan.

Influenza and smallpox did not yield to the news of peace.

Epidemics after November 11 created a much greater crisis than quick demobilization of the armed forces. Captain Dalton attempted to lessen the inroads of disease by refusing passes to his men to visit town or homes, and because of this the campus became a veritable military stockade under siege. How long the epidemics would last was anybody's guess, but now the newspaper and the public created a mood which hastened "the passing of the uniform." It was said that the appearance of men in Indiana University dressed in civvies would be a sensation for everybody but the co-eds. The girls, said the *Student*, had fallen in love with the uniforms. Now that they had just plain men on the campus they would be more discriminating.

The end of militarism was in sight by November 27, when President Bryan went before classes in "Issues of the War" and announced he had received orders from Washington to disband all university military units by December 21. He said, however, that freshmen and sophomores in the future would be required to take reserve officer training courses.

Immediate plans were made to return the university to its regular academic routine. Heads of departments were instructed to have class schedules ready for distribution by January 1, 1919. Once again students would be allowed to choose courses of major interest, and military discipline and occupancy of the campus would be ended. For the university the central question was whether or not student soldiers would remain on the campus as civilians to complete their two-year programs, or would they be influenced by a sense of the new freedom to drop out of school? Of equal importance was the impact of the battlefield veteran returning to the university. There was, of course, the question of whether or not the returning veteran would bring the more liberal social and behavioral mores of the army camp to the campus and create monstrous disciplinary problems. Finally, how soon would the American Expeditionary Force itself return from Europe?

Beginning on December 12, discharges were issued Student Army Training Corps soldiers at the rate of a hundred a day, the aim being to discharge the last ones on December 21. In an effort to convince students to remain in the university, President Bryan addressed his final remarks to the corps in the form of a letter. He told the soldiers, "Life is wonderful, more and more wonderful— if you will sail out any way on the Great Sea, taking note as you sail of the North Star." This, he intimated was the way to find one's purpose in life.

At Christmas time it was predicted that no more than half of the Student Army Training Corps would return to the university. Possibly a majority of them had come in the first place to improve their chances in future military training before being sent off to Europe to fight. They had never had a real interest in higher education.

At the opening of the new term in 1919 it became clear that students had lost their enthusiasm for military training. Like the American people generally they favored complete demobilization. Only 200 freshmen and sophomores had enrolled for reserve officer training, and Captain Dalton was left in a dilemma by the War Department as to his future responsibilities. It was not until the third week of the semester that instructions were issued from Washington that all students below the rank of junior would be subjected to sixty contact hours of military training per semester.

For the university the end of the war presented a multitude of challenges. Rebuilding the teaching staff was a monumental task, especially in light of the fact that Indiana University, said President Bryan, stood forty-third in the scale of state university salaries paid in comparison with the state's ability to support the school. Approximately a hundred staff members had gone on leave either to serve in the army or to do specialized services for the government. These either had to be brought home, or new staff members employed to replace those who resigned. One staff member, Paul Barnett Coble of the Medical School, had lost his life in battle. Others had distinguished themselves in their expert services.

The challenge facing Indiana in 1919 was that of calming emotions aroused in wartime and readjusting its whole being to a new tempo of academic developments which required a new type of approach to the educational future. National, political, and social issues crowded themselves onto campuses and into classrooms. A new moral and social code largely liberated the individual from the old taboos of 1914. In deans' offices and classrooms there was the demand for consideration of the new social and physical sciences. Even the training routine of the professions of law and medicine had not withstood revision in the war experience. Most important of all, the university had to reckon with instructional and service problems created by a new age of affluence.

An Indianapolis *Star* editorial in early January, 1919, said, "The old order was completely overthrown in colleges and universities by the necessity of making soldiers out of students. 'Cultural' education as ordinarily understood was practically dropped from the curricula with the beginning of the present school year because of the demands made on the time of students by purely military instruction. Readjustment is now taking place. Soon Latin and Greek, psychology and literature will assume their old importance in the eyes of teacher and student. . . . On the other hand are some who would like to see the 'classics' completely squelched or at best merely tolerated, in the coming educational system. Their hope that the concentration on technical and practical subjects enforced by war will become a permanent policy of American colleges is the fear of the first group. . . ." The editor admitted that not even the American Academy of Arts and Letters could stem the tide of change. The educational system would bend to the postwar age of change. He could have added, so would Indiana University.

Veterans coming back to classrooms brought with them an inordinate maturity. They also brought along the glories of the warrior, the tragedies of battle, and the martial spirit. Sergeant Dudley Woodward for instance, came to the university bearing the decorations of the Distinguished Service Medal, the Legion of Honor with the rank of Chevalier, and three Croix de Guerre. Twenty-three year old First Lieutenant Ted Johnstone, son of Professor Harold Whetstone Johnstone of the Latin Department, had gone directly from the Mexican border to officer's training school in Fort Leavenworth and then to France, the first Indiana alumnus to land on French soil during the war. The university's honor roll was an extensive one. Blue stars covered its large service flag, and it was flecked by the even more precious golden ones. Symbolic of the university's role in the war was the caption which appeared under President Bryan's picture in the Indiana *Daily Student*, "A Man Who Was in the War with all His Mind and Heart and Soul." Along with him for four years, 1914 to 1918, had gone the mind and soul of all Indiana University.

[X]

The Toils of War
in Academe

AMERICAN UNIVERSITIES as well as the course of national
life slackened their thrust somewhat after the election of
1912. The first years of Wilson's progressivism were in
fact years of institutional searching for new directions. Reading
Americans who wanted to be disturbed could take their choice
between Edith Wharton's *Ethan Frome* or Theodore Dreiser's
The Financier, and for those less literate there was Zane Grey's
Riders of the Purple Sage. In Bloomington the great crusade to
divide the university organization into new departments and colleges had leveled off. There was, however, plenty of unfinished
business, such as the search for a head of the Music School, the
establishment of a school of journalism, and the maturing of the
programs of all the new colleges.

Professors and students were largely concerned with the daily
routine of classes, and with the social affairs of a dance-crazy age.
A few had divided minds and spirits about the visible clouds which
darkened the world's political horizon. The ominous rising of na-
tionalism in Europe—especially in Germany—promised a general
European war, the vortex of which America must avoid. David
Starr Jordan travelled the national circuit raising his voice loud
and clear in the cause of peace. In Bloomington in 1914, and again

two years later, he conducted what amounted to a revival meeting on the theme.

Within the sound of Jordan's oratory for peace were rising chauvinists who had already stirred public sentiment for intervention in the affairs of Mexico. Countering this were the peace essays of seniors Howard W. Hornung and Olive Beldon awarded prizes by the Lake Mohawk Peace Conference.

Bloomington church congregations were in full cooperation with the objectives of the Indiana Peace Society, and on three different occasions in October, 1914, William Lowe Bryan, society president, spoke on the subject of peace in the spirit of Jordan. He supported resolutions commending Woodrow Wilson and William Jennings Bryan for their diplomatic policies toward Mexico and Europe. There certainly was no immediate thought that America would be asked to do more in that quarter than exert threat of intervention.

Reflecting general campus tempo, the *Daily Student* boomed on November 18, "Well let's try to get an early start and maybe Old Indiana will produce some of those prize winning essays. Those of last year evidently made a poor impression in Europe." Ironically this date about marked the end of the peace crusade. Occasionally news of one of Jordan's impassioned speeches was noted in the local press, and he was back in Bloomington in 1916, but more pressing national incidents brought war into clearer focus and nearer reality.

Many Indiana professors were personally interested in the threat of war in Europe. Some studied abroad in German and French universities, others still had direct family ties on the continent, and many travelled in all of the western countries. In the summer of 1914, several university families were in Austria and Germany when the conflict began—among them the Moenkhauses, Lintons, and Voses who were with a party of tourists. Professor Vos observed war preparations in both Germany and England. John Hess was in Marburg, and Arthur Pflueger was in Paris where he was mistaken for a German spy and was held by French authorities for a time. He saw the French army march away to the Rhine front and gained a first-hand notion that a general war was imminent.

Because of the outbreak of war in Europe, Indiana and Purdue universities began a cooperative movement in the fall of 1914 to raise a fund of $10,000 for the YMCA war services. Before the subscription lists closed, subscribers had exceeded the goal by $1200. At the same time the Indiana University Union conducted a separate drive to collect funds for the aid of Belgians. Soon it seemed almost everybody was conducting some kind of charitable campaign to aid victims of Prussian might. Perhaps the good intent of American humanitarianism had never been higher. During the next decade people would be called upon for assistance to Belgians, French, English, and everyone else injured by war. Indiana students supported all these drives. They sold candy, staged home talent plays, sold tags, danced, and did everything else ingenious youth could think up to make money. Throughout the war there was charitable concern for displaced persons, wounded soldiers, homeless children, and university students and professors from disrupted universities. So fervent was this concern that in March, 1917, Indiana University boasted that it was the first school in the United States to adopt a Belgian town, Vyle-et-Tharoul.

There is no way of calculating what amount of human energy and oratory was expended on chapel drives, preparation of handbills and posters, writing news stories, and accounting for funds. The Red Cross and YMCA conducted continuing solicitations for support using the services of hundreds of people. U. H. Smith's Bursar's office became more a collection agency for war drives than a business office for the university.

By the spring of 1915, the influx of pro-Allied war propaganda began to have an effect in Bloomington. First it was passed around as bits of jocular whimsy. It was said, for instance, if the Kaiser had his way the romance languages would be placed on the dead list. The *Student* asked, late in 1914, "How would you like to wear white socks all the time? Likewise, white shirts, white ties, white hats, in fact, how would you like to go about all the time dressed in imitation of a snow scene of the western prairie?" This, it said, would happen if the war in Europe were not ended at once. Ernest Marshall Linton of the Political Science Department wrote a thesis on Belgian neutrality which made both sensational local news and pro-Belgian propaganda.

Horrors of a brutalizing war were revealed not only in reported cruelties to the Belgians, but likewise in the imprisonment of European professors and students. Wellington H. Tinker of the International Committee of the YMCA spent several days on the campus helping to organize a university relief campaign. Plans were made for an Indiana professor to visit each fraternity house to explain the plight of academic persons abroad and to solicit aid from members. At the same time a student committee solicited support for the small French hospitals which cared for civilians and soldiers, and by November, 1915, it had gathered 355 "comfort bags."

In February, 1917, Robert Whitington of the English Department began what proved to be a long series of similar experiences of bringing graphic descriptions of the war close home to convocation audiences. He described his work with a rescue and relief mission in Belgium and told of his services in Antwerp and Limbourg. Audience interest was heightened even more by his saying he was honor-bound not to discuss political aspects of German occupation. Whitington's objective was solicitation of funds for the aid of children of Neuville.

For the first time in the opening months of the war the moving picture became an effective instrument for spreading propaganda. *The Battle Cry of Peace*, "One of the most stupendous spectacles ever prepared for the motion picture screen," was shown in connection with mobilization for peace. Its slogan was POWER, and it portrayed on the screen a milling mass of 16,000 national guardsmen, 800 GAR, 5000 horses, 17 airplanes, submarines, and dreadnaughts, all brought together in an early Hollywood spectacle of military might. The picture made a forceful impression when it was shown in a Bloomington theater. A succession of Triangle Pictures followed, which portrayed experiences of college boy ambulance drivers in action in France. These pictures produced a genuine tingle of excitement because Professor Frank Davidson and several Indiana University students had earlier volunteered for this kind of noncombatant battlefield service. Usually the propagandist films were accompanied by Mrs. Charles Alfred Mosemiller at the piano. By mid-1917, the whole university community was fully mobilized for both humanitarian and military purposes. Everybody had been intellectually conditioned to look upon the war as a great moral and humanitarian battle against a godless Prussian might.

The editor of the *Alumni Magazine* wrote that year, "No institution can go 'as usual.' I. U. for its part was vigorously upheld the course of President Wilson, & has sought to adapt its work to the needs of the emergency. We believe we should enter this war not only for the vindication of American rights & for the honor of America's name, but for the preservation of those ideas of justice and humanity upon which security of the world must rest."

Following Woodrow Wilson's positive response to Germany's announcement of unrestricted submarine warfare on February 3, 1917, the *Daily Student* told its readers this did not mean war. Congress was, however, making preparations as if war were a certainty. In less than a month the *Laconia* was sunk, and almost immediately a box in the paper carried the slogan, "Now is the time to show your patriotism." This was followed by other outcries of war hysteria such as "Why not learn *America* & *The Star Spangled Banner* as the 1st duty of preparedness." From the outset the *Student* became fervently pro-Allies and pro-war.

On March 6, a mass meeting of faculty and students was held in the gymnasium in which W. D. Howe, chairman of the English Department, and chairman of the arrangements committee, declared the assembly "to be an American meeting." In this assembly everybody would "voice faith in no uncertain tone in American ideals and our loyalty to the flag that symbolizes all that we as liberty loving people hold dear." He thought no one could be so indifferent as to stay away—this was not just another student convocation, it was to be a gathering of free men affirming in the stoutest possible way their faith in human rightness and democracy. Indiana University, said the *Student* on March 5, was neither pro-Ally nor pro-German, but it was decidedly pro-American and favored a strong policy of armed neutrality. There was no room in the institution for a lad unwilling to serve his country.

If the student editor and Professor Howe were urgent in their statements, William Lowe Bryan was even more impressive. "I wish," he said, "most of all that we may become ready in the most austere sense for the worst that is before us." This pronouncement appeared in bold face type in the *Student* that day. Not to be outdone in democratic fervor the Cactus Club, made up of bachelor professors, wired Senator James E. Watson that it stood foursquare by President Wilson. The great mass meeting took similar action. James Albert Woodburn read Wilson's war message to Congress, and it was greeted with enthusiasm. Eloquent resolutions which contained the charged words, "sacred," "unanimity of spirit," "American rights," "menace," and "terror" were adopted.

Male faculty and students did not stand alone in their support of the presidential message and congressional action. The university women said they favored military training as well. Dean Ruby E. Mason made her views known with characteristic certainty in this area, but Dorothy Drybread of the Home Economics Club made a startling pronouncement: "Military training is a fine thing not merely from the standpoint of militarism but for the excellent physical training." One wonders what Miss Drybread thought a war involved.

From March on the Indiana campus literally resounded with the babble of patriotism in and out of class. At some time in the past an iron flag pole had been erected on the campus, but the *Student* editor assumed the university did not own a flag, an unbelievable lapse which evoked righteous indignation under the title, "Oh Say Can You See?" In fact the University did possess a flag, but it was so tattered and soiled that the institution was ashamed to display it. Later the paper announced that at last Indiana had acquired a proud new banner it was not ashamed to fly.

If the institution was caught short on the flag issue, President Bryan demonstrated on March 29 that it would do as much for the country without as with the colors. He wired Governor James P. Goodrich that all the resources of the institution were at the command of the state and national governments. Bloomington and the university were mobilized for war, and in describing the school's service capabilities he submitted a detailed inventory of its properties and facilities.

On March 29, another general mass meeting was held on Courthouse Square to hear patriotic speeches and to cheer the "Indiana Army." So excited did the crowd become over the chauvinistic speeches of Reverend C. H. Taylor and Joseph Henley that it appears to have lost all sense of reality. Henley said his father was a Union veteran, and, in remembering, he waved the "bloody shirt" in a truculent tirade. The crowd responded by singing *Dixie* and *Marching Through Georgia*, repeating many times the chorus of Sherman's fiery marching hymn. On April first resolutions were adopted to declare immediate and vigorous war on Germany, but at that point an impartial observer might well have wondered whether the crowds supported war against Germany or Georgia. Authors of the resolutions were William Lowe Bryan and James A. Woodburn.

Classwork in the university was almost completely disrupted by the first of April. Organization of all kinds of special services was begun as a step toward winning the war in which America was certain to become an active combatant. R. V. Sollitt was asked to prepare for the government a list of Indiana University graduates and citizens who would be able to respond quickly to government calls. T. Rymer of the university YMCA, who had served Company I in Texas went away to Europe with Battery F to organize recreational services for troops, and soon he had need for funds and materials.

President Bryan and the university's professors stirred further hysteria with frequent and impassioned speeches, some of which were shockingly hostile. The president seems to have become so emotionally aroused by the war that he presented himself as a speaker at most of the war gatherings and even donned the uniform on occasion and drilled with students. For him the war had assumed the dimensions of an ancient Hebrew fight against all of the evils of mankind, and he was against evil in every form. The flag became a holy guidon of human rightness. So much emphasis was placed on it in gatherings, speeches, and pledges that students purchased flag stickers as decorations for notebooks, texts, fountain pens, and even as marks for future assignments. Embroidered ties, flag adorned celluloid collars, and all other visible articles of clothing took on a patriotic tone. At last the flag craze approached the point of ridiculousness and the *Student* editor disparaged its use *ad nauseum*.

In other areas student patriotic zeal outmatched the actual needs of the moment. By April 5, five dances had been cancelled, but throughout the rest of the war dancing remained a prime subject of discussion. There was a feeling that dances without expending money should be continued, yet this form of pleasure and social intercourse seemed sacrilegious in the face of grim world events. The juniors, for instance, decided to forego their prom and to contribute their money to war needs. The *Student* declared the sororities' decision to cancel the Panhellenic dance a fine example of patriotism. This was a major social sacrifice because the girls had planned for the event throughout the year. "Wartime," said the campus editor, "is no time for frivolities." Dancing at Indiana University was not a frivolity, it was a way of life. Giving up dancing seems to have caused more grumbling and discussion than all of the "wheatless" and "meatless" days put together.

Hysteria, like fever, could not burn at peak level forever, and soon there was some rationalization of conditions if not a cooling of ardor. Some dances were held from time to time, and even the track team resumed practice with hopes that it could find competitors for joint meets.

Two incidents occurred in the midst of the war excitement which momentarily shifted attention away from the European tragedy. One of southern Indiana's famous tornados shook the riverbank town of New Albany apart, and Sherman Minton, a devoted native son, rushed back to the font of his training to plead for help. At a convocation, following the rousing wartime singing of *America* and the *Star Spangled Banner*, lawyer Minton delivered a touching description of the suffering of his people and pleaded for help from students. President Bryan added his blessings to the plea and suggested that it was more blessed to give even if it did mean giving up social functions. Who could refuse to be generous in the face of all the drama on the stage? The university's large service flag was lowered slowly to the dying strains of the *Star Spangled Banner* and Minton's eloquence with electrifying results.

Every war hysteria in history has had its stock character or villain. For good measure Indiana University had three. One of these was a poor bedeviled creature whose life story had been written in the sordid blood of racial discrimination and human tragedy. He was "Hatless John" Edler, a Jew who had been forced to stand by and undergo the traumatic experience of seeing his parents murdered in cold blood in a Russian pogrom. In 1917 Edler was a junior in the College of Arts and Sciences, and amidst all the war excitement he had talked of anarchy—a word as despicable as Hun. The *Daily Student* without compassion said the lonely Jewish waif was regarded "as a dangerous enemy to the nation." He had threatened, it was said, to blow up the Bloomington *Telephone* because he disagreed with its war editorials. Calmer people, however, believed the troubled Edler was insane because he had tried openly to purchase cyanide from the chemistry laboratory. Chief among Edler's adversaries were postmaster John Cravens and the local police. They searched the boy's room looking for incriminating evidence, and they found it in the form of a pitiful handful of dog-eared anarchist tracts and several clock mechanisms, "which are taken," said the *Student*, "to indicate that he has been attempting to construct infernal machines, bombs, etc." Edler was an expert clockmaker, and rightly explained that the cogwheels and springs which the local patriots had snatched up were as harmless as the Hansel and Gretel figurines who so faithfully paraded the incessant passage of hours. A more understanding lunacy commission found "Hatless John" entirely sane, his machines harmless, his intentions pure, and it secured employment for him in Indianapolis where he proved a model employee.

The faculty, too, had its villains. In 1914 Professor James Grover McDonald, doughty Scotsman and Indiana graduate of 1910, assistant professor of history, was swept up in the swirl of opening drama and prepared a pamphlet for the German Alliance and another culturally pro-German organization. He took a moderate view toward the first accusations of bestiality against the Germans. Four years later, and after long and devoted service to the great national cause, the United States Senate turned up his name as a subversive who had questioned the truth of pro-Belgian propaganda, and he became the subject of investigation, apparently without the Senators stopping to ask about him before and after publication of the mild little statement. In an interview published in the Indianapolis *Star*, Professor James A. Woodburn defended his young colleague, even though he had expressed some doubts about the wisdom of the publication in the first place. Woodburn said McDonald's manuscript had been perverted in publication by deletion of a "no" or "not" in an important connection, and that his language had otherwise been twisted.

A more troublesome case was that of Professor W. H. Zeuch, Iowa-born third generation German, who had been appointed to the Indiana staff in the fall of 1917 to replace Professor Frank Stockton in the Department of Economics. On November 12, 1917, the Bloomington *Telephone* published a sensational story under the head, "I. U. Professor Denies Hun Atrocities!" The paper said Professor Zeuch had run amuck. "He has taken pen in hand and gone to the defense of the German warlords, denying reputed German atrocities. He had entered the lists by excusing the crimes of Belgium on the ground that those crimes are the crimes of all men in all wars. The professor has covered a lot of territory and either is a very brave man or a very unwise one, and the professor is going to travel a rocky road for the next few days."

He did indeed travel a rocky road. This was red meat for the Monroe Defense Council, for his was the first case of alleged disloyalty to come before it. Council members hustled out Kirkwood Avenue to discuss the Zeuch case with President Bryan. The *Telephone* reported, "The President, generally a mild and even tempered man, is reported to be looking for a large and pliable war club with which to top the nut off the professor." It also said Zeuch had joined the faculty while everyone was looking the other way. Information about his publication or letter had been sent to Bloomington by some unfriendly person in Hopkinton, Iowa, where it had appeared in the letters to the editor column of the *Hopkinton Leader*, and had struck immediate fire.

President Bryan was not stampeded by the press, and refused to comment on the case until he had talked with Professor Zeuch. The Iowa letter had protested the intemperate editorial policies of the Iowa weekly. Zeuch said its statements were insults to every American of German descent, and he felt the editor had maliciously intended to give his readers the impression that German people were by nature bloodthirsty brutes. He felt it dangerous to stir American passions in this way. "I have kept my tolerant attitude," he wrote, "even under the lash of this insane abuse hoping that you would see the folly of stirring the bitter resentment of German-Americans by such misrepresentation. The article in your last issue under the caption, 'Why We Fight,' is a little too much for me to endure and I must protest."

Professor Zeuch said allied powers had made plans before America entered the war to peddle choice atrocity stories to influence "our people" and had employed preachers and lecturers to do the job. Especially had they chosen the Reverends Hillis and Newton to adorn and present the allied messages of horror. This had needlessly hurt 15 million loyal Americans of foreign extraction.

The professor's readers in both Hopkinton and Bloomington had failed to credit his statement, "Being an American of pure German blood you [the Iowa editor] may realize how offensive your policy has been to the German-Americans. I hope you may see my point of view. If you confine your policy to an attack upon German autocracy and militarism I will gladly cry amen! and shall be happy to think that we radicals who have been struggling against autocracy and militarism from time out of mind have received a rather belated recruit."

Heedlessly the *Telephone* called Zeuch the Kaiser's friend. His case was to go to the District Attorney for action. Before this happened, however, the professor resigned on November 13, 1917. He told the *Student* he had no intention of being disloyal to America. He only wished to refute unfair attempts to create hatred against loyal people. Professor Ulysses Grant Weatherly kept his reason and courage and defended his colleague against what he felt to be groundless charges of rendering treasonous statements. He thought Zeuch's act more a matter of slight indiscretion in the face of so much public insanity than a matter of disloyalty.

Zeuch's grandparents had come to the United States in 1848, and were proud, gentle people. They had left the fatherland because they were bitterly opposed to monarchist oppression and Prussianism. President Bryan was less circumspect in his statement. He told the press, "We do not know much about Mr. Zeuch. He came to us at the very last moment in September to fill a temporary vacancy. In his published letter he professes loyalty to the United States and the cause for which we all are fighting, but without going into all the details, makes statements and implications about our soldiers of the Civil War and the present war which are untrue and intolerable. The University has no place for such a man." Surely President Bryan had not read Zeuch's letter. What the professor had said about the Civil War was, "If we are to believe the Confederates the northern men were brutes in the South."

Professor Zeuch had been an active supporter of the YMCA because he felt it lessened the brutalizing impact of the war. He left the university to enter the United States Army provided his defective eyesight did not prevent him from doing so. Otherwise he would accept a job in Mexico. The *Telephone* felt deprived of its own private devil and accused him of running up the white flag and departing under fire.

By the time Professor Zeuch resigned, things in Bloomington and the university began to look a little foolish, even in this time of so great a national crisis. The editor of the *Student* turned introspective. He thought all had gained revealing insight into themselves. "We admire the person who can go ahead with the present in the midst of any crisis as if there were no future, the man that carries things thus to the end as thoroughly as he would do under ordinary conditions, even if the heavens threaten to descend upon him the next instant is to be admired." The editor remarked that there had been little calmness on the campus for the past few weeks. Students had almost forgotten about classes, and when they did attend it was a frustrating intellectual experience. Everything that was attempted in the classrooms was done in a neglectful or disconcerted manner. Professors made only half-hearted attempts at lectures, but conditions seemed to settle down and there was still hope that sanity would return.

As spring advanced in Indiana in 1917, thoughts of many students naturally turned to the land as a place where they could make tangible contributions to the war effort. Now that so much emphasis was placed on the conservation of food, this was a productive place to apply student energy. At potato planting time some Greek letter fraternities engaged in growing gardens. Delta Tau Delta, for instance, started the move by planting two of its vacant lots in potatoes.

On a much broader scale was the organization of the "Soldiers of the Soil." President Bryan outlined this program, by which a boy could register properly with Bursar and Registrar and devote a certain amount of time to gardening or farming and receive academic credit for his work. He addressed students on the subject, saying, "The food campaign is just now the most essential part of our great war. We wish, therefore, to provide for the enlistment for the food campaign in a manner as nearly as possible like that required of those who enlist in the army. Students who wish to enlist at once for this service may do so by signing at the Bursar's office the following form prepared by Dean Rawles." This latter paper was a somewhat austere student commitment under oath to do farm work with the same degree of devotion, as "Soldiers of the Soil," as soldiers of the army did in military camps. The *Student* reported on May 1, there was an unbroken line of boys in front of the Bursar's office taking the farmer's oath, and not all of them were farmer boys.

Not to be outdone by the boys in demonstrating their patriotism, women students organized their own program of preparedness. The Women's Athletic Association called a meeting and distributed pledges which asked co-eds to promise to sleep eight consecutive hours each night, to refrain from eating between meals except in conformity with training rules which permitted fruit, crackers, malted milks, and plain ice cream. They promised to take an hour's exercise a day, in the gymnasium, in recreation, or in manual labor, to observe hygienic rules, and to wear sensible clothes—this meant low-heeled shoes. "No high heels," was the women's slogan.

All of this was explained by Judith Maxwell as a suitable conditioning for first aid and Red Cross work. One hundred and sixty-seven girls signed the pledge. Two girls, Dorritt and Lorena

Degner of Winamac enlisted as "Soldiers of the Soil," to the horror of Dean Rawles. He refused to permit them in the program even with their mother's consent. The spunky girls, however, were not to be denied by a dean. They appealed to President Bryan who bade them return to the land, "Go, & God bless you!"

In other ways students aided the war cause. President Bryan suggested that instead of up-coming sophomores burning their green caps, as had been done traditionally, they should send them to Europe to aid war orphans. He thought the moral effect on the boys in learning the lesson of conservation would be a salutary one. Then they would also have the satisfaction of knowing they had "capped" a cold European orphan.

While "Soldiers of the Soil" labored along potato rows and co-eds slept away eight consecutive hours every night with patriotic fervor, professors engaged in all sorts of projects. One delivered lectures on war preparedness in the summer schools of Indiana. He discussed "How Germany Makes War," "What's Wrong With Germany?," and "American Ideals and the War." Many members of the staff were granted leave to render technical service to the government. Professor Frank Davidson of the English Department went to France with the Ambulance Corps. Samuel Bannister Harding was with the National Board for Historical Service in Washington. In fact, Harding rendered perhaps the most distinguished service of any member of the staff, unless it were Rolla Roy Ramsey of Physics who taught so ably in the radio program. In Washington Harding was associated with Guy Stanton Ford, Evarts B. Greene, Dana C. Munro, James Wilford Garner, Robert McNutt McElroy, and Albert Bushnell Hart. He helped to classify war information, to prepare the *War Cyclopedia*, and wrote pamphlets for popular distribution. Harding was chief editor of the Committee on Public Information Materials. When the war ended he had just completed a revised edition of the *War Cyclopedia*. His publication, *The Study of the Great War, A Topical Outline, with Extensive Quotations and Readings References*, was said to have been a full and instructive popular aid on the war, perhaps the most useful of the publications of the National Board for Historical Service.

W. W. Black of the School of Education was an organizer of local councils of defense, Will D. Howe did special work in examinations for government services, so did Amos Shartle Hershey.

Twenty-seven Medical School professors and doctors were in active military training service. Georgia Finley, instructor in home economics, became chief dietitian of the Lilly Care Hospital and was the first woman staff member. Mason Edward Hufford of the Department of Physics was employed by the United States Bureau of Standards and was engaged in sensitive war work.

Both students and professors had made full commitment to the war by May, 1917. If they gave primary thought to the educational responsibilities of the university it was only in moments between drives and campaigns. In 1914 and 1915 these same people had exhibited extreme caution about becoming involved in the troubled affairs of either Mexico or Europe, but two years later they rode the full tide of emotions and carried the banner of patriotism and morality high. An interesting reversal of attitudes was that of the International Polity Club. On April 16, 1917, this organization discussed "Why Are We at War." Leaders of the discussion were Harding, Kohlmeier, and William Evans Jenkins. The latter was a member of the Department of English with a Stanford University background. It was his opinion that German ideas and open democracy could not exist on the same planet.

So pro-French had the university become by 1917 that Professor Logan Esarey sketched for an audience on May 7 (Lafayette Day) the history of Lafayette's brief visit to the Ohio bank of Indiana on his famous tour of the nation in 1824. Miss Ruth Maxwell's French class sang the *Marseillaise*, while the audience waved French flags. President Bryan and Samuel B. Harding paid glowing tributes to the "great Frenchman who helped America in her time of need." A special collection was taken up for the blinded and wounded French soldiers in the European hospitals. This outpouring of Gallophilia was followed two days later by the showing at the Princess Theater of *Fighting For France*, which gave a fairly realistic view of "glorious battles, & the terrible results."

On the same date that Hoosiers poured out their hearts and cash for the cause of France, John W. Cravens, representing President Bryan at the Conference of the National Association of State Universities, proposed that 180 university and college administrators pledge their institutions to support the federal government in every way possible. In a moment of hysteria William Lowe Bryan wired Woodrow Wilson asking him to state whether or not colleges and universities should remain open. "These universities, whose men are everywhere pressing forward to enlist," said Bryan, "are ready, if necessary, to nail up their doors." Wilson replied that there was no necessity whatsoever for suspending sessions of the colleges. Such an action would in fact be very much against public interests.

Indiana University during the remainder of the war stepped up the tempo of its drives and crusades, if not the pulse of its classrooms. Almost constant campaigns were underway to support the Red Cross and the YMCA, to sell war bonds and stamps, to produce food, gather clothes, organize local patriotic efforts, and to equip local military units.

Samuel Bannister Harding and John J. Pettijohn prepared a pamphlet detailing the services of the university. The campus became a Red Cross training center in which women from all over the state came to learn how to make surgical dressings and other hospital supplies. Ralph V. Sollitt, State Adjutant for the Intercollegiate Bureau, sought to meet the Surgeon General's call for 1400 volunteers for the medical corps, and Indiana University was called upon to supply a trained team of thirty-six medical men. At commencement in 1917 the trustees and faculty presented President Bryan with $500 to be known as the "Bryan Fund," in honor of his fifteen years at the head of the university. The money was to be used in war services abroad.

In the midst of the great burst of patriotism and energy, news reached Bloomington that a university audience in 1914 had been duped by James Archibald, public lecturer and magazine writer, who now stood charged in England as a confirmed German spy. He was said to have accepted $5000 from the German Embassy to further that nation's propaganda. At Indiana he had assured his audience that all was well with America. It appeared he had been trying to lull Americans into a sense of complacency.

President Bryan worked overtime to support the war effort. He organized a group in cooperation with the Indiana Union Board called "Back the Sammies." He appealed to other colleges and universities to organize a similar movement. In May, 1917, he suggested to the presidents of member institutions of the Association of Colleges and Universities that they prepare plans by which their institutions could give even more support to the nation. He explained Indiana had offered all its facilities which included the gymnasium to be used as an armory, its athletic grounds for drill fields, sixty acres of campus grounds to be planted in potatoes, the facilities of the School of Medicine, and the services of the university staff. The purpose was to make sure that every person in Indiana University be a backer of men in training or in the trenches. Students were divided into groups to work each congressional district of the state. "The Union," said the *Student*, "means to prove once and for all that the men here are really behind the men behind the guns. . . ."

On May 9, the old Mexican hospital corps was reactivated and hastened away immediately to a secret destination, and a new regimental infirmary was organized to take its place. Earlier 300 co-eds had registered in a nursing course looking forward to being able to do Red Cross work wherever their services were needed. Dean Ruby Mason mobilized her charges behind the "Sammy Backers" and by mid-October had pledges from 400 co-eds, faculty wives, and townswomen to send every Indiana University man at the front a Christmas box.

By October it was clear that the war was going to be frightfully costly in terms of human suffering and life. It promised to sap the last unit of human energy and spirit, to test the courage of every American. It had already proved financially costly. In a bold front page editorial in the *Student*, President Bryan lamented, "We must pay. We have not begun to pay as the people of Europe have had to pay in work and money. We must sacrifice. We have barely touched with our lips the cup of sacrifice which our friends & our enemies in Europe have drained almost to the dregs. We are fighting to keep what our fathers at Valley Forge were fighting to win for us. . . ." The president set the tone for a sackcloth and ashes existence for every person in Indiana University.

Sacrifice was to be practiced in the university community in many forms. In November the conservation sermons of Hooverism were impressed upon the university community. Pledge cards were given the students to sign on which they promised to conserve food to the utmost. Sugar, fats, and wheat products were to be used sparingly. The sugar bowl on the university dining tables had already been banished, and there began "meatless" and "wheatless" days. No one went to bed hungry, it was said, because Herbert Hoover had made adequate suggestion of substitute foods. Students were told the Food Administration could do little to help win the war without their help, and the least they could do was to sign the pledge cards and keep their promises.

Hoover appealed directly to Indiana senior women in March,

1918, to take courses in food management, chemistry, physiology, and economics. He hoped they would also acquire some capacity to present food facts in public discussions. "Today," said Hoover, "your country asks you to resolve to do what you can in this hour of extreme peril to the democratic peoples of the world." The food campaign gathered momentum as the months passed, and by 1918 there was a general crusade, not only to produce more food products, but to conserve those already in existence.

The war drives took on the fervor of great moral and religious awakenings. The YMCA worked both sides of the street with unflagging zeal. This organization had been established in the university at the inception of the movement, and it could now make a strong traditional appeal for funds on familiar ground. Beginning November 6, 1917, and ending ten days later Indiana students raised $11,200, as a part of the drive in the central division of the national "Y" to raise $7 million. Indiana colleges were the first in the nation to reach their goals, and their faculties contributed a third of the total sum raised in this drive.

Perhaps no war in history involved women in various phases so much as did World War I. Indiana co-eds and female faculty members involved themselves in all sorts of war projects. Under the leadership of the very active Women's League they did everything from studying political issues of the war to learning to knit socks and sweaters. Harriett Nebe Bircholdt, Chief of the Bureau of Public Discussion, prepared a syllabus for guidance in public meetings which was adopted by the National Council of Defense. The outline was part propaganda and part information. It was basically for women's clubs to use.

The league promoted a propagandizing exhibit in the Student Building. Professor Alfred M. Brooks selected the works of famous contemporary English, French, and Italian artists who had turned their talents to producing war posters. It was said the Indiana exhibit was representative of art work done in the war. Copies of the posters on exhibit were offered for sale in order to create a yarn fund for the Belgian Relief knitters. Funds from other sources were forthcoming, and by January, 1918, knitting had ceased to be a fireside pastime and had become a patriotic industry.

While co-ed knitters plied their art, other women students made and gathered garments and layettes for the relief of Belgian and French children caught in the tragedy of war. The first consignment of clothing from the university contained 1400 garments. Doubtless the most vital service rendered by women students was the making of surgical dressings. They were challenged, "Have you made a surgical dressing yet? If not, make it today!" It was said the big battles were on in France and there were not enough dressings in the United States to care for the wounded from a single battle. The *Student* informed the co-eds that every surgical dressing sent to France helped to save a wounded soldier. In fact, it might save two men, the injured one and his substitute.

War relief funds were also short, and a frantic drive was on to increase them. Approximately fifty subscription lists were in circulation. The Red Cross was in perpetual need of support, and Indiana University subscribers responded to its calls with generosity. In February, 1918, the institution added the white star for every person connected with the university who had made a contribution. The yarn fund lagged behind because the knitters needed more yarn than there was money for buying it. A sum of $550 a month was pledged, and it was prorated to the Yarn Shop, surgical dressings, French relief, the YMCA, and civilian relief.

The west parlors of the Student Building were turned into a yarn shop and knitting rooms. Girls were given lessons in knitting, and on Tuesdays and Fridays they worked industriously at making socks and sweaters. By April, 200 girls were thus employed as members of the new campus organization, the Thimble Club.

A phenomenally successful project was the packing and shipping of Christmas boxes. Each co-ed chose an Indiana University boy in service and prepared a box for him. She was given a candle, a message from President Bryan, a pound of rock candy, and a pound of fruit cake for inclusion. The cakes were baked especially for the boys by university and Bloomington women. The girls were permitted to add a personal gift. Despite a shortage of sugar, fats, and flour 648 pounds of fruit cakes and tallow candles were prepared, and the university community and town raised $719.13 to pay shipping charges. Not all of the boxes, however, reached the boys. One was sent to Georgia Finley of the Lilly Care Hospital Corps.

Women students engaged in a morale building project which had great potential for future romance. A campus drive asked girl correspondents to write the boys in France about affairs at home. In March the *Student* piously warned the co-eds the lazy days of spring were at hand and not to put off writing. At the same time the editor cautioned them not to write frivolous letters, because "Everything received by soldiers abroad is of the utmost importance." What that pompous young lad did not realize was that, since the days of Sparta and before, men in battle have placed great store by touches of feminine frivolity. President Bryan helped the project along by contributing $100 to Battery F, apparently to help defray expenses of the correspondence program.

The drives which came close to home indeed were those which promoted so passionately the sale of liberty bonds and war saving stamps. Workers were everywhere proclaiming the glories of free men and the soundness of emotional and financial investment in the future of the Republic. Through three stout campaigns speakers and workers sought an investment from every person on campus. Characteristic of the liberty bond sales was the one that started on April 6, 1918. Students assembled on the steps of the Student Building and, accompanied by the band, sang the popular songs of the war. They then moved to Jordan Field and band, students, and soldiers paraded down Sixth Street to arouse townsmen to the cause. This rally set off a month-long sales campaign in which cartoons, placards, slogans, and sermonettes were posted everywhere.

There were posters which showed soldiers at the front under fire, waved the flag, showed women and children suffering the brutalities of battle, stretches of No-Man's Land, muddy trenches, and wounded and dying boys. The composite message was that the purchase of a bond was not merely a financial transaction but the sacred extension of a helping hand to a battle-worn soldier, and to a nation bent on victory. An outside bond quota of $285,000 was set for the third loan drive in Monroe County, a good part of which was supposed to come from the university community.

More modest savings clubs were organized on the campus to sell the small denominations of savings stamps to students. Everywhere students gathered—the Student Building, the Library, Maxwell Hall, dormitories, boarding clubs, and the Book Nook—there were stamp salesmen. The *Daily Student* ran the melodramatic *Century Magazine* cartoon under the title, "After an Air Raid," a bereaved man sat beside a shrouded figure on a cot, upon which rested a crucifix. A child on his lap asked, "But Daddy, Mother didn't do anything wrong," and got the answer, "Mother made the sacrifice, and the babies wonder why, make such sacrifices impossible! Buy War Saving Stamps."

A more direct advertisement in late October, 1918, said, "In the vicious guttural language of Kultur, the degree A.B. means Bachelor of Atrocities. Are you going to let the Prussian python strike at your Alma Mater, as it struck at Louvain?" Students were told the Hohenzollern fang struck at every element of decency and free culture the college stood for. It had ripped away the old romance of war and reduced the science to bloody, filthy carnage. The paper begged its readers to put away every possible dollar for the purchase of liberty bonds, because every stamp and bond bought fired a bullet point-blank at the heart of Prussian terrorism.

Even the aesthetic side of the university was devoted to war-making. The old and revered convocation series saw a constant stream of speakers pound away at the atrocious Hun, the bravery of the Allies, the suffering of battle victims, and the holy cause of citizen support. A University of Michigan professor told his audience that the cause of it all was the fact Germans had shaped their social and political philosophy after the ideals of Nietzsche. Two weeks later Robert Frost of Amherst College read his poetry of the comfortable New England folk scene. Frost seems to have been the only visitor to the campus in that three years who reminded an audience that men still lived and died within the context of American folk ways and institutions.

It was indeed a far cry from Frost's "The Death of the Hired Hand" to the death of the handsome ship *Lusitania* with its precious freight of humanity as described by Rita Jolivet, French woman. Mme. Jolivet not only described German brutality on the high seas, she damned its barbarity in Belgium and France. She was in America on a lecture tour in behalf of the French War Relief.

The months came and went and tension grew tighter. For college-boy soldiers who plodded up and down Jordan Field in closed ranks and lived in familiar surroundings of college and campus by the regimen of war, life became a dull routine. The most exciting thing that happened was the return of the girls in November. A tingle of excitement suggested that at least one aspect of college still remained intact.

There was even reason to hope that boys then in training would never see France from a troop transport ship. The *Student* described this shining autumn of hope a week before the fighting ended.

[2 3 5]

"Somehow," it said, "the weeks passed at last and the Sunday came, the day which was 'to bring the girls back.' Sunday morning the fellows turned out in full array, fresh hair cuts, clean collars, and shoes shined till they would have made the lieutenants' cordovan puttees look sick. Never before has the Monon and I. C. station[s] seen so many fellows come to meet the girls, but can you blame them? Every train was quickly swamped by soldiers, each one making a grand dive for his 'special one.' "

President Bryan was stirred by deeper feelings than for homing co-eds. In a public letter he announced that it seemed there would be peace at last. Ending the war, however, did not mean the end of human suffering. It was still time to make gifts to the various war work drives as "a thanks offering and prayer to God for the greatest blessings—world peace with justice."

Then came the end, like the ringing down of the curtain at the climax of a dramatic thriller. At 12:30 A.M., "American time," on November 11, Bloomington natives were aroused by a ringing of the courthouse bell, and within a few minutes the streets were filled with celebrating people. They were emotionally linked by bonds of sorrow and joy. Kirkwood Avenue, of recent years the scene of so much preparing for war, "echoed with the tramp of 1500 men in service, the coming of the University S. A. T. C. The khaki lines under the orders of Captain Dalton moved along the streets with military precision. The sound of marching broken only by the cheering of spectators followed by a hush—a greater tribute than speech." The twelfth was topped off by a grand review on Jordan Field of every person in military service in Bloomington.

University co-eds marched onto the field in full phalanx, and "Daddy" Woodburn, that ubiquitous man of history, delivered a short valedictory in which he declared the armistice had "the momentous significance of the outcome of the war in the destruction of autocracy." Both U. H. Smith and James B. Wilson pleaded with the crowd to stand by the boys in France until they could be brought home and discharged from the service.

President Bryan was in Chicago at the time of the armistice celebration and missed the joy of marching to victory with the army. Nevertheless, in peace as in war, he was enthusiastic. He celebrated with the shouting, shoving crowds through the wide streets of the city, deliriously happy that the war was ended. Someone bumped into him and cocked his hat perilously onto one side of his head, giving him the appearance of an intoxicated man. He was—by the news.

Victory was scarcely four days old before the Committee on Student Affairs was engaged in a discussion of the central collegiate issue of permitting the dances to begin. An elaborate set of rules was drafted, and in the minds of faculty, students, and the Women's League, a social status as before the war would be established.

This was not to be true for Indiana University. The war years had wrought irrevocable changes in world and national society which all but wiped away the old codes of past relationships. The university now moved onto another plane of existence in which it not only had to reckon with human problems within an entirely new and strange context of revolution, it had to readjust and devise an academic program within the demands of the new age. This would become a more complex task with the advancing years than had been true at any time in the first century of the university's existence.

[X I]

"The Brass Tack":
Financing a University

I N 1918, WHEN WORLD WAR I ENDED, most Hoosiers, if they
gave the subject any thought, no doubt believed their state
institutions would return to their financial and educational
status of 1914. In fact the 1851 Constitution, and the body of
statute law then in existence pretty well assured that this would be
true if possible. There was little actual reckoning with the fact that
every aspect of American civilization had undergone revolutionary
and inflationary changes. Public attitudes toward the support of
higher education in the state had changed imperceptibly. To meet
the new and highly competitive demands for staff members, Indiana University was called upon to double its salary scale and
general budget, although it was utterly unable to do so under the
prevailing tax structure of the state.

Remarkably, Indiana University went through the war with
all of its distractions and displacements without significant losses
from its faculty. Even William Lowe Bryan was amazed at this,
and in his numerous comments about it to the board of trustees
he praised the loyalty of his staff. The majority of the senior core of
the faculty were older men who had served the university for two
decades or more. Professors who were heads of departments had
become "institutions" and either refused offers to go elsewhere or

were not invited to join the faculties of other universities. For men who had graduated from other schools, but whose wives came from Bloomington or neighboring towns there were extraordinary emotional attachments. Each of them felt loyalties to students, and most of them in these associations were repaid in generous measure with student affections and regard. Though difficult to define, the kind of parental and charismatic influence William Lowe Bryan exerted over his colleagues had holding power.

Yet it is easier at this point to give reasons why men might not have remained on the Indiana faculty than to explain why they did. In 1914, the president suggested a faculty budget of $238,-277.90 to the board of trustees. His own salary was $6,000; Woodburn and Weatherly were paid $3,000 each; Fernandus Payne, a promising young biologist with almost a decade of service was paid $1,700; Judge Enoch Hogate of the Law School received $3,300. Other full professorial salaries averaged about $2,000, and the pay of instructors was as low as $700.

In the commencement trustees' meeting that year, Bryan sang a refrain that was to be repeated many times over in the future. He told them, "Nothing could be done that would be of greater benefit to the University than a higher scale of salaries." He said faculty members felt they had lived through long lean years with hopes the university would eventually pay better salaries. Their minimum expectations were that Indiana could equal the salaries paid by neighboring state schools. His colleagues also pleaded for the establishment of a salary scale which would recognize merit in the setting of salary rates, not just whether they were married, had a long service record and were loyal, or simply were present in the university family. In Bryan's opinion in 1914, if salaries were not raised there was no hope left. Faculty members, including the least self-seeking, would be thrown into a state of despair, a despair that would linger with them for the rest of their lives.

The university would lose men because of the low rate of pay and would be unable to hire comparable replacements. To Bryan there was something even more fundamental than loss of faculty members, the university would be forced to choose an inferior status for itself if it continued to offer such low pay. Professors' salaries in his opinion should be raised to a median of $4,000, "No matter what sacrifices this should involve. If it were possible to do this, the result in ten years would appear in a totally different kind

[2 3 9]

of university here." Deans at Purdue, said Bryan, were paid $4,000, and professors received $3,000, "Thus there are ten men who are paid very much more than anyone is paid here. It is certain that such a difference in salary scale [if] maintained would make Purdue a university of distinctly higher grade than Indiana." Perhaps Bryan spoke only of the exceptional Purdue salaries, because in 1918 a federal survey indicated that the school's overall salary scale was appreciably lower than that of Indiana.

After four inflationary war years, Indiana University's salary scale in June, 1918, still fell well under the $4,000 level suggested in 1914. Professorial pay ranged from $2,400 to $3,400, associates were paid $1,900 to $2,300, assistant professors received $1,500 to 1,900, and instructors $500 to $1,500. At this point the salary scale leveled out for several years. In June, 1919, Bryan reminded the trustees of the gap between the rising cost of living and the university's static salary scale. Married men in the lower ranks were hard-pressed to sustain their families. He said that two men on the faculty had attempted to commit suicide, one of these cases he could verify personally. "It is becoming apparent that the University cannot maintain a faculty of standard quality with the salaries we now pay." Only recently he had undertaken to hire a University of Chicago instructor at a salary of $3,000, only to be told the candidate had an offer of $10,000 from private industry.

Professors at Indiana University faced a financial stringency of another sort. The institution paid salaries in quarterly installments, which required astute management of personal finances. Letters from professors appear in university correspondence asking for advances or loans against their earnings. In the early 1920's, Guido Stempel was traveling in the West and found it necessary to write U. H. Smith, the bursar, that he needed an advance in order to get home. Providing for their families often imposed genuine hardships on the professors, in some cases it bordered on being impossible.

While Bryan was confronting the board of trustees in 1919 with the desperate facts of university salaries, he in turn was being confronted with the same problem by E. R. Cumings of Geology. In his annual report the highly respected professor wrote, "I wish to call attention to the absolute necessity of increasing very materially the salaries of the University and especially of the younger men who are doing research work. The University has no future unless it can secure and retain scholarly and energetic young men. It cannot do so on the present salary scale. Everything else we do is of little consequence if we let the faculty retrograde. Everything else should be sacrificed to the one aim of keeping here a faculty of high quality."

In desperation William Lowe Bryan took his campaign for better salaries to the public in January, 1920, under the heading, "They Take Our Men." He wrote, "I wish that every citizen of Indiana could know that Indiana ranks forty-third among forty-eight states in the amount which it gives for higher education in proportion to its wealth. I have before me the figures in an official bulletin of the United States Government. Only five states of the Union do less for higher education in proportion to their wealth than Indiana does." He said in states of every size, from Delaware to Texas, this was true. Other schools robbed Indiana and Purdue faculties of their promising men, and these raids were conducted not by the great universities alone.

In a strong vein of evangelical rhetoric Bryan pricked Hoosier pride by saying, "I have lived in Indiana all my life. I love Indiana as Riley did. I have said and I believe that Indiana is our Holy Land, near to heaven as Jerusalem or Sinai. But when I see the vast procession of states marching toward the intellectual leadership of the world and when I see where Indiana is willing to march in that procession, I burn with shame. This is no matter of rhetoric. They take our men. Every year they take our men."

The Indiana president labored against the mountain. A letter from Hiram Jones, obviously an anonymous correspondent, spoke the stingy countryman's piece when he wrote, "Take the school superintendent and the college professor whose only investment is the education which in many cases is no more than that of the best businessmen of the community, and yet they drew salaries of from $2,000 to $4,000 for five day weeks and a nine month year, while the average businessman will work six and sometimes seven days a week for twelve months for the same or less salary. Hasn't this 'poor pay' propaganda gone pretty near far enough? With taxes now almost confiscatory it would seem these professors who are getting fair salaries for short service with free club rooms, golf links and swimming pool thrown in at the expense of the tax-payer, ought to have a little modesty. . . ." This was not the first time a Hoosier "Hiram Jones" had confused issues and stirred naïve public opinion on the subject of professorial duties and salaries.

While the snaggers and Hiram Joneses carried on their petty bickerings the university faced the postwar world with staggering challenges. Coincidentally, the centennial year of the institution fell in that watershed of national history itself, 1920. William Lowe Bryan informed the trustees in April, 1919, that the occasion of the centennial was imminent and that they and the institution would need to celebrate it. He asked for the organization of faculty and alumni committees to plan a proper observance of the occasion on the following January 20, 1920.

The *Daily Student*, July 25, 1919, announced the following year would be a festive one, "a year," said the reporter, "that will doubtless live in the memory as long as memory lasts. Next year is Centennial Year, the hundredth birthday of old I. U. And what won't be going on! Pageant drills and pageants, calls for meetings and meetings, celebration plans and celebrations. There are now a number of committees at work on plans for next year and the men of these are the kind that will have something doing for next year. Yes, there will be a lot of fun, and excitement and celebration." The coming year, continued the paper, would generate as much fun to boast about being a student "as say your great-great somebody who belonged to the first class of the University when the University was not like it is now where it is now."

This was a fair statement. There were all sorts of committees and sub-committees plus a veritable confusion of ideas as to what should be done in celebration. Various main ideas emerged: there would be a ceremonial parade, a striking centennial poster portraying a view of the campus from Dunn Meadow, a plethora of oratory, a host of visiting dignitaries, a dinner, a dance, a speech contest, and a commencement time pageant. Of more lasting proof of the celebration would be a series of centennial publications under the watchcare of the publications committee chairman E. R. Cumings. On April 15, 1919, Cumings reported that a preliminary canvass of staff members revealed there were ten or fifteen finished books in prospect.

W. D. Howe of the English Department was speaker and pageant chairman. There was some emphasis on raising approximately $15,000 in gifts to be used largely in financing the celebration. Apparently there was little or no thought of raising funds for a permanent endowment, or to support a part of the university's

program. Three years before the university community had celebrated the Indiana Centennial with a historical pageant written and
produced by William Chauncey Langdon. Howe's committee employed him to prepare a pageant for the university's anniversary
to be given in pleasant weather during the forthcoming commencement.

The board of trustees appropriated $6,000 in October, 1919, to
pay the university's part of the centennial expenses. It was anticipated most of this sum would be recovered by solicitation of large
groups of alumni. This they did, because alumni appropriations
amounted to $8,700. Provisions were made for special trains to
bring crowds into Bloomington in January, and a canvass produced
a listing of rooms available for visitors. There was also a discussion
of providing dining facilities for the crowds.

The famous dean of the Brown County artists, T. C. Steele,
was engaged to paint the centennial poster, and this was to be
printed in such a manner that the descriptive caption could be
clipped away and the poster prepared for framing. Someone observed that this was as near as most Hoosiers would come to owning
a Steele painting. Steele had painted a portrait of William Lowe
Bryan for the Senior Class of 1907, and in 1916 the institution had
honored him with a doctorate. Steele's diary for 1919–20 contains
some penetrating observations about the university. He attended
some of Alfred Mansfield (Dudey) Brooks' classes and was much
impressed with his instructional capabilities. It was Brooks, in
fact, who had persuaded Steele to come to the university in the first
place, and to agree to exhibit four of his better paintings on the
campus.

Speakers for the centennial gathered in the battered and worn
Assembly Hall: President William Alfred Millis of Hanover College, Jacob Gould Schurman of Cornell University, Governor
James P. Goodrich, and Will H. Hayes, Chairman of the Republican National Committee. In a politically insipid speech Governor
Goodrich told the centennial audience that teachers and professors
must be paid in keeping with the economic standards of the day,
even if a raise did mean an increase in taxes. He predicted that
prices of goods and services might actually go down, but Hoosiers
would not live "to see the day when the old wage scale will prevail. So the just thing is to legislate with such knowledge in view."
The governor's address added not one cubit's measure to the cen-

tury-old monument to higher education in Indiana. He apologized for the failure of the state to support its schools and then took refuge behind the great political generality, "but I am sure the work of our universities compares favorably with the work of others. Indiana University has a record of which it may well be proud and the celebration of this hundreth anniversary is a most significant event. . . ."

To Jacob Gould Schurman, then in the midst of a campaign to raise $10 million for Cornell University, Governor Goodrich's offering must have actually sounded defeatist. Schurman spoke in much clearer terms about "The University Today and Tomorrow." He viewed the opening of the new century for Indiana as one of possible frustration. He, like Bryan and the trustees, felt professors' salaries had to be brought into line with the economic realities of the moment. Young men all across the country were leaving faculties for better paying jobs in private industry. The educational challenge itself was now placed in a new context by the very industry which robbed faculty rosters. President Bryan closed the oratorical part of the celebration by saying that even though the past had its grim moments, and economic fog still shrouded the university's immediate future, the institution would branch out in greater adventures in the field of learning.

The centennial parade was colorful and included nearly everyone on the grounds. The four classes and the law students marched almost completely around the inner campus. In the forefront were the members of the Reserve Officers Training Corps who earlier had limbered their legs by escorting the university's special guests from the Bowles Hotel to Assembly Hall. The band, decked out in brand new uniforms, played Professor Winfred Merrill's special music, and Professor Henry Thew Stephenson was on hand with a movie camera to record the whole display. Apparently the entire student body of 2,356 members participated in the ceremony. If there were absentees they were rare exceptions.

In June W. C. Langdon produced his grand outdoor pageant, under the title, "Tho Torch of America." This extravaganza involved at least two thousand students, 500 of whom participated in a ceremonial dance. Again Professor Merrill prepared special musical compositions. An added dash of color was the parade of the G. A. R. Veterans who were meeting in Bloomington in a grand encampment. Previous to the production of the pageant

"Flying Squadrons", in fifty cars with three Bloomington business-men each, set out from the Chamber of Commerce to distribute advertising material in all the principal towns of Indiana. David Starr Jordan was the commencement speaker, and he brought back to the campus some of the old fire of the past, although he had just gone through a long, harassing peace campaign. Thus June 1 and 2, 1920, saw Indiana University move irretrievably into its second century with the color and éclat of Langdon's pageantry, the sooth-ing music of Winfred Barzille Merrill, and the shouts of encour-agement from the ancient warrior Jordan.

For William Lowe Bryan, however, the realities of Jacob Gould Schurman's speech more nearly stated the future course of the university. Mere pageantry and oratory did not drive away the immediate need for economic improvement. Bryan in his ardor to increase salaries and bring about an improvement of the univer-sity's general financial situation perhaps did his cause some injury by the fact that he had consistently, since August 1, 1914, refused to accept more than $6,000 of his $7,500 annual salary. This drew from the faculty the criticism that the lower figure became, in the mind of the trustees, a ceiling when they considered other profes-sorial salaries, and as a result the salary scale was artificially depressed. At the March, 1920, meeting of the board, Bryan sub-mitted a communication signed by heads of the departments of the College of Arts and Sciences seeking immediate salary adjust-ments. The president, however, thought such adjustments should be held off until the regular salary budget was presented in June. At the same time he told the trustees there had accumulated in the treasurer's office a sum of $5,168.00 of his back salary, and he wished to donate $1,000 of it for the purchase of furniture for the girls' annex dormitory, and to use other small amounts for like purposes. Wisely the board ordered a warrant drawn to pay the entire sum to the president, but even so he asked for time to con-sider accepting it.

In May, 1920, the faculty budget was $402,067.50, and in the following October the range for individual professors was moved upward somewhat. Heads of departments averaged about $4,200, professors received about $3,000, and associate professors approx-imately $2,700. Alfred C. Kinsey, assistant professor, received $2,000. In comparison a young professor at Columbia refused an offer to come to Indiana at the sacrifice of a $5,000 salary. It was in this year that the total university budget for all expenditures exceeded a million ($1,010,471.86) dollars.

The financial gloom thickened in the early months of 1921 when the General Assembly refused to grant either a $.10 or $.07 levy on assessed property. This was blow enough, but the rate of assessment itself was reduced, leaving greater financial uncertainty than before. This statement implies a simpler situation than actually existed in the state and the university. In September, 1920, an appeal was made by Indiana, Purdue, and Indiana State Normal to the Indiana Tax Commissioners to increase the property levy in behalf of the schools. The agents of the three colleges told the commissioners it was either this or face bankruptcy. They asked specifically for an increase from $.028 to at least $.078 per hundred dollars of assessed evaluation. The Bloomington *Daily Telephone* said, "The Board was shown that the very heart of state education is being destroyed through loss of professors owing to small salaries, and the high cost of maintenance." Later that year William Lowe Bryan expressed the opinion that every effort should be made to re-establish the $.07 tax levy, and that Indiana should be awakened to the fact that it must take a long step forward or fall hopelessly behind its neighboring states in the field of education.

Farmer members of the Indiana Legislature in January, 1921, in special caucus, favored a $.05 levy but took no formal action. Governor Warren T. McCray announced that he favored an increase in the tax levy, but did not specify an amount. The House of Representatives early in February approved a $.05 levy, and out of this Indiana University would receive two-fifths of the total return, which was estimated to be in the neighborhood of $1,125,-000 in contrast to its previous income of $700,000. This bill was finally passed by the Senate on February 14, 1921, with only one negative vote. In his annual report to the board of trustees, Bryan said the university's income was $1,063,690.05. The salary budget totaled $492,396.58. Before the year was out the *Alumni Quarterly* predicted the institution's income for the year 1922 would approximate $1,626,800, a sum which changed remarkably the economic condition of the hard-pressed university.

With a very much more promising financial condition after the adoption of the new tax levy, President Bryan suggested to the trustees that they study the situation, and so far as possible cooperate with the university in paying adequate salaries to the best men.

Bryan was concerned with the employment of new personnel in the faculty because much of the present faculty was growing old. In presenting the June budget he asked for a $500 to $800 raise for the entire faculty list, but ventured for the first time to voice the faculty's desire for a new meritorious salary scale. By March, 1922, the faculty budget had been increased to $606,466.17, but even this was only a partial solution to the chronic needs of the university. When John Hill, Professor of Spanish, resigned to accept a research professorship at the University of California, Bryan reported to the trustees, "Nothing could better illustrate the fact that our salary problem is not chiefly a question of retaining in the services of the University and the state first-rate men." A year later the salary scale showed some improvements. Bryan's salary had been advanced to $10,000, professors averaged approximately $4,700, and there seemed bright promise for another raise in 1924.

In the latter year, D. M. Mottier of Botany wrote the board of trustees through Bryan, "The professor who has 30 years of faithful, efficient and loyal service to his credit; who has attained a high standing in his profession; whose productive work has stood the test of time and criticism; who is still carrying a teaching load of 15 hours per week of undergraduate work along with directing graduate students and his younger colleagues in research, and who is engaged actively in research himself—such a professor should receive a salary of $5,000 per year, not including summer session, or as large a salary as is paid to any professor in Indiana University residing in Bloomington." No doubt what Mottier said was true because he outlined the characteristics of a professor well-nigh indispensable to any university, but the tone of his letter no doubt impressed Bryan and the trustees as being a recommendation for a raise for himself.

In nearly all the communications concerning salaries over the years, two issues were clearly defined. The first was simply securing enough money to operate the university at even a minimum level of efficiency and effectiveness. The second, however, had almost as much fundamental meaning in establishing the quality of the university. No objective historian could view the first century of the institution's history without being made aware that the practice of establishing salary scales on the basis of length of service, nominal position, loyalty, and public esteem, was a faulty one. Again the headship system was a barrier to change in this area. Young and promising men no doubt were almost impelled to seek employment elsewhere in order to advance in their professional fields.

The tone of William Lowe Bryan's statement to the trustees in May, 1927, had changed imperceptibly from that of his communication in 1914. "The most important problem for the present meeting of the Board of Trustees," he wrote, "is the readjustment of the salary roll. For reasons which are well understood, the problem is one of unusual difficulty. I have worked at the problem with great care, deriving all possible assistance from the heads of departments and Deans." The problem was the latter asked for three times the sum of money available to the university for salaries. Even in a reconsideration, the amount of the requests were still well beyond the institution's resources. So desperate was the situation, said Bryan, "The most distinguished men in the College of Arts and Sciences have urged strongly and repeatedly that their salaries not be increased too much so that the best of the younger men might be taken care of." He assured the trustees there was no reflection on men who chose to leave the university, but the school had to make definite plans to keep men of promise and distinction.

So desperate did professors, students, and alumni consider the university's financial situation in 1929 as it related to hiring and keeping promising young staff, that they opened a propaganda campaign in behalf of the institution called "Brass Tack." This group not only showered Indiana with pamphlets dealing with the university, but it interviewed people all across the state in efforts to secure support for the institution. It collected comparative data from all the Midwest state universities which revealed that Indiana and Purdue were receiving 40 percent less public aid than their neighbors. It told the taxpayers that boosting Indiana University's budget request to $2,630,172 would mean only $.21 on $1,000 property assessment, or the price of a package of cigarettes. This represented a considerable boost over the legislative committee's recommendation of $1.4 million. Law Professor W. E. Treanor's speech before the Huntington Rotary Club in February, 1929, was characteristic of statements made to the public. He said, "that Indiana University will have to receive largely increased support from the present legislature or continue its present program of denial of education to hundreds of Hoosier applicants annually, and denial of many state-wide services which are vital to Hoosier people." Treanor was a member of the speakers' bureau who appeared before Rotary Clubs. He was successful in getting this body of business and public-spirited men to ask that budgets of all the state schools of higher education be increased.

On February 13, 1929, the Bloomington *Daily Telephone* reported the combined alumni of the three state schools had made a strong case before the legislature that higher learning in Indiana was facing a crisis. Again this group produced data to show that the state was giving less than half as much support to the three schools than were other states in the Midwest. At the same time the alumni started distributing its pamphlet, *Brass Tack*, which described the loss of professors during the last few years caused by lack of a satisfactory salary scale.

The "Brass Tack" campaign yielded results, but not as generous as friends of the schools had hoped. Indiana University received $1,795,000 for 1929–30, or an increase of $335,000 over the $1,460,000 the university had received in 1928–29. President Bryan, who directed the "Brass Tack" campaign, served notice that the drive for adequate funds would be carried on into the future until the legislature did appropriate adequate funds for the university.

In the 1929–30 faculty budget Bryan's salary was raised to $15,000, thus setting a new ceiling for the professorial range. The latter was elevated to approximately $6,000. The head librarian received $5,700, Fernandus Payne the same amount, Logan Esarey in history received $3,800, and Stephen S. Visher in geography was paid $3,300. Two years later, early in the Depression, the salary scale was stabilized at the former 1929–30 level.

The total salary budget for the first time exceeded a million dollars, but the university's stance on this pinnacle was indeed shaky. In July, 1932, Albert Walsman, a Democratic legislator from Indianapolis, proposed a flat 20 percent cut in both Indiana and Purdue professors' salaries. In response the administrations of the two institutions said they were willing to accept a 10 percent cut, but any larger figure would be too drastic. Bryan proposed that Indiana cut out all professional travel expenses and save funds in every other way, but not cut salaries. His proposed salary budget for this year reflected this fact. He also reported that enrollment figures had dropped less than in other state universities, and statistically this was true. In 1929–30, there were 3,591 students on the Bloomington campus, and in 1932–33, there were 3,337; in 1934–35 there were 4,082, which brought enrollment up to the level it had reached just prior to the Depression.

Despite the monumental struggle Indiana University had endured to establish an acceptable salary schedule, it had, in the Depression year of 1936, a total budget of $1,059,176.27, and Depression cuts in salaries varied from approximately 10 to 12 percent. This condition was somewhat ironic—the university had struggled hard to raise its salaries, and had eventually been able to do so by most astute management of funds. When the general economic pinch came its financial situation was not artificially inflated. Internal savings were made by eliminating travel funds, not filling vacancies, and by not replacing men who went on leave. In addition a careful review was made of eight bond issues in order to keep the university from getting caught in demands for interest and capital payments it could not meet.

From long experience Bryan and the trustees knew how to live with financial stringency. They were fortunate, however, in the depression years to have a friend in the Governor's office in Paul Vories McNutt, an Indiana graduate and a former Dean of the Law School. In 1934, for instance, he held up the Indiana and university budgets after the state budget committee had reduced them sharply. McNutt expressed the notion that several important items had been cut from the institution's budget which must be restored, and he proposed to wait until the legislature had acted on all financial matters to see if there were not enough funds left over to maintain the university budgets intact. Two years later the faculty and administration of the university sought to have all cuts restored and salaries adjusted to the 1932 level. This meant a new budget high of $2,259,485 as compared with $1,875,000 in 1932 and $1,490,000 in 1936. This request reflected the additional fact that Indiana University was having to provide matching funds for five new buildings then under construction with the assistance of Public Works Authority funds.

On January 29, 1937, Ward G. Biddle, State Senator from Monroe County, wrote Trustee John S. Hastings that the governor and the budget committee of the legislature had agreed to a sum of $2,240,000 for the university, as compared with the final sum of $1,735,043 for 1936–37. This was indeed in sharp contrast with the total budget of $173,000 on which the university operated in 1902, in the first year of William Lowe Bryan's presidency.

The Depression years had indeed been transitional ones for Indiana University. Never before had the institution been forced to live so close to the problems which beset all Hoosiers in their daily affairs. By 1933 the bite of the Depression had become so serious in the state that even rural Monroe and its neighboring counties felt it in the form of staggering unemployment and human need. The newly created Federal Emergency Relief Administration offered assistance locally during the winter 1933–34. This federal agency was to have its greatest impact through the work-relief branch of the Civil Works Authority. In late November William Lowe Bryan submitted to the Civil Works Authority a number of projects which he believed worthy. "It is obvious, however," he wrote Professor Thomas Rogers, Civil Works Administrator for Monroe County, "that the University can provide only a limited amount of money for material and this will limit greatly the amount of work which may be done here under the Civil Works Program." Bryan then outlined nine projects which included cleaning and straightening the course of the River Jordan, repairing sewers and drains, roofing and caulking of older buildings, painting interiors, and general repairs on other structures. In all, the president's request amounted to $84,054.15 in labor costs, and $60,067.90 for materials. These projects promised employment to 246 men "for a considerable time."

The day following receipt of President Bryan's letter a part of his proposed labor program was approved. Already work on the River Jordan was under way. Because of the university's inability to supply materials several of the other projects were delayed until the board of trustees could make some provision for funds. A distinct advantage of the federal grants was the fact that students could be employed. Deans C. E. Edmondson, C. J. Sembower, Agnes Wells, and librarian William A. Alexander were appointed to assign student jobs.

This was the beginning of a significant new era in Indiana University history. Federal aid was to bring phenomenal physical and professional changes and expansion to the institution—a campus building program, student employment, and refurbishing of buildings and the wooded campus in a way the university might never have accomplished with only state aid. Federal aid, although it came in the form of emergency employment and grants for physical improvements, was to bring about some fundamental restructuring of the university's academic programs. This became possible in the initiation of an extensive new building program.

Aside from the actual impetus given university expansion, the institution's officials quickly learned that their governmental relations in the past had been primarily with partisan agrarian state legislators; now they had to confront federal emergency program administrators who, though slightly more urbane and sophisticated, made the procurement of funds far more complex and confusing. The New Deal administration itself was uncertain in the first place how to tackle the evils of economic depression. Added to this was the growing rivalry between Harry Hopkins, relief administrator, and Harold Ickes, Secretary of the Interior. In time, however, university representatives and the trustees became expert in undoing red tape, making contacts, and establishing lines of communication to Washington.

By December, 1933, the Civil Works Administration had made genuine headway in completing the original work projects on the campus for which the university could supply materials. The total cost of work had been increased to $167,052.05, of which the institution supplied $65,403.24. By the latter date the CWA program had become a major refurbishing venture in which buildings were rescued from depressing shabbiness. Walks and roadways were built and repaired, and the grounds were reworked. For the first time the campus was to be lifted out of mud and snow, and the old walks which had been cherished by some were consigned to memory and tradition.

The biggest project undertaken by this agency was the completion of the Memorial Union. Ward G. Biddle, Union director, announced in January, 1934, that four six-hour shifts of workmen would be employed with the hope that this structure could be completed by mid-February. Alfred Granger and J. C. Bollenbacher, the Chicago architects for the original building, were employed to supervise an addition of fourteen sleeping rooms on the sixth and seventh floors of the central tower section. These were to be used to house graduate students and unmarried faculty members. The basement under the cafeteria was to be finished as a general dining hall, and the ceiling of the spacious Alumni Hall was to be treated with a special acoustical material. This had been planned originally, but the memorial funds were exhausted and the room had been left unfinished.

At the same time the Memorial Union was being completed, forty-two workmen cleaned and re-painted the interiors of Kirkwood and Maxwell Halls, the Student Building, and the Library. Stone carvers adorned the south entrance of the latter building with the noble legend, "A Good Book is the Precious Life Blood of a Master Spirit." The artisans also carved a tulip tree over the two east portals, labeled the Business Building, and adorned the entrance to the Biology Building.

President Bryan announced in February, 1934, that it was the intention of the New Deal agencies to employ 100,000 college students across the nation in CWA jobs in libraries, laboratories, offices, and other university areas.

He assured Hoosiers unable to attend college for financial reasons that they would be given employment assistance at a minimum wage of $.30 an hour. The CWA officials requested that universities help further by waiving tuition and other institutional fees. Indiana college officials, however, objected to this proposal on the grounds that it hardly seemed fair to collect tuition from students who were equally hard pressed and who were working their way through school.

On February 13, 1934, an announcement was made that 350 Indiana University students would be given employment under the CWA program. Deans Fernandus Payne and C. E. Edmondson, Bursar U. H. Smith, and Thomas A. Cookson were named a committee to receive and review applications. Within a single day approximately 500 students had requested employment. The *Daily Student* said, "It is probable that no special projects will be instituted under the plan to absorb the employment. The greater part of the work will be done on the grounds, in the Union Building and Cafeteria, in the Library, and assisting various departments of the University." Students would be permitted to work sixteen hours a week, and would be allowed to earn no more than $20 a month. One restrictive provision was that 25 percent of the 350 positions allotted to Indiana University would be assigned to new students. This requirement was impossible to fulfill at registration time and the university was permitted to hire students already registered.

Hardly had students been employed and the other CWA projects placed under way before work was halted. It was said, "The projects must be reconsidered and judged as 'useful' before the work can be continued, according to provisions formulated by the Governor's Commission for New Relief Programs. . . ." Work was halted on the Union Building for twenty-two days until FERA inspectors could evaluate what had already been completed. Finally on April 21, 1934, CWA officials declared the Union a worthy project and work was resumed.

In July it was announced that FERA student aid would be continued into the next year at the reduced rate of $15 a month, but this time 50 percent of the grantees must be newly registered students. There seemed, however, to be an air of uncertainty about how long even this limited employment would be made available because affairs in both Indianapolis and Washington were in a constant state of flux. Earlier in 1934, CWA was halted largely because of the criticism that FERA projects were "boon-doggles," and workers were "boon-dogglers." An early historian of the New Deal, Dixon Wecter, explained, "When, within limits of seasonal fluctuations, it grew clear that the New Deal policies were not reducing but apparently augmenting the number on relief, the administration decided to scrap the FERA, returning direct relief wholly to local governments and devoting federal outlay to able-bodied clients and projects of durable value."

On June 16, 1933, Congress approved the organization of the Public Works Administration and gave it an initial appropriation of $3,300,000. In April, 1934, William Lowe Bryan, inexperienced and uninformed as to the intricacies of securing one of the new federal grants, addressed a simple letter request to Secretary of the Interior, Harold Ickes, for $400,000 with which to construct a new administration building. He sent a copy of this letter to Granger and Bollenbacher which alerted them to the possibility of a new architectual fee on the campus. This firm became exceedingly active and influential in procuring the grant for the university. In the meantime William Lowe Bryan's brief letter request opened a new era for Indiana University, and the beginning of the mastery of federal red tape for its officials. Between April, 1934, and July 11, 1935, an enormous amount of correspondence and frequent personal visits were undertaken between Bloomington and Indianapolis and Washington. Much of this reflected confusion at each end. The Indiana applicants were confounded by New Deal and federal red tape and legal uncertainties.

On May 21, 1934, J. C. Bollenbacher wrote James W. Fesler that he had learned on a visit to the PWA Washington offices that a major question concerning the administration building was the fact it was not a revenue-producing structure, and some way had to be found by which the board of trustees could guarantee payment of the annual interest on the government debt. The architect also told Fesler that while he and his partner had supplied the necessary architectural information about the building, the trustees would have to complete the application concerning legal guarantees. Quickly U. H. Smith reported that the board had established an amortization schedule and would report it at its June meeting. This was sent to Washington on schedule but was promptly lost in the haystack of applications from every university in the country.

Indiana University, however, had its aggressive agents on the scene in Granger and Bollenbacher. Once the application was recovered they persisted in pushing it through the various agencies toward approval. Congressman Arthur H. Greenwood was enlisted to prod Ickes' office, and other channels of influence and communication were opened. Late in June, 1934, President Bryan and the trustees persuaded Judge Ora Wildermuth and George Fullen Heighway to visit Washington and prepare a report on what was happening to the university's application. This proved an astute move. Judge Wildermuth was adept at getting at the heart of the problem and with his legal background he could communicate readily with the WPA lawyers and the federal expeditor, all of whom assured him the grant would be made as soon as the Interior Department reduced its $46,000,000 over-allottment of funds.

Despite Judge Wildermuth's success at getting information and assurances, a serious legal barrier to the university's negotiating a final loan with the Public Works Authority remained. The institution had an endowment of $775,028.67 which in the past ten years had yielded $460,516.76. The PWA officials were unsure whether the increment and capital of the endowment fund could be used as collateral to insure the government loan. They suggested that the board of trustees institute a friendly taxpayer's suit to test the legality of pledging university funds. Judge Wildermuth balked at this, saying that he was not certain that anyone could properly phrase such a suit so as to yield desired results.

Too, he thought such an action would absorb far too much time. He suggested that the legal division of the PWA agree to accept instead a special legislative mandate. He wrote John C. Cravens on November 7, 1934, "I am rather inclined to think that such a program might appeal to the legislature." Then he observed, "I will be working on the test in the meantime, but if the PWA approves the legislative act, I think that question then should be submitted to the Board of Trustees, by letter, for their suggestions." Ten days later Wildermuth told Bryan the PWA lawyers would accept the legislative act in lieu of a taxpayer's suit.

By January, 1935, William Lowe Bryan's appetite for federal money was whetted. He now sought appreciably more funds than he had requested in his original letter to Harold Ickes. He was confronted not only with the problem of expanding the physical plant in Bloomington, but of greatly enlarging the Medical School and the School of Nursing in Indianapolis. He suggested broadening the scope of the impending legislative act to grant the trustees power to use the university's endowment as generously as possible to secure more money than would be needed for the administration building alone. In reply Judge Wildermuth suggested that the president discuss the more comprehensive bill with Governor McNutt. He believed "a more general bill may be more difficult to get passed." Such a bill was drafted by Dean Bernard Campbell Gavit of the Law School, and Judge Wildermuth revised it to suit what he considered a practical situation. It was then sent to Governor Paul McNutt and Herbert A. Schneider of the PWA office in Washington.

At that point Judge Wildermuth, Senator Ward G. Biddle, and six legislators held a strategy meeting. Senator Fred Eichelhorn of Lake County was asked to sponsor the university's bill, and U. H. Smith was asked to supply such information as Senator Biddle would need. Judge Wildermuth informed his colleagues that he had no information concerning the university's original application because he had given attention only to legal details. Biddle proved a capable strategist, and at once obtained "the signatures of a powerful group of legislators to Senate Bill 133." That he was eminently successful was demonstrated on February 5, 1935, when the Senate voted 43 to 1 to allow the university to involve its credit to the extent of $1,207,000 in obtaining a federal loan.

Again President Bryan's desire for money was stimulated. Two days after the Senate passed the university bill authorizing it to contract the largest debt in the institution's history, he wrote Judge Wildermuth that it might be possible that the federal government would make money available to the states to finance the construction of public buildings. He said Governor McNutt was having prepared a list of buildings which might be needed in the state institutions. If it were to share in this possible grant of federal funds, the university had to have its request ready by February 11, 1935. Bryan said he was submitting such a list with the proviso that the trustees could modify it in future meetings.

On return from one of his Washington visits, Judge Wildermuth had lunch with Dwight Peterson of the City Securities Corporation, at which he was told that the bank would buy the PWA bonds at a premium of $2,000 to $2,500. Early in February following this conversation a Major Fleming of the PWA authorized Wildermuth to sell the university bonds to private investors if that appeared to be the best market. On February 25, 1935, the judge wired President Bryan that the Indiana House of Representatives had adopted Senate Bill 133 by a vote of 79 to 19, and the university was now free to approach purchasers of its bonds. He also informed Bryan that an attorney general's decision friendly to the university was being written that afternoon, and that Paul McNutt had signed Senate Bill 133 two days earlier.

Immediately after news of the legislature's favorable action was published, considerable excitement arose on the Bloomington campus as to where the new administration building should be located. Bryan favored the site occupied by the ancient Assembly Hall just east of Owen Hall. However, he had to confront other notions about the proper location. As early as 1932, Granger and Bollenbacher had drawn tentative plans for an administration building. They had designed a structure to house the president's office, and offices for the registrar, bursar, special committees, a board room, and an adequate file unit for university records. J. C. Bollenbacher (A.B. 1906) was astute in recognizing one of the main sources of decision-making on the Indiana university campus. He wrote Miss Ruth McNutt, the president's secretary, on March 15, 1934, "You have already contributed more to the picture which I now have of the requirements of a new administration building than anyone else and I had hoped to have your further advice on the space requirements, relationships of departments, necessary access of personnel to the public and to the students, etc." He said further he was attempting to design a building for the next forty or fifty years, and asked that Miss McNutt assist him in achieving "a perfect solution of the plan problem." Modestly Miss McNutt protested that the building she had in mind, "is all a dream of my own." Dream or not, the secretary projected her ideas in many ways.

Bollenbacher was indeed forehanded. On March 28, 1934, long before anyone knew whether a federal grant could be obtained, he informed William Lowe Bryan that plans were ready for inspection, and they were being sent by mail to him and Miss McNutt. His tentative drawings encompassed a very modest 1,560 square feet of floor space for the president's offices, and Bollenbacher estimated the building would cost approximately $250,000, including equipment and architectural fees. Bryan replied gloomily in April that he saw no immediate prospects of securing such a building.

While Bryan and Miss McNutt corresponded with Granger and Bollenbacher, and with Governor Paul McNutt and Harold Ickes, the field examiner for the Indiana Department of Inspection and Supervision of Public Offices of the State Board of Accounts submitted a searing report to President Bryan concerning the efficiency, or lack of efficiency, of the university's administrative offices. "The offices," said the examiner, "are poorly ventilated and sadly over-crowded, many of the offices occupied are semi-basement rooms and as a result are damp and consequently unhealthy. Employees are continually suffering from colds which are apparently due to the conditions outlined." The inspector was critical of space allotments and availability, saying the university's records were constantly threatened with destruction. Staff efficiency in the administrative offices was low, and the operation of the university itself was seriously hampered by these facts.

President Bryan and Miss McNutt were thoroughly conscious of all the problems outlined by the state inspector; they had to live with them day by day. The president's office was overcrowded by a huge desk, a table, and the stiff-backed chairs used by the board of trustees. Miss McNutt's office was perhaps even more crowded, as were the bursar's and registrar's offices. Thus it was with unusual anxiety that almost everybody with any administrative responsibility sought the construction of a new administrative building.

Once the Public Administration's 45 percent grant to the university became a near certainty the problem of finally defining clearly the purposes of the building, its location on the campus, and the details of its construction had to be reappraised. The purposes were left almost unchanged from those stated in the original application to the federal government. There arose, however, some considerable concern with termites. President Bryan wrote Judge Wildermuth on February 26, 1935, that should these insects gain access to the institution's records they would destroy them. "The termites are in the town in many houses," he wrote. "If they should have access to the files they would eat up the papers. This may be thought a reason why the files should be placed on the upper floor."

The location of the new building proved to be the most difficult of the three issues. No one could have anticipated in 1934 the emotions that would be engendered by this problem. Bryan repeated to Judge Wildermuth his earlier desire to see the new structure erected on the site of the shabby old Assembly Hall, but he suggested that perhaps his idea should be reexamined. "I have had all along the thought that the Administration Building should be located where the Assembly Hall now is, although the site is not for various reasons an ideal one. I am inclined to think that the whole question should be considered anew. A secondary reason for this reconsideration is that the huge, ugly Assembly Hall is very useful. It now houses and would continue to do so a number of utilities which it would be better on the whole not to include in the Administration Building." He then told the president of the board that he had walked across the campus from a point south of Maxwell Hall and he favored the knoll in the woods directly opposite Kirkwood Hall. This in his opinion would not break the quadrangle grouping of university buildings.

A fortnight later the trustees selected the site of the Administration Building east of the Kirkwood Observatory and north of Fourth Street extended. Immediately students protested the decision because they felt this would spoil the beauty and symmetry of the woodland campus. In a tactful open letter they said to president and trustees, "The student body of I. U. does not wish to appear presumptuous, but it believes that 'tis not overstepping its bounds in voicing objection to location of the new Administration Building on the site recently designated." The students admitted they were inexpert at building location, but they felt the beauty of the campus would be seriously marred by the trustees' decision.

"While every student regrets very much that Assembly Hall has been spared he is not greatly concerned over retention of the old eyesore as he is over the prospect of being deprived of the unspoiled beauty of the forest plot east of the Kirkwood Observatory and north of 4th Street extended."

Again on March 9, 1935, the *Daily Student* discussed the building location, saying that the recent totally unexpected decision had made students even more cognizant than ever that Indiana University had one of the most beautiful campuses of any American university. The paper pleaded that the natural scenery not be injured. The wooded area was one which the paper thought students would regret the most to lose. Students enlisted faculty support for their contentions. Alfred C. Kinsey thought the building should not be located in the woodland, and he suggested the university should work out a comprehensive campus plan at once which would prevent future controversy over this subject. F. Lee Benns favored a site all the way across Indiana Avenue. John R. Moore, Henry Carter, and Alex Judson opposed the woodland site, while Dean Agnes Wells and William Evans Jenkins supported the board of trustees. Miss Wells said the board had spoken and that was the end of the argument. "The architects know what they are doing," she said. Professor "C. B. H." in an extended poem capped the argument:

> Nearest the heart. Is there no other way?
> Must man's art conquer God's I doubt you not.
> I know your skill, your high intent, but oh,
> Ere yet you make your final sacred choice,
> I pray you, Architect, consider well.

President Bryan was positive in his response to professors and students, the board of trustees had made its selection and that was comparable to Aaron of old driving his rod down on the spot. A month later, however, he was more conciliatory in his statement, "I do not believe there is another location on the campus which could meet with as universal approval as this site will." He undertook to assure the critics that the entrance to the campus would be dramatized. He was speaking then of the new site on which the trustees had thrust the heel of their boots. This was now a place out of the woods on the corner of Indiana Avenue and the campus drive near the head of Kirkwood Avenue. Bryan thought perhaps a triumphant archway would be erected over the campus entrance at this point.

On April 15, 1935, the trustees announced their change of mind, and the *Daily Student* commented, "The new location for the building is one recommended by many students, faculty, and alumni who were opposed to the original selection." The woods had been saved, feelings were placated, and students generously congratulated the trustees upon their display of wisdom. "They have demonstrated conclusively," said the campus paper, "that the beauty of the campus and the proper conduct of University affairs are safe in their hands."

In approving the Indiana Administration Building grant, the Federal Emergency Relief Administration agreed to appropriate $120,000 outright and to underwrite $280,000 worth of bonds. This was the beginning of the 45 percent or matching fund program which was to play such a vital role in Indiana University expansion in the future. On June 27, 1935, President Franklin D. Roosevelt approved the 45 percent grants for non-federal projects. By waiting to receive the more liberal terms it was said the university had saved $60,000 on the Administration Building.

By mid-September, 1935, the Administration Building bonds were ready to be placed on sale. Professor David Andrew Rothrock of the mathematics faculty told President Bryan faculty members were ready to purchase the securities if this were legally proper, and if they could do so without having to pay a brokerage fee. On September 16, Judge Wildermuth wrote President Bryan that the law required advertisement of the sale of the bonds so they could be sold to the highest bidder. He thought, "It would be splendid for the faculty and the University both if this arrangement could be made. It would furnish the members of the faculty a sound and substantial investment, would renew their faith in the University and would present a happy situation all around."

The ink had hardly dried on the minutes of the board of trustees' final approval of construction of the Administration Building before other projects were planned. By October funds had been granted to finance the construction of the last of the walks and roadways, and by April of 1936, Indiana University had ended its woes with plank and dirt walkways and roads. In the previous July, President Bryan wrote Judge Wildermuth that he, Val

Nolan, and J. W. Fesler had visited the assistant administrator of the Works Progress Administration, F. M. Logan, who had suggested that Indiana University apply for funds with which to construct other buildings. Bryan suggested that plans be submitted for a women's dormitory, a School of Education, a medical building, and a music hall. He also recommended that a committee of the board of trustees be authorized to file an application with the Federal Emergency Relief Administration for funds, and that he be designated to supply proper information and sign the applications.

With extensive expansion of the physical plant of the university in prospect by the end of 1935, Charles R. Ammerman informed President Bryan that any further addition of buildings would necessitate an increase in the capacity of the heating plant. Bryan told Wildermuth in a letter that an application to the Federal Emergency Relief Administration was being prepared for enlargement of the heating facility.

At the same time plans were made for expanding the physical facilities on the Bloomington campus, arrangements were made to enlarge the Long Memorial Hospital, the School of Medicine, the School of Dentistry, and the School of Nursing in Indianapolis. This Indianapolis improvement and expansion appears from the record to have been treated largely as a separate operation from the rest of the university. Perhaps this enabled the institution to use its applications and credit to greater advantage.

On the campus in Bloomington by the end of 1937, the new buildings which had either been completed or were under way completely changed the plan of the campus. Bryan Hall, as the new administration building was named, set the new pattern. On February 19, 1937, the *Daily Student* gloated, "Maxwell Hall never looked like this!" It compared most unfavorably the "two-by-four" offices once occupied by the administration with the more opulent ones in the new hall. More than this Bryan Hall gave the university a new and more sophisticated image with its beautifully paneled Board Room, spacious president's offices, and its impressive hallways and archival stacks.

Before final approval was granted the university for the construction of Bryan Hall, Governor Paul McNutt declared the institution needed a new education building, and on June 1, 1935, he announced that "The new $100,000,000 works relief fund allotted to Indiana is not 'pork barrel' legislation and must be expended where the need is greatest. . . . Whether I. U. gets the new school building depends probably upon the number of unemployed persons on relief after assignment of projects in Monroe County. Monroe County ranks high in the number of unemployed. The entire battle is to take care of these unemployed by consummation of useful projects." The university did get the grant for the Education Building, and in time support for construction of the Music Building, the new astronomical observatory, a women's dormitory, the School of Medicine, an underground heating tunnel, and a power plant extension. These additions practically doubled the floor space available for classes and institutional facilities.

In July, 1936, nearly all of the Public Works Administration projects on campus were brought to a standstill. Common laborers on the projects struck on July 3, 1936, after their demands for an increase in wages from $.40 to $.50 an hour was denied. The contractor, Leslie Calvin, told an arbitration commttee of foremen, workers, and WPA representatves that the wage scale was set by the construction contract itself, and he said the heart of the issue was whether or not his laborers were to be secured through the government employment office or through a union of the workers. On August 7, the workers were back on their jobs, having won an increase to $.50-an-hour wage, and the Works Progress Administration agreed to assume the additional cost.

In all the feverish activity of making applications, drawing building plans, exerting influence here and there for grants of funds, settling labor disputes, and placating disgruntled campus groups, it would have been little short of a miracle if someone had not shouted "Scandal." On February 1, 1937, Judge John S. Hastings of the board of trustees wrote Ward G. Biddle that Chester Davis of Bedford had come to his courtroom and asked to talk with him about a scandalous rumor concerning the WPA projects at the university. Judge Hastings said, "So we went into a huddle and he asked me if I had heard anything about any pending scandal of a serious nature which was about to break against both Indiana and Purdue and, of course, I replied in the negative. He then said that he was in Indianapolis a few days ago and a friend of his started to tell him about it and then seemed to get suspicious of Chester and said no more." Judge Hastings could get no further information except a veiled charge that Indiana and Purdue had been illegally issuing bonds to finance their building programs. Wisely Judge Hastings dismissed Davis' report as wild gossip. Someone had tried to repeal Senate Bill 133 which would have left the Indiana trustees without authority to issue bonds, and might have left the university with such enormous fiscal responsibility as to have wiped out its endowment funds. "It also may have had its inception," said Judge Hastings, "in certain other sources known to be hostile to the present administration of the University." He informed Biddle he was placing no stock in the rumor but felt he should be kept informed. This proved to be no more than rumor, and the university's legal obligations held up under the scrutiny of both state and Federal Emergency Relief Administration attorneys.

Because of the assistance given the university by the various federal agencies, William Lowe Bryan was able to bring his administration to a close in 1937 in an unusual burst of energy. The past five years of Depression and readjustment had in fact thrust Indiana University into an entirely new role as a functional social institution which figured directly in the solution of economic and human problems which arose well beyond the borders of the campus itself. Internally the university began to realize its full educational possibilities within a physical plant which permitted material expansion of staff and educational programs.

[XII]

"Stardust" and Sub-Culture

BOTH HOOSIERS IN GENERAL and members of the Indiana University community in particular heard the word freedom as it was so vociferously proclaimed during the war years in the context of the classical idyll. They almost completely overlooked its definition in terms of people living in their towns and countryside functioning as liberated Americans. Doubtless freedom to most Hoosiers meant the imposition of an earlier behavioral and institutional pattern upon everyone in the name of social and national security. There was clearly evident in Indiana University a desire to keep the institution in the ancient pattern of trustees-president-faculty parental control. This was the direct implication of presidential and professorial speeches delivered during the war. It is now difficult, however, to fathom precisely what the propagandist did conceive individual freedom to be.

Clearly the homefolks in the cornfields and the courthouse circles realized that the boys returning from the western front could have a shattering effect upon the future course of Hoosier life. Only a few short months before, large numbers of these callow-faced lads, many still in their teens, had gone away to fight in what they were told was a holy cause. Now they were swinging home men, veterans in the same sense their grandfathers had come home from the "Grand Review" and the Union Army at the end of the Civil War. These lads had not spent all of their spare time singing the mimeographed gospel hymns distributed in YMCA huts. In Bloomington they broke the silence of Kirkwood Avenue with booming renditions of "Mademoiselle from Armentières" and other ballads. They had learned first-hand many of the young ladies' innermost secrets. Where Professor Selatie Stout and Mr. Edgar Allen Menk waited in Latin and Greek classrooms at the head of the Avenue to discuss the private lives of the Romans, to read selections from Livy, and to explore Latin and Greek mythology, veterans advanced on the campus, their pockets bulging with Captain Billy's *Whiz Bang*, *College Humor*, lurid accounts of the girls' private lives, and John Held, Jr.'s cartoons. This was the immediate freedom which grassroots veterans savored, while blowing the suds off schooners of beer.

Away in Indianapolis a dedicated legislator devised a bill to fix by legal fiat the standards of social life by regulating the length of feminine dress at a point between the instep and first tendon. Thus enshrouded in ample textile modesty, a major source of temptation would be carefully packed away to await the ritual of matrimony. In other areas of society attempts were made to chain the present steadfastly to a comfortable past where morals could be worn on coatsleeves or pinned to the hems of flowing dresses. It was already too late, change was impending.

In Indiana University there was more than an idle wish for campus and classroom to reinstate the status as before 1914. There were prophets, of course, who predicted that major changes were upon the people, and American higher education would be forced to accept new attitudes, new demands for popular education, the introduction of new modes of scientific instruction and techniques born of wartime exigencies, and to accept the forced application of views of worldwide consideration of mankind's problems.

The university would continue to expand its basic program; it would take up unfinished business left off in 1915, reexamine the curriculum, add new faces to the faculty, and seek more support from the legislature. Most important of all, however, would be the on-rush to the campus of the new breed of more sophisticated and "liberated" students. Nobody, not even the students themselves, knew what effect the postwar sense of personal and social freedom would have on the social mores to which the institution had adhered so tenaciously in the past.

In the president's office William Lowe Bryan clung stead-fastly to his concepts that a major function of Indiana University was to set a pattern of social and moral rectitude for student and citizen alike. On the campus, it was said, the strictest code of be-havior would be maintained in harmony with the past. Clearly Bryan and his colleagues were unprepared to comprehend or accept the impact which the revolution of 1914 to 1919 had wrought upon American history and attitudes. Like their fellow countrymen everywhere, they seemed not to have understood the new social matrix in which religion, politics, and social intercourse would be fixed. Jordan and Eigenmann's earlier emphases on biology and evolution now, in the burgeoning twenties, assumed altogether new dimensions. Religious fundamentalism stood chal-lenged in the basic area of human creation in Bloomington.

American capitalism had indeed contributed heavily to the winning of the war, and it emerged as an almost wholly new and dominant force in postwar American life. During the years of conflict, middle western Indiana began to emerge from an agrarian state to one assuming heavy industrial commitments. Along with an increasing industrial tempo came a new breed of Hoosier in the northern cities—immigrants or first generation Americans. With the opening of each new plant there came heavier demands on politicians and government. Indianapolis became an industrial and banking center. In South Bend the wagon-making Studebaker brothers spread their name around the globe on automobile labels. So did the steel companies around the Lake Michigan industrial crescent. Along with the rising industries came organized labor with its economic and political influences and demands. These were the new forces with which the university had to deal in curriculum planning and staff appointments.

Victorians suffered no greater setback on the campus than in the revision of youthful attitudes toward relationships between the sexes. The end of the war, the coming of prohibition, the speak-easies, the automobile, and the growing popularity of the cigarette helped bring emancipation of the American girl. She shortened her dresses, rolled her stockings, painted her face, discarded the bustle, sought more public employment, smoked, drank, and en-gaged in many other forms of free social intercourse. It was impossible for the president, the faculty, or the dean of women to return to the past. Without their knowing it there had grown up on the campus doorsteps a new "sub-culture" of university life and student decorum. The rise of the speakeasy revealed things to American men about women they scarcely suspected before. They were as interested in "sinning" as the male population. They engaged in franker and more open discussion of birth control and placed sex on the campus in a new light.

Later Hoagy Carmichael, reminiscing about the era, wrote of this period in Indiana University: "We saw jazz already in the dives and moving into the speakeasies, set the tone and color of the country. We all dreamed of super jazz bands. Jazz didn't change the morals of the early twenties. But it furnished the music, I noticed, to a change in manners and sexual ideas. Women wore less and wore it in a slipping, careless way on the dance floors. Every girl wore silk stockings—and many rolled them beneath the knees so that every sitting down showed the American female thigh, nude and lush, anywhere from kneecap to buttocks. ('You just know she wears them,' said the ads.)"

What liquor, cigarettes, and automobiles failed to accomplish in breaching the barriers of the past between men and women, the new dances—the Charleston, Black Bottom, the shimmy, the strut, the toddle, and a dozen other sill shattering stomps—and jazz completed. This era rang with the discordant notes of "Show Me the Way to Go Home," "Making Whoopee," "Collegiate," and "Crazy Over Horses," all sung to the proper stimulation of "smoky" jazz in musty holes, latched and barred behind speakeasy doors.

In this era a new generation of professors, trained in more modern graduate schools, made radical transitions in academic views from those that had been advanced in earlier classrooms. Instead of giving a more or less ministerial tone to their profession, the modern and emancipated instructors became more nearly professional men of the twentieth century. They were not averse to visiting a speakeasy, many condoned liberal social, sexual, political, and economic attitudes. They often condemned bigotry, and even discussed with students the failures of state and church to meet their social responsibilities. They criticized American industrial and fiscal systems and revised views of politics and economics and constitutional government. Charles Austin Beard of Spiceland had set tongues of American scholars and laymen alike wagging over the delayed discoveries of the conclusions drawn in his seminal *Economic Interpretation of the Constitution of the United States* (1913). Moreover, in this rising moment of American isolationism, professors concerned themselves with foreign affairs and the nation's international relationships. They organized new courses in this field, bought books of broad geographical and political interests for the library, organized foreign relations clubs, and went through the countryside speaking in favor of the League of Nations, postwar treaties, and the reconstruction of Europe, and criticizing the new immigration laws.

William Lowe Bryan and his older colleagues had to meet the challenges of a free-swinging jazz-crazed America with the limited experiences of a cloistered rural university for doing so. Bryan revealed this fact eloquently in dealing with Samuel Bannister Harding's divorce in 1916.

There were still more challenges to the university and its way of life than the throbbing paroxysms of the jazz age and unleashed adolescence. William Lowe Bryan and his faculty colleagues had supported the prohibition movement to the hilt. In doing this, however, they failed to foresee what would happen to the tenor of society in Indiana. It made almost no difference that most Hoosiers were of "dry" inclinations. The state was quickly caught up in a network of law-breaking. Its geographical location, and especially its river and lake borders proved to have greater significance. David M. Chalmers in his book, *Hooded Americans*, wrote, "Booze, women, police, and public officials were for sale in Indiana during the 1920's as the rum-runner crisscrossed the state from Hammond to Jeffersonville, Terre Haute to Fort Wayne. Indianapolis by geography and fate, was always in the center of things." At the same time the state was beginning to feel the impact of illicit liquor trade, it also became the hunting grounds for the rising Ku Klux Klan.

The first Ku Klux Klan klavern was organized in southern Indiana at Evansville in 1920 by Joe Huffington, but it was the Texan, David Clarke Stephenson, who gave it spirit and direction. By 1922 the Klan was becoming well organized in Indiana, with a membership approaching 5,000. In September, 1921, the Bloomington *Daily Telephone* announced a chapter of the Klan was being formed in Monroe County. The paper reproduced a letter addressed to the editor which solicited members for the new klavern. The editor denounced the order as illegal, saying, "the very theory of night-riding should be nipped in the bud." Nevertheless the *Tele-*

phone ran the Klan's letter containing twenty questions which it asked of prospective members. Among these were place of birth, gentile or Jew, race, color of eyes and hair, education, religion, politics, and "Do you honestly believe in the practice of *REAL* fraternity."

In June, 1922, a paid advertisement in the *Telephone* assured the people of Bloomington, "The Knights of the Ku Klux Klan are here to assist in law enforcement—to aid in raising moral standards, to create a real brotherhood and insist upon clean politics. . . ." The order's post office box, however, was located in Ellettsville. In November, 1922, the town got its first view of the Klan, when 125 hooded men marched to the public Square. At the head of the column of white-sheeted nobles were three horsemen who led the way, followed by an unmasked drum corps of Indiana University students.

Later that month the *Telephone* accused the Klan of being behind the kidnapping of Halson V. Eagelson, the Negro band member, near Spencer. There was a hint that students involved in the incident might have actually been associated in some way with the Klan. The following February a pair of hooded horsemen announced that the Reverend R. C. Blair of Bloomington would speak in an open meeting on the purposes of the Klan. In the meeting the bigoted preacher denounced the idea of the Jews being God's chosen people, the Catholic hierarchy, and declared "It is time for the scum to be thrown from the melting pot." A month later the Reverend Allen C. Trusty of the Bloomington Christian Church estimated there were at least 291,000 Hoosiers in the Klan. Monroe County, he said, had a strong Klan organization.

While the two Protestant preachers blasted Jews and Catholics, Eugene O'Connell, a Catholic student from Fort Wayne, responded hotly to the charge that members of his faith were unpatriotic. He denied that they owed political allegiance to the Pope and cited the fact 12,000 Catholics had died in World War I. He denounced the Klan's version of the Knights of Columbus' oath as a bogus document. While O'Connell spoke, four hooded men drove around the town square displaying electrically illuminated crosses in the national colors.

The Klan reached into the university still further when Hugo Fisher, assistant athletic director, was arrested on a charge of operating a small still and homebrew vat in his house at Nashville.

It was said that Fisher was reported to revenue officers by local klansmen. In many other areas they made their presence discernible. None was more obvious than the brazen Grand Dragon, David Clarke Stephenson. By the summer of 1923, the Klan had become so bold as to announce that it expected to purchase Valparaiso University for $500,000, to conduct a teacher training institute. The *New Republic* responded to this bit of publicity by saying there should be a "Mob Hall," and a chapter of Phi Beta Ku Klux Klan men. "It would be a bold yearling," said the periodical, "who would dare to lynch a professor within two blocks of the dining hall or light a fire in a synagogue on any day but Friday." "Mob Hall" was never dedicated because it was discovered that the Valparaiso charter forbade sale of the institution to a fraternal, religious, or charitable organization.

In an even more meaningful way the Klan moved closer to Indiana University in its support of the Republican nominee Major Edward Jackson for the governorship. It supported all but two Republican candidates for local offices in Monroe County. This pattern continued throughout elections into 1926. In commenting on his defeat for the Bloomington mayoralty in 1925, Jesse A. Howe said, "The Klan won, that's all I have to say."

Later the university faculty was brought into conflict with the hooded order when Professor Ernest M. Linton, ex-preacher, professor of history and political science, and popular lecturer, spoke out against the Klan in Auburn. Professor Linton directed extension studies in the university, but on this occasion he addressed a teachers' institute. He was charged with saying the framers of the Constitution of the United States were heavy drinkers. Linton responded to his overheated critics by saying, "I have always fought the Ku Klux Klan and I strongly suspect that I have this organization to thank for these unfounded charges against me." Judge William P. Endicott of the DeKalb Circuit Court issued a less than judicious statement, "The people of this state had better stay away from Indiana University if such teachings as contained in the professor's address are advanced there." Linton admitted, "I hit the Klan hard in Auburn." The garbled statements issuing from the town, however, were in fact misstatements. The professor said he had quoted from J. M. Beck's United States history which contained a foreword by Calvin Coolidge. What he had said was that in the days of the Confederation and even before, it was an American custom to drink, and some Americans drank heavily. He was emphatic, "I stand for the principle of academic freedom because it is in danger from unscientific men who speak without knowledge." Clearly Judge Endicott was one of the dangerous "unscientific men."

The Klan threat to university freedom reached its height in 1925, when 100 percent Americans and conservative voters disregarded party lines and turned to the fiery cross for political refuge. In this period when all America was concerned with grave foreign issues, Indiana Klansmen regarded such interests as subversive. Professors such as Amos Shartle Hershey, Ernest M. Linton, Albert Kohlmeier, and other social scientists were subjected to criticism and suspicion. The International Relations Club was under scrutiny from the American Legion and the Klan. There can be little doubt but that there was an awareness at least of this in the making of curricula changes. In 1925 insidious forces controlled the governorship, the legislature, and the Indiana mind.

David M. Chalmers commented, "Not all the credit for the Klan's triumph of the will in Indiana should go to D. C. Stephenson, however, Indiana was equally deserving, for while Stephenson provided the organization and the leadership, it was the people of Indiana who listened and knew it was for them." From 1921 to 1926 Indiana was too heavily dominated by the bigoted monster, the Ku Klux Klan.

Up to 1925, David C. Stephenson, Grand Dragon of the State since 1923, largely had his own way in the Republican Party, the governor's office, the legislature, and along the main streets of many Hoosier towns. From his Central States Coal Company offices in Indianapolis he ran his ever-widening empire. A part of this enterprise concerned itself with a flourishing sale of Klan literature to the faithful. While in the full flush of this "literary" success in March, 1925, the Grand Dragon sent William Lowe Bryan word that the university should purchase its books through him. Herman B Wells said in a taped interview in January, 1968, "Dr. Bryan told me, shaking in his boots, he sent back word, either written or oral by messenger, that the University would have to buy them where it could get them appropriately, at the lowest prices. Dr. Bryan thought that was also a ploy to begin control of the curriculum because then they [the Klansmen] could say, 'you buy such-and-such biology book, you buy such-and-such political science book. . . .' "

Fortunately D. C. Stephenson's even baser passions, stimulated by drink, paved the way for Indiana University's escape. Stephenson had Madge Oberholzer, a maiden employe of the Superintendent of Public Instruction's office, brought to his Irvington house, where it was said he forced drink and personal attentions upon her. Then the Grand Dragon and his bodyguards loaded the tottering woman into a stateroom in a Chicago-bound pullman where she was undressed and assaulted by Stephenson. In his ardor, it was said by the public press, he "chewed all over her body." At Hammond the couple left the train for a room in a hotel. Miss Oberholzer slipped away and purchased poison, which she swallowed. She was returned to Indianapolis, where she died a few weeks later. A sensational trial followed which held the Klan's brutality up before the gullible rank and file of the order. Once behind the gates of Michigan City Penitentiary, Stephenson was no longer a force in state politics, and his "book" order to Indiana University passed without further incident. The institution narrowly escaped what could well have been its gravest challenge to freedom of inquiry and instruction.

Less disturbing to the university administration than Ku Klux Klan antics were those of the denizens of the Book Nook, who sat squarely in the front entry to the campus on Indiana Avenue. During the years in which this student rendezvous was so much a part of student life no one had heard the term "sub-culture." That, however, was what developed in the emporium on Indiana Avenue. The Book Nook became as much a part of Indiana University student tradition as the Well House, and perhaps as much a "classroom center" as the second floor of Wylie Hall.

Like all university campuses, Indiana grew its ring of small businesses catering to the peculiar demands of students. One of the first of these was the Candy Kitchen operated by George Poolitsan on North Walnut Street. In October, 1919, he purchased the Book Nook from C. D. Fetzer and C. W. Jewett, former mayor of Indianapolis. The little confectionary was a wooden shack which had existed on Indiana Avenue for approximately a decade and had passed through several hands before those of the Greeks. Contemporary observers described it as a shabby dirty student hang out with a sawdust-strewn floor. In its beginning the establishment had actually been a bookstore, but the co-operative bookstore on the campus had robbed it of business, and books were dropped in favor of cold drinks, stationery, and sandwiches. Too, the place originally catered only to male customers.

Poolitsan, the new owner, was a shrewd merchant and announced at once that he would clean up the place and ban smoking because co-eds demanded it. Actually what he was saying was he would admit co-eds to a row of booths on the left side because the place had been a strictly stag tobacco-chewing haven, hence the sawdust floor. The other booths were reserved for the he-men of the campus. Other concessions were made to "emancipated" feminine customers, and the Book Nook took on an altogether different meaning and place in campus life.

Hardly had the last of the grime of the old establishment been cleared away before George Poolitsan, "the candy king," died in October, 1919, and his widow and sons sold their title and business good will to their cousins Peter, George, and Harry Costas of Chicago. The Poolitsans also leased the building to the new owners for ten years. The Costases were natives of the tiny mountain village of Arna in Sparta, and had come to Chicago as poor Greek immigrants. Unable to speak English upon his arrival in America, Peter Costas, for instance, made his way as a clerk in his uncle's fruit store on State Street, and within the Chicago Loop at a time when that area was being reconstructed into a new and modern commercial district. He learned both English and American business methods in this heart of mercantilism. The four brothers paid a family debt back in Arna, sent their family a monthly stipend, and accumulated a small nest egg of capital with which they purchased the Book Nook business and moved away from the raucous cries and sharp dealings of burly Chicago.

George Poolitsan had left a mild student protest. There were shrill cries from angry students protesting the raising of prices of "coke" to $.10, sundaes to $.25, milk shakes to $.20, and ham sandwiches to $.15, when other places in town charged a nickel less on each item. There was, despite these groans, a sigh of relief that the store would be continued in operation.

Peter Costas and two of his brothers, Harry and George, arrived in Bloomington glad to exchange the Chicago fruit trade for the relatively gentle atmosphere of a university student gathering place. They made generous promises that they would perpetuate the good parts of the Book Nook "atmosphere," they would conduct a scientific business, and would "sanitize" the place. They possibly meant they would redeem the latter promise by using a different coating of sawdust on the floor.

The thrifty young Costases learned fast about the vagaries of student customers. Almost the first day in business they discovered that quick-fingered filchers had consumed their first day's profit by emptying their cigar boxes, and daily afterwards they were left holding unpaid checks for drinks and sandwiches. Students, however, had not reckoned on the ingenuity of the young merchants. Soon they were writing customer's names on checks at the time they were served, and they presented the unpaid ones to fraternity brothers and other responsible persons, much to the cheaters' chagrin. While George Costas reacted to all of this in anger, Peter was patient and long suffering, believing they would win more in the long run in student good will. He was a handsome personable young Spartan with a close-cropped black moustache, willing to repay student abuses and pranks with serious fatherly counseling and pleas for offenders to reform. In time the Book Nook became the off-campus headquarters for the organized students, members of every fraternity and sorority made it almost a daily port of call. In time Peter Costas was to type each group, and he could spot members and new pledges of any order by their personality traits. During the day life in the Book Nook moved at a lackadaisical pace, but at night it throbbed with all the activities of the smoky, jazzy activities of the age; this until its doors finally closed at 2:30 A.M.

No one has left a more graphic or odoriferous description of the Book Nook than has Hoagy Carmichael in his autobiography, *Sometimes I Wonder*. "On Indiana Avenue," he wrote "stood the Book Nook, a randy temple smelling of socks, wet slickers, vanilla flavoring, face powder, and unread books. Its dim lights, its scarred walls, its marked up booths, unsteady tables, made campus history. It was for us King Arthur's Round Table, a wailing wall, a fortune telling tent. It tried to be a bookstore. It had grown and been added to recklessly until by the time I was a senior in high school it seated a hundred or so coke guzzling, book-annoyed, bug-eyed college students. New tunes were heard and praised or thumbed down, lengthy discussions on sex, drama, sports, money, and motor cars were started and never quite finished. The first steps of the toddle, the shimmy, and the strut were taken and fitted to the new rhythm. Dates were made and mad hopes were born."

This was Indiana University in the true Don Herold and John Held, Jr., beat, and it was all just across the street from the domain of William Lowe Bryan and Agnes Ermina Wells. It was at the

Book Nook that a segment of jazz was gestated and born. Pecking away at the keys of a battered old upright piano, Hoagy Carmichael "doodled" out such popular blues rhythms as "I'll Get By If I Have You," "As Time Goes By," "Barrelhouse Stomp," and "Tillie's Breakdown." It was there that he composed "Boneyard Shuffle" and "Riverboat Shuffle." From this smoky, smelly student hangout, far more than from Paul Vories McNutt's law classroom in Maxwell Hall, young Carmichael drew his inspiration and the courage to follow a musical career. As a matter of fact, to the youthful law student, Paul McNutt was not an especially imposing teacher. He wrote in later years, "Paul was clever as an instructor. He had the faculty of scanning his notes from right to left with a broad sweep of the head and the eyes as though he was trying to recall his vast store of knowledge. I was highly impressed until one day I discovered he had every word he said lying face up on his desk."

Perhaps Hoagy Carmichael and many of his contemporaries were on more familiar terms with the interior of Pete Costas' Book Nook than with those of campus classrooms. It was here that Carmichael made headquarters for his college band called the Syringe Orchestra. He went out from this place to play with jazz orchestras over the Midwest, and then as far away as New York City. He, as much as Pete Costas, gave the place its personality.

Perhaps as influential as the professors of literature and sociology across Indiana Avenue were Ed Wolfe and William E. Moenkhaus. They supplied the touch of genius, if such it could be called, to the nightly Book Nook assembly. Wolfe was an imaginative jocular fellow who seems to have passed into oblivion. William E. Moenkhaus was what Hoagy Carmichael called "clock-faced." He was the crippled scion of Professor William J. Moenkhaus of the Department of Physiology, and was a man about the world. He said he had viewed a part of the universe from the perspective of an Atlantic cattleboat. He told his eager and provincial audience of milk-faced Hoosiers, "Once you've seen an Alp you've seen 'em all." "Monk" was the mastermind and father of the Bent Eagles, a band of lads bent on doing as little academic work as possible, and with almost no other defined purpose. He was also the "poet of Indiana Avenue." His abstract poems and playlets are like the earth —nebulous, without form. Perhaps they had meaning to coke-dazed Book Nook patrons who gorged themselves on Peter Costas' fifteen-cent ham sandwiches, but they meant little to any one else.

Writing in the campus "literary" magazine, the *Vagabond*, under the scarcely concealed *nom de plume* "Wolfgang Beethoven Bunkhaus" he no doubt brought blushes to his eccentric father-professor's face and sometimes generated a burst of anger from the university faculty. "Monk" was safely out of reach of the professors in his aerie across Indiana Avenue, but not so the *Vagabond*, and in that publication's friskier moments it was called into harsh council by the faculty to answer for its license.

Not all the smells which gave distinction to the Book Nook came from the sources listed by Hoagy Carmichael, or so thought the county authorities. Costas and his brothers were victimized in the prohibition years by students who brought hip flasks with them and spiked "cokes" and even coffee. The Greeks realized the grave danger of being charged with running a speakeasy, but they had little or no control over the students' drinking. As Peter said, students drank in fraternity houses, the Student Building, about town, in Indianapolis, and everywhere else. Nevertheless there had to be a goat, and in these dry years some vigilant observers of Monroe (Dean Edmondson and Dean Wells) thought they detected the aroma of bathtub gin, kerosene-laden moonshine; and basement homebrew. On April 28, 1927, the *Daily Student* said the case, *State of Indiana* vs. *Book Nook*, had been set for trial. The Greek owners were charged with maintaining a common nuisance. Forty-five summonses were issued, the overwhelming majority to students friendly to the defense.

Students were loyal to the Costases. They testified they had not seen any drinking in the Book Nook—even though they had seen drunks in the place. The Costases were charged with knowingly allowing drinking in their hangout and of allowing other social and moral indiscretions. Their accusers, Dean of Men Charles E. Edmondson and Dean of Women Agnes Ermina Wells, were determined to strike at student drinking, and the Book Nook seemed the place to start.

The state leveled heavy legal guns at the Costas brothers in the battery of Professor James J. Robinson of the law faculty, Judge James B. Wilson, and Simpson Robertson. Schuyler Livett of Martinsville and George Henley defended the owners. On May 19, the jury handed up its verdict against Peter Costas, his brother Harry, and the Book Nook, and recommended a fine of $500 and a suspended state penitentiary sentence of thirty days for Pete.

The Costases paid the fine and suffered through the suspended prison sentence. This was a modest drama, however, beside national efforts to enforce prohibition laws, and to stem the tide of moral and social deterioration which neither Dean Edmondson nor Dean Wells could comprehend, let alone control.

The court debacle no doubt chastened the Costas brothers, who before 1927 had not taken a careful enough look around Bloomington and Indiana to get a true sense of public attitudes. Hoosiers may have drunk themselves, allowed their state to be crisscrossed by rum-runners, and have watched public officials fail to enforce laws, but they wanted to keep their youth innocent of these things.

The Costases were occupied with keeping fresh sawdust on their floor, sloshing together chocolate milk shakes, and the eternal clatter of jazz. By this time, Hoagy Carmichael had earned a law degree and had gone on to harvest fame and wealth from "Stardust," "Lazy Bones," "Maple Leaf Rag," "Lazy River," "Rockin' Chair," "Georgia on My Mind," and "I'll Get Along Without You." The jazz age itself was sagging and the youth of the nation had developed a more refined subtlety in its social relationships.

Along Indiana Avenue there were to be only a few more audacious flings of juvenility. In 1927 with the collaboration of Peter Costas the Book Nook ringleaders and some of the fraternities planned the first of the famous mock commencements. The jokesters organized a "university" with colleges which represented in title the principle areas of the hangout's interest. Peter Costas was made "president," and he had a faculty of "deans" and "professors" who looked after his intellectual domain. They devised a long list of degrees, "earned" and "honorary," which in time became cherished sentimental mementoes. One person so honored was the young instructor in Economics and Sociology, Herman B Wells, who was awarded the degree of Doctor of Nookology, and was made "Supervisor of the Faculty Emeritus" in the 1931 "commencement." There was a fairly long list of other persons who later in their careers proved the wisdom of their being chosen for Book Nook honors, among them, Howard W. (Wad) Allen, saxaphonist in Carmichael's band, and later a vice-president of the Johns-Manville Company.

The Book Nook "professors," largely under the leadership of William E. Moenkhaus and Ed Wolfe, parodied the Indiana University exercises. Many of the stunts reflected Moenkhaus and

Wolfe's humor plus the jovial cooperation of "president" Peter Costas. Following the last of these "exercises" the Bloomington *Evening World* said on June 5, 1931, the Book Nook diplomas awarded with all pomp and ceremony by Peter Costas "are the only ones many students ever received at the University." This certificate was later given a place of honor on many office walls, and it may have represented about as much fundamental education as the university's own richly adorned parchment.

In 1929, on the eve of Depression, the mock Book Nook commencement reached a high level of ludicrousness. Where William Lowe Bryan and the board of trustees had led their flock of faculty, seniors, and families onto Dunn Meadow in a parade that rivaled a medieval mustering of forces, the Costases and William Moenkhaus across Indiana Avenue staged their own parade: a waddling duck, Keyser Cheese Freyerberger riding a donkey, three "seniors" or "antiquities" in invalid chairs audibly recalling their long years laboring with "cokes," 175 barbarians dressed in bathrobes, whose only "credits" were faithfuless to the club. Four robed seniors played bridge in the forefront of the proceedings, and others behaved as befitted the occasion. Peter Costas had cancelled a trip to Greece and his beloved Arna in order to be present and preside. Karl Thornburg, an Indiana University graduate, delivered the commencement address on the subject "Such Unfatal Work." Twenty-four degrees were conferred by the College of Hearts and Appliances, and an honorary B. O. L. P. (doctor of hearts emeritus) was conferred on Bob Walker. Bailey Lewis was knighted KISS or Master of Hearts Count-out-Laude. The Book Nook Orchestra clad in burlap sacking played a jazzy requiem. All of this frivolity was performed before the lenses of Pathé World News to be projected in movie houses all across the country.

For the last time the irreverent students packed themselves in encircling layers along Indiana Avenue and in the edge of the campus woods before Peter Costas' Book Nook door to celebrate "commencement," 1931. Police blocked the streets off from Fourth to Kirkwood Avenue and the land belonged to the revelers. The celebrants awarded degrees, drank cokes, listened to jazz, cavorted in general. Hard times on the shadowy eve of the Hoover era knocked at the Book Nook door, and before another commencement season, the Depression had settled on American businesses and individuals alike. The Costases felt the sting of financial string-

[2 7 9]

ency. Their lease expired and Mrs. Poolitsan and her sons proposed to double the monthly rate in its renewal. Almost tearfully the *Daily Student* halted figuratively before its scuffed door jambs long enough to observe nostalgically, "With its passing go many of the traditions that set if off as a distinctly Indiana institution."

Two doors down Indiana Avenue at the corner of Kirkwood, the new Book Nook opened its doors as a general restaurant with staid and dignified booths and appealing Greek food to attract a more sophisticated clientele of faculty and townsmen. To a large extent the student rabble was left behind to patronize the Poolitsan's new Gables, but the spirit of the old site vanished with the ending of the age. The mock commencements were no more, and with more automobiles available to courting couples they wandered far afield to find a quiet spot to enjoy their individual versions of collegiate "star dust."

Hundreds of Indiana University students, of course, had little or nothing to do with the Book Nook and its particular manifestations of the American age in which it thrived. They nevertheless fell under the influence of the times. Indiana University ground its way through what George Louis Beer called the "Mauve Decade" with all the student razzle-dazzle of the times. This was a transitional phase in the university's history in which the whole structure of American society underwent challenges and revisions. The closing of the old Book Nook indeed symbolized the closing of the era. Peter Costas observed with Greek wisdom, "Students of today are dignified persons, and not rowdy collegians of a few years ago." With the advancing thirties they demanded more polished and sophisticated catering.

Across Indiana Avenue the establishment itself was undergoing a revolution in social mores. Dean Edmondson, Dean Wells, and President Bryan discovered that youth—or the younger generation—had problems they could neither understand nor solve. The code by which families and their offspring had lived since the 1880's without material revision was now all but inapplicable. Girls no longer looked forward to romantic love matches which led them to the altar with the "right man" unkissed and uninstructed in the facts of life. Legislators and moral crusaders had no impact on female dress—skirts grew skimpier, so did blouses, and corsets and bustles went away with the day's trash. This was a physical age in which people everywhere either became more conscious of their bodies or more open in displaying them.

In this passing phase of extremity in dress and flamboyant taste, Hoagy Carmichael might well be considered an astute observer on the Indiana campus. In his more meditative later years he wrote what is one of the most vivid physical descriptions of the college co-ed of his day. "Our girls were trying to make he-men of us but we were still hicky kids. Every girl I knew wanted to own a long strand of pearls in a hangman's knot and borrow the college boys' pull-over sweaters of fuzzy wool, to which were pinned Greek letter frat pins; the more the merrier. Flat chested girls were the rule, with no shape visible from arm pits to thighs; the mammary glands had not yet become pin-up art.

"Ball bearing hips, jello haunches free of girdles or even under-wear. Soft felt styles and the first of the shoddy, shiny rayons. Seated on their spines, legs in the air, in Stutz Bearcats or the high-nosed Packards, wrapped in school colors at games, kicking the lock step in hotel rooms and country clubs, while the band played *I'll Get By If I Have You* and *As Time Goes By*."

What of the "hicky" lads? They were around during the 1920's with their long stringy hair pulled back in bear-oil plastered pompadours, wearing silk shirts, sailor-legged britches, shoe-string width four-in-hand ties, coats with wide lapels, and all of this stuffed under the cover of bright yellow oil-skin slickers which smelled more of Gloucester and Moby Dick than even the Book Nook. Painted on the slickers were nude figures which undulated when the owners walked about the campus, there were naughty words and slogans brought fresh off the men's room walls, and other juvenile mouthings of the time. Pointed "French" toed shoes helped many a country boy cut the shimmy and Charleston capers on dive floors. Those who could afford it bought a Ford run-about and began exploring the rolling hills of Southern Indiana. This was the age in Indiana University when the "hicky" boy actually began to disappear from the scene. Students were now coming from the cities and large towns where they caught fewer hayseeds in their oiled locks and were more oriented "men of the world" where girls, cars, and the return of legal beer and red liquor were concerned. In 1938 the faculty self-study committee was startled to find that only one-eighth of the Indiana student body came from farm homes, and over 50 percent came from metropolitan centers. The times and changing structures of the locations and attitudes of Hoosiers had indeed outrun the social knowledge and experience of the administration and faculty in Bloomington.

[2 8 1]

For the university administration the problem of social decorum was greatly intensified by the modern technology. The automobile and the coming of better roads gave students a mobility that took them well beyond the folds of the home, and at the same time removed them from the clutches of the tottering system of institutional chaperonage. The deans of men and women could cry out in anguish at the lowering of moral standards, but the open car, the rumble seat, and the speakeasy, and then the return of the open liquor bar and free sale of alcohol widened the breach. Where Miss Carrie Louise Denise cried out against the single-seated buggy in 1912, the "run-about-tin-Lizzies" from Detroit lifted the curfew. Students read F. Scott Fitzgerald's novels, nice girls smoked cigarettes on the public streets in rumble seats, and discussed all sides of life with abandon. Now in the new society it was almost impossible to identify the crimson woman of history.

Student dress and nocturnal cavortings were not the only concerns of the central administrative authority of Indiana University in the closing 1920's. Those of the faculty who had been schooled in the standards of the 1880's Victorian code were embattled on all fronts because of changing attitudes in American society. William Lowe Bryan closed the rowdy decade by making one last gallant stand in the pre-Rooseveltian era of prohibition by attempting to maintain a "dry" stance for the university. In the summer of 1931, the Department of English employed Leslie Bigelow of Oberlin College as an instructor. Before the new professor set foot on the Jordan Banks, however, the press alleged he had been arrested for driving while introxicated and in the possession of liquor. President Bryan commented to a *Daily Telephone* reporter that if the report were true Professor Bigelow would not be allowed to come to Indiana University. Nevertheless time ran against the Victorians, and in the immediate future the wall of prohibition crumbled before the onslaught of American voters. This did not occur, however, until a considerable body of campus folklore concerning the administration's attitude toward liquor was passed about by professors and students, and in time this too became a part of the institutional legend.

William Lowe Bryan, Fernandus Payne, and their academic colleagues were aware of most of the facts of this age so far as they demanded academic considerations. The decade had opened with a student enrollment of 600 students, and had closed with a total all-university head count of 11,068. There were demands for more and better teaching, a liberalization of university-students relationships, a greater awareness of internal university responsibilites and more response to the demands of recurring national problems. The analysis made by the self-study committee in 1939 revealed innermost results of the reshuffling and reevaluation of the values of life itself and especially in the implications of higher education in the conditioning of modern Hoosiers to meet and accept the changes which would constantly be upon them. Clearly, in the history of the university there would never again be such a long interval of time in which an established moral and social code would be observed with so little disruption. For Indiana University the age of innocence was largely ended by the time Franklin D. Roosevelt and his new dealers assumed power in Washington. On the River Jordan both state and federal legislation and largess began to transform the institution into a less patriarchical, more sophisticated place where the off-campus subculture of college life became as much an accepted fact as the automobile and the chain grocery store.

[XIII]

Faculty Lights in a Waning Era

ORLD WAR I with all its excitement of military activities, fund and special humanitarian drives, and pageantry of crisis did not completely submerge Indiana University into forgetting its role as an institution of higher education. There were several significant pieces of unfinished business left over from the great organizational crusade prior to 1915 which demanded a degree of concerned attention. One of these was the organization of an acceptable music program and the continuing search for a head professor. Bryan and the trustees perhaps had only limited personal appreciation for musical art itself, but they appreciated its curricular significance in a liberal arts university. There were two problems, the provision of decent quarters for a school of music, and the employment of the right man to develop such a program.

William Lowe Bryan took great pride in the performances of the Glee Club on its tours about the state of Indiana. To him it was a showcase exhibit for the university's talents and accomplishments which could be displayed before the homefolks. In a more practical way the offering of good music training had very real signifiance in the terms of enrollment. This was especially true in areas where university-trained teachers taught popular courses in public school music in Indiana high schools. Bryan knew, however, because of his earlier frustrating experiences, that establishment of a school of music was fraught with problems. He had wearily given up the search for an off-campus professor and had appointed Charles Divin Campbell, associate professor of German, to the post on a contingent basis. Some of Campbell's philosophy concerning music training has been presented elsewhere; he felt Indiana should pattern its own efforts at music instruction after that of the Michigan School, which he said was a credit to the artistic world. He asked of Bryan and the trustees, "Why should Indiana not have an institution just as worthy of admiration as that of Michigan, but one not affiliated with, but belonging to the state university?" In his opinion music was a misunderstood art among people who were accustomed "to taking music lessons." Instruction in the art, "on the average," said the professor, "is of the most primitive sort, comparable in many ways, to the state of education in the early history of our state." A year later (1916) Campbell reported he had worked at music instruction for a decade and he felt his accomplishments fell short of his ideals. Some progress had been made. He requested that he be promoted to a professorship, saying handworkers in Indiana were many, but competent music instructors were indeed few in number.

Campbell struggled on with teutonic doggedness, gaining tiny advantages here and there with his music instruction, even in wartime. He suggested in March, 1917, that Archibald Warner, the janitor in Mitchell Hall, be made director of the band at a salary of $1,000 a year, an increase of $376 over his janitorial earnings. Mitchell Hall, said Campbell, was a dreary pile, and the sophisticated art of music deserved a more fitting physical setting. Two years later, in the intense heat of postwar excitement, the music professor suggested that Mitchell be rebuilt at once. Its walls bulged and plaster dropped off in ever larger slabs. Even the colors of the place were jarring distractions.

Through the dust of despair and the clatter of falling plaster, "Old Mitchell" had somehow stood the ravages of time and the arts. In the face of decay and abuse in professorial and administrative reports, there, however, shone through the shambling studs a tiny ray of hope in November, 1918, when Bryan announced that Tolerico of Milan and the Indianapolis College of Musical Art would offer piano instruction in Indiana University. Gaylord Yost of the same institution would give lessons in violin, and Adolph Shellschmidt would teach cello. John L. Geiger of Indianapolis,

Frank Senour of the Department of English, and Harold Eicholtz Wolfe of Mathematics, were asked to give other courses.

Before the newly organized faculty could make a dent on the establishment of a school of music, Charles Divin Campbell died in 1919. Again music at Indiana was without a head professor. William Lowe Bryan once more searched for a "practical" artist who could organize a school of music on a starvation budget, and at the same time fit himself into the less esoteric phases of university operation which involved concern with majors, grades, and credits.

The *Daily Student* announced on July 22, 1919, that at last Actaeon was home from a ten-year hunt and brought glad tidings. Bryan had hired Winfred Barzille Merrill of the Department of Music of Iowa State Teachers College. Merrill was born in Elgin, Illinois, in 1864, and appears to have been a self-taught musician. He had directed the Tacoma, Washington, Academy of Music, and the Atlanta Symphony Orchestra. In the latter city he had also been director of the proprietary Merrill School of Music.

Once in Bloomington the new professor had hardly unpacked his music and instruments before he informed President Bryan and the trustees in October, 1919, "in the first place we are not in evidence in the state as a place where boys and girls can come for a musical education in piano, violin, or public school music, and this means a course of state-wide advertising."

No doubt an advertising campaign paid off, because a year later the Professor said there were 600 students enrolled in music, forty of whom had come to Bloomington specifically to take courses in the department. At the same time E. E. Birge of Indianapolis was appointed professor of public school music with the hope that even more emphasis would be placed in this area. The seven pianos of the Music Department were in constant use from 7:00 A.M. to 7:00 P.M., and there was no additional room in creaking Mitchell Hall in which to place another instrument. There were applicants for instruction in organ as well, but there was no organ, and none was available to the university in the Bloomington churches. In fact there were so many applicants for music instruction who could not be accepted that Winfred B. Merrill concluded it was useless to advertise further the work of the Department of Music.

The Bloomington churches refused to rent their pipe organs for practice purposes for the valid reasons they neither wished their instruments injured nor their church sanctuaries turned into classrooms. Anyway, Professor Merrill regarded the aged church instruments as unsuitable for sophisticated music instruction. He suggested to President Bryan that the university meet its need for instruction in organ music by purchasing a "one stop" instrument and employing an instructor to use it. Again came the refrain that Mitchell Hall was an improper structure in which to house even so simple an instrument.

The old frame structure was ever the nemesis. In his annual report in 1921, Merrill said, "It would be a great satisfaction if Mitchell Hall could be painted the same color as the annex so that it might be more attractive and less disfigure the beautiful spot in which it is located. The feeling would be that the School of Music is an entry and the impression abroad among students would be improved."

Despite the repressive physical setting of his department, Professor Merrill was enthusiastic about the progress of music instruction in the university. In the spring of 1921 he began major agitation for the organization of a professional school which would be used to train music teachers from Indiana and the country at large. By that time he felt the staff had been enlarged sufficiently to justify a more formal organization, a conclusion which was approved by the board of trustees in the creation of a school to supersede the department.

The new status of music in Indiana University under the more dignified designation of "school" called for innovation in modes of instruction. In January, 1922, Rolla Roy Ramsey of the Department of Physics assembled radio facilities so as to transmit the nightly concerts of the Chicago Opera to the stage in Mitchell Hall, a simple effort which was to begin a tradition that in time grew into a history of major accomplishments in the operatic field. While Ramsey and his experimental radio instruments rattled the homey rafters of Mitchell Hall with the incongruous sounds of the Chicago Opera performance, Merrill busied himself with more fundamental details. He began a campaign to convince the faculty that the university should grant a Bachelor's degree in music. Supporting the new dean in his efforts, the *Daily Student* in April boasted the Music School "stands second to none in Indiana in four or five areas." Promptly the faculty and trustees approved the granting of a degree in music, and the initial phases of establishing such a program in the university's curriculum was ended.

Happy results in elevating his program to the status of a special professional school and the recognition of its instruction in the form of a special degree could not entirely conceal Winfred B. Merrill's disappointment in the university's inability to improve its physical facilities. No amount of paint and beaver board could hide Mitchell Hall's deficiencies for use as a music school. The dean wrote President Bryan in April, 1924, during the great Memorial Fund Drive, that he envisioned a combination music and public art building on the campus. "I notice, however, that the memorial rumors seem to point toward the embodiment of the auditorium in the Union Building. My great desire is to see here a music school of solid dignity and worth; to see frivolous and false notions of music held by a great majority of our students, supplanted by a serious-minded true conception." The new dean said when people complained about the music building he answered that it was men who counted, but deep in his heart, "I know Polonius was right in the matter of his son's apparel, and that the student who joyfully announced to me that he is going to a 'conservatory' next semester, only voices the general feeling that we haven't a 'school of music' here because we lack the visible sign." Merrill was certain that Indiana University failed to attract good students because of this need.

Little more than this was added to the essential history of the Music School during the rest of the Bryan administration and until 1941 when Winfred B. Merrill himself retired. The school lacked proper space during almost all of his years as dean, the aesthetic environment was often disharmonious, and the school needed proper instruments and teaching equipment. Two innovations, however, were successful—one, the organization of a preparatory department for the purpose of enabling defectively trained students to prepare themselves for entry into the school, the other, the conduct of the "school" of music in Munich during the summers of 1929 and 1930.

The Indiana University Music School under the administration of Winfred Merrill came within sight of realizing the dream of both professor and president. After 1935 it had the promise of proper housing through the assistance of the Federal Emergency Administration matching funds arrangement. Students of music on the campus gave Dean Merrill assistance by circulating a petition addressed to Governor Paul V. McNutt asking state approval of the music building loan. They hoped an adequate number of class and practice rooms could be provided in the new building to accommodate a large enrollment, and that a 400-seat recital auditorium would also be included. By October that year the request for funds to finance the new building had been approved, and it was located east of Memorial Hall and facing on Third Street.

On the evening of January 15, 1937, Indiana University seriously dedicated itself to the fine arts when the first recital was given in the new Recital Hall; at least the sophisticated art of music was at last freed from the tortuous caverns of Mitchell Hall which were now abandoned to the use of more prosaic tenants.

Music was only a single intellectual interest of Indiana University during the significant transitional years after 1914. In almost a century of institutional history, with the exception of the Long Memorial Hospital gift, the school had not received significant monetary donations. Graduating classes had planted trees and erected class memorials, the campaign in behalf of the Student Building and subsequently the memorial buildings had been gifts, but no individual had endowed a chair or given appreciable support to a university program. Thoroughly aware of this fact was Carl Eigenmann who had worked with the Carnegie Foundation and Museum, at Woods Hole, and with other endowed scientific bodies. He was ever alert where possible funds were concerned. In some way, maybe by direct association, he learned Dr. Luther Dana Waterman, professor emeritus of the Medical School, might make a substantial bequest to sustain scientific research. Perhaps Dr. Waterman and his family wished to endow a chair, and Eigenmann may have changed their minds. The dean was easily excited where research money was involved, and he pursued the Waterman prospect with proper diligence.

Dr. Luther Waterman no doubt kept his friends in the university guessing while he made up his mind as to what precisely he did wish to do. He announced in May, 1915, that he planned to give Indiana University four pieces of property located in the City of Indianapolis with the proviso that the institution would not gain full possession of them until after his death. The gift consisted of a business block at 133 South Illinois Street, four business rooms on Massachusetts Street, a residence on North Rural Street, and an unspecified amount of intangibles. The record is not entirely clear whether Dr. Waterman had in mind at the outset a research professorship or whether that was Eigenmann's idea.

The board of trustees was asked to bind itself to appropriate annually an amount of money equal to the increment from the Waterman bequest. In June, 1916, Eigenmann prepared a report on the accumulation of the special fund, revealing that it then amounted to between $11,000, and $12,000. At the same time the Indiana General Assembly had appropriated $17,000 in matching funds to be used by the Graduate School. The Dean recommended to President Bryan that two Waterman professors be appointed. True to character, the ebullient dean predicted that if everybody worked together the Waterman bequest would accumulate a half million dollars' worth of endowment funds in the next decade. He advised the trustees to develop a policy of handling such endowments ahead of time so Indiana University would not suffer future loss or confusion at the hands of other prospective donors.

President Bryan accepted Eigenmann's advice, and at the June meeting of the trustees in 1916, he recommended that a Waterman Institute be established. He explained that it was his belief such a division in the university would be analogous to a department, or perhaps to the Graduate School itself. In October of that year Dr. Waterman presented bonds worth $11,000, and the following June he appeared before the board of trustees and again offered his gift of $100,000, this time stipulating even more emphatically that the income and an equal amount of money from the university should be devoted to scientific research. At the same time the retired professor gave $2,500 to the Robert W. Long Memorial Hospital. The record at this point becomes somewhat blurred. Either Dr. Waterman had not fully made up his mind about his gift, despite past board and legislative action, or he felt himself under pressure from his heirs to provide for them. In his second statement of the gifts he provided that his beneficiaries should have use of the property and a share of the income. Too, it appears from the record that the $11,000 in bonds may have been an additional gift, but in April, 1917, President Bryan listed the Waterman gift as $102,500 which included the hospital stipend.

At its meeting in June, 1919, the board of trustees appointed a special endowment committee comprised of Dr. Waterman, chairman, and Bryan, Eigenmann, J. W. Fesler, and Theodore Frelinghuysen Rose as members. The year before Arthur Lee Foley of the Department of Physics had been appointed the first Waterman Institute professor for one year. From this beginning both the Institute and the professorship grew into a prestigious expression of Indiana University's dedication to pure research in various areas of the physical and biological sciences.

There are hints in Carl Eigenmann's personal papers that he would have cherished full-time appointment to the Waterman Institute professorship. He, however, was too deeply involved in a multiplicity of administrative and research interests to have confined himself to the highly specialized purposes of the institute. Following World War I this gift became an important precedent in the development of a university research program.

The Waterman Institute came into being during the feverish war years when no one really had time to devote much attention to anything other than the demands of international conflict. Bryan was obviously absorbed with the emotional demands of the war, with renewing the search for a music professor, and with further realignment of the university's departments and schools. In this period, also, he allowed himself to become a central figure in what he considered to be a righteous cause. He considered Samuel Bannister Harding's divorce from his wife in 1916 too great a moral and social shock to be endured by the university community, and he took direct disciplinary action.

The Bloomington *Evening World* carried the story of Samuel Bannister Harding's divorce under bold headlines and the *Telephone* gave it even more space. The latter paper said Harding "Was His Own Chef and Hired Girl . . . and because of these Reasons and Others Samuel B. Harding, of the History Department, Seeks His Freedom." The professor gave as his reason incompatibility. The paper said "Indiana University faculty received a shock in a divorce suit which has just been filed by Samuel B. Harding of the history department against his wife, Caroline Harding White [sic]," then gave many details of the private lives of the couple. Finally on December 21, 1916, the sensation ended with the granting of a court decree which awarded Mrs. Harding custody of her son and a property settlement. Apparently there had never been a divorce in the university's faculty. This case must have lingered on in local gossip because in May, 1917, when the university was so deeply involved in wartime affairs and Samuel Bannister Harding was away in Washington working with the War Information Board, William Lowe Bryan took time out from his wartime speaking engagements to deliver an address to a Bloomington audience on the evils of divorce. As a result of the speech, an H. M. Hudelson was stimulated to write the president a letter about what he called the love affair of Professor Harding and a co-ed, a letter that reopened the earlier social wound.

Samuel Bannister Harding had joined the university staff in 1895, after receiving two degrees from the institution. In 1898 he was awarded the doctorate by Harvard University. Harding was a productive scholar and author, but also was well known as an able classroom teacher and enjoyed the esteem of students and colleagues alike. His name was displayed in half of the classrooms of the country as editor of the *Harding History Maps*. In fact, he appears to have been one of William Lowe Bryan's most esteemed colleagues.

H. M. Hudelson's letter to Bryan was full of hearsay and innuendo; its intent was to give the appearance that Samuel B. Harding had carried on an illicit love affair with the young woman he married on May 1, 1918. Hudelson had written, "Wonder if you would not like to know that some years ago one of your faculty members was in regular correspondence with a certain young woman, and when in Bloomington, was frequently with her and supposedly engaged. At any rate he signed himself 'your devoted husband.' He is now divorced and some late developments look suspicious. This is a matter of history in our house and I know absolutely whereof I speak. If you care for names and particulars, please see me either at the store or at home." The nose of the meddler could not have been more clearly revealed than in the harness-maker's letter, and it deserved only enough attention to pitch it into a waste basket. Instead President Bryan gave it credence, partly because he was emotionally aroused at the moment by the divorce, because of his wife's reactions to it, and by local newspaper stimulation. Both the Bryans knew intimately of the Hardings' marital troubles, and rumor had it that Mrs. Bryan agreed with Mrs. Harding that her husband in some way bore responsibility for the physical invalidism of their son.

It must have been with genuine shock that Harding read President Bryan's letter of May 13, 1918, in which he said it was his painful duty to write about the divorce. Bryan expressed in positive terms that he believed separation from a virtuous wife and mother of his son was a grave sin on Harding's part. "Your subsequent marriage," he wrote, "constitutes a grave wrong. . . . For the University, the question is not a technical one. The question is as to what moral principles and moral influences the University will assume responsibility for and commend to its students and to society. I am aware that there are those who make light of the moral principles involved. For my part I believe that those principles are as vital to mankind as any we are fighting for in Europe." The president attempted to soften his blow a bit by telling Harding, "The writing of this letter is one of the most painful acts of my official life, but I cannot do otherwise."

A fortnight after President Bryan wrote Samuel B. Harding he had a second letter from H. M. Hudelson apparently in response to a request that the harness-maker supply further information. Hudelson said, "Mrs. Hudelson's attention was called to the first letter she read by her eye falling on the subscription, 'Your devoted husband, S. B. H.' " Hudelson failed to explain the moral issue of how his wife happened to be reading surreptitiously private letters not addressed to her. The rest of the meddlesome letter was filled with gossip prefaced with well-worn phrases of the talebearer, "I understand," "quite brazen," "I should think," and "my own opinion." Then Hudelson raised the point that Harding had given his daughter Vista a "C" on final examination when she should have had an "A". Self-righteously the merchant concluded his letter, "Her work is done and I have no interest in this matter except the good of humanity."

Bryan was seriously disturbed by this matter, and perhaps would have taken a very close look at the issue had he received Hudelson's second letter prior to writing Harding. He wrote his trusted friend James Albert Woodburn, head of the Department of History, on June 6, 1918, a month after Harding's second marriage, "I have thought of calling the faculty together to state the case of Dr. Harding. I shall certainly do this before presenting the matter to the Trustees if any members of the faculty desire it." He sought from Woodburn advice on two points: first, the calling together of the faculty to explain his action, and, "second; my position in the matter is like that of the British Prime Minister who makes not minor but major proposals to Parliament. I would as a matter of course resign if the proposal were not sustained." He expressed fear that any statement from him would unduly influence some faculty members and he hoped Woodburn would tell him how to proceed.

All of this question was discussed against a background of strict public adherence to the tenets of the sanctity of the home, motherhood, and the permanency of the marriage vow.

On June 8, 1918, William Lowe Bryan addressed two letters to the board of trustees saying he did not recommend Samuel Bannister Harding's reappointment as professor of history; "the University should not be asked to assume responsibility" for a basic act of immorality. He again informed both Harding and the trustees, "I am aware that there are those who make light of the moral principles involved. For my part I believe those principles are as vital to mankind as any we are fighting for in Europe. And I know of no good which a university can do which can counterbalance the evil it does if it condones the violation of these principles."

Harding had faithful friends in Bloomington among his colleagues. Those named were Amos Shartle Hershey, Oliver Fields, William Evans Jenkins, James Grover McDonald, and Alfred Manfield Brooks. His attorney, Judge James B. Wilson, also of Bloomington, was a loyal supporter. In a long letter addressed to Theodore Freylinghuysen Rose, President of the Board of Trustees, Harding explained that he was engaged in an urgent and sensitive task for the Office of War Information and it would be against national interest for him to leave Washington. He cited twenty-three years of devoted and honorable service to the university, and expressed fear his Carnegie retirement stipend would become involved. He denied stoutly there was any color of truth in the allegation that he had at any time breached the proprieties of the prevailing social code in his second marriage. He and his second wife had collaborated on a perfectly respectable book, just as he and his first wife had done in 1909.

The two Hudelson letters held by President Bryan Harding branded fabrications, malicious gossip, spite, and hearsay. A complaint he had kept Vista Hudelson from being elected to Phi Beta Kappa was one which should be examined on the authority of the Registrar's record. Harding told the Muncie banker-trustee that his life during the latter years of his first marraige had brought him to "the time when I could not face the prospect of a crabbed, isolated old age, to which her [Caroline Hurst Harding] course condemned us both." His "afflicted" first wife had withdrawn more and more from social affairs until he had become a prisoner of her will.

In this moment of anger and frustration Professor Harding

delved deeper into what might have been no more than campus gossip. He wrote both the trustees and President Bryan, asking the latter for definite "charges of wrong doing by known accusers, instead of cowardly anonymous allegations." He intended to prosecute for slander anyone who dared assume responsibility for the scurrilous charges.

Theodore F. Rose told Judge James B. Wilson on June 7, on the eve of the board of trustees meeting, that he had "looked it [Harding's letter] over casually," and that if it was a matter of town gossip he thought it likely the board would not care to take action on it. This was before Bryan's letter of the 8th had been prepared, and which repeated the moral charge against divorce and remarriage. The president told the board, "I recommend that Professor Samuel B. Harding be not re-elected Professor of History in Indiana University."

On June 8, at 1:00 P.M., and without presence of counsel, accusers, witnesses, defendant, or presentation of formal evidence, the board of trustees concluded, apparently solely on the basis of the president's recommendation, not to retain Harding as a member of the university faculty. The board entry in the formal minutes is curt indeed. Bryan was instructed not to present the plaintiff's name for reelection. There seems to be no available evidence that Harding took further action in the matter. His attorney expressed the opinion that an actionable wrong had been committed against his client which had resulted in great damage. The board, he said, had the power within itself to hire and fire professors without being influenced by an outsider. He was sorry, however, that body had acted "without any knowledge of the facts." There still remained the courts before which an appeal could be taken and the facts presented.

If the facts in the Harding case were unknown to the board of trustees at the time of its action, as Judge Wilson claimed, then it was fully informed by the Bloomington *Daily Telephone* which ran a full page story detailing the whole issue, even to publishing the private letters of Bryan and Harding. How the paper came by those letters is left unexplained. For reasons best known to Samuel Bannister Harding he never took his case to court. Apparently he accepted the decision of the board of trustees as final and beyond change by litigation.

James A. Woodburn replaced Harding in the Department of

History with Paul L. Haworth. When Harding left the Office of War Information in 1919 he became editor of *Compton's Pictorial Encyclopedia*, and in 1921 his wartime colleagues in Washington, Guy Stanton Ford and Evarts B. Greene secured him the appointment as professor of modern history in the University of Minnesota; later he became director of university extension, a position he held until his death in 1927.

The Harding incident left some scars on Indiana University. It was clear that the president of the institution had wielded a decisive influence over the board of trustees, and that the board acted without holding either hearings or otherwise gathering information, or sifting evidence. Bryan, as he had told James A. Woodburn, had put himself in the position of a British prime minister and had declared he would resign if the action of the board went against his wishes. How strong he made this point in oral communication with board members cannot be determined from the record. What is clear is that Bryan did communicate fully with the trustees as he told Judge James B. Wilson when he said he had been instructed by the board to refer all requests for information to that body.

A local membership of the American Association of University Professors existed at Indiana. Some vagueness shrouds the beginning of this organization on the Indiana University campus, but the *Bulletin* in December, 1916, listed James Albert Woodburn as president at Indiana and George Davis Morris, Associate Professor of French, as secretary. The local organization had thirteen members, and the list was made up almost altogether of "old-line" professors. By 1921, and following the dismissal of Samuel Bannister Harding, the AAUP had a record enrollment of forty-nine members, and a year later a national constitution was adopted and the Indiana society was organized into a chapter. It seems strange that James Albert Woodburn, local president of the organization in 1918, and E. R. Cumings, a national councillor, did not raise their voices in the Harding case. The AAUP was elevated to chapter status with sixty-nine members; E. R. Cumings was president and George Davis Morris continued as secretary.

Throughout its history, Indiana University was successful in keeping a core, at least, of faculty members who had long-time service records. In 1920 there were at least twenty members who had been in the faculty long enough to become "fixed personal campus institutions." Among these were William Lowe Bryan, James A.

Woodburn, Carl Eigenmann, W. A. Rawles, Bert John Vos, Daniel Myers Mottier, Burton Dorr Myers, W. E. Jenkins, Schuyler Colfax Davisson, Carl W. F. Osthaus, U. S. Weatherly, E. R. Cumings, Alfred M. Brooks, Charles M. Hepburn, Rolla Ramsey, and Enoch George Hogate. These were largely the men of the inner core of the faculty; otherwise faculty members, both able and feeble, came and went with recurring semesters. It was clear by 1920, however, that the day of the old residual "institutional professor" was drawing to a close.

Presaging things to come Paul Leland Haworth, a bright and productive young historian with a Columbia University doctorate, replaced Samuel Bannister Harding. Haworth went on to Butler University where he distinguished himself as the main author of a multi-volume history of the United States, and became the standard authority on the famous Hayes-Tilden dispute and the Compromise of 1877. He would have added luster to Indiana University had he remained on its faculty.

W. D. Howe held a doctorate from Harvard and joined the Indiana faculty in 1906. He was a solid scholar who served as head of the English Department, but in 1919 he left the institution to become an editor in the house of Charles Scribner's Sons. On the heels of Howe's departure Henry Holland Carter was employed as head of the English Department in 1923. He held a doctorate from Yale, and from his arrival on the campus until his retirement in 1941 he exerted a strong scholarly influence.

Carter was a man of sound ideas who contributed heavily to departmental administration, teaching, and writing. His most worthwhile books were *Ben Johnson, Every Man in His Humor* (1921) and *English in Action* (1937). No one in the field of English and literature at Indiana, however, overshadowed Alexander Corbin Judson. He, too, held a Yale doctorate and had joined the faculty in 1923 with Carter. Judson became an authority on Edmund Spenser, publishing *Edmund Spenser in Ireland* (1933), and the *Life of Edmund Spenser* (1945).

Of the same vintage and high academic quality with Carter, Judson, and Howe, was Stith Thompson, a Kentucky-Hoosier from Indianapolis. He joined the faculty in 1921, coming to Bloomington from the University of Maine. He was a graduate of Wisconsin, California, and Harvard. Before he arrived in the university he already had produced a considerable list of publications, and between 1921 and his retirement in 1955 he was unusually productive. His monumental *Motif-Index of Folk Literature* (1932–1937; revised, 1955–1957) displayed its author's broad knowledge of folklore, and made Indiana University a focal center for the study of the subject. He approached the study of folklore from an international, universal viewpoint, rather than local Hoosier or national settings. Thompson's numerous publications comprise a modest library in folklore. Besides teaching and writing, he served as Dean of the Gradute School from 1947 to 1950.

Coming up from the prewar years was the bright Columbia doctorate, Ralph Leslie Rusk, a member of the Department of English, 1915 to 1925, who resigned to accept an appointment in Columbia University. The impact of Indiana nevertheless was reflected in his two-volume landmark study *Literature of the Mid-Western Frontier* (1925). Later Rusk edited the prestigious *American Literature*. Frank Davidson of the same department was to distinguish himself less in the field of publication than in teaching. A native Hoosier and graduate of the university, Davidson rendered yeoman service in the classroom and in student counseling. In the eyes of graduate students his services were finer than an extended list of printed tangibles. He sent many a young apprentice instructor on his way to a successful scholarly career with his counseling.

Coming up from the ranks was one of Indiana University's strongest professors and campus personalities, Fernandus Payne. Dean Payne was born on a farm in Shelby County, Indiana, where he received the most primitive sort of elementary education in a poverty-stricken township school. He attended the Valparaiso Normal School, dropping out on occasion to teach country school to earn enough money to continue his education. In 1903 he entered Indiana University and became a devoted student of Carl Eigenmann. Later Payne entered Columbia University to work under E. B. Wilson and Thomas Hunt Morgan. In 1909 he returned to Bloomington to begin a long career of research, teaching, and academic administration. He was a well disciplined scientist who had learned much from Eigenmann, Morgan, and Wilson about research in the pure sciences.

Fernandus Payne was forthright in his views, determined in his pursuits, and dogged in his opposition to loose academic standards. He looked upon his beloved Eigenmann's Graduate Council in 1925 as senile and inefficient; succeeding the old crusader he set out to reconstruct graduate work in the university. In time he played a central role on a much broader scale as chairman of the important classification committee of the Association of American Universities. He served this body as the sole representative of Indiana University because President Bryan for some reason never attended the meetings of the presidents' section.

From the vantage point of his prestigious committee chairmanship Dean Payne was able to view Indiana University critically against the backdrop of other graduate schools of the country, and he was often critical of what he saw. Nevertheless he fought at home to raise standards, and in doing so gained the confidence of a good segment of the faculty. Later in the transitional years between the Bryan and Wells administrations, Dean Payne's colleagues documented trust in his honesty and judgment by voting in 1938 to make him a member of the self-study committee, despite the fact no administrator was to serve this body.

Contemporaneously with Payne, Thompson, and Davidson was Stephen Sargeant Visher, a geologist, geographer, and climatologist. A native of Chicago and a graduate of the University of Chicago in 1914, Visher joined the Indiana University staff in the latter year as an assistant professor in geology under the administrative watchcare of the redoubtable E. Roscoe Cumings. In time he was to become a distinct if not eccentric character in the faculty. Possibly no other professor in the history of the institution generated so much folklore as did Stephen S. Visher. His memory remains green. He gave his colleagues and their wives many stories, tidbits of gossip, and possible reason for anger.

In 1921 Professor Visher was sent by the United States government into the South Pacific on a research journey to produce a geographical outline for educational purposes. A year later he published an article setting forth the pioneering theory that the major storms of the continental United States had their origins in the tropics. He expounded for his Hoosier neighbors the theory that weather changes in their states were governed by currents and climatic changes far removed from Indiana. Between 1922 and his retirement in 1955, Stephen Visher was a productive scholar, a "popular" writer, analyst of unusual statistics, and a tireless correspondent. After analyzing the Indiana entries in *Who's Who in America*, he told a Bloomington *Daily Telephone* reporter, "Indiana's production of distinguished persons is far more significant than its production of limestone, rye, or sheep." In 1954, he published his *Climatic Atlas of the United States* with Harvard University Press.

Visher presented his administrative colleagues with recurring dilemmas. The calm and usually imperturbable E. R. Cumings of the Department of Geology told Bryan and the trustees in his annual report in 1922, that Stephen Visher should be promoted to an associate professorship. Cumings regarded him as a man of broad and thorough training and with wide experience. He had traveled extensively and Cumings was impressed with Visher's discovery of the tropical influences bearing on continental weather conditions. The fact he had collaborated with the famous Ellsworth Huntington on a book was also impressive. There were, however, reservations. Cumings wrote Bryan, "As you know from our former conversations his personality leaves certain things to be desired; but I have made up my own mind that in view of his positive scholarly merits we may overlook these faults, and advance him at this time."

Visher stalked through Indiana University like a one-man horde, and Cumings had changed his mind by 1924. "The case of Professor Visher is more difficult than any situation that ever has confronted me," he wrote Bryan. "While he has remained relatively quiescent during the year, I constantly feel that he has no loyalty to the department, and that he thinks only of his personal interests. He apparently is not concerned about the welfare of the department as a whole, but would like it if geography swallowed up everything else. His ability and scientific productivity I fully recognize and appreciate."

A much more equable scientist who brought distinction to Indiana University during Bryan's administration was Edgar Roscoe Cumings. For nearly half a century, 1898 to 1944, he was a member of the Indiana faculty. In 1903, the year he received his doctorate from Yale, he became head of the Department of Geology at Indiana. Cumings and his colleagues, Joshua William Beede and Clyde Arnett Malott, carried on the strong geological tradition established by the Owen brothers in the university. Cumings' handbooks and special reports on Indiana geology were of major importance in the search for new mineral resources during World War I. Between 1920 and his retirement in 1944, he made significant contributions in his specialty, stratigraphy. In his latter years, 1930 to 1944, Cumings devoted his attention to the study of the ordovician and silurian ages of northeastern North America.

Cumings was an active member of the faculty. He was the chief consultant in the effort to create an adequate water supply for the university and was in charge of the design and construction of the university lake. During World War I he served as acting dean of the Graduate School, and his name appears frequently in the university records. He was a charter member of the American Association of University Professors, and served a term as member of that body's council.

Associated with Cumings was the Lincolnesque Clyde Arnett Malott. This scholar was born near Atlanta, Indiana, and he earned three degrees from the university. He joined the staff in 1915 and served the state Geological Survey until 1921. Robert Shrock, head of the Department of Geology at Massachusetts Institute of Technology, said of Malott, "He knew more about the geology of Indiana than any other person of his time." His major contributions were in the fields of geomorphology and stratigraphy.

In the Bryan faculty were men who represented by background training and philosophical outlook the substantial values in early twentieth century American higher education. One of these was Ulysses Grant Weatherly. Educated at Cornell, Heidelberg, and Leipzig, he joined the Indiana faculty in 1899 as sociologist and historian. As his career progressed he pioneered in the field of applied social work. He was one of the most active professors on the campus. He promoted the new field of social work, especially in connection with commissions having to do with child labor, charities, and industrial education. Professor Weatherly had a well-developed sense of the dynamics of social change in Indiana during the decades of his service, and he dealt with this subject professionally in a pioneer study. In the university Weatherly impressed students with both his energy and his mature scholarly competence, thus giving the Bryan administration a solidity comparable to that of Wisconsin and Chicago in the newer fields of public and social concern.

In the midst of wartime Henry Lester Smith was elevated in 1916 to the deanship of the School of Education. In the postwar years he was to exert a major influence in Indiana University over curriculum matters and in the state of Indiana in the area of public education and teacher training. Dean Smith represented the educational philosophy of the College of Education of Columbia University and brought to Bloomington fresh concepts of teacher training which sharply revised university traditions in this area. Between 1914 and 1938 he published a phenomenal body of educational analytical materials. Inside Indiana University Dean Smith and Dean Payne polarized points of view and philosophies concerning the standards and nature of graduate education, and many times they sharply disagreed as to the fundamentals of university education itself. Smith's influence on public education was significant.

In botany, Paul Weatherwax continued a long tradition of scholarly investigation. A native of Worthington, Indiana, with a farm background, he received his degrees from the university. In 1918, D. M. Mottier recommended his appointment to the faculty because of his research with maize. Both Bryan and Mottier hoped the appointment of Paul Weatherwax would be an answer to the institution's need for a course in agriculture which could be offered to public school teachers, without encroaching upon Purdue's major field of interest. Bryan had earlier proposed work in agriculture which would deal with crops and plant diseases, soils and fertilizers, and animal husbandry. To sustain his recommendation Mottier submitted to the trustees papers which Weatherwax had written in the study of corn or maize. Briefly Weatherwax accepted an appointment in the University of Georgia, but in 1919 he returned to Bloomington as an associate professor. In the next three decades this scientist enlarged the scope of his special studies, and became an international authority on the subject of maize.

Rivaling the English Department in good quality teachers and publishing scholars were members of the Department of History. The historians had a tradition of service to the liberal arts dating back to the founding of the university. After 1884 there was a fairly distinguished procession of young scholars who served the department for varying periods of time. The man who came to personify history on the campus from 1883 to 1924, however, was James Albert Woodburn. Descended from South Carolina émigrés of the 1830's, Woodburn possessed the grace and gentility that were personally distinguishing marks. From the immediate post-Civil War years in 1885, when he was delivering chapel lectures on the race problem in the New South, until his retirement in 1924, Woodburn was a dominant member of the university faculty.

In 1889 as a graduate student in The Johns Hopkins Graduate Seminar, Woodburn delivered a series of adult lectures in Washington, D.C. The following year the board of trustees elevated him to the "Chair of American History" in Indiana University. He was a conscientious scholar with a creditable list of books and articles published and papers read. In 1925–26 he served as President of the Mississippi Valley Historical Association and later became chairman of its executive committee.

Woodburn was Republican, Presbyterian, and conservative; nevertheless he engaged in an extensive debate in the Bloomington *Daily Telephone* with Dr. W. L. Whitted on the subject of bimetalism. Woodburn damned the "gold standard" as unworkable and advocated "cheap money." Subsequently while teaching at a summer chautauqua in Bay View, Michigan, in July, 1894, he invited Eugene V. Debs to give a lecture on American labor problems in Indiana University. After the Pullman Strike, the Bloomington *Daily Telephone* carefully noted the invitation was withdrawn.

During World War I Woodburn engaged in both written and spoken propaganda before state and national audiences. In his mind, "The Potsdam Gang" had planned the war over a long period. The Germans had hoped to master western Europe, without becoming involved with Great Britain. In 1918 he said, "Now that [the] United States has entered the war we must not only check German aggression, but defeat once and for all these 'Prussian Warlords.' If this is done there won't be another war." Woodburn, along with most of his fellow historians, was a rampant chauvinist during the war years and wrote things that in calmer moments after 1920 they must have considered extreme. When there was a rumor of peace feelers in October, 1918, he gave the press the statement, "The Kaiser, with his accustomed hypocrisy and infamy, is again graciously offering his enemies 'an honorable peace.' He speaks like a conqueror and says he 'offers his hand for no other.' Let him look upon his hands. They are red with the blood of the slain, of French women, of Belgian children, of massacred Armenians, of countless thousands of brave men who have died fighting to resist his brutal conquest of the world." To Woodburn, Americans should not make peace with the Kaiser's gang;

the "peace offers" were camouflage to allow the Germans to revamp their forces.

In 1922 Woodburn announced his retirement, and the Indiana *Daily Student* proclaimed, the "Grand Old Man Completes Service of Forty-Six Years on Faculty." This, however, proved a premature announcement. Bryan persuaded him to remain for two more years as head of the department and research professor of American history. In 1924 Woodburn made positive his intentions to retire, this time to head the Bok Peace Opinion Group.

One of Woodburn's significant contributions to Indiana University was the preparation of the first volume of the history of the institution from 1820 to 1920. In this book he edited six chapters prepared by Judge David Demaree Banta, a trustee from 1877 to 1889. He then reworked articles he had published in the *Alumni Quarterly* and prepared afresh the remainder of the text.

Rivaling Woodburn as scholar and teacher was Amos Shartle Hershey of the famous Pennsylvania chocolate family. He received the doctorate from Harvard in 1892, and a second one from Heidelberg in 1894. He came to Bloomington the following year as an assistant professor at the annual salary of $600. Hershey's initial work at Indiana University was a study of the Cuban crisis in 1898, for which the university rewarded him by withholding part of his salary while he was on leave to collect documentary materials. In 1907, he published "The International Law and Diplomacy of the Russo-Japanese War" and in 1912 *The Essentials of International Public Law*. Upon the appearance of this book William Lowe Bryan wrote the trustees, "It is my belief that the University never does anything more directly in line with its main function than when it enables such a man to do such work."

Hershey received more tangible reward in 1913 when the Kahn Foundation granted him a $3,000 scholarship in recognition of his work in international law. This enabled him to travel abroad with the powerful backing of Elihu Root and John Foster. At the same time the French Societé Conciliation Internationale awarded him a gold medal honoring his pioneering study.

During the war years Hershey worked overtime speaking and writing propaganda pamphlets. In March, 1917, he wrote of the German rapprochement with Mexico, "It is an attempt to form an alliance for hostile purposes. . . . It is an act in the highest degree unfriendly. We should go farther than a mere protest. The proper reply would be a declaration of war. We should line up with the

Allies for otherwise we will have to fight Germany by ourselves. . . ." In December, 1918, Hershey went to Paris with Woodrow Wilson's peace commission as an expert adviser. At the time he was conducting a peace survey for the Carnegie Endowment for Peace.

By this time Hershey had become head of the newly formed Department of Political Science and gave a new sense of direction to his discipline on the Indiana campus. When he returned from France he began an active campaign in behalf of the League of Nations, and in 1922 he traveled extensively in Europe and Asia making a first-hand study of current political developments in more than a dozen countries. This journey brought him little comfort because he viewed conditions as chaotic and unpromising of future order. The next year he predicted "the worst is yet to come," and expressed the belief the United States would soon be feeding millions of starving Germans because France was bankrupting its former enemy in demands for indemnities.

Amos Hershey became incurably ill in 1932, and was hospitalized for the remainder of his life. With the possible exception of David Starr Jordan, he was Indiana University's first professor to gain an international reputation, and he was easily the most notable scholar on the campus. Hershey was the butt of much community humor about his absentminded antics. Once his wife had called the departmental secretary to inquire discreetly whether Amos was wearing his trousers. She had found his time-honored pair hanging in his closet and had forgotten, herself, that he had just purchased a new suit. To students "Doc" Hershey rated high, as an editorial sage advised in the *Arbutus*:

> But freshman, softly in your ear
> I'd whisper. This man you'll not fear;
> For he's the best good-tempered man
> That you could find in all this land.

Complementing the work of Hershey was that of F. Lee Benns of history. Benns received the Ph.D. from Clark University in 1920, and that year came to Indiana as an assistant professor. Within a decade he had produced four important books, one of which won the coveted Justin Winsor Prize of the American Historical Association in 1920.

As time went on Benns earned the esteem of historians nationally. He was elected secretary of the modern European history section of the American Historical Association in 1934, and in the same year was made a member of the George Louis Beer prize committee to select the best study in American diplomatic history.

Where Benns won broad recognition in the area of Modern Europe, William Thomas Morgan built a solid reputation at home and abroad in the field of eighteenth century British history. In fact he became the leading American authority on the age of Queen Anne and early eighteenth century British political history. He came to Indiana University in 1919 from an instructorship at Columbia University, and a year later was awarded the doctorate by Yale University. The year following Morgan's arrival in Bloomington he won the American Historical Association's Herbert Baxter Adams essay prize. In succeeding years his publications became both numerous and meritorious. Much of Morgan's most important scholarly contributions were made in his fifty essays which appeared in first-rate journals. His work received fine critical appraisal, and the British recognized it by electing him to a fellowship in the Royal Historical Society. Like Hershey and Benns, Morgan was an internationally significant scholar.

When James A. Woodburn retired from the headship of the Department of History in 1925, he was succeeded the following year by Albert Ludwig Kohlmeier, a native of southern Indiana, a graduate of the university in 1908, who received the doctorate from Harvard in 1920. He was appointed an instructor in 1912, and was promoted to a professorship in 1921. Though not as productive a scholar as some of his colleagues, Kohlmeier was an impressive speaker before Hoosier and professional audiences, and no doubt an effective teacher. Like Woodburn before him, he was active in university administrative affairs, and he gave his department a calm and dignified leadership. During his years he either employed or encouraged such colleagues as Roscoe Carlyle Buley, Oscar O. Winther, Donald F. Carmony, Chase Mooney, and John D. Barnhart. He also had for colleagues William O. Lynch, Logan Esarey, Prescott Winson Townsend, and John Carl Andressohn, all of whom made material contributions to the university's reputation, and who impressed students with their teaching and scholarly concerns.

In his struggle to broaden the professional base of the university William Lowe Bryan and three or four colleagues were able to make a beginning in the field of journalism. Building on a flimsy curriculum of established courses the department gained momentum when Joseph W. Piercy of the University of Washington was brought to Bloomington in 1911 to pioneer in the organization, first of a department of journalism, and then to prepare ground for the creation of a school. From 1911 to 1938 the Department of Journalism graduated a score or more of major newspaper men who served their profession with significant newspapers and news services. Among these was Don Mellett, who was killed by gangsters in Canton, Ohio, in a sensational national crime, when he conducted a strong publicity campaign to drive this element out of the city. *The Canton News* was awarded the Pulitzer Prize as a result of Mellett's reporting.

Joseph W. Piercy's services on the faculty are to be measured in terms of creating a productive department in the pioneering era of training professional newspaper men. At the time of his death, the *Indianapolis Star* said his career bridged the transitional period between old-time "sandlot" reporting and the appearance of the modern graduate of professional departments of journalism. When Professor Piercy retired in the Bryan-Wells transition in 1938, the Indiana *Daily Student* on November 24, 1944, said he had organized a highly respectable department which consistently earned top ratings among competing departments of journalism in other schools.

There were many other Bryan faculty who proved their worth in different ways. Guido Stempel and Bert John Vos were bedrock yeomen who sent students from their classes with new skills in languages and literature and new perspectives on the learning process. Stempel came to Indiana University as an instructor in English in 1896, and in 1904 became Associate Professor of philology. To hundreds of students Guido Stempel personified Indiana University. The same was true of Bert John Vos, graduate of the University of Michigan, 1888, and holder of a doctorate from The Johns Hopkins University (1892) in the exciting years of that institution's expanding graduate program. As Professor of German he went through the vicissitudes of World War I and struggled during the postwar period to reinstate his subject, not only in the university, but in the public schools of Indiana. Dean of Men Charles Jacob Sembower impressed students with the beauty of English poetry and the substance of English novels. Don Herold looked upon the dean as a man who was able to combine the metaphors of campus athletics with those of the classics of literature and somehow get both into the heads of reluctant students.

Limited space no doubt causes injustices to be done such men as Enoch Hogate, Bernard C. Gavit, and Charles McGuffey Hepburn who trained many of Indiana's best lawyers. There were many other professors like Agapito Rey, Lander McClintock, William A. Rawles, Ulysses Grant Weatherly, Henry Lester Smith, Selatie Stout, Wendell W. Wright, Oliver P. Fields, Herman Thompson Briscoe, Kenneth P. Williams, Frank Curry Mathers, and Mable Thatcher Wellman who were teachers and scholars of great worth. These were the people who with scores of other colleagues accomplished many of the objectives of a people's university through the trials of war, inadequate public financing, radical changes in challenges to higher education, and aging administration, and a rising sense of student and faculty independence. They were the ones who took hundreds of Indiana's "first college generation of children" and turned them into men and women ready to accept intellectual maturity.

William Lowe Bryan and some of his deans and heads of departments were limited in perspective if not eccentric in the hiring, discharging, and encouragement of faculty members. Bryan frequently expressed pain at the loss of promising young scholars without apparently sensing the fact that the internal administration of the university sometimes had a stultifying effect upon the professors who sought greater freedom in their institutional associations. Administration critics became more openly vocal as time advanced. They opposed especially the older heads of departments who undertook to continue a type of academic feudalism into an age of ever-broadening academic democracy. Arthur Lee Foley, for instance, was said by colleagues to have actually prevented Rolla Ray Ramsey from developing to the fullest possibility the fields of radio and electronics, areas in which he had pioneered. In the face of the new physics Foley was quoted by some of his contemporaries to have said, "there is not an electron in all Indiana."

There was friction in the faculty which perhaps proved costly in terms of broadening the curriculum and advancing the university into newer fields of investigation. Eigenmann and Mottier allowed their personal and professional differences to become visible to colleagues and students. In Eigenmann's personal correspondence there are occasional notes to President Bryan referring to relationships with the head of the Department of Botany. Dean Payne had differences with the Dean of the School of Education which not infrequently spiced discussions of graduate work. Even so, Indiana University was not unique in this respect. Such clashes generally characterized the American university scene where strong-willed men strove to advance views and ambitions.

Indiana University's faculty worked and lived in a small and close-knit community where even the most intimate professional and domestic affairs were subjected to dinner-table discussion. Nonetheless a communal intimacy and friendliness prevailed, which overshadowed the petty rivalries of classroom and departmental office. The faculty had largely to create its own social background and amusement, which it did in the form of dinner parties, dances, musical events, discussion clubs, and outings. This camaraderie was possibly the greatest human asset of the Bryan years. A decidedly distinguishing virtue of the faculty in this era was fervent loyalty to the institution, and this spirit extended into the area of faculty-student relationships. In October, 1926, the *Daily Student* made a survey of student opinion regarding the price charged faculty members for admission to university activities. There was active student resentment against levying of full rates. The paper contended that faculty season tickets for all events should be reduced from $15.00 to $5.00 or $7.50. In January, 1927, 2100 students signed resolutions to the board of trustees asking that faculty members share equal status with students in the purchase of activity tickets.

There are no thoroughly dependable criteria by which a university historian can fully appraise the worth and quality of graduates produced in the university. Indiana's graduates made highly reputable showings in later life. Some of these revealed in terms of genuine human warmth the benefits they had derived from their university experiences. In this respect the less publicized yeoman professors came into their own.

Don Herold of Bloomfield, later of *College Humor* fame, looked back in 1919 upon his Indiana years from the perspective of the jazz age pinnacle of spoof and academic snobbery and sorted out what he conceived to be the honest values of his own college career:

I went to Indiana University because it was thirty-five miles from home, but I would have gone to the farthest university in the world if it had had Charley Sembower on its English staff. And I would have gone to the smallest university in the world if it had had William Lowe Bryan for president. And that's the whole story of the paradox of the proximity and mediocrity and the glory of Indiana for most of us. It's the old story of Rasselas and the Blue Bird and all the other yarns of good things being near at hand, close to home.

Farmer boys and girls, and small town boys and girls, and a few from Indianapolis and other larger Indiana towns, all go to Indiana because it is near and comparatively inexpensive, or because their high school chum went there—an easy, lazy way to choose a university, but maybe about as good as any in the long run. If you find a Sembower or a Dr. Bryan (and I use these in somewhat of a symbolic sense), you have found about all that any university can offer you; and if you don't find them, you might as well go to college at a Sears Roebuck warehouse. . . . Half of Semmy's students had not the slightest idea what he was talking about in his classes; the others were enjoying the keenest hours of their intellectual lives. He was much too mystic for the masses. He would talk Keats in terms of baseball, or Shelley in terms of household dust. . . . William Lowe Bryan, President of Indiana, is one of the grand souls of this earth, one of the smartest of living men and one of the finest writers of English prose in all the world. A lot of Indiana boys and girls go through the University and completely miss William Lowe Bryan and I pity them.

I may dwell on these two personalities perhaps to too great length because they were, to a large extent, Indiana University to me. Other men were Indiana to other students; in almost every university there are two or more professors, I dare say, who are that university to certain students. What I am getting at is that, to a great degree, all this comparing of universities is pure applesauce. You take potluck at any of them, and it is partly accident whether or not you come in contact with faculty men who set you aflame. I had plenty of pinhead profs at Indiana, and I don't imagine ten-million-dollar annual appropriations can keep them out of any university. I had a Spanish prof who meant an hour of the deepest dank depression because he was that kind of human being, and I had others who were just inoffensive blah. . . . But as I think back, there were torchbearers aplenty who could not have been beat at any price: Guido Stempel, fine, rare; "Dudey" Brooks, the best of all pedagogues, who gave me about the only facts that I ever remembered about anything and fired me with a capacity for some enjoyment of architecture, which had meant fun to me for many years; "Doc" Campbell, who did the same for me in music; "Doc" Eigenmann, who knew more about blind fish than anybody else in the world and who could give you a passionately romantic interest in an amoeba. . . . Most boys and girls at Indiana are first generation college goers. In this way, Indiana differs most distinctly from some of the larger Eastern universities. Some of them come down to Indiana eating with their knives. Families have to start going to college somewhere and sometime, and, as a geologist reckons time, a generation one way or another is nothing over which to get a swelled head.

The latter two decades of the Bryan administration were changing times in which both student and professor tried to identify themselves with the era of intellectual revolution. The Bryan faculty, though subjected to rather harsh appraisal in the self-study report in 1939 in comparison with other American universities, had served the university with faithfulness and capability. Don Herold may have been as nearly right as the self-study committee when he wrote, "And all the time there was a yell that the richer schools were hiring our best men away from us. All I know is that there are a lot of them left there even now. In the sciences, of which I know little, it may be possible to put a finger on the best men and hire them away mechanically; in the arts, I imagine that it is only the students who know exactly who the best men are." The retirements and shifts made in faculty personnel after 1937 brought to a close the day of the feudal headship, and ended at last the domination of the inner core of the Bryan faculty. Too, Herman B Wells' acceptance of the presidency in much larger measure brought a radical break with the nineteenth century Victorian concepts of faculty morals, freedom, and internal associations. Emphasis came to be placed more upon academic qualities and accomplishments than upon mere institutional loyalties and communal sentimentalities.

[XIV]

Grist for the Mill

A s the day of transition approached in the late 1930's, some of the university administration began taking stock of almost a century and a quarter of the institution's accomplishments. They attempted to evaluate them in terms of its chief product—its graduates. Spread over a broad expanse of time, and with the confrontation of so many problems, it seemed on the surface the numbers of individuals coming and going in its classrooms were much greater than actually was the case. Throughout most of the period of the university's history there was, in terms of modern numbers, a relatively light enrollment. By 1939, and after one hundred and nine years of degree granting, the institution had graduated 27,273 candidates, and of these 26,136 had completed their work since 1902, 24,063 of these since 1920. In all it was estimated that approximately 40,000 students had been enrolled in some classes in the university by 1938. The graduating class of 1902 numbered 124, and that of 1938, 758. Of the 124 graduates in 1902, ninety-one received the Bachelor of Arts degree; there were fifteen lawyers, and eighteen Bachelors of Science were preparing for the practice of medicine. In contrast in 1938 the institution granted thirteen different degrees, with Bachelor of Science degrees in eleven fields. In the first hundred and twenty years of its history the university had granted 17,405 Bachelor of Arts degrees.

This elementary recitation of statistics eloquently reflects the fact that Indiana University was overwhelmingly an undergraduate liberal arts institution to the end of the Bryan administration. Perhaps one more statistical fact has relevance. The registrar said in 1931 that, of 13,624 graduates from 1830 to 1929, 11,893 were still alive, and of these, 6,966 were still living in Indiana; the rest lived in other states, and 165 graduates lived abroad. The professional distribution of these graduates further sharpened the institutional profile. Out of 13,624 living graduates 4,073 were teachers or educational administrators. Approximately 1,500 degree holders became housewives, there were 1,383 doctors, and the rest were lawyers, dentists, nurses, merchants, manufacturers, journalists, politicians, and government employees.

In the years 1930 and 1931, with the rising rate of unemployment, 90 percent of the Indiana University alumni were employed or were housewives as of June 1, 1931. There were also some inconclusive statistics which undertook to prove that graduating from the university was economically profitable in the rate of personal earnings.

University officials and boosters repeated so often the statement that a disproportionate number of Indiana graduates were chosen college presidents that the boast became trite. In 1926, it was said, there were fifty-nine sons who headed some kind of educational institution. Several of these—Lotus Delta Coffman of the University of Minnesota, Ernest H. Lindley, a former professor of philosophy and psychology, president of Idaho and later chancellor at Kansas, E. B. Bryan of Colgate, and Robert J. Aley of Maine—held significant posts. It was stretching the facts a bit, however, to list David Starr Jordan as being among the fifty-nine honored sons. Most of the others were presidents of smaller institutions, many of them were heads of teachers' colleges.

The fact that so many presidents had been chosen from among Indiana alumni reflected, of course, the personal and professional qualities of the individuals. Somewhat more meaningful for the university was the restricted emphasis in its curriculum and staff upon the liberal arts. An overwhelming number of graduates chose teaching as a profession. There were no specific courses in the curriculum which were designed specifically for the training of college administrators. Even without clear documentation, however, little doubt remains that the faculty emphasized teaching careers for their students.

In February, 1923, the *Daily Student* announced the results of a campus survey which revealed a change in focal direction among students. The paper expressed the opinion that Indiana University would soon exchange its "academic presidential" image for the laurels of corporation presidencies. Out of 1,511 students who answered the career questionnaire, 1,380 declared they intended to enter either business or non-teaching professions. Twenty-five respondents said frankly they intended to do nothing when they graduated.

Already by 1925 some Indiana graduates had demonstrated high business capabilities. Earl Blough, A.B., 1899, had worked his way up the industrial ladder from a frustrating public school teaching career to become vice president and director of the Aluminum Company Limited of Canada. Building on his major in chemistry, he had become one of America's important entrepreneurial chemical engineers in the vital field of aluminum manufacture. He had helped materially with the organization of the Aluminum Company of America. Before Blough, graduating in law in 1893, Harry R. Kurrie became president of the famous Monon Railroad Company. In time he either exerted or attempted to exert a considerable pressure upon the university in the selection of trustees and the making of other internal appointments. He with George Ade had presented the Oaken Bucket athletic trophy to the rival schools. Also hard by the university's doors, Sanford Teter, 1893, became a major administrative official in the Showers Brothers furniture manufacturing company.

Of a later generation, Herman B Wells became a key figure in Indiana and national banking reform during the trying years of the Depression. It was he who analyzed the problems of antiquated state banking procedures and helped to devise more progressive legislation to regulate the business. In the years of the New Deal he also made a personal contribution in the revision of national banking procedures.

Who's Who in 1938 listed 479 Indiana University graduates out of a total of 5,782 entries. The vast majority of those recognized were educational administrators or professors. There were however, Byron K. Elliott, 1920, who was general solicitor for the John Hancock Mutual Life Insurance Company of Boston; Dick

Miller, 1894, was a major Indianapolis banker; and other non-educational men were lawyers, doctors, authors, editors, and three were engineers. James A. Stuart, 1901, became editor of the Indianapolis *Star*. Kent Cooper, a student in 1898–99, was general manager of the Associated Press for twenty-six years. On the campus he was associate editor of the *Daily Student*. Edwin C. Hill (1897–1901), the well known "voice" of the Columbia Broadcasting Company's "Human Side of the News" in the 1930's was a student in the university, 1901.

No graduate of Indiana University, however, gained so much universally warm human recognition as Ernest Taylor Pyle of Dana. Pyle attended the university from 1919 to 1923, and apparently left with some self-inspired encouragement from the institution. After leaving Bloomington he was a reporter for the Washington *Daily News*, aviation editor for the Scripps-Howard papers, then managing editor of the *News*, and later roving reporter for Scripps-Howard. In 1944 he was awarded the Pulitzer Prize for distinguished war reporting.

While enrolled in Indiana University Ernie Pyle was too busy savoring life on the run to be an entirely serious student. He was involved in one caper after another. In October, 1923, he and Evanson Earp set out for Boston to see Indiana play Harvard. Their old car caught on fire and burned up. They then bummed fifty free rides in continuing their trip, missed the game, but took in the sights of Boston and had scores of adventures in their 1,600 miles of charity rides.

Pyle, then news editor of the *Daily Student*, ranged far and wide for his stories. The year before he, Harold Kaiser, Warren Cooper, and Joseph Benham, set out for Kobe, Japan, to see the Indiana baseball team play the Japanese. They hitchhiked to Seattle and signed on as deckhands on the *Keystone State* which transported the baseball players, but when they reached Kobe they were not allowed to jump ship and had to continue on to Shanghai. During this caper the boys picked up a young Filipino named Eugene Velbelbrot and smuggled him into the United States, bringing him on to Bloomington. Pyle persuaded the local Rotary Club to support the boy and entered him in the Bloomington High School.

On June 30, 1922, the Bloomington *Daily Telephone* commented, "It is needless to say that Pyle is a 'live wire,'—and he will be much heard from in years to come." A modest prophecy!

[3 1 5]

However, there were people in the registrar's office who may have had reasonable doubts. Pyle surfaced next in a LaPorte, Indiana, newspaper office reporting on the activities of the Ku Klux Klan. He was able to attend a secret klavern meeting unnoticed and gave the public an inside view of what the Knights had in store. This venture won him several threats of violence.

As a roving correspondent Pyle turned up in all sorts of places gathering those tidbits of human interest stories which he presented in his warm Hoosier style. Then came World War II, with its thousands of homesick GI's who did not want to be forgotten at home, and Ernie Pyle assumed the job of telling their story as it unfolded from day to day on three battle fronts and of keeping their memory green. He was in Africa, in western Europe, and in the Pacific. It was on the sprawling Pacific front that he used a quarter-century of newspaper experience with great effectiveness. On April 18, 1945, he was killed by Japanese machine gun fire on Ie Shima Island. He went to his grave, however, with an honorary doctorate of Humane Letters from Indiana University which he had been awarded on November 14, 1944. A special convocation was held to pay tribute to this son who was too busy as a student to earn a degree. Former classmates were on hand to greet him, and all Indiana had a day out from the war reminiscing about his student escapades.

Less folksy and adventurous than Ernie Pyle was Wendell L. Willkie. A second generation German, Willkie, like his father and mother before him, had a mind of his own. Born in Elwood, Indiana, one of six children, he was competitive from birth. His mother was the first woman to be admitted to the Indiana Bar. His father, an outspoken man who had urged President Bryan to fire Zeuch in that controversy during World War I, sent his four sons and a daughter to Bloomington. Three of them, Robert, Wendell, and Fred, were in school at the same time. The Willkie brothers formed an aggressive triumvirate who tolerated little or no opposition and no abuse. Wendell was tough-minded on the one hand and a "college man on the other." He belonged to the Boosters Club. He organized and promoted the first state basketball tournament, wore the star of a campus marshal, and served as a second lieutenant in the First World War. Later he served as counsel without charge to soldiers before courts martial.

Wendell Willkie received the Bachelor of Arts Degree in 1913 and two years later graduated from the law school. After the war he established a law office in Akron, Ohio, but within a decade he was in New York City as a public utilities official. Soon thereafter he was chairman of the board of the Consumer Power Company and of the Ohio Company, a director of the Illinois Light Company, and of the Indiana Gas and Electric Company. His most distinctive corporate association, however, was as president of the Commonwealth and Southern Power Company. In the latter position he was brought directly into confrontation with the evolving public power movement, and into opposition to Roosevelt's New Deal. The rise of the Tennessee Valley Authority threatened the basic structure of the Insull empire and the private power complex of the South. After the Supreme Court handed down its famous decisions in the *Aswander Case* (1933) and the *Tennessee Electric Power Company* v. *The Tennessee Valley Authority* (1940), which were adverse to private power interests, Wendell Willkie had no choice but to discontinue his fight.

In 1940 Willkie negotiated the sale of the Tennessee Company along with a cluster of other private electric groups to the Tennessee Valley Authority for $74,425,095. In making this transfer he dealt with David Lilienthal, another Hoosier. In presenting the government's check to Willkie, Lilienthal commented jokingly that it was a lot of money for two Hoosier farmers to be kicking about. This remark did not appeal to Willkie's sense of humor; instead he launched into an impassioned lecture on the virtue of private enterprise.

On July 2, 1940, the Board of Trustees of Indiana University revealed a political turn of mind when it officially congratulated Wendell Willkie on winning the Republican nomination for the presidency of the United States. "We record our profound pleasure, satisfaction, and pride," resolved the board, "in this great and unique distinction which has come to one of our most esteemed, respected, and beloved alumni." The board in its jubilation offered Willkie the thirty-five thousand seat Memorial Stadium as the site for his official notification ceremonies.

The *Daily Student* outdid even the trustees in its burst of jubilation. "Only a football victory over Purdue—and some doubt even that," said the reporter, "could cause the outburst of pride and excitement in Bloomington and on the campus resulting from Mr. Willkie's nomination. . . . Local Democrats have joined Republicans in paeans of praise, joy, and triumph for this 'patriot— no politician.'

"To Indiana University—long called 'mother of college presidents'—would come the greater maternal honor should one of her sons be the next President of the United States. . . ." The *Alumni Magazine* carried an extensive article about Willkie, and the Republican campaign was underway. Four years later the university community held a solemn convocation to the memory of this son of 1913.

Hoagy Carmichael wrote in *Sometimes I Wonder* that Wendell Willkie and Paul Vories McNutt were roommates. At least they were campus front-runners. McNutt was president of the senior class and Willkie was president of the time-honored Democratic Jackson Club. The lads shared political views and both burned with ambition. In his senior year the debonair McNutt was president of the Union Board and editor-in-chief of the *Daily Student*. On top of this he was initiated into Phi Beta Kappa. Since his high school days in nearby Martinsville, McNutt had been involved in almost everything going on in the university.

After graduating in 1913, Paul McNutt went on to the Harvard Law School, where he was elected to the presidency of the Harvard Legal Aid Union, was a United Press correspondent, and graduated in 1916 with a good classroom record. Returning to Martinsville he entered the practice of law with his father, but the quiet of this conservative town lacked the luster to hold the interest of so ambitious a young barrister. The next year he was back in Bloomington as a member of the staff of the Indiana University Law School, but almost immediately he went into the army with the rank of captain in the Field Artillery, and two years later he held the rank of lieutenant colonel. He was promoted to colonel in 1923 and given command of the 325th Field Artillery Reserves. At the same time he was elected president of the Reserve Officers Association of Indiana.

When Dean Charles McGuffey Hepburn retired from the deanship of the Law School, McNutt was promoted to that position. It was said at the time of his promotion that he was the youngest Indiana faculty member ever to attain the rank of dean. Hardly had this bustling young professor settled himself into the dean's chair before he cast his lines into other and more exciting places. He got himself elected president of the Alumni Association in 1923 and threw himself into the great memorial fund drive which absorbed so much faculty and alumni time and interest. In the midst of all this he was awarded the Thayer Teaching Fellowship at Harvard to pursue work toward a doctorate of jurisprudence, an honor he finally had to surrender. He reapplied the following year for the fellowship, but in the meantime the changes in the law school again prevented his accepting the grant.

In August, 1926, McNutt was elected commander of the American Legion of Indiana and became most active with this body in a crusade to combat un-American activities in the state. Although unwilling to speak publicly on the woes of the Law School, he had his concerns about his and his colleagues' salaries. There were many conferences on the subject of money, and at the time he assumed the presidency of the Legion, six of his professors left Bloomington for more alluring salaries in neighboring universities. McNutt warned Bryan and the legislators that Indiana University Law School professors averaged $1,175 below those of other north central law schools.

Just as he had raced up the scale of local fame in the Martinsville High School, in Indiana University, at Harvard, and in the army, Paul McNutt maintained his ambitious pace. At its national meeting in San Antonio, Texas, in 1928 he was elected national commander of the American Legion. In Bloomington, town and gown turned out for a rousing welcome for the local hero. William Lowe Bryan greeted his peripatetic dean with a cheering speech, but his mind must have been divided as to whether or not he was welcoming home an unusually energetic dean of a law school or a bird of political passage. He had given the university national publicity, and McNutt was now a well publicized figure. No doubt by this time he had set himself a schedule which would take him through the governor's office in Indianapolis to Pennsylvania Avenue by 1940 or 1944.

In Lansing, Michigan, at a Legion convention, legionnaires who had supported the Colonel in San Antonio boomed him for appointment to the presidency of their state university to succeed President Cecil Cooke Little. There is now no way of determining how serious this latter proposal was or what it really meant. Paul McNutt had other plans that he hoped would lead to more prestigious positions even than the presidency of the University of Michigan. In Indiana he was constantly on the circuit, shaking hands, making friends, huddling with the ambitious and the influential, making "non-political" speeches, and otherwise making himself known. In 1931 he went before Herbert Hoover's cabinet to advocate removal of profits from war-making. He also advocated policies to be followed in case of war which attracted the attention of Secretary of War Patrick J. Hurley.

At home there was at least one critic: B. W. Bradfute said McNutt's speaking campaign in Indiana was only stirring up future disaster for the university. Never before had a staff member been so active in what appeared to be a political campaign. Bradfute admitted the Dean of the Law School or any other professor had a right to engage in politics, but not "to play politics by methods which will raise half or more than half or any part of the state against the University. . . ." He asked, "is Indiana to be sacrificed to the burning ambition of Professor Paul McNutt?"

Bradfute no doubt was right in the observation that Paul V. McNutt was creating a demand for his services among a majority of the voters. In June, 1932, the curtain was lifted a notch higher on the dean's ambitions when Indiana Democrats nominated him for the governorship. The following November he was elected to the office, and from that time on he received almost as much national publicity as Wendell L. Willkie. The fate of history, however, was to cause both of their ambitions to be blunted by Franklin D. Roosevelt.

McNutt was to figure prominently in the transitional period of the university in the 1930's. Although Joseph Wright was the first former Indiana University student to be elected governor, McNutt was its first graduate to hold the office. The latter's correspondence, now contained in the Lilly Library Collection, reveals how thoroughly astute a politician Dean McNutt was. He gathered about him a cluster of clever managers who were diligent in supporting their candidate and governor.

There was a distinct outside interest, if not attempted interference, in the appointment of a new dean of the Law School. On December 29, 1932, H. R. Kurrie of the Monon Railroad wrote Elmer Stout, president of the Fletcher National Bank, that he was backing Alfred Evans to succeed Paul McNutt as Dean. Professor Fowler Harper, without knowing about these backstage manipulations, appealed to McNutt to influence the appointment of Bernard Gavit, an able and respected professor. Harper wrote, "It would be a downright shame for him not to obtain the appointment." All of this sounds strange in face of the fact that the president had been such a decisive factor in every appointment made in the university. Some people, however, evidently believed McNutt, not William Lowe Bryan and the trustees, would make faculty appointments. McNutt offered his resignation from the law faculty on January 4, 1933. In acknowledging the governor's letter of resignation, Bryan wrote, "you are to be congratulated upon the fact that the quality and morale of the Law School have been brought to the highest level in its history. You may be sure that we share your ardent hope for the continuance of these excellences." The board of trustees granted McNutt a leave of absence instead of accepting his resignation, but the governor had plans for the future which did not necessarily include returning to the deanship of the law school. Immediately after he settled into the governor's office, rumors were set afloat that he would be the next president of Indiana University.

For Indiana University the election of Paul McNutt to the Indiana governorship in 1932 was indeed fortuitously timed. In the years he held office he was influential in securing increased appropriations from the legislature. He knew first-hand what it meant to lose professors to other universities because he had seen members of his own law school staff drawn away when he had no funds with which to hold them. Too, McNutt gave substantial help both in Indianapolis and in Washington in the procurement of money to finance the physical expansion of the university during the active years of FERA and its associated agencies. In many ways Paul McNutt became one of the most responsive graduates of the university. As Commissioner of the Philippines in later years he was to play a central role in a land where the institution had made such a heavy investment in the educational talents of its sons in the post-Spanish-American War years.

Graduating classes between 1902 and 1915 produced some of Indiana University's most distinguished graduates. A classmate of Wendell L. Willkie and Paul McNutt, Sherman Minton of tiny Georgetown, Indiana, brought glory to the institution in his career. It would have been hard to imagine a university student with a more unpromising social and economic background than that of Sherman Minton. Sitting on the United States Supreme Court as an associate justice years later he must have recalled those days when as a child he trimmed neckbones in a packing-house at pitifully low wages. One summer he was said to have existed in Bloomington on $10 in cash, eating two-for-a-nickel loaves of stale bread and blackberries when he had time to pick them.

Sherman "Shay" Minton graduated in law in 1915 *summa cum laude*, and went on to Yale University the next year to earn the master of law degree. He practiced law in New Albany before he entered politics. In 1935 Minton served briefly as public counselor for the Indiana Public Service Commission just before he took the oath of office as United States Senator. He was an ardent and militant New Dealer, as a matter of fact he was an active defender of Franklin D. Roosevelt against his detractors, and especially against those who criticized the famous "fireside talks." Because he was angered at the newsmen Minton introduced legislation designed to silence the president's critics. His seat in the Senate chamber was next to that of Harry Truman. Times changed in Indiana, however, and in 1940 the Hoosier Republicans defeated the eloquent Democrat from New Albany. Roosevelt immediately made him an administrative aide, and soon thereafter appointed him to a judgeship on the bench of the Seventh Circuit Court of Appeals, Chicago.

Minton's senatorial seat-mate and friend did not forget him, and when a vacancy occurred on the Supreme Court Harry Truman appointed him an associate justice. It was indeed a long way from Georgetown—clinging to the slopes back from the big bend of the Ohio—to the United States Supreme Court chambers.

In the academic field Indiana graduates achieved as much glory as the politicians. Frederick Austin Ogg, son of the superintendent of grounds William R. Ogg, was born in the sleepy village of Solsberry. He was also the nephew of Robert A. Ogg, trustee of the university from 1923 to 1934. Frederick Ogg received the Master's degree in 1900 and was a teaching fellow in the Department of History in 1902–1903. As a professor of political science in the University of Wisconsin Frederick A. Ogg wrote or edited fifteen books, as well as numerous articles. His best known work was the *Introduction to American Government* (1921) in collaboration with P. O. Ray. This famous textbook went through many editions and revisions and had a marked influence on both the teaching of political science and the organization of separate government departments in scores of colleges and universities.

The name of Clark Wissler almost epitomizes earlier scholarly work in the field of American anthropology. Like the great mass of Indiana University students prior to 1935, Wissler came from a rural farm background in Wayne County, in east central Indiana. He was awarded a Bachelor of Arts degree in 1897, and the Master's degree in 1899. He became curator of the Columbia University Anthropological Museum, and during his career he was consultant to many other museums, including the American Museum of Natural History. Like Frederick A. Ogg, Wissler became a highly productive author. Clark Wissler was not only a successful anthropologist in the professional sense, he was a highly successful interpreter of the science to a vast audience of lay readers.

Carl O. Lampland, A.B., 1902, made significant astronomical history in 1905 when he was able to reproduce on twenty photographic plates the rills or crevasses of the planet Mars. Working in Harvard University's Lowell Observatory near Flagstaff, Arizona, he recorded irrefutable photographic evidence of this phenomenon which had long puzzled astronomers. Up to that date many astronomers had had doubts that the rills actually existed. Some said they believed they were simply optical illusions which appeared on the discs of the telescopic images. The *Daily Student*, on May 29, 1905, commented that Lampland's findings would set to rest forever the controversy over the contours of the major planet. Almost seventy years later *Mariner II* of the United States Space Agency was to take fairly close pictures of the volcanic area—comparable in size to the state of Missouri—and of the long jagged gash across the Martian surface.

Out of William Lowe Bryan's pioneering classroom in psychology came a major scientist in that field. Lewis Madison Terman of Johnson County graduated with Carl Lampland in 1902, and the following year he was awarded a Master's degree with major emphasis in psychology and pedagogy. During his career he was professor at Clark University, the University of Pennsylvania, the University of California, and Stanford University. Terman's major professional contributions were made in the field of intelligence testing.

This Indiana scientist was a member of the famous but controversial committees for psychological examination of the United States Army recruits in World War I, and of the Committee for Classification of Personnel for the United States Army, 1918. Because of questions raised about the Army's testing procedures,

Terman and four other psychologists were asked to revise the procedures in administering military intelligence tests.

Besides being most active in the direct testing field, Lewis Terman was a diligent author, producing a long list of articles and special treatises, and more than fifteen books. He distinguished himself, however, as the author of the Terman Group Tests, 1920, and the Stanford Achievement Tests, 1923. Earlier he had helped to revise the pioneer Binet-Simons Intelligence Scale. Terman either devised or assisted in the preparation of other mental testing procedures. In recognition of his achievements the American Psychological Association elected him to its presidency in 1923.

Indiana University's broadest contributions to American scholarship were made largely in the field of the sciences. The third edition of *American Men of Science*, published in 1921, listed twenty-nine graduates of the institution as "starred" names. This reflected the vitality of the Owen-Jordan-Eigenmann-Coulter-Mottier-Lyons tradition. There is no way for a historian to appraise with certainty the impact university graduates had on teaching and the sciences particularly in secondary schools, colleges, and universities. For instance, modest but scholarly William Ray Allen, Eigenmann's assistant on the famous Latin American collecting expedition lived to be one of the University of Kentucky's finest scholars. Late in his career he published one of the ablest studies of South American icthyology. Other of Eigenmann's students distinguished themselves in this and associated biological sciences.

Thus far the treatment of the accomplishments of alumni of the university has been almost altogether in terms of what they achieved beyond the campus. Actually one of the institution's most important rewards is to be measured in terms of the contributions of graduates who remained in Bloomington as faculty members. This was at once a source of biting criticism and of virtue. During the years 1865 to 1937, if Indiana graduates had been barred from faculty appointments, the university would have lost its basic core of professors and administrators.

In other areas literally hundreds of Indiana University alumni justified their training. After the Civil War alumni and former students began to have a significant bearing upon state and local politics. As the number of graduates of the Law School multiplied so did the loyal sons who turned politicians. There were 103 graduates who sought public office in the election of 1928. Three years before, five of fifteen Indiana congressmen had attended the university. After the turn of the century alumni wielded significant influence in the succeeding sessions of the Indiana General Assembly. In 1924 there were seven graduates in the Senate and the same number in the House of Representatives. Eleven Law School graduates sat on circuit benches as judges, and twenty-two prosecuting attorneys had studied law in Bloomington. As time passed and law training procedures changed in Indiana, the influence of the university's graduates became even more noticeable.

John Simpson Hastings of Washington in Daviess County was a shining example of the Law School's handiwork. Between 1936 and 1959 Judge Hastings was to prove one of the most influential trustees in the history of the board of trustees. He finished his first two years of academic work in 1918 and transferred to the United States Military Academy, from which he graduated in 1920 with a Bachelor of Science degree, as a second lieutenant. He was soon back in Bloomington after a brief military career, and enrolled in the Law School where he was awarded the Bachelor of Law degree in 1924. He then went back to Washington, Indiana, to practice law and later to sit as circuit judge. As a student "Jack" Hastings was highly active, but in no student effort did he exert greater energy than in the Memorial Fund Drive. His eloquent persuasion accounted for the contribution of a considerable part of the money which was raised. His most distinguished service was as Judge and then Chief Judge (1957–1968) of the United States Court of Appeals, Seventh Circuit.

Enrolled in the Law School at the same time as Judge Hastings was Hoagland Carmichael. Few individual Americans of the 1920's and early 1930's so nearly personified the jazz age in American history as this alumnus. He entered the university in 1920 and received the Bachelor of Law degree in 1926. It was not as a lawyer, however, that Carmichael won fame. It may even be doubted that he learned anything in university classrooms which contributed directly to his fame and fortune. The environment on the edge of the campus was far more important.

Hoagy Carmichael still remains a popular American figure, and his occasional appearances on television are somewhat like viewing a sentimental national album. Long ago several of his songs became classics. This is especially true of *Stardust, Lazy River, Come Easy Go Easy Love, Ol' Rockin' Chair,* and *Lazy*

Bones. In 1936 Indiana students solicited funds with which to purchase from the publishers the copyright to *Chimes of Indiana,* and to make it the property of the university.

Hoosier pride in Hoagy Carmichael's success ran high. On November 23, 1946, Governor Ralph F. Gates proclaimed *Hoagy Carmichael—Stardust Day* in Indiana. The composer returned to the Indiana campus for a day of "easy-going shenanigans." Two years later the Wells administration offered the use of the campus to Triangle Publishers for the filming of the movie version of Carmichael's life. In 1950 the Indiana Theater on Kirkwood was selected by Warner Brothers for a "Multi-city simultaneous state-wide" tribute to the boy who had hammered out some of his earliest songs on Indiana Avenue in Peter Costas' Book Nook.

Where Hoagy Carmichael achieved fame in the music world, Ross Franklin Lockridge, Jr., and Roscoe Carlyle Buley reached peaks of literary fame as prize-winning authors. Lockridge won the Houghton Mifflin Literary Award with his novel *Raintree County.* This widely known book was set in the author's maternal homeland of Henry County. Young Lockridge was the son of the local historian and lecturer, Ross Franklin Lockridge. His father had been Law School librarian, extension and public speaking instructor. The son had grown up near the Indiana campus and in 1930 had enrolled as a student. He revealed outstanding aptitude in language, and in 1933 was awarded the Delaware Scholarship, which enabled him to spend the years 1933 to 1935 at the University of Paris. Three years after his return to America, Lockridge was awarded the Master's degree in English, and for the next four years was an instructor in that department. At the time he won the Houghton Mifflin Award he was a member of the English staff of Simmons College in Boston.

Roscoe Carlyle Buley, also of Georgetown, graduated with the Bachelor of Arts degree in 1914, and two years later received the Master's degree. Through the teachings and counseling of Logan Esarey, Buley developed a deep interest in the history of the Old Northwest and spent almost a professional lifetime gathering research notes on the region.

After graduation he was an assistant principal and head of the history division of the Springfield, Illinois, High School. In 1925, and just before he received the doctorate in history from the University of Wisconsin, he returned to Indiana University as an instructor in the subject. In 1945 Buley shared with Richard

Hofstader the Alfred A. Knopf Fellowship for Literary Achievement in History. Buley's award was made in recognition of *The Old Northwest, 1815–1840*. This manuscript was published by the Indiana Historical Society in two large volumes in 1950, and on May 7, 1951, Buley was notified that he had won the Pulitzer Prize in history. In characteristic Buley fashion the professor commented on his Pulitzer award that it was the second piece of good news he had received in a week. His wife Evelyn had picked the winner in the Kentucky Derby.

With few exceptions the alumni mentioned were of rural origins and either poor or suffering severe economic limitations. This no doubt was true of the great mass of Indiana University students down to 1920. The university itself was cast largely within the rural middle class social context. Isolated Bloomington with its many limitations offered some distinct economic advantages to students. Here they were able to secure cheap boarding and lodging in the first decades of the twentieth century, and in the latter decades, with the building of dormitories, the university offered reasonable bed and board. Farmers from the surrounding countryside flocked onto Courthouse Square with cheap farm products and firewood for sale. In 1911, the *Daily Student* estimated that room rent ranged from $36 to $150 a year, and board from $100 to $180, entertainment cost $12.50, fuel and kerosene $20, and laundry $10 to $25 per annum. Thus the annual cost ranged from a modest $198 to $445. The paper said most students spent $230 to $300 a year, exclusive of clothing and railway fare. This condition has not prevailed without modifications down to date. A majority of modern students come from larger urban centers, but their needs remain as urgent.

On the eve of World War I, the editor of the *Daily Student* expressed the opinion that more than a hundred male Indiana students were entirely self-supporting, and one out of eight men enrolled earned all his way through the university while meeting a full schedule of classes. Others sustained themselves by doing summer work. These students did almost every sort of job to earn money. Most, said the paper, "helped pa on the farm, store, or office." Some became summertime book "canvassers." Leota Ray of Ellettsville substituted for her father as principal of the high school. M. E. McFerren of Hartford City was said in 1907 to have earned more money than any other student. He worked in the co-operative bookstore, owned and operated a dancing school, managed a dancing club, ran the Vandette—a 5-cent theater, sold pianos, and played professional baseball. A lad from Vincennes attempted to establish a shooting gallery but was prevented from doing so because town officials insisted on his paying a five dollar a week privilege fee. They said they believed such a business would be detrimental to the best interest of the university.

President Bryan's oft-printed lecture to students advised them to "Go to work today. Work steadily every day for so many hours. Don't consent to be a failure in everything you undertake. Don't let yourself live along through demoralizing days with your work falling in a wreck about your ears. Face the most tedious thing you have to do, if not with a joyful spirit then with a fighting spirit. If you do this you will at least have the firm joy of self-respect and you may arrive at the place where the hardest work turns into the finest game in the world." Thus a large proportion of the 40,000 students enrolled in the university were exposed in some fashion to the American ethic of hard work and thrift. The background of large numbers of the alumni might very well have comprised the opening chapters of Horatio Alger's novels. Though a psychologist interested in the processes of the mind, so many of William Lowe Bryan's remarks to students stressed the hard work ethic rather than pure devotion to things of the intellect.

Not only was Indiana the university of the common everyday people of the state, it was also an institution which throughout a century and a quarter developed very warm family ties. A wag said instead of the institution being called the alma mater of college presidents it should be known as the chief match-maker in the commonwealth. On the face of the record it is evident, without precise statistics to quantify fully a general statement, that a large number of campus courtships resulted in marriage. The family tradition since the day of the Wylies and Maxwells has been strong. In 1930 John W. Cravens, Registrar, made a study of families which sent more than four sons and daughters to the university, and of parents who were themselves alumni.

Of greater significance, however, was the fact that so many students who enrolled in the university were "first generation" college registrants. Behind the alumni rolls are almost endless stories of human sacrifice and parental ambition expressed in desires to improve the lot of the children. Such a story was that of Albert Schneider Kunz, a music teacher, who sent thirteen children through Indiana University. For twenty years this German immigrant farmed near Corydon and eked out enough income from his meager land to partially support children in school. In the Depression he moved to Bloomington and gave private music lessons to sustain the others. For thirty-two years at least one member of the Kunz family was enrolled in classes on the campus.

Nine members of the James Smith family attended the university, four of whom were awarded degrees. John Diedrick Haseman and his wife sacrificed through their labors to send eight children through the university. Seven of this family received degrees. Five of the Haseman sons were supported in school by sale of river-borne sand from a family farm near Linton. John D. Haseman, an assistant to Carl Eigenmann, discovered an unusual specimen of fish in South America which was deemed to be a connecting link between fish and salamanders, thus establishing further evidence of the evolutionary process in living forms.

On the faculty Professor Harold Whetstone Johnstone of classics and athletic fame and his wife produced eight university registrants, six of whom received degrees. Just one step behind the Johnstones were Dean and Mrs. Charles McGuffey Hepburn. They saw seven sons and daughters graduate, and for a span of years the student body rang with the names of Johnstone and Hepburn.

Enrollment data which reveal the registration of numerous members of individual families also reflect the fact that cost of attending the university was kept sufficiently low that parents with even modest incomes could aspire to higher education for their progeny, and down to recent years the university has appeared to foster this family loyalty. In fact the central institutional image has always been maternal in concept, despite the strong patriarchal behavior of presidents, trustees, and professors.

Appeals which the institution made to the public in its various drives were couched in the context of family loyalties. In May, 1930, Cravens outlined suggestions of what alumni could do for Indiana University. Among these were, "Tell the people your alma mater is entitled to the name 'mother of presidents.' " They should discuss the growth of the institution under the father image, William Lowe Bryan, and he added, "You had teachers to whom you owe a debt of gratitude for the inspiration given you. Write them letters from time to time, and let them know that they are partly responsible for your upward climb." There is no doubt but that it was the *pater-mater familias* concept of Bryan and his professorial colleagues that gave the university such a strong, sentimental hold on its graduates.

With the great transition in 1937, upon the retirement of William Lowe Bryan and many of his veteran colleagues, Indiana University definitely crossed the threshold of time and destiny. The departing stalwarts could look back upon a hundred and twelve years of institutional history with the satisfaction that, in the context of stated hopes and aspiration as contained in the 1820 charter, in keeping with the experiences in American public higher education and the turn of public mind in Indiana, the university had produced positive results. Throughout more than a century it had moments of functioning under most trying circumstances as a public liberal arts institution. Now in the late 1930's it was just beginning to grow into a university meeting the broader public demands for more professional and advanced education.

It is ironic that a state university, with all of its concern with academic testing and evaluation, cannot determine with any degree of precision what it does accomplish in the changing of conditions of human intellectual thought and reaction, or in revising social and political procedures. The only certainty left to the historian is the attempt at drawing the highly generalized conclusion that Indiana University repaid its commonwealth ten times over on its fiscal investment in the supplying of teachers, doctors, lawyers, office-holders, housewives, businessmen, scientists, musicians, nurses, dentists, bankers, and even gentlemen of sophisticated leisure.

To single out a few star graduates of the university and cast the institution's record of accomplishments in their image is no doubt to adopt a false standard of measuring actual achievement. Clearly exhibited in the historical record was the central fact of conscientious teaching. This was what John W. Cravens meant in his advice to alumni in 1930. He asked graduates to focus on that intellectual pebble which professors had cast in the pool of their minds, and which had created spreading and concentric waves of ideas and insights. In a final analysis it was, after all, the modest alumnus, who succeeded as county clerk, legislator, merchant, school teacher, small town doctor, lawyer, or cultivated housewife, who so eloquently fulfilled the original aims and objectives of a Jeffersonian people's university.

[X V]

"It's the Last Yard that Counts"

ALTHOUGH THE TURMOIL of world conditions after 1914 had a marked impact on Indiana University athletic programs, there were other facts involved. True the institution lacked proper physical facilities and financial backing. This condition had been prevalent since the first Indiana athlete had raised a home-made baseball bat in the corner of the old college yard in the 1870's. The coaching in recent decades had been makeshift if not poor. Horne, Sheldon, and Clarence Childs, however, had all proved capable coaches. Childs was an innovative fellow. For instance he and Frank H. Gentry conceived the idea of using Gentry's famous circus whippets to pace track men, and as automobiles became more common he used a large bullseye attached to the rear of the car to train runners. His theory was that by having the athlete focus attention on the target and by gradually speeding up the automobile he would have his trainees running at top speed without realizing their exertion.

Despite good coaching many fans were actually convinced a jinx hung heavy over Jordan Field. In 1915 the jinx was unusually strong during baseball season. Indiana beat only Indiana State Normal at Terre Haute, Rose Polytechnic, and Ohio State out of an eight game schedule, and had its annual dispute with Purdue over the accuracy of score-keeping.

As a football coach, Childs had the same flair for the spectacular. In September, 1915, he announced that the famous Indian athlete Jim Thorpe would join him as assistant coach. This led the fans and even the *Daily Student* to believe that the new season would be a promising one. For the first time the football team played a Virginia institution. Before their journey to Indianapolis for the game, United States Senator John Worth Kern called on that great football fan in the White House, Woodrow Wilson, and invited him to come to Indiana to watch the Hoosiers trounce Washington and Lee. Had Wilson accepted the invitation he would have seen the red and the gray struggle to a 7 to 7 tie and argue over the referee's failure to see that a punted ball had touched the rebel quarterback's leg.

All those who knew Clarence Childs, and they were numerous, seemed to be convinced that he was a football expert. When not dealing with the practicalities of the game on Jordan Field he held his forum in the "Coach's Corner" of the Bowles Hotel lobby. The Bloomington *Daily Telephone* reported, "It is said that more football battles have been fought in the corner between Coach Childs and his friends than has [sic] ever been played on Jordan Field."

Child's weekly battle on the gridiron was a test of moral courage. Like thousands of fans before him he hoped for a miracle which maybe Jim Thorpe and Gentry's whippets could help to shape. Thorpe, said the *Daily Telephone*, was the world's greatest athlete, and his visit to Bloomington would be important in preparing the Hoosiers for the annual fight with Purdue.

The Purdue game in 1915 was played in Bloomington, and the Chamber of Commerce planned to capitalize fully on it. "Plans are to make the entire week preceding the game a homecoming," said the *Daily Telephone*. "Committees will be appointed in surrounding towns to make the event a holiday." One would have thought the football players were being fattened for the arena lions. They were consuming 120 pounds of sirloin steak a week and almost the entire Indiana potato crop. This was to be their week of glory. The upcoming game, it was thought, would be the last played on Jordan Field, as the new field was to be ready for the next year. Local papers were quick to write the old gridiron's obituary. Students of both Indiana and Purdue roamed the town by Friday morning. Two moving picture machines were on hand to record the historic pageant and to symbolize the entry of Indiana sports into a new era in athletics and technology.

In order to protect his players from the throng, Clarence Childs hauled them off to the tranquil surroundings of Martinsville. Just before game time he returned them to Bloomington, a trip which was almost as big an ordeal as meeting Purdue. As it turned out, Childs and his men might as well have stayed home and enjoyed the pregame fun, because Purdue defeated them 7 to 0 and set off a hue and cry against the Hoosier coach. Some alumni and students demanded that Indiana get rid of both Childs and Jim Thorpe. The big Indian had not brought a streak of primitive luck; Jim himself was beneficiary of the tribal misfortunes of his ancestral Sac-Fox forebears.

Rumor circulated that the Athletic Board at its latest meeting had already changed coaches, although that was denied publicly. The faculty and students were said to be about evenly divided in their attitude toward Clarence Childs. The local athletic oracle, Frank H. Gentry, informed the public that his private survey had revealed that the trouble with athletics in Indiana University was with the squad and not the coaches. It was said that some players were arrogant and disobeyed the coach. They broke training rules, and failed to perform properly on the field.

To cap a dreary athletic season off with fire, Frank Aydelotte of the class of 1900, Associate Professor of English in the university, published a highly critical article about spectator sports in the *Indiana Alumni Quarterly*. "The feeling of American college professors toward intercollegiate athletics is one of growing hostility," he wrote. "On every hand one hears more and more talk of the necessity of their abolition, if our institutions of learning do not wish to lose their standards of scholarship and their moral prestige." He went on, "by a million subterfuges and devices athletes and their sponsors dodge the requirements or satisfy them in irregular ways." Aydelotte belittled tutoring, snap courses, summer make-up work, and the bringing of other undue and unwholesome pressures on students. Games he thought which were run for the benefit of the spectators always degenerated morally. Professional baseball was a good example. The only way intercollegiate athletics in America could be cleaned of their evils was to get rid of the public spectators.

There were few ears in Bloomington attuned to the biting words of the young English professor. Few, also, shared Frank H. Gentry's belief that Indiana University's athletic woes sprang from the inadequacy of the players themselves. Childs' hours were numbered, and early in January he departed the River Jordan, but not before he had coached a successful women's track team, of which one member, Pauline Sieben, cleared the pole vault bar at six and a half feet. On the eve of Child's departure the Bloomington *Daily Telephone* reported that rumors were afloat that Ewald O. Stiehm, a former Wisconsin star, would be employed as coach at a salary of $4,250, second only to President Bryan's.

Ground was broken that winter for the site of the new gymnasium and for the football field to the north. On March 10, 1916, a large gray eagle was captured near the site and proclaimed an omen of good luck. It was said he had come to bring victory over Purdue in basketball. To cap off this piece of majestic folklore, Coach Stiehm, in one of those grandiose new-coach gestures, said he placed more stock in Indiana's future athletic success. He went on, "if the enthusiasm shown by the men is any criterion, Indiana will certainly have a good football team next year." Perhaps some of his optimism was based upon the fact that he, unlike Jimmy Sheldon, would not go along with Alonzo Stagg's arbitrary assignments of dates for the Chicago game. Indiana and Chicago would not meet in 1916. In fact there was almost as much dissatisfaction with the behavior of Minnesota, Illinois, and Wisconsin, other members of the "Big Four."

It is interesting that in 1917, and at a time when travel was severely limited by wartime conditions, the Indiana baseball team took its first spring training trip through Kentucky, Georgia, and Tennessee. On this jaunt the team played seven games and brought home only the meager satisfaction of having tied Vanderbilt University. This was the beginning of an extended series of southern trips following World War I. There might have been a notion of turning more Hoosier athletic interest southward because the Athletic Committee met with President Bryan on March 30, 1917, in a closed door session to discuss "freely" its "western" athletic schedules. It was true that the war crisis had most to do with the discussion, and as a result President Bryan wired each of the Big Ten presidents for an expression of opinion as to whether or not athletic schedules should be abandoned during the rest of the war. Indiana was the first of the midwestern schools to follow the lead of the eastern universities in this area. The other Big Ten schools, however, wished to continue their schedules, even if it did mean playing the teams of small neighboring schools.

From March on, Indiana University's athletic and physical education programs felt the sharp impact of war. Military drill took precedence over all other physical activities. Coach Harvey Cohn disbanded his track team. The baseball team began official organized military drill supplementary to practice. There was a running debate up until the middle of April as to whether or not all schedules should be cancelled. On April 15, Bryan and the trustees voted to proceed cautiously with the policy, "but these [athletic schedules] may be suspended when the services of the country requires." In a magazine article Coach Stiehm maintained that Indiana University played its part in the war effort by making available athletic training to its men students. By mid-September he must have wondered if his contention had any validity because only fourteen men reported for football training. Even so these made an unusually high scoring record against Indiana small college teams, and included a 37 to 0 victory over Purdue.

To ease guilty consciences the football team was required to take a half hour drill every day to give semblance to serving the war effort. As further recognition of the war the band played both the French and American national anthems before the games. It took more than playing of nerve soothing anthems, however, to smooth ruffled feathers after the Purdue game.

For the second time in the long period of troubled athletic relations, the Lafayette school on the eve of the big game charged Indiana with knowingly allowing two professional players to remain on its team. It was established by the Big Ten Committee that Howard William Ewert of Hammond and Lynne Wales Howard of Bloomington were ineligible.

Barring Ewert and Howard raised such a commotion in Bloomington that the Indiana football players threatened to strike. A tremendous amount of sentimental publicity had been given out about this final game on the revered spot, and relations between Indiana and Purdue had become so highly sensitized that any incident was likely to touch off pandemonium. President Bryan notified President Stone that Indiana University would make every effort to avoid trouble, and asked the Purdue officials to agree that, no matter who won, there would be no post-game demonstration. The Bloomington *Daily Telephone* said, "The spirit of the Indiana team was like nothing ever witnessed in the athletic history of the University." After the game, however, Purdue again threatened to break off athletic relations with Indiana.

The argument was carried to the December meeting of the Big Ten Conference and became somewhat more tense when it was decided that body would allow football to continue the following year, in spite of wartime stringency. Purdue refused to schedule Indiana, and the two schools were left with the lightest programs in the conference. In 1918, Indiana played Kentucky State (now Transylvania), Camp Taylor, Fort Harrison, and DePauw and won only the latter game. It was not until 1920 that it again played Purdue.

In the midst of the period of uncertainty about Purdue relations, the Bureau of Internal Revenue informed Indiana University that it owed $1,500, or 10 percent of the gate receipts, from the Purdue and Ohio State games. At this point athletics promised to become downright expensive from the standpoint of taxes, travel, and maintenance of facilities. It was now necessary for the university to provide temporary playing fields. Jordan Field was being trampled into the mud by the constant drilling of cadets, and the new field was only in the formative stage. The old grounds near Mitchell Hall were again brought into use, and temporary grounds closer to Tenth Street were made ready.

While the so-called major sports program showed signs of being interrupted by the war, co-ed athletes came to life and were more visible in Indiana's athletic activities. The girls played baseball and basketball, swam, and performed on the track. Plans were underway for holding a local tournament in Bloomington and for conference play. In April the co-ed baseball team defeated Chicago in the national conference, and swimmers placed second and third in two events. With the accomplishments tucked away in the record books the girls then turned to war work. The leading female athlete, Wilma Lloyd, joined William Lowe Bryan's "land army."

By September 26, 1918, military restrictions had become so binding on travel, personnel, and physical facilities that the Big Ten Conference abandoned its control of intercollegiate sports in the following resolution: "Whereas, The Rules and regulations of the Conference are superseded by the rules of the War Department; now be it Resolved, That the Western Intercollegiate Conference suspend its activities as a controlling body during the period of the emergency, the same as now existing, to be resumed at the end of that time."

Each university athletic committee was left to its own initiative in the formulation of schedules and in exercising of control over rules. Indiana games with Minnesota, Michigan, and Iowa were cancelled; Indiana played instead DePauw, Camp Taylor, Fort Harrison, and Kentucky State. On November 22, it abandoned football practice altogether. The naval forces occupied the gymnasium and there was no place on the campus for the basketball players to practice. They turned to the Bloomington High School gymnasium, but prospects for the basketball schedule promised even more frustration.

Allied victory early in November quickly reversed the thinking of members of the Big Ten Conference, and universities began the formulation of schedules for the coming year. At Purdue Oliver F. Cutts had resigned as head football coach. It was said that he had opposed resumption of relations with Indiana, but now that barrier was removed. Rumors were circulating by June, 1919, that there might be a Purdue game in the fall. Admittedly the annual game was important to both institutions, and without it the football season lacked its full measure of excitement. Neither school had been happy about the break.

At Bloomington the *Daily Student* believed it would be a happy day when Purdue and Indiana were on speaking terms again. While the olive branch was being waved vigorously between Lafayette and Bloomington, Indiana developed its own homegrown problem which threatened temporarily to put it out of the football business. In September, 1919, the faculty athletic committee expelled Captain James William Ingles of Indianapolis from the team for social rule infractions. His teammates, egged on by "old grads," threatened to strike. The alumni were aroused, even though the team, as usual, reconsidered and did not strike. The Indianapolis alumni undertook to single out an individual professor against whom they could direct their wrath. In almost incessant long distance telephone messages they conveyed their feelings to Bryan.

Each successive meeting of the alumni seemed to generate more heat. The "old grads" even issued an ultimatum through Dick Miller saying that either Jimmy Ingles would be re-instated or they would take direct action. This order was really formulated and delivered in the heat of a pep session on the eve of the Wabash game. Following this rally Miller drove to Bloomington from Indianapolis and presented the "facts" to an audience of local

[3 3 7]

alumni. He said, "The old grads are not going to tolerate the faculty handicapping the football team without giving battle to the faculty."

The 1919 stormy football season saw Indiana win three games out of a seven-game schedule. It suffered defeat by Centre College, Minnesota, Notre Dame, and Northwestern. There was some grim satisfaction in the defeat of Syracuse. The Bloomington *Daily Telephone* said on December 3, "Indiana's place in the sun on the gridiron map is assured if pep, enthusiasm, and backing on the part of the alumni will have anything to do with the 1920 football aggregation." Part of this pep was chilled the following day when the overactive George Cook, alumni member of the Athletic Committee, was asked to resign. "The request for Cook's resignation," said the *Telephone*, "has been the largest sensation that has broken in Crimson athletics for some time. Cook has long been prominent as a booster of I. U. athletics, and his work has caused much friction. During the past football season he headed a movement which attacked various members of the I. U. faculty because they sought to make certain members of the football squad obey the rules of the University. Cook has long been obnoxious to the authorities of the university."

Thus Indiana entered the "dazzling twenties" of postwar America with old values tarnished by conditions of war and its immediate aftermath. The relationship between "big time" athletics and higher education underwent a reappraisal by those who supported the intellectual objectives of universities. Fans, alumni, and "I" men in Indiana, however, saw in the game only the glory of victory, and a successful season in football was as valuable as an unusually good crop of graduates at commencement. New and powerful athletic pressures were revealed in the recurring skirmishes between rooters and faculty rule-makers. Since 1908 and the final shaping of the Big Nine Conference, the Midwest had been growing into the center of national football power, and Indiana found itself caught in the terrific pressure to compete with other members of the conference.

No longer could the Indiana University Athletic Association operate from year to year on a rising and falling budget. After 1920 members of the Big Ten were fixed on the financial treadmill. In order to have good teams they had to collect increasing gate receipts, and there had to be money with which to recruit players to attract fans. Recruiting was not a new activity among the Northwest schools, but it now became both recognized and highly competitive. A star quarterback, like a good experiment station herd bull, became an immensely valuable asset to the big land-grant universities. From the standpoint of gate receipts many Indiana supporters thought their athletic teams suffered because they had to play in a lightly populated center. Like the ancient attempts to move the university itself, this handicap was to cause irritations for years. Indianapolis could produce the crowds, and a large corps of Indiana graduates lived in the city and wanted the games brought to them.

One solution to the stabilization of Indiana's athletic income was to levy a set fee on each student as he enrolled in the university. This subject was first introduced by students themselves in February, 1920, and a month later the trustees received a petition requesting approval of a $5 fee for which students would be given season tickets to all athletic events. Members of the athletic fraternity thought the faculty and trustees should go even further by requiring each candidate for a degree to swim fifty yards. Some of the faculty elders might have been sorely embarrassed if their promotions had depended upon a similar test.

The football team in 1920 finished third in the conference, defeating Minnesota, Northwestern, and Purdue. This cheered everybody and made the mandatory fee a more acceptable idea. Former athletes organized a committee of seventeen to promote sports and to recruit players. One of the things which accounted for Hoosier success at this time was the return of several mature war veterans who still had eligibility. In this flush of success a debate arose over the desirability of playing a good part of the football schedule in Indianapolis. The Athletic Association could expect twice to three times the returns over those received in Bloomington games. The Notre Dame game in 1920, for instance, grossed more than $12,000, and that with Northwestern $10,000. Despite these heartening returns, the Athletic Association would still finish the season $14,000 in debt.

At the end of the football season that year a committee of thirty-three men representing the university, the alumni, and Bloomington businessmen met to discuss athletic fortunes. The main subject of their talk was how could Indiana have a major football team and continue to play its important games in Bloomington. The other concern was maintenance of college spirit while playing away from the campus. It was finally decided, however, that only one game a season would be played in Indianapolis.

Equally important was the abiding issue of recruiting stellar players for the teams. There was an almost desperate need for men who could be trained to become outstanding athletes and at the same time maintain acceptable academic standings. There are hints that course contents were not always comparable. For instance, the faculty on May 14, 1921, approved seventeen courses in the theory and practice of football to be offered by the Department of Physical Training in the coming summer session. Doubtless no one could answer positively whether there existed in the Indiana curriculum certain "snap" courses favored by athletes. Yet reports were made almost annually that athletes equalled or exceeded the general grade point average of the student body.

Athletic excellence seems to have been measured in instances by the dual standards of what did and did not appeal to public spectators. In the minor sports—wrestling, swimming, track, and tennis—Indiana accumulated an unusually good record. In 1921 both the wrestling and tennis teams won Big Ten championships. But the conference itself placed major emphasis on football.

Surprisingly, Indiana waited until 1921 to seek a fighting name for its football heroes. For some time remarks were made about the soft connotation of the "Cream and Crimson" or the generality of the name "Hoosiers." In September of that year the players initiated a search for a suitable designation. Quickly a list of twenty-one proposals was compiled, many of which were even more bizarre than Thomas Jefferson's proposed latinized names for the new states in the Northwest Territory. One can well imagine difficulties in raising nine stirring rahs for the "Red Clovers," "Bloodhounds," "Cher Kees," "Fighting Foxes," "Unlicked Cubs," "Wampus Cats," or "Arbutarians." Luckily none of these names appealed; the rooters had to content themselves with the time tested "Scrappin' Hoosiers." It would have seemed downright undignified for the "Jordan Ducks," for instance, to go against the Harvard Crimson or the Wisconsin Badgers. It was difficult enough to have to play against the Gophers of Minnesota without being called "Wampus Cats." In the first week of October, 1921, the Hoosiers were to play the elite of the East, Harvard. The Bloomington *Daily Telephone* announced on October 4 that several carloads of local fans had left to cheer the Hoosiers on in their first game against Harvard in Cambridge. This was an adventure in itself because fans had heretofore depended largely upon travel by train. Too, the good roads movement in America was still a gleam in official eyes. Nevertheless the Hoosier fans were cheered, said the *Daily Student*, in block high headlines by the "Attention of Football World on Indiana Conflict Today." Special arrangements were made to receive news of the progress of the game back in Bloomington by radiogram. When the 19 to 0 score was announced, however, it was far less cheering than the idea of playing Harvard.

No real progress had been made by the end of 1921 in the preparation of the new football field for use the next season. An anonymous alumnus offered to match funds in amounts from $1,000 to $25,000 to finance the preparation of this facility for early use. In the meantime a newly revised athletic body began a drive to enroll members in the Indiana Athletic Association. It was said every male student could earn a monogram by participating successfully in one of sixteen sports.

By the time Indiana met Notre Dame late in October, the dogs of dissatisfaction were nipping angrily at the ample heels of Coach Ewald O. Stiehm. A brave group of defenders started a movement to support him, using the slogan "I'm for Stiehm and the Team." This year ended Stiehm's football coaching on the Jordan. At the time the new practice season opened in the following September, he had entered the Mayo Brothers' Clinic, seriously ill. In May, 1923, he resigned as head coach. In the meantime Pat Herron, assistant coach at the University of Pittsburgh, was employed temporarily to assume coaching responsibilities. William "Navy Bill" Ingram, an ex-Navy star and a native of Jeffersonville, was hired as head coach, and in June the board of trustees appointed Zora Clevenger athletic director, with Leslie Mann assistant director.

The disastrous season of 1921 again cut deeply into the financial resources of the Athletic Association. Net profits dropped to $2,500 in 1921, as compared with $10,624 the year before. Gate receipts had amounted to $36,054.96, and expenses were $33,874.33, and $11,000 was used to pay off temporary bank loans. Despite the sharp drop in profits these figures marked the beginning of the upward spiral of athletic finances.

[3 4 1]

In an interesting diversion from the usual athletic schedules, Coach George Levis, between March and June, took thirteen Indiana baseball players across the Pacific to play Waseda University in Tokyo. The Japanese agreed to pay the $15,000 necessary to transport the Hoosier team abroad. In past years Waseda's teams had visited the United States, and on their visits had played Big Ten schools. On their return home the players said they had their biggest thrill of the trip out West when they saw cowboys galloping along the road, "just as we used to see Bronco Billy do."

Everybody wanted to have a hand in promoting the athletic fortunes of Indiana University in the 1920's. No group however, was so majestic in its proposal as the commencement committee which promoted the million dollar drive for funds to finance building of the new gymnasium and the athletic field and two other memorial buildings. The committee proposed building a dam across the Jordan in the end of Dunn Meadow to form a placid lagoon. A large platform would be raised in the middle of the lake for a bandstand, gondolas would float around the pavilion, and aquatic events would take place before the reviewing stand. In an amphitheater on the side there would be a dance floor, and the Jordan River Revue would present its productions. Circus animals would be brought up from West Baden to give a Junglesque flavor. To climax all this, athletic games would be played on a nearby field, and games would be followed by fireworks displays. Even Cecil B. De Mille would have been staggered by this setting, and Frank Aydelotte would have gone into shock.

This flight into fantasy had little to do with either education or athletics, and it was strangled a-borning. On May 16, the *Daily Student* said, "The inadequacy of outdoor athletic facilities has long been recognized at Indiana, but the need for more grounds has become pressing since the Intramural Athletic Association has drawn large numbers of men away from loafing centers and set them to exercising their muscles."

At last the date arrived when positively the final football contest would take place on Jordan Field. Store buildings and trees in town were cluttered with signs block letter high reading, "Scrappy Hoosiers get Purdue's Goat," all for old times sake. The entire student body was to act as pall bearers, mourners, and singers of the dirge in the tearful closing ceremony. The Bloomington police were out in full force. For the first time of note in Indiana athletic history, traffic patrolmen were assigned about the Square to prevent jams and accidents. Chief Fred Campbell served notice there would be no store rushing after the game. Truly this event ended one era and opened another. A. B. Leible wrote the dedication song, "Jordan Field," which may also have ended an era of its kind. Since 1891 Indiana had won 75 of 95 games played at home. In the Purdue rivalry it had won nine and tied three, and Purdue had won eleven times. By a meager 3 points to 0 Indiana added the tenth game as it closed the gates of history on November, 1923, on the muddy old battleground.

Assistant Athletic Director Leslie Mann resigned as baseball and basketball coach in 1924, and Everett Dean of the class of 1920 was appointed in his place. Dean was to serve in this capacity until 1938. His baseball teams were successful in holding their own in the balance between games won and lost and in maintaining highly respectable standings in the Big Ten conference. He played heavy schedules and did a considerable amount of traveling, especially in meeting the southern spring practice schedules. The same was true of his basketball teams. Measured in terms of games won and points scored, Dean was one of Indiana University's most successful athletic coaches. In his fourteen years as basketball coach he made opponents conscious of Indiana's capability in this sport.

The new football stadium was not ready for the playing season of 1924, and games were played that year either on the freshman field or in Indianapolis. Possibly no greater frenzy ever gripped an Indiana University throng than that of the night of October 10, 1924, and on the eve of the game with Louisiana State University. The *Daily Student* said, "Yells, howls and cries of frenzy shook the very foundations of the huge Claypool Hotel last night during the eighth annual Pow Wow and loyalty conference attended by several hundred University students, alumni, members of the 'I' Men's Association, and friends of the University." Indianapolis was the very den of the lettermen, and like the ancient braves of the Wabash on the warpath they all assumed victory would come as a matter of course the next day. They whooped and howled for Zora Clevenger and "Navy Bill" Ingram. There was no mention of what they drank, but it was said, "Tempting viands furnished by the Claypool chef were slighted or gulped down hurriedly, and sometimes flung at the head of a too enthusiastic reveler with a Bacchanalian freedom seldom known in the big establishment." Sleek-haired bellhops were kept busy explaining to strange guests in other parts of the hotel that the harsh noises were merely vocal expressions of Indiana's confidence in the Scrappin' Hoosiers. Women rooters also held a powwow in a segregated tearoom in the hotel, but if they threw things and sang *Indiana*, no one noticed.

After a rowdy "nine" for "Navy Bill" led by Eddie Brackett, William Lowe Bryan reassured the assemblage:

> While I have been mostly in the background as regards athletics, I have been there steadily suppporting the men in command while they were in command whether they were succeeding or not. A man who is not succeeding cannot expect to continue in command, but while the fight is on, he is my man. I wish, however, to name those of our successful commanders.
>
> First, Sheldon: I went out alone east and west to find a man. I found Sheldon and for a half dozen or more years, his brain and his character gave Indiana a great succession of clean victories.
>
> Second, Ingram: He was selected by others, but he is none the less my man. Those who know him best believe most in his strength as a man and superb ability as a coach.
>
> Third, Clevenger: Unexcelled athlete and leader of men. He is a man I have long wanted as our lieutenant-general. He has the intelligence, the rectitude, the energy. It is an unfailing joy to stand back of such a man from year's end to year's end.

This was good history, and no doubt blunted the pie throwing and yelling, but it failed next day to impress the Louisiana Tigers, who dragged their host opponents down 21 to 14, after the Hoosiers had led throughout the game. Louisiana braced on the one-yard line, and tacklers rushed through and kept Indiana from tying the score, or maybe winning. It was this failure to break the Louisiana line which inspired William Lowe Bryan to write his famous homily, "The Last Yard."

On the evening of the great powwow in the Claypool, the Indiana fans hoodwinked themselves with food, drink, and oratory about the ultimate strength of their team. Too, they might have let the blinders of sectionalism conceal from them the possible strength of an extra-conference foe. To date the Hoosiers had defeated Rose Polytechnic Institute and DePauw by high scores, but almost by tradition neither of these games had been true indicators of Indiana's strength or lack of it. Louisiana was actually the first real test, and Louisiana's "last yard" stand foretold a season of disaster. On the following weekend, Alonzo Stagg's men piled up a score of 23 to 0, and a week later Northwestern opened the wound even deeper with a 17 to 0 defeat. Chicago generously shared $20,000 in gate receipts, which was some consolation, and the defeat of Ohio State on November 10 by a score of 12 to 7 in Columbus revived hope. This game was of historic significance. A radio receiver had been established in the Book Nook, and almost the instant the final word came that the Hoosiers had won, six or seven bonfires were set in the street. Students turned back the Bloomington firemen, and a lone policeman appeared on the scene to try to restore order. He called upon firemen to return to the fires, and there ensued a general melee in which three students were arrested on charges of disturbing the peace. Angrily, students said that instead of combatting the fires the firemen had turned their hoses on the crowd, including townswomen, co-eds, and children. One curious fact about these perennial outbreaks was that the ladies and children of Bloomington always seemed to be caught in the crossfire between students and policemen. What ardor the police and hose-waving firemen failed to dampen Purdue finished the next weekend in Lafayette by a score of 26 to 7 in the dedication of that schools Ross-Ade Bowl.

Shortly thereafter, the university found itself in an unexpected public hassle over the next season's game with Syracuse University. The new football stadium was certain to be ready for play in the fall season of 1925. In making the football schedule that year, Zora Clevenger followed tradition and scheduled the game with Syracuse in the smaller stadium in Indianapolis. A vigorous protest appeared in the *Daily Student* on February 2 from Kermit R. Maynard, a former Indiana athlete. He expressed surprise that a game would be played away from the campus now that the new stadium would be available. He labeled the 1925 schedule an injustice to thousands of alumni and friends of the university who had subscribed to the Memorial Fund and said this was a desecration of the memory of the war dead whom the stadium honored. Maynard charged that officials had given in to the pressures of Indianapolis hotel proprietors and merchants who stood to make a good profit from the crowd.

Maynard's letter pulled the thumb out of the dike. The public hue and cry grew louder with each mail delivery. A stream of letters and petitions from all sorts of organizations poured into the president's office. Dean Fernandus Payne and professors Fred Davidson and W. A. Cogshall favored the stadium site for the Syracuse game. No doubt they spoke for most of their colleagues. On May 30, the decision was made to cancel the Indianapolis date to bring Syracuse to Bloomington. That October, coming on the heels of a humiliating defeat by Michigan of 63 to 0, the Syracuse defeat of 14 to 0 was somewhat gentler. Yet it seemed anticlimactic indeed to the furore in the spring over the schedule.

Memorial Stadium was dedicated during the Purdue game on November 21, 1925. Elaborate preparations had been made for this ceremony. Banners were attached to buses going out from Bloomington advertising the event. Window show cards were distributed widely in Indianapolis and other towns, and extensive newspaper advertising was purchased. Arrangements were made for the first wireless broadcast play-by-play of an Indiana game. Original plans fell through, but the local Indianapolis *News-*Merchants Heat and Light Company station carried the broadcast across Indiana. The Bloomington *Daily Telephone* said sixty-two newspapers were to be represented by reporters and photographers in the new stadium press secion. Two newsfilm companies had men on hand to record the actions of the day.

Highlight of the stadium dedication was the presentation of the old oaken well bucket by the alumni of Indiana and Purdue as a victory trophy for the annual games of the future. The idea of this token originated with Wiley J. Huddle (1901). He suggested a joint meeting of a small group of Indiana-Purdue alumni of Chicago to discuss presentation of some sort of trophy in keeping with the practices of other schools. Subsequently a committee recommended an oaken well bucket as a sturdy symbol of rural Indiana. The bucket, said the committee, should come from a well in Indiana, and the chain should be an ever-growing one composed of "I's" and "P's" as the athletic fortunes of the schools unfurled in the future. Fritz Ernst (Purdue) and Wiley J. Huddle were sent in search of a bucket, and they found it on the Burnet Farm between Kent and Hanover. In the dedicatory service the bucket was carried on to the field by George Ade of Purdue and

Harry R. Kurrie and presented to presidents Bryan and Elliott.

While sentimental alumni and fans dedicated the new stadium and watched the teams fight to a tie to add the first "IP" link to the well bucket chain, a new athletic problem for Indiana sprang up. Inevitably the blanket issuance of student ticket books at greatly reduced prices would lead to ticket scalping. Many students either could not or did not wish to attend games and sold their tickets. Others undertook to sell their passes at a profit. In March, 1925, forgers of numbers on student ticket books were caught and made to forfeit their tickets, and if they attended future games were required to pay full prices. A stern warning was given that future ticket scalpers would be suspended from school. Any student ticket presented in the future and not in the hands of the original holder would be confiscated. The Syracuse and Purdue games brought out the largest football crowds in history to Bloomington. With the university's enrollment approaching 3300 and increasing yearly, the problem of student identification was intensified. Controlling scalpers became more complicated.

Despite the fact football fortunes sagged mightily in the middle twenties, Everett Dean's basketball and baseball teams made highly respectable showings and created real respect for Indiana's athletic capabilities. The basketball team tied in a curious four-way statistical situation with Michigan, Purdue, and Iowa for first place in the Big Ten Conference in 1925–1926, and in 1925 the baseball team finished its schedule in first place in the Conference. The Hoosiers built up a most impressive lead in wrestling, and its track accomplishments wavered between notable and mediocre performances.

Financially, athletics at Indiana by 1925 had become significant business as compared with the past. First the cost of the athletic facilities were greatly increased with the addition of the new gymnaisum and football stadium. Football yielded $68,-084.27 aside from student fees. The Purdue game alone produced $27,047.50 in 1925, and the next year the successful basketball team attracted an attendance of 23,023. In 1926 football alone yielded $77,057. On November 3, 1926, the Bloomington *Daily Telephone* said, "With some $47,000 from the game of football [three games] is the best evidence of the wonderful popularity of the contest. Indiana's share of the Purdue receipts Saturday was about $13,000. The athletic management received $20,000 from

Notre Dame, and about $14,000 for the game played with North-western at Evanston."

The 1925 season with it monotonous defeats, however, was too much for the "old grads" to take. They were hungry for victory and opportunity to take pride in their team. As a result William Ingram's last season with its high score losses was the end of his coaching career at Indiana. He must have looked back like a traveller over a craggy road to see lying in ruins below him Clarence Childs, Ewald Stiehm, Pat Herron, and maybe even James Sheldon. Quickly pressures built up against the Athletic Committee and it hired Harlan (Pat) Page as head coach. Possibly no one to this day can fully explain all the pressures, although the Big Ten Conference five years later seemed to believe Indiana alumni had been a little too willing to supplement his salary from their own pockets.

Page reached Bloomington with a highly promising coaching career behind him at Chicago. This three-letter athlete had excelled as a quarterback in football, a baseball pitcher, and a basketball guard. He had coached all three sports, having performed a miracle in redeeming a droopy Chicago basketball season by turning it into one of championship caliber. In football he seemed to have Stagg's magic touch. Page was a member of the Chicago baseball team which toured Japan in 1909 and which had won all of its ten games. On the record a new day seemed to have dawned over the Jordan and football fortunes shone bright in the firmament.

Everybody looked to the handsome and rugged Page to produce a winning football team. The fans appeared to have wanted this at almost any cost. The Chicago coach assumed his duties with ample foreknowledge of the school's athletic history, and of what his employers expected from him. If, however, for some reason he was vague on the latter point the Indianapolis *News* stirred his memory late in January, 1926. "It may be a difficult task to interest a first class director in the prospects of a job at Indiana;" said the metropolitan paper, "the school had been termed the athletic graveyard as a result of the army of men who have been here in a football coaching capacity during the last several years." "Navy Bill" Ingram and the others no doubt muttered "amens!"

In his first season Page learned dramatically, if he had not

[3 4 8]

already known, what a zero meant, or what it meant to have Indiana appear so regularly in the right hand column of game results. In December he could thank God for DePauw, Kentucky, and Mississippi A. & M. College. When the last shout or moan had died away in the Memorial Stadium he was no nearer an answer to the oft-asked question, "What is the matter with Indiana University football?" than had been his predecessor at the same time of the past year. Although the Bloomington *Daily Telephone* did not know an answer, it gave the coach some disturbing reading matter. "Why is it an assured fact that the Crimson team will be weak year after year?" it pleaded.

> Why has the Bloomington campus become known as the graveyard of coaches? The above questions are asked from time to time by people who are interested in Indiana University. Until these questions are answered, until the trouble is found and the fundamentals changed, the Crimson grid teams will continue what they have been in the past. Weak Indiana football teams are not a matter of coaching or coaches, since I. U. has had good coaches in the past and the records have still been poor.
>
> There is some connection between a school's growth and its football team and Indiana has lagged far behind. The present coach, Pat Page, was brought here by the old graduates who want a winning football team even though Page was unliked among other circles of coaches and schools. This will not be the answer though it seems a new system—a championship system, whatever that is—must be started and built up.

Maybe Page in this unhappy moment believed there was some magic in President Bryan's toe. He asked him to open the coaching season in September, 1927, by kicking the first ball to the players. Page held and Dr. Bryan punted. Anticipating this historic act, the eloquent president informed readers of the *Daily Student*, "This afternoon I'll kick the first ball as requested and then I shall be requested not to kick another this season. I cannot make the team. I would like to. I hate to sit on the side lines. I like to be shoulder to shoulder with unconquerable Youth." Many Indiana backers, like President Bryan, liked "unconquerable youth," and that was the central problem.

Bryan's kick was too short that season to do more than beat Michigan State, Northwestern, and Kentucky, tie Minnesota, and hold Chicago to thirteen points. Only once in five years did Pat Page's team beat Purdue, and that was a weak 7 to 6 in his final game in 1930. On October 4, 1929, despite losing seasons, Indiana rooters made a minor bit of university history. For the first time men and women fans held a joint powwow on the eve of the homecoming game with Notre Dame. Page expressed disappointment at a lack of student support. He told students that week if there were 2000 of them before the stadium gates by 4:20 P.M. he would hold a full scale open practice drill. Students, said Page, could either support the team, "fool around the campus or hide away in organization houses while five full teams of Indiana's men go through a tough practice session in preparation for the Notre Dame game." The *Daily Student* added, "the day of 'whoopee' pep sessions on the eve of the game with a big bonfire and destruction of property has passed, and in its stead is an organized mass meeting of students." Notre Dame won 14 to 0, and on succeeding weekends Indiana was defeated by Chicago and Colgate. In the wake of these disasters a resolution appeared on the campus signed by male students promising not to shave until Indiana won a football game. The male animals, said the signers, had been accused of being too fond of dates. If the co-eds wanted dates they would have to be "satisfied with bewhiskered eds, as we are not going to shave until we win a game. We are sacrificing personal appearance to prove to Pat and his men that we are willing to do our bit." It was not until afer the game with Northwestern on November 16 that the co-eds could celebrate the loss of their men's whiskers. Rudely Purdue put them on again by a score of 32 to 0.

The season of 1929, in the height of the prohibition era, was dismal enough to stun even the most ardent temperance crusader. From indications in the stadium, it did chill alumni into drinking. The Culls J. Vayhinger chapter of the WCTU petitioned the Student Council asking that intoxicating liquors not be consumed at football games. They may have had a point; even Pat Page was upset over a show of poor sportsmanship following the Ohio University game that September.

If determined alumni in 1926 hoped for improvement in Indiana's football fortunes in the near future, the results of the season discouraged them. Indignity was compounded that year when the new football schedule was published and only one conference game was scheduled in Bloomington.

Only one bright star seemed to shine through the clouds of the murky athletic season of 1929–30 in which the football team won but two games: the basketball team won 7 and lost 5 conference games, and the baseball team drew the curtain by standing third among the Big Nine. A proposal was made by Professor Hugh E. Willis of the Law School that the university develop its reservoir watershed just off the northeast corner of the campus into a golf course as a means of promoting student recreation. President Bryan expressed favor for this idea which finally became a reality.

Football fortunes went unimproved in 1930 except for the fact that Indiana defeated Purdue 7 to 6. An incident earlier that month reflected the degree of indifference that beset the campus. When the team departed the Illinois Central station on is way to play Southern Methodist University in Dallas, Texas, few people were on hand to cheer. The *Daily Student* observed, "As if the I. U. football team was not already laboring under a burden of handicaps that is nearly overwhelming, there appears to be on the campus an utter lack of loyalty to the Scrappin' Hoosiers that makes that burden all the more crushing."

Following the humiliating defeat (25 to 0) by Northwestern in the homecoming game on November 8, 1930, it became clear that Pat Page's days as head football coach were severely limited. The cry of "What's wrong at Indiana?" was said to echo throughout the state, and with every touchdown scored against the university it was said to grow more menacing. "People are wondering," said the campus daily on November 11, a fortnight before the big game with Purdue in the Ross-Ade Stadium in Lafayette, "if it is lack of material in the players; poor coaching staff; poor football spirit at I. U., whatever the cause, everyone will have to pull together to beat Purdue and bring the Old Oaken Bucket home."

The one-point victory over Purdue touched off one of the last of the great battles between students and firemen and policemen. The mob appeared to think these city functionaries were stand-ins for the Lafayette school. Clothes were torn off people, bonfires threatened destruction of buildings around the Square, people were run over, traffic was halted, and there was commotion everywhere. There was only one difference between this maniacal seizure of the town and all others in the past; there was a threat to set fire to the old gymnasium on the campus. University officials had to post tight guard around the structure to save it. When the train bearing the team arrived on Saturday night at 9:30, the fans went wild again, but Pat Page foiled them. He had his players slipped out the rear of the train and into waiting taxis and driven away from the mauling crowd. This was his final act for the football team.

Page returned to Bloomington from Lafayette with the howl of fans ringing in his ears. He, however, was undeceived. A one-point victory over Purdue was not sufficient to erase the memory of a disastrous season. When the shouting died down and bonfires had smoldered into beds of lifeless ash, the dogs of removal would again be unleashed.

The ebbing tide of enthusiasm over the Purdue victory was prefaced by an extensive soul-searching in the Athletic Committee. On December 3, 1930, a perceptive editorial appeared in the *Daily Student*. This expressed student point of view undertook to put the Indiana football situation in perspective. The paper said the past season had provoked "columns of comment on questions of whether athletes should be paid, whether receipts of large gridiron contests should be devoted to charity or whether the stressing of athletics over scholastic achievements has not gravely affected the standards of our present higher education system. Football has been a big industry on college campuses; millions of dollars have been spent during past seasons and it is safe to assume that in future seasons there will be no decrease in box office receipts." The editor felt that educators should accept the fact that football had become an established "big sport" on the American college campus. Professors and presidents had to fit it into university programs. It had its place in the modern life of a university, if for no other reason than its pageantry. The public demanded support of the game, and the editor inferred Indiana had to bend its academic and social programs to accept this fact.

There was quick acceptance of the basic principle of the student editorial. Rumors had it that Harlan (Pat) Page was being considered as successor to Alonzo Stagg at Chicago, and that the highly popular E. C. "Billy" Hayes, track coach at Indiana, would be made head football coach in his place. Before the rumor advanced beyond the stage of speculation, the Bloomington *Evening World* on January 15, 1931, announced that Page had mailed his resignation to the Athletic Committee from Chicago. In the latter city he told newspapermen that President William Lowe

Bryan had asked him to leave Indiana. He said, "while I knew a certain alumni group was attempting to undermine me in Bloomington, the request for my resignation was a surprise and a disappointment. No matter whether I am successful in obtaining other employment I shall insist the University pay my salary until the expiration of my contract in 1932. I am willing to fulfill my end of the agreement." Page, however, had only an oral contract with the university, and when the actual terms of his original employment were publicized they created a sensation in the Big Nine Conference, especially when Page threatened to sue a member of the conference. Even more disturbing was the revelation that alumni had added a secret bonus to the stated university salary paid the coach.

Twenty-eight lettermen submitted a resolution three days later praising Page. "We the undersigned lettermen," read the resolution, "of the Indiana University football team do hereby go on record heartily endorsing Pat Page as coach. We also wish to state that there was undying team spirit throughout the hard season. We believe in Indiana's football future with Page." The Faculty Athletic Committee and the alumni did not share this view, and they made the decisions.

The *Daily Student* had its own view of the Page resignation. Sports writers and editors during the past year had been inhospitable to Indiana. "In recent years," said the paper, "Indiana has been referred to as the 'door mat' of the Western Conference rather than the 'Scrappin' Hoosiers.'" It was thought this condition of being a "door mat" was caused by failure to secure the cooperation of students, alumni, and faculty rather than failures of the coach.

The Faculty Athletic Committee voted to terminate Page's period of employment on April 1, 1931. Page in turn went to Indianapolis to search for evidence to sustain his contentions in his suit and perhaps to consult counsel. Professor W. J. Moenkhaus, chairman of the Athletic Committee, informed the coach that positively his agreement would not be renewed after April 1, and that he would be paid no salary beyond that date. Page took his case to the federal court in an effort to collect $15,000. President Bryan denied publicly that the university had a formal agreement with Page and hoped he would not press charges further. Perhaps at this point Page ceased to do so. Nevertheless the publicity was

[3 5 3]

injurious. It was revealed that Page had been paid an extra salary by a group of football supporters. This irregularity, it was said, led to a Big Nine decree against the practice.

When the Faculty Committee appointed E. C. Hayes as temporary coach it engaged in a bit moralizing. Hayes was extremely popular on the campus, and the thought was, of course, that he could produce a good football team in the midst of the Depression of the 1930's. Even beyond that it was hoped he would be able to reestablish a good balance between scholarship and athletics. "That an intimate relationship exists between scholastic success and athletic success is [a theory] which the Indiana faculty committee has long held and one which is regarded as basic by Coach Hayes." In a bit of ambivalence the faculty was said to want to put football on an even balance with the institution's scholastic achievements. The professors, however, proposed to make some compromises of scholastic requirements for a winning team. Actually Hayes did no better, if as well, in his first year than had Page in 1930, with one exception, his team beat Chicago 32 to 6. Pat Page no doubt felt after this game that the evils of the past four years had followed him onto the Midway. This was the first time Indiana had defeated Chicago since 1910, and only the second time since the two schools began playing in 1902.

Almost obscured by the football doldrums was the success Indiana athletes had in other sports. E. C. Hayes was an exceedingly fine track coach. In December, 1931, while the football wolves sought Pat Page's bleeding carcass, the Indiana cross-country team was said to have "gained a position unequaled by any other athletic group at this University." It won both the Big Ten and the National Amateur Athletic Union title. In the following years, despite the Depression, Indiana won conference championships in wrestling and track. The Hoosiers in May, 1932, either won first places or placed in every event in the Penn and Drake relays, and the distance medley team broke a track record which had stood for seventeen years.

Henry Brocksmith set a new collegiate record in the two-mile run. As a result of Hayes' coaching Charles Hornbostel and Ivan Fuqua were selected as members of the 1932 American Olympic Team. Success in track sports continued throughout the remainder of the Bryan administration. No track star shone brighter than Donald R. Lash. In June, 1936, he set a new world record of

8.58.3 in the two-mile run at Princeton University. Later that month he broke his own record and qualified for the Olympic Games to be held in Berlin by also running the 10,000 meters in 33.45.4.

Six Indiana trackmen and wrestlers and coaches Hayes and W. H. Thom went to Germany. Hayes and Thom were official coaches. Dick Voliva placed second in the light heavyweight wrestling, but the Indiana runners suffered disappointments. Lash unhappily finished eighth in the 10,000 meter finals, and third in the 5000 meter semi-finals. In the finals, however, he was fourteenth.

Track thrived at Indiana while other sports felt the impact of the Depression. Zora Clevenger anounced in the fall of 1932 that the Athletic Department would be forced, because of financial stringency, to discontinue support of golf, tennis, and swimming. Expenses were deeply cut in all other sports. Gate receipts fell off drastically, and at the same time it became necessary to reduce admission prices as much as 60 percent. Attempts were made to hold "dollar" football games, a misnomer because many seat prices had dropped to $.40. The football games with Iowa and Michigan suffered a reduction in attendance of 14,349 from those of the previous year, and a cash loss of $37,603.01. By January of 1933, there had been such a drastic shrinkage in athletic income that it was thought the university would have to borrow enough money to operate the next year. Income in 1934 took another plunge. Gate receipts were $60,615.00, but expenses exceeded this by more than $30,000.

The Depression manifested itself in another and somewhat surprising way on the Indiana campus. It became unsafe to park a car to attend a football game because thieves might ransack it. In November, 1933, the entire Bloomington police force, some of it in plain clothes, was called to duty during the Purdue game to prevent looting of cars. It was not until after 1936 that there was perceptible improvement in the economic fortunes in Indiana athletics. Then it was boasted that no sport was actually abandoned during the hard years because individual contestants in golf, tennis, and swimming had financed themselves in taking part in the meets.

Billy Hayes' accomplishments as football coach were no more spectacular than those of his predecessors. His teams won six out of twenty-five games. His most exciting achievement was the defeat of Chicago in 1931, otherwise the "floor mat" of the Conference continued to function. Even in the depth of the economic depression there were enough solvent alumni and fans to clamor for the appointment of a winning coach if somebody could identify one.

Despite Hayes' failure to achieve victories in football he was popular with the students, and some of them began a campaign to have him appointed Director of Athletics in the place of Zora Clevenger. This was not to be. Instead, Hayes, a bosom friend of Clevenger's, returned to track coaching and continued to assist with football.

Before progess could be made in the search for a successor to Hayes, someone had to find answers to the riddle of why Indiana football teams were so consistently unsuccessful in the Big Ten Conference. A fact finding committee was appointed to investigate this question. If the results of its findings were published no trace of them seems to have survived. Perhaps the findings were reported orally, and the search for a new coach was begun in February, 1934. William Lowe Bryan, Zora Clevenger, Judge O. L. Wildermuth, and Charles M. Neizer met in Fort Wayne to interview Don Peden, a former Illinois star, and coach at Ohio University. The Indiana representatives tentatively offered Peden the job and Clevenger told the press only a few details needed adjustment before Peden would finally consent to risk his coaching fortunes at Indiana. Two days later, however, Peden wired Clevenger that he preferred to remain at Ohio University.

Perhaps, if he saw it, the Ohio coach was disturbed by a *Daily Student* editorial. The paper said, "The Hoosier football coaching problem, riled into turbulency after a discouraging season, assumed a new angle Saturday afternoon when Athletic Director Z. G. Clevenger and Coach E. C. Hayes admitted there was to be a re-deal in Hoosier athletics. Three sweeping changes were announced for the program: First, that Clevenger was to be given more executive power; second, that Coach Hayes would retain his position as head track coach and would act as assistant football coach, and, third, that a new head grid coach would be selected." This prophecy was fulfilled early in March, 1934, when Alvin Nugent (Bo) McMillin, head coach at Kansas State College in Manhattan, was employed at Indiana. President Bryan had given

Zora Clevenger and E. C. Hayes the assignment to find a coach who could win games for the university and get the institution out of the losing syndrome of the 1920's. Bryan told Clevenger, "You go and get us a man and don't tell anybody but me." Clevenger asked that he be permitted to confer with "Billy" Hayes and Bryan consented. Clevenger had coached at Kansas State before returning to Indiana, and he had several direct personal sources of information in the school. One of these was the Dean of Education, who was himself an Indiana graduate. When Clevenger asked about Bo McMillin the Dean said he was a Catholic, but "I'll tell you this. He'll go out in the state and make you the best Methodist speech you ever heard." That was what Indiana wanted, a Catholic coach who could win football games and make Methodist speeches to the alumni and public.

Almost without consulting anyone Clevenger and Hayes secured a commitment from Bo McMillin to accept the Indiana job, and he was employed before the press and alumni had opportunities to comment upon his capabilities. In Bloomington "friends" of the university had helped compile a list of more than a hundred possible coaching candidates. In an interview in November, 1969, Clevenger said there was only one candidate considered. Bo McMillin's employment had the blessings of President Bryan and William J. Moenkhaus; there was no alumni fund this time for unstated salary to scandalize the school. Bo McMillin saw to it that Indiana paid him a good salary to move.

Bo McMillin was one of the most colorful characters to join the Indiana University staff in its long history. Texas born, he was one of twelve children, and he told sportswriters that his mother kept three or four other children around for company. He combined in his personality the flamboyance of Texas, a southern sense of humor, and a directness of manner which drew people to him. At the end of World War I, Bo and four classmates set out for Kentucky in the wake of their coach, "Chief" Bob Meyer to play football at the tiny Presbyterian foothold, Centre College. The lads, however, lacked the proper credentials to admit them to a school which took some pride in its academic standards. They then went down into the eastern mountain rim and enrolled in the Somerset High School, presided over by that most human of city superintendents, Porter Hopkins. Quickly the boys were able to meet Centre's standards of admission. In the meantime the Texans had found blood cousins in "Red" Roberts, Ed Diddle, and other hill country lads, and combining forces they became a formidable small college football team. It was "Uncle" Charlie Moran who honed the gaps out of them and taught them the game.

On October 20, 1921, in Cambridge, the wiry McMillin galloped through a big hole opened by Roberts to score a thirty-five yard touchdown against Harvard in the only score of the day. Little Centre with its wild Texans and mountain boys had turned back the mighty, a thing Indiana University had been unable to do. The good Catholic kneeling before each game in fervent prayer won instant fame. Perhaps no other modest football score in American athletic history was ever cherished so long as this one.

After leaving Centre McMillin coached at Geneva College in Pennsylvania, and then moved to Manhattan, Kansas, to take Zora Clevenger's old job as head coach. He arrived in Bloomington on a chilly March 13, 1934, to be welcomed warmly to Indiana University. No new professor, and, possibly no new president, had been received with so much fanfare. A grand reception was held in Alumni Hall of the Memorial Union. The university band introduced Bo to *Indiana Frangipana* and the other fight songs in a half hour concert. He was then all but drowned in oratory from William Lowe Bryan, Dean Charles Jacob Sembower, Judge Ira T. Batman, Billy Hayes, and Zora Clevenger. Topping off the ceremony, Bryan read a letter which was as much prayer as greetings from Governor Paul V. McNutt. This was yet another new beginning for Indiana.

Zora Clevenger had scheduled for the 1934 football season a rugged series of games which meant more to Bo McMillin than all the oratory in Indiana. He faced such maulers as Ohio State, Chicago, Iowa, Minnesota, and Purdue. The only "breathers" were Ohio University and, maybe, Maryland. McMillin's first year's record with this heavy schedule, with the exception of the 17 to 6 Purdue victory, was no more impressive than those of Bill Ingram and Clarence Childs. The defeat of Purdue was dramatic, and the fans chose to see in it a happy portent of the future. They began to believe that the new coach meant what he said when he told a friend, "They're (Indiana football players) used to losin' and I'm used to winnin', but I'm the boss so these pore lil' boys are gonna have to get used to *my* way of doin' things."

Bo McMillin proved a rugged drill-master and soon had his

players begging for academic mercy. By mid-November of 1934, a rumor was afloat that members of the football team were petitioning the faculty to reduce the number of classes and shorten recitation periods because the prevailing system offered too much competition with football practice. In a more serious note McMillin undertook to change another Indiana tradition. Just before the Purdue game he appealed to students to behave themselves. "I do not want to say anything that will dampen the fine spirit & loyalty that was manifested by the students thru-out the football season, but I am asking in behalf of football that the leaders on the campus see to it that there is no breaking of classes for the Purdue game. It hurts football more than anyone realizes, and personally I do not think that it helps school spirit." "Breaking classes" had become a nuisance in the university, not so much because of occurrence of actual disturbances as by the constant threat of disruption. The committee on student affairs voted that any student trying to break up classes on the eve of a football game and charged with inciting to riot should be expelled.

Despite changes in athletic coaching personnel, the effects of the Depression lingered on in 1935–36, even though President Bryan did inform the trustees that all athletic sports had been restored to the active roster. McMillin was paid $6,500, more than twice the salary of Everett Dean, and well above the maximum professor salary range. Students and alumni seemed to have felt even more the financial pinch when on October 25, 1935, they voted to make a collie dog official football mascot, but were unable to raise enough money to purchase a suitable animal.

Bo McMillin's coaching rewarded the closing years of the Bryan administration with football success. It did not, however, serve up Purdue's head on a platter at the end of the 1937 playing season. The Indiana team, nevertheless, missed a perfect season by loss of three games and twenty-six points, and the board of trustees gave the Texan a ten-year contract. Even if Indiana did lose to Purdue in the final year of his presidency, William Lowe Bryan no doubt was charmed by the happy refrains of a *Daily Student* editorial. The "Indiana University football team," said the paper, "is becoming known as a strong team rather than a stepping stone with the new coach, Alvin (Bo) McMillin."

Three decades of dampened football fortunes had made Indiana University a highly self-conscious member of the Big Ten Conference. This condition created internally many complex problems of relationships between the popular spectator sports of football, baseball, and basketball and the improvement and maintenance of high academic standards. Even so precious a fact as freedom of teaching and classroom management was threatened at times by irate alumni and lettermen. Students caused woes for the university by their uncontrolled victory riots on campus and along village streets, and by their threats to "break" classes. On the other hand there were worries about lack of student support to cheer teams onto victory, and to help assume the constantly rising costs of maintaining a modern gymnasium, stadium, and outdoor playing fields. The financial burden of athletics after 1925 at times approached that of maintaining the university itself.

The overwhelming zeal for victory on the part of overwrought alumni and fans involved the integrity of the university itself. It was not pleasant to be charged and proven guilty of playing ineligible players, or of abusing the code of ethics of the Big Ten Conference, even though the code itself was poorly defined in some areas.

Since 1910 a question uppermost in the Indiana professorial mind was whether or not pressures to produce winning teams in Indiana University had a direct bearing on academic standards, and especially on the work of athletes. This was frequently the subject of formal faculty discussion. Almost annually someone undertook to determine objectively the facts in the case by making comparative studies between athletes' and non-athletes' academic achievements. Repeatedly it was asserted that if there were any differences, athletes might be a shade better. It is impossible to tell whether or not the comparisons rested upon grade evidence alone, or if so, upon grades in comparably difficult courses. Athletes sometimes gave clues to the academic problems which they faced by threatening to petition for more lenient class work, or by asking for more considerate scheduling of classes.

No single aspect of Indiana University's program received more constant publicity after 1910 than did its athletic contests. As the twentieth century advanced this became an even more pronounced fact. The postwar years of the 1920's saw greater national emphasis placed on collegiate sports in America. The multiplicity of metropolitan sportswriters not only created an ever watchful public eye which saw and reported every word and deed of coaches and athletes, but the writers, no matter how inexperienced, editorialized on many things relating to the university and its educational programs. Movie news cameramen came onto the campus to record not only athletic games, but to gather background shots of the physical plant and of university activities, and schools with winning athletic teams received national publicity. The same was true with the appearance of the radio sports commentator who broadcast descriptions directly from playing fields and courts. Bloomington was no longer isolated. Even the good roads movement in the United States in the 1920's and 1930's had a bearing on Indiana University athletics, by enabling larger crowds to come to Jordan Field and later to the memorial gymnasium and stadium, and by creating parking troubles. There is no doubt but that all of the new agencies of publicity helped as much or more to create in the public mind an image of the university than did the soberer efforts of university administration and faculty.

It has generally been assumed that athletic success has had a bearing on public support of state universities. No one at Indiana University has undertaken a definitive study of this contention, or, so far as is known, to measure the impact of success or lack of success upon the legislative mind in making appropriations for the institution. It is not possible here to say more than that there appears to have been a high degree of sensitivity about this subject. It would be difficult indeed to say precisely that failure of Indiana University football teams to achieve the reputations of some other Big Ten schools held the university back in legislative budget considerations, or that a successful season helped. The record is clear, however, that Purdue with a generally more successful athletic record fared no better at the hands of the legislature.

There is almost no room for reasonable doubt that alumni and "fans" were deeply influenced in their personal attitudes toward the university by athletic success or failure. How constant alumni and "fans" were in their feelings was an open question. They perhaps were the most concerned, at least momentarily, of any segment of the institution's constituency. The further away from his college days an alumnus advanced in time, the more concerned he appeared to have become about athletic fortunes. Large numbers of alumni seemed to look to football players to bolster their pride in their alma maters and to give them a vicarious sense of virility.

Bo McMillin arrived in Bloomington just as it became discernible that the great Depression was slackening. Once again Indiana University athletics surged forward as expensive sidelines of the institution's operation. The Bryan administration constantly had to adjust its thinking and emotions to the rising demands for expenditures of large sums of money to remain competitive among its neighboring universities. There is no doubt that the new brand of campus chauvinism disturbed the Victorian in the president's chair.

By the time William Lowe Bryan retired from the presidency, Indiana athletic fortunes were brightening. Whether coincidental or not, the university began to make strides in its athletic programs at the same time the academic revolution was underway, as a result of adoption of the searching self-study report, retirement of over-age professors, selection of aggressive young administrative leadership. The new administration showed acute concern for every facet of Indiana University's public image, and athletics was one of its most important public image makers.

[XVI]

Self-Study and New Directions

THE RETIREMENT OF so many persons at the same time in 1937 revealed in clear outline two cardinal facts, both of which proved weaknesses in a time of urgent educational demands for progress. First, departments in many cases were left leaderless; and, second, the entire program of the institution needed serious reappraisal at this point. In far too many cases departments were left without men of the maturity and capacity believed necessary to become leaders in their various fields of instruction. The challenge to advance the instructional program onto a new plane of operation was as great for the professor as for the president, and good quality men had to be employed to do this. Specifically, much of the structure of Indiana University existed in framework only, and the next advances had to be made in the direction of setting well defined aims and objectives for the institution. This meant in biological terms the fleshing out of the existing skeleton with qualitative teaching and research. Before the university was the timely mandate to take three steps: first, a deeply searching and revealing inventory was to be taken of every phase of institutional operation. Second, this inventory had to be made well beyond any question of its being an administrative venture and without allowing the formation of party and academic factional lines. Finally, a search for new personnel had to be started at once, even though it would have been most desirable to have had the results of the survey committee in hand first. Wells already had underway a diligent search for the best possible men to replace those who had retired and to fill new vacancies. Perhaps the acting president could have done nothing to convince the faculty more forcefully of his seriousness of purpose than by making the new appointments after a thorough search for the best quality professors obtainable.

Some observers believed that Wells, as Dean of the Business School, had sensed need for such a survey and had acted quickly to make certain that one would be made. There were others who believed they saw in the proposal for a self-study possible unfavorable criticism of the preceding Bryan administration. The records reveal that neither of these points had much, if any, validity. At the inception of the plan it is true that Wells was Acting President and for an unspecified length of time. But anyone who took the time to look into his professional background could have predicted he would have favored a searching inventory of the university's programs. He was a young man with an unusually mature experience in the field of surveying banking procedures in the troubled decade when they had reached a watershed. His research bureau housed on the university campus had been engaged in assessing current conditions and in setting new aims and objectives for the banks. It would have been strange indeed if he, as an aggressive acting president who said so often the university could not afford to lose momentum, had pursued any other course when chances of success were so promising, even more so than they had been in 1934 in the field of banking.

This background notwithstanding, there were few universities in 1937 which either had not been surveyed or were in the process of intensive self-examination. The University of Chicago had finished its famous survey by 1933, and Floyd W. Reeves and John Dale Russell had published their impressive two-volume report, *Trends in University Growth and The University of Chicago Survey*. A decade earlier Yale University, caught up in an immediate post-war flurry of dissatisfaction, was shaken from stem to stern by self-appraisal and reorganization. This modern survey was comparable with the famous Yale *Report* of 1828. Nearer Bloomington, Northwestern University underwent a searching inventory which seemed to have proceeded along an organizational plan later to be followed in Indiana. The Northwestern survey and methods employed in its compilation were cited by the various academic deans to the Indiana Board of Trustees on November 22, 1937. In the same year Walter Crosby Eells published a voluminous book entitled *Surveys of American Higher Education.* Preparation and publication of Eell's widely publicized book was financed by the Carnegie Foundation for the Advancement of Teaching and covered in whole or in part almost 1,900 educational institutions.

There is, however, among the Indiana University documents a note stapled to the university *News Letter* indicating that a faculty committee as early as 1936 had under way a reexamination of the old Jordan "Major Subjects." It was felt, said the committee, that a marked trend had set in toward "the recognition of groups of departments and toward provisions for achievement tests and comprehensive examinations preceding graduation." Included in the manuscript records is another interesting and undated document written on the backs of three French Lick Hotel envelopes in Herman B Wells' hand which might be considered the first germ of the idea of a self-study in Indiana University.

On August 9, 1937, in a much more extensive document entitled "A Memorandum Concerning A Fact Finding Program for Indiana University," Acting President Wells said when the new president was selected and was installed in office he would have to make quick decisions concerning internal problems. No matter whether a stranger to Indiana or someone thoroughly acquainted with the institution, he would need precise knowledge of every phase of the university's operation. "In the interim," said Wells, "between the opening of school in September and his [the new president's installation] I wish to propose that the administrative offices and faculty be mobilized and started on an extended program of fact finding." He then outlined ten areas which he felt should be examined. He said, "I should like to have the authority from the Board of Trustees to make contact with the administrative officers prior to the opening of school in September and have them begin such studies as their staffs will allow. I should like to have the authority further to present to the faculty and to its various affiliated groups such as the University Council, the A. A. U. P., etc., a proposal for the undertaking of such of these studies as the time of the members of the faculty will allow." He said he also wanted to seek advice on this subject from the advisory committee. The acting president said that aside from being of great value to the new president, the self-study would produce sidelights upon the university's needs which would facilitate the making of a better case before the legislature. Too, if the data could be formulated in the interim period while the board searched for a new president there would be a minimum loss of momentum when he took office.

The acting president presented to the academic deans in September, 1937, his plan for self-study which that group quickly adopted as its own. At first the deans expressed the thought they might undertake the survey, but finally decided that it should be conducted under the sponsorship of the trustees. They procured a copy of the Northwestern survey and talked with the chairman of that university's committee. They further decided against seeking outside professional survey assistance, and finally concluded that the Indiana committee should be composed of nonadministrative faculty members. They indicated they were familiar with the Carnegie study and understood the implications of a searching self-study. A prospective committee should be given free rein to use its collective judgment as to the scope of their study, and the trustees should have made available to the committee all pertinent university records. In every other way faculty, trustees, and administration should support the committee. In order that the trustees might be thoroughly conversant with the deans' proposal they were given a copy of the Northwestern report, believing such information would prepare them better to receive the results of the Indiana study when it was submitted.

Acting President Wells presented the deans' request for a self-study to the board of trustees on November 12, 1937, and that body accepted all the recommendations with the admonition that such a study should get under way at once. In a somewhat extensive set of resolutions they gave full authority to a committee of three faculty members to proceed with the self-examination, and authorized use of pertinent university materials without let or hindrance.

A month later Wells appeared before the faculty and discussed the proposed self-study and requested its members to suggest to him names for appointment to a three-man committee. There followed a revealing correspondence in which professors not only suggested an extensive list of names but also offered many suggestions about what a survey committee should do. An overwhelming majority expressed confidence in Dean Fernandus Payne despite the instructions of the board of trustees, acting president, and deans that stipulated that only professors would be appointed to the committee. Some suggested colleagues most closely associated with

[3 6 6]

them, while others made objective efforts to name able and judicious men. When the votes were tabulated a modern Solomon could not have decided, except for Dean Payne, who were the top choices for membership on the committee.

Unruffled by the diffuse vote, the acting president chose three staunch academic yeomen who brought to the committee three widely differing points of view. Wendell W. Wright of the School of Education was a conservative pedagogue who gave serious consideration to his decisions and was to prove that he had a ruggedly independent mind in his dissent. Herman T. Briscoe of the Chemistry Department was not without deep convictions but he perhaps was more conciliatory in defending them, a fact which often gave a temper of compromise to the committee's conclusions. Briscoe has been termed a defender of the student of average capabilities and pretensions. He was highly respected as a man of high integrity and proper academic standards. Fowler V. Harper, the chairman, was professor of law, and a liberal. At the time, he no doubt was considered by many to be a leftist. Thus any report which the three would submit would be sprinkled with asterisks indicating dissents among the three. Despite the fact the deans had presented to the board of trustees a copy of the Northwestern report, one can only wonder if anyone in Indiana, in the summer of 1937, had a clear idea of what should be revealed in the self-study committee's final report—or what results might be achieved. By no means was the Indiana self-study the work of three men alone. In time many people either made independent analysis of segments of the university program or cooperated as sources of specialized information and skills.

The first question asked was, what were the purposes of higher education? Then, how did Indiana measure up with the stated aims and objectives? Harper and Briscoe defined the aims and objectives of the university in the succinct statement that education was the process of developing a trained mind and the acquisition of knowledge. The two were critical of the huge organizational structure that American higher education had allowed to develop. They felt at best the university could only articulate the premise that it organize facilities and offer intellectual guidance. The process of attaining knowledge and of developing a trained mind was an individual responsibility. Here were two twentieth century Jeffersonians who tried once again to state the ideals of an intellectual

[3 6 7]

aristocracy based upon the efforts and worth of an individual man. They were emphatic that they did not "identify democracy with mediocrity in education." Since Wright made no statement of beliefs, it is not possible to present the source of his objection to this statement.

Again, Professor Wright objected to free use of the Carnegie report of the investigation of the Pennsylvania educational system which Professor Frank Davidson had analyzed for the committee. His objection stemmed from lack of faith in its thoroughness or full validity when applied to Indiana. It was this report, however, which led to a thorough survey of Indiana University student relationships with the institution's educational program.

When the committee sought from the faculty its views as to the objectives of the university, it got, of course, a diversity of replies. These statements were classified generally under four major heads, with a small miscellaneous section added. Faculty concepts ranged from 46 percent holding to the belief the general objectives should be cultural, social, and liberal, and 14 percent believing them to be research. The self-study committee generally agreed with these objectives, even if they were to be more clearly defined as time went on.

There was unanimous expression of concern with the fact that in the 1930's the university had expanded rapidly into new fields, service areas, and fields of narrow interest using specialized techniques which could be of only doubtful longevity. They criticized the lengthening in time and number of courses required to complete the professional curricula. Gazing into their statistical crystal the three prophets were less than successful with their predictions for the immediate future. "It does not seem reasonable to suppose that the next twenty-five years will witness an expansion in size or an increase in financial support of public education comparable to that of the past quarter century." They no doubt were misled by the Bureau of Census' projection which was based upon the Depression era birthrate. Gloomily the three predicted that the state of Indiana would grant no substantial increase in appropriation and that the university would be fortunate to maintain its present plant and program as it was. Already they thought the university was overextended in some fields. There were too many courses which spread the curriculum too thinly over too much territory. It was not enough to train country doctors, lawyers, and school teachers. The university "must subject them [students] to an intellectual discipline so

severe as materially to help them attain a comprehensive understanding of factors which have produced our civilization and make a
critical appraisal of the values by which it is to be judged." No
clearer statement could have been made for unswerving loyalty to
the ancient liberal arts tradition, and later this philosophy was to
develop in the university some differences of opinion. Actually the
stimulus for this declaration stemmed from twin shoots—the offering of too many inconsequential courses which drew meager
patronage and the fear of a rising vocationalism.

Since those first ten students enrolled in Indiana Seminary in
1825, the student had been the main actor on center stage of the
institution. Thus, the self-study considered him but not without
subjecting him to a most critical appraisal. Many times in the history of the university presidents and professors involved themselves
in soul-searching to keep the student from becoming a mere name
in a roll book, an aimless occupant of a classroom seat, or an adolescent waiting around the campus for the passage of four years and
for his senior graduation. In every way the university depended
upon the student, and in every way he was central to the whole
teaching and learning process. Masses of students came to Bloomington ineffectively prepared to do university level work. On the
other hand, there were those golden nuggets who brought to the
campus greater learning challenges than faculty and curriculum
could satisfy. Clearly students, not trustees or faculty, set the institutional standards and image of its graduates.

Interwoven with this matter of student relationships was the
nagging issue of Indiana institutional parity. Again those notes
scribbled on the back of French Lick hotel envelopes reveal the
anxiety of the acting president on this matter. Fiercely determined
on one hand, and verging on defeatism on the other, he was afraid
the university had already lost the race to Purdue in the area of
student patronage. For thirty-five years President Bryan's periodic
reports to the board of trustees and his office correspondence revealed eloquently the importance which he attached to student enrollment. In the 1930's total all-university enrollment numbers were
increasing—from 7,817 in 1930 to 11,752 in 1938–39—and with
this increase the deficiencies of student preparation were multiplied.
It would have proved a calamity for the university, however, to have
attempted to institute selective admissions to correct this basic
problem.

Obviously a searching report on student qualifications and educational responses in the 1930's would reveal staggering shortcomings, not only of individual students, but of the American home and the university itself. Development of a statistical image of the times revealed a façade of stagnation in so many areas, and the university did not escape this criticism. By the latter part of the decade under consideration, 57.24 percent of the university's student enrollment came from what the committee classified as city homes. The towns held their own, but country boys and girls were becoming less numerous. No matter where they came from, too few students gave an indication they were willing to make the hard core effort necessary to gain knowledge by the austere standards prescribed by the committee for excellence in classwork, reading attainment, cultural growth, and the acquisition of social awareness. Negatively it was said masses of students were unwilling to forego the trivialities of college life for the sake of concentrating effort and time on gaining sophisticated knowledge. Some 12.5 percent of the students were said never to have used the library, and 30 percent "read no books outside of class assignments during the school year."

Counter attractions to the academic program were 162 student organizations, a number which the survey committee considered excessive indeed. Many students it seemed had confused organization objectives with those of the university itself. There were other sources which absorbed student energy and time, one of which was the Memorial Union. The opinion was expressed that idle students spent far too much time in the Union, and an analysis of student application of hours revealed that 30 percent of them spent only six to nineteen hours a week in study. This revelation angered committee members and they all but shouted refutation at the oft-repeated opinion that a main function of the university was "teaching students how to mix, to get on with their fellows, and to act as a preparation for social life after college. *The principal business of the University is to advance knowledge and to train the minds of its students!*" said the committee in unanimous voice. It infuriated the members further that an analysis revealed that such a large proportion of the total student body seemed to be almost wholly oblivious to current and major social problems. "The low ebb of student thought and opinion is nowhere more strikingly evidenced than in the general field of social problems. To the committee, it is a source of wonder that in a community of more than five thousand young people that there should exist such phlegmatic indifference to the highly controversial social problems with which our civilization is plagued." Because of this condition the committee felt the university in 1937 was not properly organized to correct this situation.

The heart of the self-study report lay in the area of restructuring student institutional relationships, in improving the teaching process, and in wholesale revision of the first two years of course offerings. It was never made clear just how much dependence there was on the Chicago College plan. There is every reason, however, to believe the Chicago survey was very much in the minds of the committee. At least one or two members appeared to have been willing to institute the Chicago College plan in full. Likewise, there was not even a hint in available materials that any of the committee had in mind a junior college organization comparable to that instituted by the University of Minnesota. Several unspecified plans were examined, among them that of Colgate, but the committee concluded, "the general unrest and dissatisfaction with traditional conditions and practices indicate clearly that experimentation in techniques, practices, and organization is indispensable if Indiana University is not to fall hopelessly in the rear of the educational cavalcade." In formulating the fabric of the junior division plan the committee said it held over 300 conferences and received almost as many expressions of faculty points of view. In an analysis of materials and opinions in hand the committee outlined five core areas in which it said every well educated person should acquire general knowledge. These were the physical, biological, and social sciences, the humanities, music, and fine arts. Freshman English, physical education, and military science were to be added as compulsory subjects. Students, said the committee, would be required to demonstrate proficiency in four of the survey course areas and English before they would be allowed to advance to upper-level standing.

Basically, in educational speech of the moment, the junior division program would be organized on a horizontal relationship of courses; and the bulkheads of departmental organization would be breached, if not destroyed. The present custom of allowing a student to begin professional courses in the freshman and sophomore years would be prohibited. The ideal was that all students would have a body of common knowledge, that the quality of teaching and learning would be improved, and that a comprehensive examination at the end of the sophomore year would be an effective gauge for determining the university's educational effectiveness.

By 1940 Indiana University had involved itself in the twentieth century educational revolution which was occurring throughout American higher education. The long and detailed confidential ballot cast by the faculty in March, 1940, reflected both a profile of professorial reaction to the self-study report and to the tenor of educational philosophy that prevailed in Indiana University. The balance of the vote in many instances was delicate indeed and reflected the hesitancy with which many members of the faculty were willing to embrace change. Perhaps the most significant decision was that which, momentarily at least, rejected the lower division proposal by an almost even division of opinion. The idea itself was retained for further study in a separate ballot, and in 1942 the lower division was created by action of the board of trustees. Certainly in 1938 there was often dissent among the committee of three, as was reflected in numerous notes and dissenting sections.

Perhaps no faculty committee before 1937 would have been so bold as to examine with critical thoroughness the administrative organization as did the self-study committee in 1938. Somehow revisions of the operation of the university had to be made so as to break the tight hold of the president's office on the growing institution. The organizational chart projected by the survey committee was a study indeed in a step from rigid simplicity and personal control to one of complexity. In fact the committee's charted proposal was more a prescription for revolutionizing the administrative system of the university than anything of the sort had been since the founding of the institution. Not only was this branch of university government to be updated, but it was to be brought into proper relationship with both the institutional and professional aims and objectives set forth in the general program.

To allay any unnecessary trustee fears the committee assured the board that it recognized that body's authority for the operation of the university. But by something more than implication it told the trustees of the changes that had occurred in recent years in the field of university administration. Indiana University itself had worked in the direction of change. With the creation of semi-autonomous schools and colleges which in turn were brought under the surveillance of professional accrediting bodies, with the rising demands of younger and more aggressive professors demanding a voice in policy-making, and the broadening of the university's personnel and service base, the old straight-line trustee-president-professor administration was no longer adequate. "The duty remains," said the committee, "to be familiar at all times with the general educational and financial policies of the institution and to know and understand the conditions responsible for these policies and the methods employed to make them effective."

On the administrative chart drafted by the committee, the office of president was left in almost as powerful a position in the organization as ever. It was proposed, however, that it be cushioned by four hefty administrative supports: an educational vice-president, an administrative board composed of divisional heads, and a financial vice-president. An additional supervisory board composed of divisional heads was to oversee the junior or lower division.

The most important concept expressed by the committee in regard to administration was that the presidency should have the major function of supervisory oversight of the entire educational enterprise, should report the conditions of the university to both the trustees and the faculty, and should give special attention to the institution's public relations.

It was pointed out, with history on the committee's side, that throughout its century and a quarter of existence Indiana University had wasted some of its best professorial talent in the performance of commonplace tasks. It was rare for a man of creative talents to make significant scholarly contributions after he had accepted an administrative assignment. Appointments to headships of departments and deanships had been used as a device for holding good men in Indiana University, but it certainly had not proved to be a means of turning them into scholars who would bring the institution real notice in major fields of learning. Worst of all was the practice of appraising the worth of professors who had been given administrative assignments on the basis of scholarly achievements.

Whether a criticism of the former administration was implied or not, the self-study committee reached the conclusion that every phase of the university's operation was tied up in some way with its single strand of administration. It was evident at once that the institution had little promise of expanding or even competing with other universities in the future if it continued to tolerate a restrictive administrative plan. So many changes had occurred in American higher education in the post-World War I era that no university could fail to recognize them and continue to thrive. There was, for instance, urgent need in Bloomington not only for a centralization of the management of student affairs, but for the employment of trained personnel to deal with this important phase of the university's operation. No longer could a dean of women, the Women's League, and a bunch of loosely associated organizations serve the greater needs of students.

Despite the roaring '20's and '30's Indiana University still held onto vestiges of its historic parental attitude towards students. They came onto the campus as adolescents and needed close personal supervision. The campus was in fact an extension of the family fireside, and president and faculty assumed some parental responsibilities. Housing was in short supply, and the individual student was left pretty much on his own except for those few hours a day when he was in class. The coldly objective profile of the Indiana student which the self-study committee produced revealed how out-of-date and inadequate the administration of this central charge of the university had become. No longer was institutional responsibility to the student to be cast in the context of family simplicity and standards. The family itself had failed its children. As the committee revealed, students came from homes where there were lacking intellectual stimulus, reading materials, and even awareness of pressing social problems. The university had to assume responsibilities in these areas in such a positive manner that it would break the old mores drastically enough to revise the habits and customs of childhood. The massing of ever-increasing numbers of students in the university within so tight a social community created its own peculiar problems. Too, the whole tenor of parent-child relationships in national life was undergoing a thorough revolution, and Indiana University could not afford to ignore this fact in 1938. It was necessary to begin building at ground level in this field to institute a proper administrative organization to care for student needs. The areas of public health, student government, employment, registration, admissions, records, and social affairs all had to be served. The committee believed the time had arrived when a full-time health program should be organized, and that student personnel should be cared for by trained persons who knew something about the management of human affairs *en masse.*

The faculty was not spared the rod. In just as searching an enquiry the self-study committee set out to determine how good the

Indiana staff was in comparison with those in other institutions, and in keeping with its newly prescribed aims and objectives. Like the faculties in every other state university, that at Indiana had grown in size but not always in quality as measured by the more demanding standards of the mid-twentieth century. Herman B Wells revealed consciousness of this fact when he began his intensive search for new faculty members to replace those retiring and to find additional ones to bolster departmental programs. During the first years of his presidency he visited many campuses, inspected departments and colleges, talked with specialists in the fields where Indiana wished to build, and took counsel of the best advisors he could identify. The board of trustees itself became concerned in this matter of rebuilding the faculty, and on May 18, 1937, voted to accept James B. Conant's offer of his services to help select professors in physics, botany, and chemistry.

The times could not have favored the adoption of new principles of faculty organization more than at the retirement of William Lowe Bryan. Basing its conclusions on answers to questionnaires, the self-study committee was able to produce a composite of the Indiana professor. He spent 27.94 clock hours a week with his teaching, 14.25 doing research and writing, and the remaining 17.26 per week in administration, student affairs, and public service, or attending to his own personal interests. Much of what was classed as public service was in fact teaching extension courses. Left to their own wishes most professors preferred to spend more than half of their time in the classroom.

Law professors spent more time in research than any others and less time in the classroom. Education and business administration professors gave less evidence of doing research than their law and arts and sciences colleagues. It was the belief of the committee that the faculty had not made research a primary part of their professional activities. Indiana University itself gave no statistical evidence of being properly diligent in this area. In comparison with efforts in other institutions in the Old Northwest, the university in 1935–36 spent $21,108 annually in the direct support of research, as compared with $146,636 at Wisconsin. All of the other Big Ten schools spent more than four times Indiana's appropriation in this area.

The self-study committee made an even more precise assessment of the place of research in the general scheme of Indiana

University in 1936–37, when it revealed the institution spent only 1.7 percent of its total annual budget in the support of original investigation as compared with an average of 10.07 spent by 135 publicly controlled universities listed in the biennial survey of the United States Department of Education.

Only Minnesota had a lower percentage of members of the College of Arts and Sciences holding doctorates than Indiana. Its percentage was 37.8 as compared with Indiana's 48.5 or Illinois' 69.3. In teaching loads and research, only the Law School made a favorable showing in the North Central table of averages, and even it was slightly below the regional average. "By comparing the average of the School of Law with the average of all faculty members of the University," said the committee, "it appears that the School of Law has produced twice the average number of articles. The Committee has little doubt that the chief factor involved in the excellent record of the Law School is the low teaching load which prevails in the school." It was the committee's unanimous opinion that "It is clear that so long as teaching schedules are heavy as they have been at Indiana University, little improvement can be expected in the quality and quantity of research." In an even stronger vein the men expressed the opinion, "When the expensive character of research is considered, it is obvious that it were folly to hope to compete in achievements with institutions that make such generous provision for scientific and scholarly investigation." As confirmation of this fact the committee indicated that out of a general fund of $1,839,352 in 1936–37, the university spent $32,922 for research, and approximately half of this amount was derived from restricted funds.

Other criteria were applied to the entire faculty of Indiana University by the self-study committee. Until 1937, the institution had employed or developed only three "starred" Men of Science as compared with 30 in Michigan and The Johns Hopkins, 22 at Illinois, and 68 at Harvard. In citing this latter statistic it was clear "that Indiana has lost ground from 1906 to 1938." In another category, thirty-seven active faculty were listed in *Who's Who in America* as compared with 152 in Ohio State University and 126 in the University of Illinois. Only Purdue and Michigan State had fewer members so recognized in the Old Northwest. In its frank appraisal of the measurable quality of the Indiana University faculty, the self-study committee weighed many contributing facts and concluded,

"It is not to be denied that Indiana University has on its faculty a number of competent, and indeed a few distinguished men. The Committee in no sense would detract from the contributions made to scholarship by these persons. When considered as a whole, however, it is a fact which the Committee believes cannot be successfully denied that the faculty of the University is far from a distinguished one. Indeed, from whatever data one draws his inferences, it is clear that Indiana does not deserve to be classed with the other state institutions in the Middle West (except Purdue), much less the leading endowed schools of the country." Moreover, the committee believed that the formulation of sound policies with respect to faculty selection was perhaps the biggest task which faced the administration at Indiana University.

Ten departments in 1937 were felt qualified to do acceptable graduate work as compared with 18 at Ohio State University and 14 at the University of Wisconsin. In appraising the competence of the individual departments the committee touched on an ancient and sensitive fact in Indiana University's history of hiring and promotion policies. It criticized vigorously the twin evils of nepotism and in-breeding. Over 20 percent of the staff members hired between 1925 and 1937 were related to other faculty members. The sciences, English, mathematics, and classics departments had especially offended in this area. It should be noted in this connection that the statistical data of the self-survey committee is in sharp variance with those of Dr. Burton Dorr Myers in his somewhat defensive appraisal of nepotism and in-breeding practices of the university.

In its conclusions on the question of the hiring of new faculty with mature training and experience, the committee was clear in its admonitions. Speaking directly to the new administration its members were positive in saying, "In the judgment of the Committee, it is impossible to over-emphasize the significance of these matters and the necessity for frank and critical appraisal of past conditions and practices. Moreover, the Committee believes that the formulation of sound policies with respect to such matters is perhaps the biggest task which faces the new administration at Indiana University."

The two-volume report of the special committee was a frank and brutally straightforward document. Nowhere in the text did the authors allow sentiment or tradition to sway them in their views.

They revealed a sincerity of purpose which was laying a foundation for a modern public university, comparable to the better ones in the nation as a whole. In reading this report an uninformed person could have easily got the notion that it was a severe indictment of the Bryan administration, and even of earlier administrations of the nineteenth century. A more important implication was its indictment of the failures of the faculty then in service. Without saying so in words, the nature of the data used and the interpretations made of it revealed on the whole a weak corps of instructors. There is no doubt but that these direct conclusions raised hackles in the faculty, and many persons were quick to find fault with the report. There seems to be no dependable indication of how President Emeritus William Lowe Bryan reacted to it. As strong as was his pride in his long-time service, and as pronounced as was his ego, he no doubt saw in the report's basic recommendations attempts to accomplish most of the same objectives for which he had struggled so diligently. He seemed to have stuck to his resolve not to comment on university affairs unless asked to do so.

There was one area where criticism was pointed and well merited. The people of Indiana and their political officials had never seen in clear focus the role of a thoroughly adequate public university in their midst. Despite all of the criticism of Indiana University in the past no doubt the average Hoosier still regarded the institution as adequate. If so, and if he had been given the opportunity to read the self-study committee's penetrating report he would have been startled.

It was largely for this reason Ross Bartley advised strongly against publicizing any part of the report. He feared that its publication by the newspapers would prove disastrous indeed to the university. Copies of the report were given serial numbers, and faculty members were cautioned against letting them be seen by irresponsible persons. When discussions were ended in 1940 the reports were returned to the President's Office for safekeeping, and in time all but twenty-five sets were burned.

By December, 1939, the self-study materials were completed, and it was time for the faculty itself to decide whether or not it would accept the fundamental changes outlined by the committee. In presiding over the faculty sessions in which the committee report was discussed, President Herman B Wells prevented the debates from ending in futile and tedious arguments. He demonstrated capacity to secure free expression of the deliberative body without allowing the whole effort to be wasted away in boredom and trivial discussion. On January 11, 1940, he vacated the chair in favor of Dean Henry L. Smith and presented the faculty his views of the report. He recognized that public skepticism had tainted much of the professional view of the national educational effort. In fact, he observed that some bankers expressed the opinion that they could not remain in business if the servitors of their institutions were as bitterly critical of them as educators were of the schools. Skepticism was evident in the report under consideration. Wells acknowledged there were still skeletons in the university's educational closet, the most disturbing of which was its policy of universal admissions. Surely, he said, a faculty as ingenious as that in the university could devise some means of solving this age-old problem and of insuring admission of only qualified students.

Wells expressed reserved favor for the junior division concept largely on the basis that it offered a means by which a large body of basic knowledge could be transmitted to freshmen and sophomores. Beyond this the division promised students training in areas of learning which they might otherwise bypass if left to their individual choices. "I myself am appalled when I look at our curriculum," he said, "to realize that boys and girls are going through this university and coming out with a degree from Indiana without any acquaintance with history, the basic sciences, and other things we consider to be the inheritance of an educated man or woman. So I suspect that if we're going to create a product here that can be distinguished, that has any distinguishing characteristics from students who haven't had university training, that we've got to look at our curriculum and academic organization, as we've been doing here by the efforts of this survey committee and these discussions and as other institutions are doing." Perhaps few state university presidents were so bold in 1940 as to say, "I think that the thing for us to do is to try to do our job the best possible way and if we do our job the best possible way support will follow. I feel that as much as I can feel anything." There was not in this case the ancient defeatist refrain of "Where is the money coming from?"

There was no doubt that the self-study report was a blueprint for the future of a vastly different Indiana University. Even though many of the sections of the ballot were approved by slender margins, acceptance, however narrow, opened the way to future experimentation and readjustment. More than that, the general acceptance of a great majority of the sections was indeed a decision for future greatness for the university, because the institution could now, for the first time, set a new and more certain course to the future.

There were those professors who objected stoutly to the committee's report, in part or in whole, for diverse reasons. Inevitably, individual plans and ambitions were threatened if not trampled by it. Dean Fernandus Payne of the Graduate School, member of the presidential advisory committee and above all a trusted professor, said, "There is much in this report which smacks of the 'New Deal,' a panacea for reform by enlarging upon the sins of the past administration, the poor quality of our teachers and students, the inequities of the high salaries of heads of departments, and by appealing to the down-trodden to stand up for their rights and particularly to vote for reform or at least for change, even though they know very little about what change will do for the University." Dean Payne pleaded with his colleagues to go slowly in making decisions for or against the report. "No one," he said, "has a monopoly on wisdom. . . . As hinted earlier—I object to your open criticism of the past administration. It matters not what you think of it. This is neither the time nor place to make such a tirade. It is wholly unnecessary. Let the historian of the future make his comments. . . ." His view was supported by Dean Burton Dorr Myers.

Edmund S. Conklin, head of the Department of Psychology, thought the committee had accepted too freely the general outline of the University of Chicago's general college idea. He told his colleagues that he was informed that institution had abandoned the college because of its impracticality and the fact it handicapped students when they attempted to transfer to other universities. He did not oppose the proposal for a junior level series of courses in Indiana University, but he felt the system as outlined in the report was too elaborate and administratively complicated.

An anonymous critic, obviously a Yale graduate, was bitterly opposed to the whole report. He accused Briscoe and Wright of being weak-kneed and surrendering to the radical and aggressive Harper rather than arguing with him. He said Harper had refused to accompany his colleagues to the University of Chicago for a week of inspection of the general college. They had concluded from their observations that surveys in the natural sciences and humanities were fairly adequate, but that work in the social sciences was poor. He then explained that he and Robert Hutchins had been fellow students at Yale in Dean Cook's law classes, and when Hutchins later became dean of the Law School he discharged his old professor. Cook was the fount of Hutchins' ideas, and since he had dismissed Cook from the Yale faculty he had not since then had an idea of his own. All of his sophisticated talk (about educational reform) was simply a parroting of his professor's lectures passed off as original stuff. Ten years later, said the critic, Fowler Harper had discovered the teachings of Dean Cook and "had swallowed them hook, bait, and sinker," but the writer thought a couple of years in Roosevelt's Washington would serve to clear his colleague's mind. "But don't reorganize the University on the strength of such a compound," he warned. "A more enthusiastic, impracticable bunch would be hard to find. Hutchins [once] swore that tenure was an abomination for professors. Last year he swore it is essential to the integrity of higher learning in America. My guess is that soon he will forswear the Chicago Plan."

This was wonderful bombast, and no doubt there was more than an element of truth in it, but it threw dust in the eyes of faculty members who were asked to view Indiana University as a whole and not as an institution centering all its educational efforts on the lower division. Other and more temperate members of the faculty were shocked at the intellectually shabby image which Indiana students presented in the various categories of assessment. They suggested various remedies for correcting obvious weaknesses in this area. Professor Conklin said, "I have often wondered why our students did so little work. I never knew till I read the report. I'm not sure that the details which are being prepared here are practical, but I'm perfectly confident that the time is ripe for drastic action to make our students give up a large proportion of their excessive social activity and devote time to study." Professor Ralph Cleland of Botany expressed the hope that in some way or other the Commons could be closed in the afternoons. Wells responded that perhaps the faculty would have to look into the Book Nook and the Gables also. He then indicated that he might not feel entirely comfortable in taking such drastic steps because, as he said, "I had something of a record myself in that way at one time."

As indicated above, sections of the self-study report were accepted or rejected by a secret vote. The faculty had chosen by popular vote the 271 propositions which would appear on the ballot. Again on the advice of Ross Bartley, the taking of the vote and announcement of its results would be kept confidential for fear the newspaper press might give it damaging publicity. The report per se, aside from being highly revealing and informative, may not have been of completely vital importance. What was significant was the fact that the faculty and administrative staff of Indiana University reviewed with a high degree of thoroughness and thoughtfulness the entire program of the institution in a period of fundamental changes in American college and university education, and at the moment when the university could offer fairly generous post-retirement benefits. They did this just prior to the moment when the university would be called upon to render the utmost service to free men of the Western world again involved in a world war.

For the university the immediate result of the self-study was the aid it rendered in a realignment of the institution to recognize new educational opportunities and to meet the needs of the near future. The luck of time and history favored Indiana University in 1940. Its administration and a major portion of its faculty no doubt became aware of the currents in post-Depression America of educational reform and were emotionally and intellectually pre-pared to accept change with little loss of momentum or desecration of tradition. A distinctly advantageous sidelight was the revelation of the unfavorable intercollegiate competitive situation within In-diana itself in which the university had become boxed in prior to 1937, and 1940 was a propitious moment in which to rip away this longstanding inequality.

A more timid administration or more reluctant faculty might have allowed the time of decision to pass by default. In the spring of 1940, if not at many other moments in the university's future, the board of trustees' optimism was borne out in faculty and ad-ministrative decision. In a buoyant outpouring of oratory on March 22, 1938, when it announced the election of Herman B Wells to the presidency of the institution, the board proclaimed a hope and an ambition. "With great expectations," the trustees told the public, "we invite him to great responsibilities. His observed experience, practical wisdom, admirable temperament, and high ideals give conspicuous assurance of enduring achievement. With trust in him, we have confidence in the future."

Part of the fulfillment of the "great expectations" lay with the inauguration of the concrete decisions made in January, 1940, to restructure much of the university's operation and to undertake an educational experiment within the context of a long institutional history, and in the face of challenges presented in an uncertain social and political age which demanded high courage and imagination of Indiana University's leadership. If the institution was to escape mediocrity it had to act, and act quickly and imaginatively at this dramatic moment. Beyond this, the dream expressed in the institutional charters of 1816 and 1820 could now, and for the first time, be brought within reasonable expectation of realization. The school now had the times, the leadership, and the program in proper relationships to create a mature university.

[XVII]

Decision for Greatness

O<small>N THE EVENING</small> of May 7, 1962, at the banquet session of the National Association of State University Presidents, Herman B Wells of Indiana University delivered what amounted to a public valedictory of his presidency of twenty-five years. His speech was well padded with prefatory humor while he gave his fellow presidents some tongue-in-cheek rules for success. The first, he said, was "be lucky." At this point President Wells might well have added another maxim of equal value for presidents and universities alike—receive from history a gracious break in time, place, and coincidence.

For Indiana University in 1937, at the moment when Herman B Wells became acting president, both history and the conditions of the moment favored the ending of an era in American higher education. For thirty-five years, 1902 to 1937, William Lowe Bryan had clasped tight the scepter of power. In the end he had grown weary but was no less vigorously determined, as he would have said in Old Testament style, to "labor on the wall of Jerusalem." Weary though Bryan had grown over the years, he was reluctant to let go of the power. Bryan apparently had waited at least a year for the right time to retire. At last that time arrived in March, 1937. That he had reached the decision to leave the presidency well beforehand is borne out by hints in news stories during the spring of that year.

He was said to have had an intimate conversation with his bosom friend, an Indiana graduate, President Lotus Delta Coffman of Minnesota on their way to attend a meeting of the Carnegie Board of Trustees. He told Coffman he planned to retire, to which the latter replied, "Fine, you should have done so ten years ago." The seventy-six-year-old president supposedly was startled, but he also saw reason in the remark.

A man who had served an institution for so long a period and as such a dominant personal figure as Bryan had been would generate much folklore and considerable critical opposition. Much of his presidency was colored with excitement and drama and some of it with frustration and a sense of utter helplessness. The aged president as a personality presented several human paradoxes. It is doubtful that any other president of an American university had faced such a variety of problems, academic and public, as did William Lowe Bryan; any one of which could have defeated both man and university. The scourge of drouth, for instance, annually swept up the southern Indiana valleys like apocalyptic horsemen bearing the pangs of thirst, threatening fiery holocaust and total destruction, disease, and removal of the institution to another site. Building a medical school and maintaining an ever-expanding public service hospital, away from the Bloomington campus, administered by a professional staff, and located in the very heart-throb of medical and state politics in Indianapolis, was enough challenge for a single lifetime. There was the even greater problem of expanding the university itself from a single stem with the delicate off-shoot of a law school into a broadly based, professional institution.

World War I, with its accompanying social revolution, divided the periods of university history into two sharply distinct eras. Three biting depressions and periods of political reform and reaction in the nation and Indiana slowed, if they did not halt, state progress. The reactionary politics and developing pressure groups of postwar Indiana had indeed roiled the waters of public education, and at times they seemed to want to bend public educational institutions to the wills of little and selfish men. Even so insidious an influence as the Ku Klux Klan and its baneful leader D. C. Stephenson had threatened a barbaric invasion of the university in the postwar years. The fight for adequate financial support was a biannual exercise in frustration and disappointment. In the spring of 1937, Bryan said to Dean Wells of the Business School, "This is my thirty-fifth budget, and it is not reasonable for a man to still be alive after having made thirty-five budgets at Indiana University."

Maintaining the status and strength of a "separate" university itself in the Indiana system of higher education involved, if not perpetual anxiety, then a constant awareness that the balance among the state universities was indeed delicate. This balance was placed in constant peril by groups who wished to create a multiplicity of state colleges and thus spread even more thinly the meager resources of already inadequate finances. Repeatedly Bryan had journeyed to Indianapolis to prevail upon agrarian-oriented governors not to allow the planting of "too many grains of corn to the hill in fear of producing spindly stalks."

For thirty-five years William Lowe Bryan had personified Indiana University. One is constantly aware of this fact in reading documentary records of the institution. Awareness is made even more precise when one examines the university's administrative chart for early 1937. All lines on the diagram of institutional authority ran to the president's office; they came from departments, schools, the library, ground crews, university extension, social organizations, and even from the campus barbershops. To the professorial staff, presidential blessing was more rewarding even than that of trustees. Bryan ruled the empire of Indiana University, from business office to cafeteria cook, in the same way a lordly plantation master oversaw plow share, scythe, and sack. Below him professors raised hands in supplication, above him trustees took instruction and counsel. Thus when the end of his reign hove in sight on March 15, 1937, portals to a new world stood well ajar. As James W. Fesler had said in 1913, it would be difficult to imagine Indiana University without Bryan. Like trunk and branch the two had grown together as one, but now must be parted.

The manner in which President Bryan requested retirement, or "resigned" as he said, was characteristic of the man. Since 1885 the board of trustees had met either in the president's Maxwell Hall office or in a hotel room in Indianapolis. Perhaps, later, they met at times in rooms in the Student Building and subsequently in the Indiana Union. The president's office, said one trustee, had few virtues as a meeting place. Bryan's massive desk crowded the chamber, and the chairs were said not to be comfortable. The former trustees hinted that some decisions were made quickly and out of inspiration generated by lack of space and physical discomfort.

Trustees felt blessed relief when they moved in 1937 to their own spacious room in the new Bryan Administration Building. George Ball of Muncie was president of the board, and he felt that the new room ought to have much more elegant furniture than Indiana taxpayers should be asked to buy. He furnished an elegant board table and comfortable chairs to match. On March 15, President Ball, seated at the head of the table, was flanked by Albert Rabb and Judge Ora Leonard Wildermuth. President Bryan sat in his customary place at the foot of the table, and Judge John Hastings says that Bryan had given no previous hint of what was to happen. He went to the head of the table and delivered to Mr. Ball an envelope containing his "resignation." When Ball examined the note he choked up with emotion and asked Albert Rabb of Indianapolis to read it because he was too overcome to do so himself. Bryan asked to be retired at the board's earliest convenience. Judge Wildermuth moved acceptance of the request and proposed that the retiring president be given the title "President Emeritus" at his full salary of $12,750, and that he be allowed to remain in the president's house. Bryan accepted the board's proposal with one exception: he would take only $6,000 annually, leaving the remainder of his salary as a special fund to be spent in behalf of the university at the discretion of the trustees. Within an hour and a half the board was back in regular session discussing problems of the university, one of which was taking advantage of the so-called 45 percent grants from the federal government for physical expansion of the plant.

A story is told that soon after the newspapers announced Dr. Bryan's approaching emeritus status, he met an elderly lady friend who was profuse in congratulating him on his new honor. She said critically of the board that it should have granted him this honor a long time before. A more telling bit of folklore was that Bryan had waited until Paul McNutt's appointment as Commissioner to the Philippines was published in the press to announce his resignation. According to James Farley, in his published statement of his break with Franklin D. Roosevelt, there was truth in the fact that Roosevelt wanted to get McNutt out of the country and out of the way of the election of 1940. There seems to be plenty of evidence to indicate that Bryan and McNutt were the most cordial of friends, and nothing appears either in formal record or rumor, to indicate that Bryan disapproved of the governor.

Paul McNutt, of Franklin and Martinsville, had a long and

intimate association with Indiana University. First as a student, graduating in 1913, then as professor and Dean of the Law School, and later as Governor of Indiana. There is not the slightest doubt but what he wanted to be president of Indiana University at one stage of his career and that he had the support of powerful friends in this ambition. As the wheel of political fortune turned for him, however, neither history nor the times served this end. His local ambitions were overshadowed by a greater desire to be President of the United States.

Of far more tangible importance was the coincidence of change in Indiana University's personnel policy respecting retirement of aged professors and administrative officers. It was true that since 1919 the university had participated in the Carnegie retirement program, but this arrangement promised professors little more than a bare subsistence after they left the classroom. Because of the obvious fact that the old retirement plan was little short of being an invitation to many to end their lives in even less than dignified poverty, a move was begun in 1935 to seek a better system of changing status. A professorial committee made a study of retirement plans and reached the conclusion that the Teacher's Insurance Annuity plan was the most desirable. On March 6, 1937, the Indiana Senate approved the plan and appropriated $50,000 to finance it, and three days later the *Student* announced the House of Representatives had also approved the professors' recommendations. On March 16, 1937, President Bryan announced he would have for the board of trustees at its next meeting a full report on the Teacher's Insurance Annuity Association retirement program. He meant he would in fact be ready to recommend that Indiana University adopt it. True to his promise he produced a report and recommendation which the board accepted on May 18, 1937, and the new retirement system was to go into effect on the following first of July.

All persons who had reached seventy years of age before that date would be immediately subject to mandatory retirement, and all others would retire on July 1, following their seventieth anniversaries. The university agreed to pay 5 percent of the retirement fund, and the individual paid 5 percent. Besides, the institution would pay 2 percent of salaries earned before July 1, 1937, withholding only the sum it had paid into the Carnegie plan, thus assuring persons without accumulation of funds in the new plan much more substantial annuities.

Never in the history of the university had the way been opened for such drastic reorganization of its personnel. In the past men had remained members of the staff until they were no longer physically able to function and then "resigned." Such revered old soldiers as Elisha Ballantine, Richard Owen, and Theophilus Wylie had been forced to remain on the staff almost into their dotage. Bert John Vos asked for retirement in March, U. H. Smith retired in May, and Bryan in June. Adoption of the Teacher's Insurance Annuity plan of retirement resulted immediately in the withdrawal of Carl Wilhelm Ferdinand Osthaus, German; David Andrew Rothrock, Mathematics; David Myers Mottier, Botany; Joseph William Piercy, Journalism; Schuyler Colfax Geiger, Music; Allen Hendricks, Medical Librarian; and Mary Ethelda Roddy, Physical Education. Not since David Starr Jordan departed for Stanford with the heart core of the university faculty in tow had such a personnel vacuum come to exist. This was especially so since most of those retiring were deans, heads of departments, and the president. They all had long-time associations with the institution, and personally comprised much of its inner staff mechanism. Most had been present at the founding of the new schools and services.

Retirement of numerous elderly members of the faculty in the late 1930's involved many tangled strands of Indiana University history and emotions, and perhaps as many of fundamental institutional weaknesses. It was said that many over-age professors remained stubbornly in their positions well past the established age of academic retirement because President Bryan refused to retire. In fact some had confronted him with this fact. Of more vital concern, the university itself was locked in a vise of administrative and intellectual rigidity from which it could be freed only by drastic revision of its personnel contingent.

Tragically older staff members had, by conditions well beyond their personal control, focused their attention so thoroughly on traditional local problems of the university that many were oblivious to the impact of change which had occurred in the postwar and Depression ages. They did not understand that currents of state and national life had radically changed courses, and that worldwide social and intellectual concerns demanded more imaginative university administrative and faculty responses. No matter what individual reactions and responses to these changes may have been in Bloomington in 1937, these outside forces of revision were too strong to be stemmed. Bryan and his veteran colleagues, like Moses of old, had exhausted themselves in the valiant journey across the wide desert, and their labors had sapped them of the vitality and vision necessary to enter the fruitful plain which lay before Indiana University in the immediate future. William Lowe Bryan's name had long been synonymous with that of Indiana University, and any change in the latter tended to reflect one way or the other on the reputation of the former. Fortunately young Herman B Wells had established good rapport with President Bryan long before he was considered for the job of acting president.

Bryan was surely impressed by the banker's letters he received. Basically the two men were of radically different personalities and outlooks, but this fact seems never to have disrupted their father-son attachment. Bryan was at hand all times after 1937 to give such advice as Wells asked of him, but he repeated often that he did not volunteer advice. Wells, a master of human relationships, was careful never to allow his own actions to irritate the President Emeritus, and for almost two decades the two lived in Bloomington harmoniously.

Bryan's career was weighed in almost as many scales of judgment as there were individuals to adjudge it. Those who had served with him over a long period of years had a high regard for him, in fact they had a near worshipful, leader-follower attachment. Others were highly critical of Bryan because of his extremely patrician and puritanical views. He could be direct and stubborn when a member of the staff was in any way involved with alcohol and tobacco, and almost rivaled the New England theocrats as a strict Sabbatarian. He even sent his office messenger around to warn faculty members not to work in their offices on Sunday. Bryan's domestic life became a theme of campus gossip, possibly without many people knowing much about Mrs. Bryan. On several occasions the president was outspoken in the field of psychoanalysis, indicating his sensitivity about what may have been his wife's eccentricities. Certainly Charlotte Lowe Bryan wielded a tremendous personal influence over her husband.

Any objective and meaningful appraisal of William Lowe Bryan's connection with Indiana University must be made against two factual backgrounds. First, he had to wage a constant campaign with governors and legislators, not only to get financial support for the university, but to make himself a buffer against politicians and self-seekers who constantly tried to destroy the institution by financial attrition or to weaken its influence by creating competing colleges. On top of this the Indiana president had to be certain that he never allowed the university to get itself politically boxed in because of the competition with Purdue. This was a matter which required not only eternal vigilance but a keen insight into the Indiana political mind.

The second fact which must be remembered is that during his long administration Bryan served through at least four distinct eras in American higher learning. At the end of the first, in 1915, he told the annual meeting of the National Association of State Universities that phenomenal changes had taken place in the tenure of office of heads of educational institutions, and he labeled the job of president as among hazardous occupations. In a more extended statement he undertook to differentiate the functions of president and professor for his administrative colleagues by describing an experiment of his in 1915 in which he undertook to delegate some of the administrative responsibilities of his office to professors. Immediately they ran into difficulties in trying to organize the budget. There were other problems which they failed to solve because of their inability to comprehend the obligations of the university as a whole. In speaking of the presidency he said, "My purpose is not, however, to solicit compassion or favor for men who accept this hazard. I like to see a man make his fight and, when he fails, do so as a good soldier. What I wish to show is that taking the whole period of our history, the tenure of the president is uncertain and brief, and that if he is a tyrant he is a short-lived tyrant. Tyrant or not, he cannot, except in rare instances, maintain his place against the hostile sentiment of faculty, alumni, and other interested persons. I do not complain of this. I think it is right. Gladstone, even if in the right, cannot and should not rule England when the House is against him."

As a wartime president, Bryan at times seemed to throw calmness and reason to the wind and became an ardent supporter of the war effort, after he had been so ardent a disciple of peace in 1915. His hand was seen firmly guiding at least a dozen wartime projects, some of his own invention. So vigorous was he in his activities that the campus newspaper came close to crediting Bryan with proprietary interests in the struggle.

The post-World War I world with its rapidly unfolding events and changing human values presented many dilemmas to the Hoosier puritan. For instance, the dry crusade, which he supported so vigorously all his life failed to accomplish its objectives. In fact it aggravated some of the problems of the university, and greatly disturbed President Bryan's peace of mind. In a more subtle way the changing standards of social and moral behavior presented problems of an order he had never before conceived possible. Students had increased greatly in number, and the bases of their origin had shifted markedly so that Indiana University no longer catered to an overwhelming and somewhat amenable rural enrollment, nor were the problems or ambitions of its students those of agrarian people.

The old world of William Lowe Bryan had begun to disappear by the centennial year of the university in 1920. In that year the Bloomington *Telephone* reported that there had been ten presidents of Indiana University in 100 years.

> During President Bryan's administration the institution has gone forward by leaps and bounds and the future is bright with the promise of still greater progress. The attendance increased from 1,334 in 1902 to 4000 in 1920. The income has increased from $129,761.01 in 1902 to $999,077.86 in 1919, but the present amount is far too low. During the seventeen years of Dr. Bryan's administration [1902–1919] new schools, departments or courses have been established as follows: Graduate School, education, medicine, extension, journalism, comparative philology, anatomy, physiology, music, militarism, commerce, science, training school for nurses, Waterman Institute for Research, and combined courses in arts, law, and medicine, one of the best in the country.

The university had been admitted to membership in nearly all of the national and international academic organizations. The physical campus and the number of buildings had been expanded. These were the tangible results of his planning and his fights, and in 1937 these were still the monuments of his accomplishments.

In other ways the world of William Lowe Bryan underwent revolutionary changes in the early 1920's. In April, 1921, he and Mrs. Bryan led the grand procession in the Junior Prom. This seems to have been the first time the president acknowledged that dancing was an obsession in his institution. That fall, and on another front, he was left afoot when a ten-year-old child stole his faithful buggyhorse Bessie and rode her out of Bloomington. Sixteen months later the *Student* reported that a small iron ring imbedded in the concrete curbing in front of Maxwell Hall memorialized the passing of an era. The automobile had crowded the president and his horse off the campus driveways, and the Forest Place woods no longer could be used as Bessie's browsing ground. While changes were being wrought in presidential transportation about the campus, William Lowe Bryan was introduced to mass media communication, a science to which Professor Rolla Ray Ramsey and Indiana University had made such worthwhile contributions during World War I. On May 1, 1922, the president addressed Indiana alumni in a national broadcast, an event which was said to be the first time in the history of any university that a president had addressed so many graduates on a founder's day.

The last decade and a half of Bryan's presidency was one of national ferment, depression, and social and economic relocation. It took a daring and powerful personal thrust to make headway with the Indiana people and legislators in securing support for a public university. Indiana University was deeply involved in the Depression, despite the fact it never suffered the threat of bankruptcy which confronted so many schools. In this respect Bryan and U. H. Smith had demonstrated a rural Indiana shrewdness in husbanding the university's resources. There were, however, severely limited resources to support plans for the future, and for the construction of vitally needed new buildings. The building of even one was considered a supreme triumph. On February 18 and 19, 1937, the new William Lowe Bryan Administration Building was dedicated, and the public was invited to inspect it. Bryan Building was indeed a palatial hall with spacious offices, and made the aging Maxwell Hall and its "two-by-four offices" appear a shabby forebear indeed.

In many respects the opening of Bryan Hall just on the eve of William Lowe Bryan's retirement was symbolic indeed of the changes which were to come in the immediate future. Those persons who recited on several occasions at the end of Bryan's administration the man's accomplishments did so in terms of the schools and departments he developed. The maturing of these was a challenge for the future. Before this could be done the institution had to determine precisely where it stood in regard to its future needs. To make such a thorough inventory involved of course the revelation of many institutional weaknesses, and in some cases failures. This also involved inevitable criticism of the Bryan administration.

Some critics were quick to say that the aging president had been a phenomenal success in the academic and spiritual guidance of the institution, but he had demonstrated a decided weakness in the field of administration, a fact they could document on an administrative chart which portrayed the direct line of command from the lowliest campus position directly to the president's office. Demonstrably Bryan was not a man who could delegate authority with grace. W. D. Gatch said at Bryan's retirement dinner:

> That the public regards President Bryan as the greatest asset of the University is no cause for wonder, when we consider the length and amazing success of his administration. So great has been his prestige, and so uniformly sound his policies that he has been able to govern the University for thirty-five years without noteworthy opposition by students, alumni, faculty, or successive boards of trustees. I doubt that any board of trustees has ever failed to confirm a single major recommendation he has made to them. One of his great achievements has been the creation of the School of Medicine. He secured it for the University almost single-handed. He, also, more than anyone else built it up. His influence has permeated the entire educational system of the state—I may add the entire life of the state.

Bishop Frederick D. Leete at the Conference of the Methodist Episcopal Church said, "Indiana citizens and members of the church should thank God for W. L. Bryan, President of Indiana University, because he appreciates the importance of Christian ideals in education. I should like to see him President of the United States. The country needs another Indiana President."

Bryan may have delayed his retirement date too long, and no doubt would have retired earlier had he not been deterred from doing so by an intensely aggravating rift which occurred over the university's insurance policies, a thing which involved the institution in an unpleasant incident with J. W. Fesler of the board of trustees. Bryan clearly sensed the fact that the demands now being made on modern American state universities had to be served by younger and more daring men who could comprehend first the gauge of the times and who had the courage and audacity to meet challenges in a troubled world. Bryan perhaps realized the certainty that public education had an indispensable social and political mission to perform and he was no longer capable of comprehending the challenge. In closing the ledger on Bryan on July 1, 1937, one finds the assets of his career far exceeded the liabilities, and his personal eccentricities were negligible when compared with his fight to make his institution a university instead of a normal school. He himself recognized he was a man of a season, and that the season of his usefulness had drawn to a close in a moment of great change and seeking for new directions in national as well as world affairs. Without ever saying so, he no doubt was little surprised at the institutional profile revealed in the future self-study committee's comparative statistics. For thirty-five years William Lowe Bryan had spoken to trustees and legislators in the same revealing statistical language. As a matter of fact he himself had come to the presidency after having made a searching statistical study of Indiana University. He could not with consistency have resented the new study, and Bryan had the virtue of being a consistent man.

William Lowe Bryan was among the last American puritans to become lost in the jungle of social confusion if not a certain amount of gothic barbarism. He was a moral perfectionist who followed the admonitions of David Starr Jordan when the latter departed Bloomington for the west, "You may carve the words, if you like, somewhere upon the walls of the University. You may engrave them and forget them. But if passion for what is highest pierces through your decisions, and controls what you do then the Glory of the Divine Perfection shall abide in this place." Approach to a form of academic perfection for Indiana University was to come under conditions and in forms less divine than Bryan had in mind. Nevertheless, clothed no less in scholarly ambition and sensitivity, the university was to begin deep soundings to locate its new channel.

Thus it was a major coincidence in 1937 that there was the return of some degree of stability and promise of the American economic system. The great Depression was retreating into a period of cautious and modest prosperity. This was the strategic moment in which Indiana University had to make its advance onto a new plane of activity, if it ever hoped to do so. Confronted with rising all-university enrollment—10,591, in 1936–37—there was desperate need for classrooms, student housing, and service facilities of all kinds. The university had to find a way to break the old parity formula for the three Indiana institutions of higher learning established by the legislature in 1895. This permitted the three state colleges to share in a special millage tax on a basis of equality regardless of particular needs. In 1925 a slight change was made in the parity formula by which Indiana, Purdue, and the state teachers colleges were asked to submit general budgets in lieu of the expectancy of income from millage collections. At its next session, however, the legislature enacted the Chamberlain-Harris-Claycombe-Pittenger Bill which provided a two-cent levy on each $100 for ten years, and provided a $10,000,000 building fund for the four state colleges. Indiana and Purdue would receive $350,000 annually from this source. Purdue was in a more advantageous position than the other three institutions because it received capital outlay and operating funds from the federal government in connection with its various agriculture services.

The 45 percent matching plan of the federal government under terms of the Public Works Administration and the Works Progress Administration provided the university with necessary extra funds to enlarge its physical plant at this strategic moment. Present campus buildings give testament to this fact in the numerous plaques which bear WPA and PWA inscriptions. Quickly, agents of the university became masterful in the procurement of federal funds. Such monuments as Bryan and Woodburn Halls, the Memorial Union extension, some dormitories, the Music Building, and the university Auditorium are examples of this new era of construction. There are some individuals who more than half seriously attribute Indiana Uuniversity's successful advance to the future after 1940 to the support of these public funds.

There was more, however, to this program than mere physical expansion. The university had now an opportunity to build so solidly and extensively on the Bloomington campus that hopefully the yokes of parity and threats of removal would be removed forever. In the minds of officials and trustees it would be difficult indeed for the people of Indiana in the future either to walk away and leave a magnificient physical plant worth hundreds of millions of dollars in Bloomington, or to fail to maintain their investment properly. At the same time, necessary improvements could be made in the physical plant itself to accommodate the new university program. The internal academic structure created by Bryan in the form of schools and colleges could now be nurtured and matured. For the first time there was hope that a greatly extended scope of operation, administered by a younger staff trained in modern graduate schools, could take over where the old guard left off, and with far fewer inhibitions than had curbed actions of their predecessors. For instance, an end could be brought to inbreeding and nepotism. The quality of the new professorial staff could be substantially raised by careful employment procedures and improvement of conditions under which these scholars would be asked to function.

These were challenges which called for the energies, courage, and imagination of youth attuned to a revolutionary age in American education. According to Judge John Hastings (Trustee from 1936–1959), Bryan saw this in clear perspective. By mid-summer, 1936, a sense of change of administration at Indiana University was in the air. At first it took the form of rumor and town gossip. In October, just before the gubernatorial election, H. H. Evans of Greenfield sent up a bitterly partisan cry of despair when he declared that Governor Paul McNutt controlled the board of trustees and would have himself appointed president so he could live in the best house in Indiana and support his governor's mansion lifestyle on the $12,750 salary. The only way he could be kept from doing so, said this critic, was to elect Raymond Springer, Republican, governor in November.

A source closer to home, the Bloomington *Telephone*, said when James W. Fesler had resigned as president of the board of trustees on March 20, 1936, McNutt would become president of the university. Fesler's resignation, it was said, gave the governor a majority vote on the board. The paper even polled individual trustees for its readers and predicted that if the former dean of the Law School were made president, he would introduce a new regime in which all officials of the institution over sixty-five years of age would be replaced by younger men. The *Telephone* based its reasoning on the fact that the past session of the legislature was friendly to the university's retirement proposal; the plan was sanctioned even in the face of Purdue alumni opposition because the latter feared their institution would lose by enforced retirement the services of President E. C. Elliott.

Rumor had it that the only thing which would keep McNutt away from Bloomington would be appointment to the Roosevelt Cabinet, either as Attorney General of the United States or Secretary of War. From this point on every move that Bryan or any of the trustees made was watched with the penetration of a hawk. If Bryan went outside the state his actions were interpreted as leading to a secret rendezvous with trustees or McNutt supporters. It was even said that he and two or three other university administrators had met on the pretense of a secret budget session in an Indianapolis hotel with McNutt but rather to discuss the university presidency.

Gossip was shattered, if not cut short, by word in February, 1937, that Roosevelt had appointed McNutt to be Commissioner of the Philippines. The governor accepted this post saying he did not believe it would hamper his chances of being nominated as Democratic candidate for the presidency of the United States in 1940. His political spokesman and mentor, Frank McHale, however, was said to favor the university appointment because he believed the governor's absence from the country would injure his prospects of presidential nomination. Even the press and the political speculators so interpreted Roosevelt's intent. William Lowe Bryan's wry comment was, "Taft was once Commissioner of the Philippines and came back to become Secretary of War, President of the United States, and Chief Justice of the United States Supreme Court."

Newspaper second-guessers in Indiana thought the Philippines appointment would be for one year only, and then McNutt would be made president of the university. By March, 1937, however, the rumor-mongers were making other inspired nominations which included Glenn Frank of Wisconsin, Lotus Delta Coffman of Minnesota, Ernest L. Lindley of Kansas, and Walter A. Jessup of the Carnegie Foundation. These may have been no more than names of men whom the trustees consulted about a likely presidential candidate. During the next twelve months the state press had a field day, not only appointing Bryan's successor, but subsequently Acting President Wells' successor. Again the movement of board members was watched with certainty that, if they did more than go from their houses to their offices, they were up to something.

In an interview in Chicago in November, 1970, with Mrs. Dorothy Collins and the author, Judge John Simpson Hastings, Senior United States Circuit Judge on the United States Court of Appeals for the Seventh District and a member of the board of trustees in 1937 said unequivocally that President Bryan recommended Dean Herman B Wells of the Business School to be his successor. For some reason which remains unexplained, the trustees waited from March 15 to June 10, 1937, to select a temporary successor to President Bryan. On the latter date President Bryan asked to be retired on June 30, instead of in December as he had indicated at some time after March 15. Late at night on the latter date, board vice president Judge Ora Leonard Wildermuth called by telephone Herman B Wells at the latter's Brown County cottage and invited him to accept appointment as acting president until a permanent president could be employed. Wells protested that there were more likely candidates for the permanent position who should be considered for the acting office, and besides, he liked his job as Dean of the Business School, he thought he had a chance of being successful in it, and foresaw no future in the presidency. Judge Wildermuth replied that the trustees were not yet ready to make a choice among the other men but knew that they did not wish Wells to be permanent president and that was the reason they wanted him to accept the interim appointment. Wells agreed on condition that he would not be considered for permanent appointment and that his tenure as acting president would be brief. The trustees then appointed an advisory committee of four members to serve with the young acting president. These were Dean Fernandus Payne of the Graduate School; Dean Henry Lester Smith of the School of Education; Ward Gray Biddle, Bursar; and William Albert Alexander, Librarian.

The appointment of Wells was a major act performed in proper historical timing. To the uninformed (and even to some people on the campus), the university trustees had brought to the presidency a campus unknown. One wonders how the public arrived at this conclusion in the first place when it was soon evident that William Lowe Bryan earlier placed the hand of fatherly blessing upon his young successor. To the myth-makers the acting president had at some unspecified time roared around the campus cloaked in a coonskin coat and at the wheel of a Stutz Bearcat automobile, neither of which he has said he owned nor paraded. Another strand of the myth was that Dean Wells was a stand-in for Commissioner Paul McNutt until the latter could pursue the will-o'-the-wisp of political fortune to its point of evaporation. Board members denied, and still deny, stoutly that this latter rumor had the slightest element of substance. Wells himself said he wanted to get back at the earliest possible moment to the deanship of the School of Business, thus reiterating his agreement with Judge Wildermuth that he would only be acting president.

It perhaps is not surprising that so much myth grew about this extroverted man, even before he reached the president's office in the new Bryan Hall. No doubt he was a lively figure about the campus as both student and bank economist. Quite to the contrary of the raccoon-Stutz Bearcat tradition, however, Wells had a Hoosier family background as proper as a well-executed cashier's check. Born in the village of Jamestown on June 7, 1902, as a blood son of the soil and in the central rural Indiana tradition, he spent his youth in conformity to local custom. His father, Joseph Granville Wells, a student for a time in the state normals at Danville and Terre Haute, had taught school but left that profession to become vice president of the Jamestown Citizens Bank and an official in a larger Lebanon bank. Herman B Wells grew up in his father's banks, serving in all sorts of capacities from standing around in the way as an observant and inquisitive child to serving as clerk and assistant cashier. His youthful experience in a small village-farmer bank, and in the bank at Lebanon, was as much a part of his family heritage as planting corn was to sons of neighboring farmers. This early experience gave him insight into both human nature and the foibles and frustrations of rural people. In the process he developed a generous amount of sentimentality for their way of life and a sensitive understanding of their needs. Except for his parents' school teaching experiences there was little or no real academic influence which bore directly upon young Wells' life during his formative years, except, from his babyhood on, his parents were determined he would attend college.

Wells went away to the University of Illinois for his freshman year, but in 1921 as a sophomore came to Indiana University where he took a Bachelor of Science degree in 1924, and a Master of Arts in economics in 1927. He then went on for a year of graduate work in business administration in the University of Wisconsin. Clearly, he was destined to be a banker or a businessman. Out of college, he served for a time as a specialist with the Indiana Bankers Association and, under the auspices of the American Institute of Banking, taught evening classes in Indianapolis in banking procedures for clerks and junior bank officers. He was appointed an instructor in economics in Indiana University in 1930, and between that date and 1935, he held succeeding positions as assistant professor of economics, Secretary and Research Director of the Study Commission for Indiana Financial Institutions, and in 1933 he became head of the newly created Division of Research and Statistics, Secretary of the Indiana Commission for Financial Institutions, and Supervisor of the Indiana Division of Banks and Trust Companies and Financial Institutions. In May, 1935, President Bryan appointed him Dean of the School of Business Administration to succeed William A. Rawles. He was also named Professor of Business Administration.

The 1930's were years of the crucible for American bankers and businessmen, and especially for those in Indiana. Financial wreckage and ruin of the Depression reshaped business procedures and human destiny in almost every town and village. Men who had followed what they had believed all their lives to be sound business policies now found that they were incapable of dealing with problems of economic crisis inside a changing social and political order. Reorganization, reappraisal of methods and approaches, reconsideration of the statutory structure of operational procedures were challenges to be met if Indiana banking was to function aggressively in the future.

Two segments of the Indiana public especially stood in need of direct relief from traditional financial excesses and liabilities. First, depositors needed assurances that a generous portion of their money would be given legal security. Second, borrowers who depended upon high interest rate institutions for cash had to be protected against excesses. Out of the Division of Research and Statistics, which Wells directed from his office in the basement of the Indiana University Library, came a form of state depository insurance guarantee formula which had a direct bearing upon the content of the Federal Insurance Deposit Banking Act. Frank McHale, in a letter to the author, credits Wells with having had a decisive hand in the formulation of this key banking legislation at both state and national levels. In the high interest or installment credit area, the pioneer "Truth in Lending" law was an outgrowth of Wells' Division of Research and Statistics studies. What was accomplished in this area was the formulation of regulatory legislation which would stand testing in the courts. This was successfully accomplished, and the "log jam" was broken in the field of small and installment loans. This led to the enactment of the subsequent "Truth in Lending" law.

Nowhere was Wells' work in the field of banking more force-fully documented than in a series of letters from bankers to President Bryan in 1935, with regard to the appointment of a successor to Dean William A. Rawles. Vernon L. Sailor, Supervising Examiner, 6th Federal Deposit Insurance District, St. Louis, Missouri, wrote that while he was examiner for the Sixth Federal Deposit Insurance area he had to deal with several delicate problems. "Mr. Wells showed a very comprehensive grasp of the entire banking situation in Indiana and was most versatile in dealing with difficult cases. I also had an opportunity to observe the results of the excellent work which he and his associates in the Banking Department had done during the crucial period following the bank moratorium in 1933. His knowledge of sound economic principles and his previous wide experience in banking and educational work qualified him to cope with a big problem in a most constructive manner."

In the same vein, R. L. Hopkins of the Federal Deposit Insurance Corporation of Madison, Wisconsin, wrote, "During the greater part of 1934, I was in the Washington office of the Federal Deposit Insurance Corporation in the capacity of Assistant to the Board of Directors. During this period I had charge of the reorganization of the state banks in the western part of the United States, which includes the State of Indiana, as well as other duties which gave me an intimate incite [sic] of the work in the State of Indiana and personal contact with Mr. Wells. . . . It is my opinion that the work in the state of Indiana with respect to rehabilitation of the banks has been one of the outstanding instances of the whole country and the improvement in the banking situation in your state has been very gratifying indeed. Mr. Wells . . . deserves a great deal of credit for the highly improved condition of the banks in Indiana."

With this extensive practical business background, especially in the sophisticated area of banking, few public university administrators have ever been so well prepared to manage institutional fiscal affairs with great professional certainty. Of comparable importance, the gregarious Wells had come to know people all over Indiana, many of whom he met under adverse, if not excruciating, conditions of economic failure and panic. Some of their names were burned into his memory by these grim conditions, others were friendly associations. He easily surpassed David Starr Jordan's boast that he had been in every county in the state and had become acquainted with large numbers of people. As a Banking Commission official he came to know politicians of every stripe and saw how they worked and how they viewed public issues. His most important lesson perhaps was to know how far legislators could be coerced, without their becoming resistant and rebellious, and to get a keen firsthand insight into the workings of the Indiana political mind.

This was the man, who at 10:17 A.M., March 22, 1938, became President of Indiana University, having been nominated to that position by Judge John S. Hastings of Washington, Indiana. Judge Hastings explained in 1970 that he was prompted to do so by the fact that he felt the acting president had exceeded all of the trustees' expectations during his interim year. "I was convinced he would stay on the job," said Judge Hastings. "I was moved to vote for him . . . because one of these outstanding educators [university presidents whom the trustees consulted] in answer to my question, which was whether we should take the man who had a great outstanding reputation as a scholar or as an administrator, or whether we should risk taking some one like Herman Wells . . . who yet had neither reputation. The answer given me was this, and I never forgot it: 'Given the choice, take the man who hasn't yet made his reputation, and let him make his reputation building Indiana University.' " Judge Hastings was told such a man would develop his own reputation in building a reputable university, and "I was convinced," he said, Wells "had the potential that I personally was willing to gamble on. If we won, we would win big. That's the way I finally rationalized my own thinking."

Paul Feltus, another trustee, told reporters on March 22, 1938, "I believe him [Wells] to be the best selection which could be made, and I say this after having been a member of the committee on the Board which interviewed many possibilities, and had advice from men high in educational circles."

Seven members of the board of trustees that March morning gambled on Judge Hastings' presidential nominee, and the eighth, William Albert Kunkel, Jr., was on vacation in Florida but sent a telegram saying if he were present his vote would also be for Herman B Wells. While the trustees deliberated in their quarter-hour executive session, their minutes indicate that the acting president awaited their verdict, during part of the time anyway, with President Emeritus William Lowe Bryan.

By noon the president's office in Bryan Hall overflowed with telegrams of congratulation and flowers as the eleventh president outlined for reporters his sense of the responsibilities which confronted him. This was in fact the groom, after a year of trial marriage, explaining his ambitions on this his wedding day to the university. The Bloomington *Telephone* reminded Wells that day that a basic problem continued to be his search for a competent staff to fill the vacancies created by the new retirement system and to make retirement as palatable and humane as possible for those old soldiers who had served so long. The aged professors had labored, said the paper, under terms of tenure based upon ordinary life expectancy, and emotionally their lives had become intertwined with the routine of the university itself. Several of them resisted summary retirement and in some instances individuals were pathetic in their pleas to be allowed to contiune in active service. Perhaps no document in the University Archives reveals more clearly the velvet and the iron of the new president than does that relating to over-age staff members. In this memorandum Wells reviewed with a banker's candor the background and condition of each professor involved, and in most cases offered a charitable face-saving way for them to adjust to their new status. At the same time the president made clear that the rules of the national retirement plan would be observed to the letter.

No doubt as flowers and telegrams poured into his office, and Wells told trustees, reporters, and the public he appreciated the extent of his new responsibilities, he also had in the back of his mind the discouraging academic image of Indiana University which was already emerging in the preliminary reports of the self-study committee. These, not the eloquent words of well-wishing friends and the judgments of reporters, spelled out in cold, objective terms the realities of the job confronting the young president.

Still three months inside his thirty-fifth year, Herman B Wells became the youngest president of a major state university in the land. His youthful appearance even seemed to reduce further his chronological age. His joviality and obvious shrewdness caught the immediate attention of state and national press. His name, almost overnight, became the most publicized of any in Indiana University history except David Starr Jordan and Paul Vories McNutt. The election of Wells, however, had no connection with publicity given Paul McNutt. Perhaps it is within the realm of fact that, had the governor pursued his original ambition to be president of the institution, and had he foregone all other ambitions, he might have been selected. On the other hand, the trustees gave every indication of having carried on an extensive and conscientious search for a new president, giving no heed to Indiana or national politics.

Time Magazine told the nation on April 4, 1938, in a well-nigh factless story that the Indiana board of trustees had selected a "gourmet president of Indiana University." In its free-swinging vapid style the magazine repeated the old street rumor that the trustees had waited a year for Paul Vories McNutt to accept the university presidency, but McNutt was in search of the best road to the presidency of the nation. Ten days before, said *Time*, he had turned the trustees down, and "back he flew to the Philippines to keep in actual touch with politics." In an extremely personal manner the Luce publication gave about as erroneous a picture of the new president as could be imagined.

Time to the contrary, these more dependable facts seem clear; Herman B Wells may have borne the title "Acting President," but he never really cast himself in that role. Clearly, he acted like a president from the start. The challenges of the university were too clear at the outset for an aggressive, imaginative man to be content to slow down its momentum and to allow the institution to mark precious time waiting for the trustees' final decision about the presidency. As acting president Wells had an unusual opportunity to set Indiana University onto a new plane of operation without having to make sharp or wounding breaks with the past. The new retirement system removed men from several key posts in administrative and instructional areas with the grace and dignity of making them emeriti, rather than by fiat of trustees' action.

The elevation of Herman B Wells to the presidency of Indiana University in 1938 brought to office a vigorous young man who was closely attuned to the needs of the times. His intimate associations with Indiana banking reform, plus his brief term as Dean of the Business School, gave him a good background to lead the university into a new academic age. He nevertheless came into office on the heels of a strong personality who had sat in the president's chair for thirty-five years. Bryan had personally shaped the university, and it was this structure that Wells had to redesign and expand into a mature institution.

Bibliography

INDIANA UNIVERSITY
CORRESPONDENCE, MANUSCRIPTS, AND PAPERS

Benns, F. Lee, Correspondence and papers, Indiana University Archives.
Bryan, William Lowe, to Edwin Corr, Oct. 3, 1904; also to local stone companies, Oct. 10, 1904.
———, to John H. Edwards, Joseph Swain, Vernon Carter, and the State Auditor, April 10–April 18, 1908.
———, to J. W. Fesler and Joseph H. Shea, Jan. 7–April 8, 1908.
———, to Stith Thompson, July 23, 1921–May 3, 1937.
Eigenmann, Carl, Correspondence, 1914–1925.
Faculty Personnel Records, 1830–1940. (This looseleaf file comprises a curriculum vitae of former faculty members describing their services both in Indiana University and elsewhere.)
Harding, Samuel Bannister, Manuscript file on divorce case. Includes letters from William Lowe Bryan, Samuel Bannister Harding, and H. M. Hudelson.
Hastings, John S., Correspondence File, Sept. 23, 1937–June 25, 1940.
Indiana University, Correspondence File, 1900–1940. (This file includes looseleaf incoming and outgoing correspondence.)
———, Letter Books, 1900–1938. (This file is made up exclusively of outgoing letters and memoranda.)
———, Newspaper clipping file, July, 1938–January, 1940, Indiana University Archives.
McNutt, Paul Vories, Papers, 1932–1938, Lilly Library, Indiana University.
Self-Survey Committee, Correspondence and Papers, 1938–1940, Indiana University Archives.
Soupart, A., to William Lowe Bryan, May 17–Nov. 15, 1904.
Wells, Herman B, Speech File, 1935–June, 1962, 23 vols.
———, to Stith Thompson, July 20, 1937–May 17, 1955. (In the possession of Stith Thompson, Bloomington.)
Wildermuth, Ora L., Correspondence File, Oct. 17, 1934–Sept. 16, 1935.

Indiana University
Official Minutes and Presidential Reports

Board of Trustees, Minutes, November 4, 1897–June, 1940, 11 vols.
———, Minutes of the Executive Committee, November 5, 1921–July, 1940, 7 vols.
Faculty Minutes, September, 1877–May, 1940, 6 vols.
President's Annual Report, 1900–1940, 40 vols.
Sigma Xi, Minute Book, 1904.

Indiana University Official Memoranda

Biddle, Ward G., Conversation, May 3, 1935.
———, on Public Works Administration Grants, May 5, 1935.
Bryan, William Lowe, to, on federal grants, July 18, 1935.
Bryan, William Lowe, general letter to faculty and former faculty, December 4, 1934.
———, and Prof. J. E. Moffatt, conversation, April 24, 1935.
Committee from the Medical College of Indiana to the Indiana University and Purdue University Boards of Trustees, confidential memorandum, February 24, 1904. This concerned a statement of the position of the Indianapolis doctors on the resolution of the Medical College issue. Indiana State Library, Manuscript Division.
Gavit, Dean Bernard C., and William Lowe Bryan, conversation, May 3, 1935.
National Youth Administration, on, Wells File, July 11, 1935.
Rawles, Dean W. A., and William Lowe Bryan, conversations May 3, 1935, and May 7, 1935.
Robinson, Prof. J. J., memorandum for, on federal grants, September 20, 1935.

Indiana University Official Publications

Alumni Magazine, 1938–1940, 2 vols.
Alumni News-Letter, vols. 1–38, January, 1913–February, 1940.
Alumni Quarterly, Bloomington, 1914–1940, 26 vols.
The Arbutus, Indiana University Yearbook, Bloomington, 1900–1940, 40 vols.
Bulletin (Catalogue number), 1900–1940, 40 vols.
Newsletter, 1937.
Official Handbook: Paul V. McNutt Quadrangle, 1968–69, Bloomington, 1969.
Self-Survey Committee, Report to the Indiana University Board of Trustees, two parts, Bloomington, 1939.

INTERVIEWS

Allen, Ross. March 21, 1970.
Allen, Wad. January 18, 1973.
Barnhart, Dean, and Gill, George E. Spring, 1970. By Kemp Harshman, Joseph Kosarko, and Thomas D. Clark.
Blough, Earl. May 11, 1971.
Bradfield, Joseph L. March 27, 1969.
Byrnes, Robert F. December 20, 1968.
Chamness, Ivy Leone. January 24, 1969.
Clevenger, Zora. November 24, 1969.
Costas, Peter.
Davidson, S. Frank. January 1, 1969.
Day, Harry G., with Frank Mathers. October 25, 1972.
Fraenkel, Peter. July 30, 1970.
Franklin, Joseph A. September 29, 1969.
Hastings, John S. November 17, 1970. By Thomas D. Clark and Dorothy Collins.
Kinsey, Mrs. Alfred C. [Clara McMillan]. February 17, 1969.
Kohlmeier, Mrs. Albert. November 11, 1968.
Lundin, Leonard. October 10, 1972.
Mathers, Frank. October 25, 1972.
McNutt, Ruth J. March 27, 1969.
Nelson, Alice. April 28, 1969. By Thomas D. Clark and Victoria Cuffel.
Norvelle, Lee. February 19, March 6, 1970.
Payne, Fernandus. October 8, 12, 15, November 2, 1968. By Thomas D Clark and Oscar O. Winther.
Prickett, Alva Leroy. October 24, 1968.
Shrock, Robert. April 13, 1972.
Snow, Wilbert. May 2, 1970.
Solitt, Robert V. June 23, 1971.
Stahr, Elvis J. November 5, December 12, 1968.
Stempel, John. April, 1970. By Thomas D. Clark and Barbara Benson.
Sulzer, Elmer G. December 18, 1968.
Thompson, Stith. November 10, 1968. By Oscar O. Winther and Thomas D. Clark.
Thornbury, William D. May 21, 1969.
Von Tress, Edward. November 24, 1969 and December 12, 1972.
Wallace, Leon. May 2, 1969.
Warren, Mrs. Winifred Merrill. May 27, 1969.
Weatherwax, Paul. March 5, 1969.
Wells, Herman B. January 25, 1968, March 6, 10, 1971.

NEWSPAPERS

Bloomington (Ind.) *Telephone*, 1898–1913.
Bloomington (Ind.) *Daily Telephone*, 1914–1943.

Bloomington (Ind.) *World*, 1900–1941.
Bloomington (Ind.) *Evening World*, 1931–1943.
Indiana *Daily Student*, 1900–1940.
Indianapolis (Ind.) *News*, 1897–1940.
Indianapolis (Ind.) *Star*, 1900–1940.
The Lafayette (Ind.) *Daily Courier*, 1905–1908.
The Lafayette (Ind.) *Journal-Courier*, 1947.
The Lafayette (Ind.) *Morning Journal*, 1907–1908
Purdue (University) *Exponent*, 1903–1910.

UNPUBLISHED THESES AND PAPERS

Cumings, Edgar Roscoe, Autobiography, July 19, 1937. Prepared as an extensive communication with Robert R. Shrock, Lexington, Mass., 1957.
Deputy, Manfred Wolfe, "The Philosophical Ideas and Related Achievements of William Lowe Bryan," Doctoral thesis, Indiana University, posthumously, 1947.
Neff, Robert R., "The Early Career and Governorship of Paul V. McNutt," Doctoral thesis, Indiana University, 1963.
Shamon, Marvin, "The Traditions of Indiana University," Unpublished paper, ca. 1945, Indiana University Library.

GOVERNMENT PUBLICATIONS

Financial and Statistical Studies of Indiana University, Purdue University, and Indiana State Normal, General Education Board, 1922.
Report of a Survey of the State Institutions of Higher Learning in Indiana Made by a Commission Composed of Charles H. Judd, John A. H. Keith, Frank L. McVey, George A. Works, Floyd W. Reeves, Under the Authority of Governor Ed Jackson, Indianapolis, 1926.
Reynolds, Clifford, comp., *Biographical Directory of the American Congress, 1774–1961*, Washington, D.C., 1961.
State of Indiana, *Code of 1971*, Titles 19–21, Article 5, Indianapolis, 1971.
——, *Journal of the House of Representatives*, regular session, 1905, vol. 1, 1907, Indianapolis, 1905, 1907.
——, *Journal of the Senate During the Sixty-Fourth and Sixty-Fifth Sessions of the General Assembly*, regular sessions, 1905, 1907, Indianapolis, 1905, 1907.

ARTICLES

Blatchley, W. S., "A Century of Geology in Indiana," *Proceedings of the Indiana Academy of Science*, 1916, vol. 32, quarterly 157, copy 3, pp. 96–110, 115–124, 148.
"Gourmet and President," *Time*, April 4, 1938, vol. 31, p. 50.
"Indiana University: *Life* Takes a Farewell Look at Doomed Campus Folkways," *Life*, November 23, 1942, vol. 12, pp. 90–96.

Johnson, Alva, "I Intend to Be President," *Saturday Evening Post*, March 16, 1940, vol. 202, pp. 20–21.

"Letters to the Editor," *Life*, December 14, 1942, vol. 12, pp. 4–6.

Shrock, Robert R., "Memorial to Edgar Roscoe Cumings, 1874–1967," *Proceedings Volume, Geological Society of America, 1967*, pp. 177–183.

———, "Memorial to Clyde Arnett Malott," *Proceedings Volume, Geological Society of America, 1950*, pp. 105–110.

"Speaking of Pictures. . . . With These *Life* Makes Its Apologies for an Injustice Done to Indiana University," *Life*, February 1, 1943, vol. 13, pp. 12–15.

BOOKS

Akeley, Lewis, *This Is What We Had in Mind, An Eye-Witness Account of the Formative Years of the University of South Dakota*, Vermillion, S. D., 1959.

Barzun, Jacques, *The American University, How It Runs, Where It Is Going*, New York, 1968.

Beck, Frank O., *Some Aspects of Race at Indiana University, My Alma Mater*, Bloomington, 1959.

Best, John Hardin, and Sidwell, Robert T., eds., *The American Legacy of Learning, Readings in Higher Education*, Philadelphia, 1967.

Blake, George I., *Paul V. McNutt: Portrait of a Hoosier Statesman*, Indianapolis, 1966.

Blakey, George T., *Historians on the Homefront: Propagandists for the Great War*, Lexington, Ky., 1970.

Bishop, Morris, *A History of Cornell*, Ithaca, 1962.

Boucher, Chauncey S., and Brumbaugh, A. J., *The Chicago College Plan*, second edition, Chicago, 1940.

Bryan, William Lowe, *Farewells*, Bloomington, 1938.

———, *The President's Column*, Bloomington, 1934.

———, and Bryan, Charlotte Lowe, *Last Words*, Bloomington, 1951.

Calvert, George Chalmers, *Catalogue of Theodore Clement Steele Memorial Exhibition During the Month of December, Nineteen Hundred Twenty-Six*, Indianapolis, 1936.

Carmichael, Hoagland (with Stephen Longstreet), *Sometimes I Wonder: The Story of Hoagy Carmichael*, New York, 1965.

Carmony, Donald F., ed., *Indiana: A Self-Appraisal*, Bloomington, 1966.

Cartter, Allan M., *An Assessment of Quality in Graduate Education: A Comparative Study of Graduate Departments in 29 Academic Disciplines*, Washington, D. C., 1966.

Cattell, Jacques, ed., *American Men of Science*, Lancaster, Pa., 1906.

Chalmers, David M., *Hooded Americanism, The History of the Ku Klux Klan with a New Epilogue by the Author*, Chicago, 1965.

Cheyney, Edward Potts, *History of the University of Pennsylvania 1740–1940*, Philadelphia, 1940.

Curti, Merle, and Carstensen, Vernon, *The University of Wisconsin 1848–1925*, 2 vols., Madison, 1949.

East, C. Earl, *Relive It with C. Earl East*, Bloomington, 1963.

Eells, Walter Crosby, *Survey of American Higher Education*, New York, 1937.

Fisher, Karl W., *First Hundred Years of Beta Theta Pi at Indiana University 1845–1945*, Menasha, Wis., 1947.

Gray, James, *The University of Minnesota 1851–1951*, Minneapolis, 1951.

Hall, Forest M., *Historic Treasures—True Tales of Deeds with Interesting Data in the Life of Bloomington, Indiana University, and Monroe County*, Bloomington, 1922.

Harding, Samuel Bannister, *Indiana University 1820–1904: Historical Sketch, Development of Course of Instruction, Bibliography*, Bloomington, 1904.

Havighurst, Walter, *The Miami Years, 1809–1959*, New York, 1958.

Hepburn, William Murray, and Sears, Louis Martin, *Purdue University, Fifty Years of Progress*, Indianapolis, 1925.

Hicks, John D., *Republican Ascendancy, 1921–1933*, New York, 1960.

Hoover, Thomas Nathanael, *The History of Ohio University*, Athens, 1954.

Idea and Practice of General Education, An Account of the College of the University of Chicago by Former Members of the Faculty, Chicago, 1950.

Jackson, Kenneth T., *The Ku Klux Klan in the City, 1915–1930*, New York, 1967.

Jencks, Christopher, and Riesman, David, *The Academic Revolution*, Garden City, N.Y., 1968.

Kinnison, William A., *Building Sullivant's Pyramid, An Administrative History of the Ohio State University, 1870–1907*, Columbus, 1970.

Langdon, William C., *The Centennial Pageant of Indiana University 1820–1920*, Bloomington, 1920.

Leuchtenburg, William E., *Franklin D. Roosevelt and the New Deal, 1932–1940*, New York, 1963.

Lockridge, Ross, Jr., *Raintree County*, Boston, 1948.

Lynch, William O., *A History of Indiana State Teachers College* [Indiana Normal], *1870–1929*, Terre Haute, Ind., 1946.

Morison, Samuel Eliot, *Three Centuries of Harvard, 1636–1936*, Cambridge, 1936.

Myers, Burton Dorr, *History of Indiana University, 1902–1937*, edited by Ivy L. Chamness, Bloomington, 1952.

———, *Trustees and Officers of Indiana University, 1820–1950*, edited by Ivy L. Chamness, Bloomington, 1951.

Peckham, Howard, *The Making of the University of Michigan, 1817–1967*, Ann Arbor, 1967.

Perkins, Dexter, *The New Age of Franklin Roosevelt*, Chicago, 1957.

Perley, Maie Clements, *Without My Gloves*, Philadelphia, 1940.

Phillips, Clifton J., *Indiana In Transition: The Emergence of an Industrial Commonwealth, 1880–1920*, Indianapolis, 1968.

Pierson, George Wilson, *Yale College: An Educational History, 1871–1921*, New Haven, 1952.

Reeves, Floyd, Russell, John D., and Miller, Ernest C., *Trends in University Growth: The University of Chicago Survey*, Chicago, 1937.

Rinsch, Emil, *The History of the Normal College of the American Gymnastic Union of Indiana University, 1866–1966*, Bloomington, 1966.

Rock, Dorcas Irene, *A History of the Indiana University Training School for Nurses*, Bloomington, 1956.

Rudolph, Frederick, *The American College and University: A History*, New York, 1962.

Schmidt, George P., *The Liberal Arts College: A Chapter in American Cultural History*, New Brunswick, 1957.

Steele, Selma N. and Theodore L., and Peat, Wilbur D., *The Life Work of T. C. Steele: The House in the Singing Winds*, Indianapolis, 1966.

Stephens, Frank F., *A History of the University of Missouri*, Columbia, 1962.

Sullivan, Mark, *Our Times: The United States, 1900–1925*, 6 vols., New York, 1926–1936.

Veysey, Laurence R., *The Emergence of the American University*, Chicago, 1965.

Visher, Stephen Sargent, *Scientists Starred, 1903–1943*, Baltimore, 1947.

Wecter, Dixon, *The Age of the Great Depression 1929–1941*, New York, 1952.

Wilson, Kenneth L., and Brondfield, Jerry, *The Big Ten*, Englewood, N.J., 1967.

Wish, Harvey, *Contemporary America: The National Scene Since 1900*, New York, 1955.

Index

Index

[4 1 7]

Index

Kuersteiner, A. F., 110
Kunkel, William Albert, Jr., 403
Kunz, Albert S., 328
Kurrie, Harry R., 314, 320, 347

Lafayette (Ind.), 69, 70, 81, 83, 111, 127, 128, 165, 166, 182, 183, 190, 337, 351
Lafayette *Daily Courier*, 91, 166
Lafayette *Morning Journal*, 84, 85
Lahr House, 182
Lake County (Ind.), 256
Lake Forest College, 47
Lake Mohawk Peace Conference, 217
Lampland, Carl O., 323
Langdon, William Chauncey, 243, 244
Lansing (Mich.), 319
LaPorte (Ind.), 316
Lash, Donald R., 354
Lawrence County (Ind.), 17, 18
League of Nations, 305
Lebanon (Ind.), 400
Lecture and Concert Series, 59, 60
Lee, Floyd, 212
Leete, Frederick D., 394
Leible, A. B., 348
Levis, George, 342
Lewis, Bailey, 279
Lewis, L. A., 137
Library, 236, 253
Lilienthal, David, 317
Lilly Care Hospital, 233
Lilly Library, 320
Lindley, Ernest H., 45, 49, 58, 123, 124, 145, 146, 152, 174, 313, 398
Linton Ernest Marshall, 217, 218, 271, 272
Linton (Ind.), 225, 329
Little, Cecil Cook, 319
Little, Jessie M., 55
Livett, Schulyer, 277
Lloyd, Wilma, 336
Lockridge, Ross Franklin, 326
Lockridge, Ross F., Jr., 326; *Raintree County*, 326
Logan, F. M., 262
Logansport *Journal*, 142
Long, Robert W., 98
Long, Mrs. Robert W., 98
Lost River, 17
Louden, Theodore J., 24, 80, 154, 192, 193, 201, 204
Louisiana State University, 345, 358
Louisville (Ky.), 149, 204
Lowe, Charlotte, 8
Lowe & Bollenbacher, Architects, 156, 160

Lusitania, the, 198, 235
Lynch, William O., 306
Lyons, Robert Edward, 45, 66, 114

McAtee, Camden, 141
McCartney, Nealy, 137, 138
McClaire, Patrick, 169
McClellan Collection, 114
McClintock, Lander, 308
McCray, Warren T., 246
McDonald, James Grover, 211, 224, 294
McElroy, Robert M., 228
McFerren, M. E., 327
MacGriff, Floyd, 39, 40
McGuffey's Readers, 6
McHale, Frank, 398, 401
McKinley, William, 2
MacManus, Seumas, 120
McMillin, Alvin Nugent, 179, 356, 357, 358, 359, 361
McMullin, Harry, 185
McMurtrie, U. Z., 157, 159
McNutt, Paul Vories, 153, 160, 206, 221, 250, 256, 257, 258, 262, 276, 288, 318, 319, 320, 321, 358, 387, 397, 398, 399, 404, 408
McNutt Quadrangle, 43
McNutt, Ruth, 123, 257, 258
McShaw Bell Company, 130
Madison (Wis.), 185, 402
Maidens, Scotland, 17, 18
Malott, Clyde Arnett, 300, 301
Manchester, A. L., 59
Manhattan (Kan.), 356, 358
Mann, Leslie, 341, 343
Marion County (Ind.), 80, 83, 87, 93
Marshall, Thomas R., 52, 53, 99, 101, 190
Martinsville (Ind.), 277, 318, 333, 387
Mason, Ruby, 30, 31, 222, 231
Mathers, Frank C., 308
Maxwell, Allison, 73, 96
Maxwell, J. D., 37, 38
Maxwell, Judith, 227
Maxwell, Louise, 114, 229
Maxwell, Ruth, 229
Maxwell Hall, 55, 108, 110, 112, 113, 127, 143, 149, 259, 262, 276, 334, 386, 393
Maynard, K. R., 345
Medical School, 46, 65–100, 214, 229, 262, 263
Medico-Chirugical Medical School, 94
Mehurin, Architect, 16
Mellett, Don, 307

[4 2 3]